MW00637288

Our Century Together

100 Years of Photos, Memories and News Leader Front Pages

 • ISBN: 1-932129-90-1

Published by Pediment Publishing, a division of The Pediment Group, Inc. www.pediment.com Printed in Canada

Table of Contents

Acknowledgments

This book would not have been possible without our readers. Without their loyalty and support we would not have been able to thrive and prosper over the past 100 years.

We would also like to give our special thanks to a group of local photographers and collectors who willingly shared their material with us for the creation of this book. Among these are, David Schultz, the Waynesboro Public Library, Richard Hamrick, and Dennis Sutton. Without their unselfish contributions it would have been impossible for us to create this book for you to enjoy.

Finally, we would like to thank Charles Culbertson. The breadth of his knowledge regarding the history of our area is evident in the detailed captions he has written. Without his contribution to this project much would have gone missing in the way of context and detail for each of the photographs selected.

Foreword

To many it probably seems like only yesterday that The News Leader published its first edition. "Yesterday" however, was 100 interesting years ago. Much has happened in that time to our city, county, state and nation and we at the News Leader are proud to have brought to your homes accurate reports of what happened and the impact it had on our lives.

This book reflects only a small portion of the history that surrounds all of us. Our look at the past is informative, entertaining and hopefully will conjure up some memories that have been stored away in your memory banks. Some, we are sure, will be joyful, while others will surely be painful to some, but it is our history and we cannot change it, nor would we want to for it has helped fashion our lives.

It has truly been "Our Century Together." We hope you enjoy taking this brief but fascinating trip with us through time.

The 1900s

The Tranquil Era

When the first edition of the Evening Leader rolled off the presses in 1904, it hit the streets of a city living partially in the 20th century and partially in the century that had just passed. While modern conveniences such as indoor toilets, streetcars, electric lights and telephones had worked their way into everyday lives, the technological landscape was still dominated by horse-drawn conveyances, outbuildings and the telegraph.

STAUNTON DAILY LEADER.

VOLUME 1, NO. 1. STAUNTON VA., THURSDAY, DECEMBER 15, 1904. PRICE 1 CENT

PLANS FOR NEW CADET BARRACKS.

S. M. A.'s Brick Quadrangle to Resemble That of V. M. I. Accommodate 250.

WILL BUILD ON OLD SITE.

Temporary Class Rooms Now Under Roof and Nearly Ready for Return of Boys After Holidays.

The well known firm of architects, Messrs. T. J. Collins & Sons, has recently draughted the plans for the handsome new barracks of the Staunton Military Academy. When the buildings which these plans represent have been constructed, Staunton will have an institution which will rank in point of architecture as well as in curriculum, with the foremost seats of education in the Old Dominion.

The plans as drawn by the Messrs. Collins, show a large quadrangular brick building, three stories high on three sides, and arranged very much on the order of the Virginia Military Institute. At the open end of the quadrangle is a small row of one story rooms, for the use as baths, etc., while at the other end are ten large class rooms, an immense assembly hall, and also a large gymnasium.

The dormitories of the quadrangle, which front upon the plaza, upon tiers of porches connected with broad stairs, are arranged for the accommodation of two hundred and fifty cadets, while the inner quadrangle itself affords ample room for individual company drill, roll call, etc. The ground covered, outer dimensions, will be 150x120 ft., and the inner quadrangle will be 140x75 ft. This handsome building will crown the Kable hill, on nearly the exact site of the burned barracks.

The temporary class rooms, work on which was begun almost immediately after the recent disastrous fire, are now under roof and Captain Kable expects to be fully able to meet the exigencies of the occasion upon the return of the cadet corps in January.

ICE ROUGH BUT PERFECTLY SAFE.

The extreme coldness of the weather both yesterday and today was not sufficient to deter the large crowd of merry skaters which gathered on the fair ground lake to enjoy the greatest of winter sports. Although the ice is very rough, it is several inches thick, perfectly safe.

Silks and velvets at cost for next 30 days at Mrs. Kingeter's. 12-15-1 w.

Headquarters for "Old Prentice Whisky." Weston's Model Bar. 12-15-1-m

Handsome Percherons.

On Monday last the fire committee of the city counsel purchased two fine Percheron horses from Mr. T. J. Collins, the well known liveryman. The pair of horses weigh 2,700 lbs. and are for use in thecity fire department.

Try a glass of our Coca Cola at Thos. Hogshead.

Invincible Eagle Cigar is King.

At cost! At cost! At cost everything for 30 days at Mrs. Kingeter's. 12-15 1 w.

Invincible Eagle Cigar is King.

White Tooth Wash, the dentifrice with a character.

Invincible Eagle Cigar is King.

White Tooth Wash invigorates the mouth secretions.

Invincible Eagle Cigar is King.

STAUNTON MENTIONED IN ROMANCE OF THE SEA.

In the current issue of the Cosmopolitan, is the second installment of A Modern Swiss Family Robinson, a romance of the sea, by Cosmopolitan's well-known and able editor, John Brisben Walker. The heroine of the story is a Miss Warden, of Albemarle county, and she is described as a charming young lady who had taught a year at one of the Staunton seminaries, and was making a tour of the world in company with her aunt when the accident around which Mr. Walker has woven his exceedingly clever story, took place.

CAPT. R. C. BERKELEY SAILS FOR COLON.

Capt. Randolph C. Berkeley, who was recently visiting his father, Dr. Carter Berkeley, of this city, sailed Monday, from League Island, on board the Yankee for Colon, Panama. Captain Berkeley is in command of a company of Marines and will be absent about a year.

Mr. Ranson Improving.

The condition of Mr. J. Baldwin Ranson, who has been suffering from eye trouble for the past several days, is said to be somewhat improved today. It was at first thought that Mr. Ranson would lose the use of one of his eyes, but it is now hoped that the most serious danger is over and the patient is resting more quietly than usual. Doctor Hanger and Armstrong are administering to him, and every effort it being put forth to save his eye sight.

Train Delayed.

Train number 15, which is due here from Richmond, at 2 o'clock, was delayed an hour and a half this afternoon on account of an accident which occurred near Waynesboro. The engine of No. 4 broke down, and it was sometime before the train could switch off in order to allow the local to pass.

The local, number 16, which is due here from the west at 2 o'clock, layed over here until the arrival of number 15.

Market Glutted.

The turkey market opened a little slow today, live birds bringing only from eleven to fourteen cents, against fourteen and a half steady yesterday. The market was glutted and local buyers had things pretty much their own way.

State News in Brief.

A movement has been started in Richmond with a view to sueing the State of West Virginia, for the $15,000,000 debt alleged to be its share of the mother State's ancient obligations.

E. C. Burnett, of Richmond, arrainged before Justice Chrutchfield on the charge of murdering H. L. Fletcher, was sustained in his plea of self-defence yesterday, and promptly dismissed.

A dispatch from St. Louis says that it has just been discovered that Mrs. Maude Gochenour, of Woodstock, Va., was married in that city, to Wm. F. Pohzehl, of Michigan, on September 29th.

In order to secure a uniform freight classification the State Corporation Commission has requested representatives of all Virginia railroads to appear before it January 17th.

On Wednesday the House of Representatives sitting as a grand jury, found Judge Charles Swayne, of Florida, guilty of high crimes and misdemeanor removed him from the bench.

Among the large class of applicants for license before the State Medical Board now sitting in Richmond are fifteen negroes.

All kinds of pretty novelties at Shreckhise & Bear.

FOR SWEET CHARITY'S SAKE.

Young People of Staunton Arranging to Give Bal Poudre During Christmas Week.

PROCEEDS FOR THE POOR.

Much Interest Manifested Among Local Society People Who Will Take Part in Ball.

A movement is on foot in the city to give a bal poudre during Christmas week, the proceeds of which will be used in an endeavor to give the city poor an enjoyable Christmas. A number of well-known young people are planning for the big charity, which promises to be one of the largest and most successful entertainments of many seasons.

A bal poudre as always an attractive and brilliant spectacle, and it is reasonable to predict that every one in Staunton who dances will purchase a ticket to the proposed Christmas affair. While the plans for the ball have not been definately laid, there is little doubt that it will be carried to a successful conclusion. Application has been made for one of the largest and most suitable dancing halls in the city, and final action in the matter will be taken this evening, at which time a meeting has been called to consider the matter.

JURY CASE IN CORPORATION COURT.

The Corporation Court convened this morning in the County Court room, Judge H. W. Holt presiding. A decree was entered in the case of Cootes vs. Cootes, and a certificate of good character was issued to Mr. Taylor McCoy, in order to allow him to engage in the practice of law. Mr. McCoy will now apply to the Court of Appeals for a license.

The case of A. B. Doom vs. the Fraternal Accident Order was entered into, and much evidence was heard. There are about twenty-five witnesses to be examined in this case, which involves an accident policy of not less than $3,000. Mr. Cook, of Philadelphia, general secretary of the defendant company, was in attendance upon court. The defence is represented by Hon. A. C. Braxton and the plaintiff by Messrs. Glasgow and Taylor.

Former Staunton Man Weds.

Dr. W. Smith Shepherd, of Wright, W. Va., a former well-known resident of this city, and Miss Banks, of Madison county, were married yesterday, at the home of the bride.

Lewis Creek Bed Repaired.

The washout in Lewis Creek, under S. D. Timberlake's store, which was occasioned several weeks ago by a heavy freshet, and which might have caused considerable damage to the adjacent property had it not been discovered immediately, has been substantially repaired. The bed of the creek has been cemented by the city's hands, and no further damage is likely to occur from the water. For two weeks the workmen have labored industriously, having gained access to the creek by digging a large entrance near the intersection of Main Street and Central Avenue, and the work is now rapidly nearing completion. The street will soon be cleared of the materials which blocked the way, and the usual traffic can be carried on with less danger and inconvenience to passers by.

Jas. E. Pepper whiskey prevents grippe and is effectual on breaking up colds, call at Westons's Model Bar. 12-15-1-m

BEVERLY THEATRE TO OPEN IN FEBRUARY.

It may not be generally known that the name of the city opera house, in keeping with the times and the community, has been changed to Beverly Theatre. Contractor M. B. Stoddard, who is in charge of the remodeling of the interior of the building, stated yesterday that he thought it would be ready for occupation by the first of February. Mr. Stoddard, with the exception of some minor details, completed his work yesterday, and a force of expert workmen is now engaged in doing the frescoing and ornamental plastering. When Beverly Theatre is completed it will be one of the handsomest play houses in the State and a credit to the city. The stage and stage facilities are all that could be desired.

PROPOSED CHANGE IN U S COURTS

If the proposed congressional bill for a new judicial circuit of the United States court is passed, all in Staunton and Augusta county who have dealings with that court, will haveto go to Charlottesville instead of to Harrisonburg. The bill for the creation of a new court was draftted by Judge Henry Clay McDowell, presiding judge of the United States courts for the Western District of Virginia, and who provides for a new district, to be known as the Middle District of Virginia.

The bill proposes to abolish the courts now held at Harrisonburg, and to change the place of sitting to Charlottesville. The following counties now in the Western District, will probably be transferred to the new district:

Halifax, Pittsylvania, Henry, Patrick, Charlotte, Campbell Bedford, Appomattox, Buckingham, Cumberland, Fluvanna, Albemarle, Nelson, Amherst, Rockbridge, Bath, Highland, Augusta, Rockingham, Greene, Madison, Page, Rappahannock, Shenandoah, Warren, Clarke and Frederick.

Though the Virginia delegation has not indicated its position in the matter, it is expected that Representative Slemp will introduce a bill in accordance with Judge McDowell's measure during the present session of Congress.

The New Station.

Little has been said of late about the proposed new C. & O. Station to be built at this point, and the news, that work on the structure will be begun in March is more than welcome. The plans drawn up by Messrs. T. J. Collins & Son were accepted last Saturday, by the C. & O. authorities, and the Messrs. Collins were highly praised for the general excellence of their work. It is expected that the local firm will supervise the construction of the new station.

In the Far East.

It is reported that the Japanese have successfully torpedoed the Russian battleship Sevastopol, and that Japanese shells now reach every part of Port Arthur, the streets of which are occupied only by its soldiers.

A Small Blaze.

The fire alarm which occurred yesterday morning at about ten o'clock, was occasioned by a small blaze in the kitchen of Lincoln Jackson, a colored man who lives on West Main street. The alarm was turned in at the corner of Jefferson and Main streets, and was promptly responded to by the firemen, who extinguished the flames before any damage was done.

Prescriptions filled only by experienced druggists at Thos. Hogshead's.

Headquarters for "Old Prentice Whiskey." Weston's Model Bar. 12-15 1 m

V. P. I. TROUBLE BROUGHT HOME.

Local Cadets of the Institute Who are Affected by Resignation of Juniors.

LETTER SENT TO PARENTS.

General Request From Senior Class That Juniors be Returned and Troubled Adjusted.

A number of cadets from Staunton and Augusta county who attend the Virginia Polytechnic Institute are more or less directly affected by the recent trouble at that well known school. One of them, Cadet Reese Grubert, a member of the Junior class, returned home last night. Mr. Grubert had little to say about the resignation of the class other than what has already been published. However, he stated to a LEADER reporter that the return of the class after Christmas depends upon the further action of the faculty in reference to the expelled student. The parents of those who voluntarily left the Institute have received letters from the Senior class, requesting that no arrangements be made by them to send their sons to other schools until the final action of the faculty in the matter. These letters intimate that every effort will be made to do justice to all concerned, and in them is expressed the desire that the entire Junior class will return and things will resume their normal state of peace and harmony.

Some pacific measures have been taken toward the Sophomore class, and it is not thought that that body will follow the Juniors' example and leave the school. The Staunton boys in the Sophomore class are Cadets Lomax May and Wm. Bickle. Cadet-Lieut. Frank M. Vost, of this city, is taking a post-graduate course at Blacksburg.

It is claimed that the trouble at the V. P. I. has been grossly misrepresented, and that the Juniors acted under a mistake, as the man who conferred with the class president did not represent the faculty. It is said that the Juniors may return at their own request. The resignation as a class cannot be recalled.

Notice.

THE DAILY LEADER hereby notifies the public that R. D. Lucas is authorized to solicit subscriptions and advertisements and to collect for all such business matters as may be connected with this office.

Baltimore Dental Parlors.

Dr. G. Morgan, of Lynchburg, has succeeded Dr. A. A. Weaver, deceased, at the Baltimore Dental parlors. Dr. Morgan has had long experience as a dental surgeon, and was one of the first dentists to enlist for army practice when a branch of dentistry was attached to the service during the Spanish-American war.

WANTED—Two white girls to work in kitchen and dining-room, Apply to Hotel Weston, Staunton, Va.

Carrie Again in Trouble.

"I see by the pa-pers," as Mr. Dooley would say, that Carrie Nation is again on the war path. When last heard from she had just been hit amidships with a bung stopper thrown by an irate bartender whose establishment she was endeavoring to raid. What in the nation makes Carrie carry on so? If she doesn't "quit her behavior and learn how to don't," someone will have to carry Carrie off to the morgue.

The Celebrated Centemiri Glove can be found only at Shereckhise & Bear.

December 15, 1904: The very first edition of the Staunton Daily Leader. *Microfilm Archives*

A look at Staunton's ordinances in the early 20th century attests to just how rural in nature many aspects of life in the Queen City still were. No one, for example, could put a bell on his cow or any other animal between sunset and sunrise. The fine for such a heinous act was a crisp $1 bill.

"Any person," read another ordinance, "who shall butcher or cause to be butchered any steer, hog, or other animal on any street or alley within the city shall be fined one dollar for every animal so butchered."

Anyone caught riding his horse on a sidewalk would find himself shelling out from $2 to $10. This also held true for mules, wagons, drays, carts or "other vehicles."

For the most part, Stauntonians lived in a secure, close-knit and peaceful community. It was, still, very much a small town.

But Staunton was growing. From 1891 to 1912, architect T.J. Collins designed some of the city's most impressive structures, including C&O rail station at the Wharf; the Marquis Building at Beverley and Augusta streets; the Eakleton Hotel on South New Street; St. Francis Catholic Church; the opulent C.W. Miller House on North New Street (across from Mary Baldwin College); several structures in Thornrose Cemetery; and a number of residences in the Gospel Hill district. In all, Collins designed more than 200 architecturally stunning structures in Staunton.

In 1905, when the annexation of county land caused the population of Staunton to surpass 10,000, state law mandated that the city reorganize its government. It did, installing a seven-member board of aldermen and a 15-member common council. To boot, sometimes as many as 15 standing committees dealt with a variety of issues affecting the city. There was, not surprisingly, little if any agreement on how to accomplish any single issue, and many major capital projects ground to a complete halt due to bickering among committee members.

Common council member John Crosby, who had served as clerk for the Augusta County Board of Supervisors, came up with what he thought was a better way to run a city and tirelessly sought support for it. Crosby's system featured an elected city council which, in turn, would hire a professional business manager to handle Staunton's administrative needs.

Crosby, who said this form of government would result in increased services and decreased taxes, lobbied for a year before his plan was adopted in January 1908. Three months later, on April 3, 1908, Charles Ashburner of Richmond became Staunton's – and the nation's – first city manager.

Just down the road in Waynesboro, the dawning of a new century presented residents of this quaint yet industrious town with a fresh set of challenges, not the least of which was educating its young people. On March 10, 1904, Waynesboro's city fathers authorized the issuance of a $5,000 bond to pay for the town's first public school building which, two years later, opened for both elementary and high-school students.

In April 1904, council appointed members of a school board and passed an ordinance making Waynesboro a "separate and single" school district from Augusta County.

Five years later, in 1911, the number of school-age children had grown to the point that council voted to build a new school building next to the one erected in 1906. This structure became Waynesboro High School.

In the waning years of the 19th century, sometimes the greatest problem for Waynesboro's city fathers had been keeping livestock off the streets. Now, the smoking, belching behemoth called the automobile began appearing on city streets, forcing council in 1908 to pass an ordinance setting the speed limit at 8 miles per hour.

One of the vehicles that the speed limit didn't affect was the Dawson Auto-Mobile, which was produced in Basic City in 1900 and 1901. It was the first automobile to be built in Virginia, but was ultimately unsuccessful as the industrial giants of the Midwest consumed more than 2,000 of their competitors. By the time Waynesboro got a speed limit, the Dawson was long gone.

By the early 1900s, Stribling Springs in Western Augusta County had been a popular resort since 1817. During the Civil War, "Stonewall" Jackson used the 1,400-acre site as his headquarters following the Battle of McDowell, and for years before and after vacationers from all over the world visited the springs for its pastoral, peaceful location. The Stribling Springs Hotel, pictured here, had to be torn down in 1940 because a spring of water had undermined part of it. *Schwartz Collection*

The Brunswick Inn was one of Waynesboro's premier hostelries from 1890 to 1938, when it was demolished. *Waynesboro Collection*

Streetcar service began in Staunton in August 1890 with a fleet of 12 mule-drawn cars. In 1896 the lines were converted to electricity and controlled by the Staunton Light and Power Co. Pictured here are (1) a typical Staunton streetcar and (2) the unloading of a streetcar in the Wharf, near the C&O station. The growing availability of automobiles slowly killed the city's streetcar system, with the tracks being taken up in 1933. *Waynesboro Collection*

The grocery store of J.L. Henderson was located on Main Street in downtown Staunton just west of its intersection with Augusta Street. The brick building just to the left of the grocery is the Staunton Telephone Exchange. *Sutton Collection*

An early view of Stuarts Draft. *Sutton Collection*

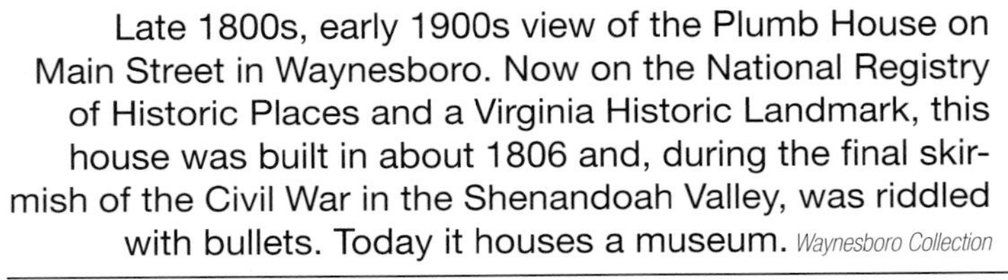

Late 1800s, early 1900s view of the Plumb House on Main Street in Waynesboro. Now on the National Registry of Historic Places and a Virginia Historic Landmark, this house was built in about 1806 and, during the final skirmish of the Civil War in the Shenandoah Valley, was riddled with bullets. Today it houses a museum. *Waynesboro Collection*

View of Waynesboro's Chesapeake and Ohio passenger station, looking east toward the Blue Ridge Mountains. This station was built in 1873 and torn down and replaced 1907. *Waynesboro Collection*

This circa 1890 photo shows the bucolic nature of Waynesboro and Basic City at about the time they really started to grow. Pictured are a field in the foreground with scattered houses in the middle distance, and Basic City and the mountains in the distance. *Waynesboro Collection*

Charles Ashburner, Staunton's – and the nation's-first city manager.

Panoramic view of Basic City, Waynesboro, and the Shenandoah Valley, taken sometime in the early years of the 20th century. The open areas pictured here no longer exist, having given way to development. *Waynesboro Collection*

This early photograph of Basic City shows the Brandon Hotel on the hill (middle, right) and the N & W Railway. The view looks east. *Waynesboro Collection*

Photo-postcard showing a view of Staunton's central business district taken from the summit of Sears Hill. In the immediate foreground is the old American Hotel (center, left) and several warehouses along the C & O railroad tracks. *Waynesboro Collection*

If You Want anything try the Want ad column	STAUNTON DAILY LEADER	We Get all the News and it's all here.

VOLUME 7 NO. 37 STAUNTON, VA., TUESDAY EVENING, JANUARY 28, 1908. PRICE ONE CENT

Oysters on Shell

We have just installed an oyster saloon and are prepared to serve oysters in all styles. Oysters fresh every day. On half shell a specialty. Cohen's Restaurant.

Mrs. Florence Flood Dies in Far West

Intelligence was received here today announcing the sudden death of Mrs. Florence Wentworth Lyons, as known here while living in this place. She after locating in the West married a Mr. Flood, who has made Montana their home for a number of years. Mrs. Flood will, as Mrs. Lyons, be remembered by a large circle of friends in Staunton, as an accomplished and attractive lady, whose bright mind and winning manners made her a favorite with those who were fortunate enough to know her. She leaves four children by her first marriage, Mrs. J. E. Robertson, and her two sisters, Maud and Hilda, and brother, Harry, all of whom are married and live in the West. Mrs. Robertson lives in El Paso, Texas, but was on a visit to Chicago, expecting to visit Staunton before returning to her home, when a telegram announced the sudden demise of her mother.

Local Pick Ups

Rain in southeast; rain or snow in north and west portion Wednesday warmer tonight in south portion. Colder Wednesday in north and west portion.

The Poultry Show is now a memory and Secretary Henton is going to work to take the conceit out of the Staunton Bowling team. Here's a bet—Harrisonburg News. We take that bet. Stakes?

Another big fire in Baltimore yesterday. It seems that the Monumental City is doomed to burn before its time.

A bill has been introduced into the Legislature to substitute the electric chair for the gallows in Virginia, but we would much prefer to die a natural death.

Holden, a mining town in West Virginia, will, after February 1st, have the unique distinction of running a saloon for charity. Complaint was made to court that the miners would not work where there was nothing to drink, and court agreed to grant license, provided the money be used for such charitable purposes as it shall direct.

A teacher in a certain country school had a pupil who answered to the name of Johany. Johnny always had an offensive odor about him. The teacher wrote Johnny's mother, saying, Johnny was a good boy and a bright one and did very well at school, but she would be much pleased if she would give him a bath occasionally. The mother, feeling somewhat incensed, wrote back—"Johnny aint no rose and I send him to school for you to larn him and not to smell him."

Two fatal fires in adjoining counties. In Alleghany, Mrs. M. M. Gillaspie was burned to death Saturday night and yesterday two little children in Augusta suffered a similar fate.

All those who wish to know what "roller polo" is are respectfully directed to the skating rink on Friday night where they will get a few pointers and be thoroughly entertained simultaneously.

How many times must we write that we cannot publish unsigned communications of any description? This is an invariable rule, in force in nearly every newspaper office in the country. The author's name is not wanted for publication, but as a guarantee of good faith.

Mr. Leonard Dawson, who was recently appointed to a $5,000 position as treasurer of Samar, P. I., is a graduate of the Dunsmore Business College, of Staunton. Mr. Dawson's rapid rise on the road of success is but another instance of the thoroughness and efficiency of Dunsmore's.

For Rent

Nice office room in the Witz Building. Choice location and commodious business quarters. Heat and janitor. 1-1-1mo.

Drop in and we'll open your eyes: we have all the weight in underwear wool and cotton.

TUTWILER & PARRENT.

MAYOR APPROVES CITY MANAGER

Action Certified to Clerk of Council in Document Setting Forth Advantages which Should Accrue From Centralized Municipal Government.

Mayor W. H. Landes has added the weight of his approval to the "General Manager" ordinance, recently passed by the Common Council and the Board of Aldermen. This approval, which has been certified to Clerk Argenbright, is in the following words:

To the Honorable Council for the City of Staunton:

I have carefully considered the ordinance adopted by the Common Council on the 13th of January 1908, and concurred in by the Board of Aldermen, the 16th of January, 1908, creating the office of a Business Manager for the City of Staunton, prescribing the mode of his appointment and defining his duties, and return the same with my approval. The ordinance was adopted upon a report made by a Joint Special Committee appointed for the purpose of looking into the expediency and advisability of creating some method or devising some system, for the conduct of the business departments of this city by a Board or Commission. This report furnishes much valuable information upon the subject of municipal government by a board or commission, and the Committee deserves special commendation for the researches made as well as for the great care with which the report has been drafted.

It is clearly shown by this report that it is impossible for the City of Staunton to adopt the Galveston-Houston plan of municipal government by a Commission composed of the Mayor and four citizens, elected by the people, by reason of the fact that the Constitution of this State provides for the retention of Councils and the government of cities thereby, together with the Mayor. It is equally as clearly shown by this report that ample authority is given the City Council under our Charter, as well as under the Code of Virginia, to create the office of a Business Manager for the City of Staunton, and to prescribe his duties and define his powers. There is no denying the fact that our present system of municipal government is defective, in that it lacks centralization of power and authority in the various business departments. The Galveston-Houston plan of government of the entire municipality by a Commission of five, would in my judgment, come nearer the crying demand for municipal reform than any other method yet suggested; but as this plan is impossible of adoption in Virginia, under the existing organic law, the next best thing to it, now receiving much attention by the various cities throughout the State, is a Board of Control, such as is now in existence in the City of Norfolk.

I attended the "League of Virginia Municipalities" which recently met in the City of Richmond. Many valuable papers were read at this meeting, bearing on the subject of centralizing the various business departments in Boards, or Commissions. A very able paper was read by Judge Old of Norfolk, who was chairman of a Commission appointed to look into, and devise some method of municipal government by Boards of Control, or by Commissions. The Chairman of the Board of Control of Norfolk also read a paper full of valuable information upon the working of the plan in that City. After one year's trial it was clearly demonstrated by this report that there has been a considerable saving to Norfolk's finances during the one year of the operation of the Board, with prospects of a still greater saving in the future, as the plan gets better under way.

Other valuable papers were read at this meeting by persons who had given much study to the subject, and of almost one accord the opinion was expressed that the business departments of Cities should have a business head, whether that head be a board composed of more than one, or a Business Manager, with equal powers of a board. These paper will be printed in pamphlet form, and will furnish us with much valuable information for future reference in the management of the business departments of Staunton.

While the ordinance which was adopted on the 13th of January by the Common Council and concurred in on the 16th by the Board of Aldermen, seems to cover pretty generally the plan suggested by the Special Committee in the report upon which said ordinance is based, at the same time I have no doubt but that it will be found wise to revise the same from time to time as necessities may demand. Too much care cannot be given to the power and duties conferred, and sought to be conferred, upon the Business Manager, in order to avoid conflict with the other departments of

Continued on 4th page.

Man Assaulted And Shot At His Own Threshold

Curtis Reedy, a Rockingham man of 33 years, is in jail at Harrisonburg, to await trial on the charge of shooting his own father, Philip A. Reedy. It is said that four men assaulted Philip Reedy at his home Saturday night and that his son Curtis was one of the party. The accused, however, denies that he was in the neighborhood at the time and says he can prove an alibi.

Many rumors are afloat as to the cause of the shooting, which it is generally understood was done by members of a posse. Mrs. Philip Reedy is not living with her husband, but makes her home in the neighborhood with a married daughter, Mrs. Dove, the wife's place at home being occupied by a younger woman recently employed as housekeeper. The presence of the younger woman in the house is alleged to have caused resentment upon the part of some of the neighborhood and it is intimated that the visit of the posse was in the nature of a whitecap mission. This view is given additional weight by the fact that the posse shot out all the windows in the house.

Young Man Says Ghost Was 12 ft. Tall

Mr. Earl Gabbert believes in ghosts. At least he insists that he saw a real one Sunday night at Thornrose cemetery. According to Mr. Gabbert's description, it was twelve feet high, with great red eyes as big as ones fist and wore the usual flowing white mantel of the time-honored and much maligned spook. When first seen it was sitting on a tombstone weeping over the sins of the world, but when Mr. Gabbert endeavored to catch it in a butterfly net, it glided around a vault and disappeared, greatly to his relief. Motorman Yeager, whose car passes the cemetery, and another street car employer, also claim to have seen the apparition but they insist it was only six feet tall. And now the good people going the neighborhood, of a... recrude... g men's engaging in rather ... tain your... sport. dangerous...

Would Substitute The Electric Chair

If the ... wishes of Legislator Williams, of Southampton, prevail, all persons condemned to death in this State for capital crimes will die in an electric chair at the penitentiary.

A bill providing that all criminals on whom the death penalty is imposed shall be ... proposed by Delegate ... of Henrico, and has been favorably reported by the Committee on Courts of Justice.

The Southampton solon believes that electrocution, in the long run, would prove far more economical than hanging. He ... says that the operation of the gibbet at the penitentiary would cost from $50 to $150 a man, according to the county or city in which the prisoner was convicted. Moreover, the Southampton lawmaker regards hanging as a barbarous medium for executing the sentence of the law.

Miss Woods to Wed

Captain and Mrs. Micajah Woods of Charlottesville have issued invitations to the marriage of their daughter, Miss Mary Watts Woods, to Dr. Frank Allemong Lupton. The wedding will take place on February 12th at 8:30 o'clock in Christ church, Charlottesville.

For Sale

A nice weanling colt, 8 months old. Sired by Lawson Red. Address A. C. Thomas, 5 S. Augusta street, Staunton, Va.

Mrs. E. F. Wayman Drops Dead at Home

The community was greatly shocked last night by the sudden death of Mrs. Edward Franklin Wayman, who dropped dead at her home on North Augusta street about 6 o'clock in the evening. Mrs. Wayman was apparently in good health and had been out during the day and her sudden death was a severe shock to her family and friends. Heart failure is supposed to have been the cause of her death.

Mrs. Wayman was Miss Hattie Flecker before her marriage to the late Dr. E. F. Wayman and was from Eastern Virginia. She was about 50 years of age when death came. She was a devoted member of the First Presbyterian church, being a lovable and conscientious Christian woman.

Surviving her are her mother, Mrs. Frances B. Flecker, of Staunton, and seven children, Mrs. Fanny Gray, and Misses Cassell and Elizabeth Wayman, of this city, Dr. Walter Newton, of Staunton, Mr. Edward Franklin, of Kansas, Mr. Jenifer Wayman of Culpeper and Master Joseph Wayman of Staunton.

Mrs. Wayman's funeral will take place Thursday afternoon at 3 o'clock from the house and will be conducted by Rev. Dr. A. M. Fraser.

Will Cost State $100 To Get L. R. Sexton

Sheriff Arthur Willson expects requisition papers here on the 4 o'clock train this afternoon from Governor Swanson, authorizing him to go to Arkansas to get L. R. Sexton, who surrendered at Texarkana last week for shooting Dorsey Tyler at Augusta Springs on the morning of Tuesday, Jan. 21st. Mr. Willson may leave tonight or tomorrow Texarkana and take Sexton into custody. He will stop at Little Rock to see the Governor of Arkansas in regard to giving Sexton over to Virginia authorities, and will bring him back to Staunton for trial. The trip will require about ten days.

It is not believed that Sexton would refuse to return without requisition but the papers and incidental formality are necessary in order for the Sheriff to procure expenses for the trip from the State. It is said that Sexton's return to Virginia will cost the State about $100.

Sexton's younger brother, over whom the difficulty of last Tuesday arose did not accompany him west, but returned to his home in Buchanan county. Mr. T. D. Sexton, his father, was here last night to investigate the trouble and to make arrangements for his son's defense.

Has Spinal Meningitis

The little son of Mr. and Mrs. F. H. Wheeler, whose critical illness was mentioned in these columns Saturday, shows little signs of improvement, says yesterday's Clifton Forge Review. Nearly all the physicians of the city have held a consultation over the little sufferer in the hope that some relief might be secured, but late this afternoon there was no material change for the better. The physicians have diagnosed the case as spinal meningitis and they are resorting to every means to save the life of the little boy who is the idol of his parents.

Jack London Returns Home

San Francisco, Jan. 26.—Jack London, who left here last May on a seven-year trip around the world to procure material for literary work and for whose safety fears have been entertained, returned to San Francisco today in the steamship Mariposa, from Tahiti.

London is accompanied by his wife. He says that he came back to attend to business. He will leave again on the Mariposa on February 1. The Snark, the fifty foot boat in which London is making his trip, was left at Tahiti for repairs to the engine.

Major Boisseux Resigns Commission

The resignation of Major C. Gray Boisseux of Richmond was accepted yesterday by the governor and the adjutant-general. Major Boisseux gave as his reason for resigning that his military duties took a great deal of his time from his business and forced him to resign.

Major Boisseux started in the Seventieth regiment thirty-two years ago as a private and has held every office in the regiment up to the majority.

Milk For Sale

Delivered to any portion of the city.
tf. P. J. Landes, Staunton Va

He Knew Where to get it

When last seen he was going to the C. & O. depot with his shoes in his hand saying let Dave do the work Shoes shined and tans dyed with neatness and dispatch. 1-17-6m.

THAW DEFENSE CLOSES CASE

Rebuttal Evidence Today, Justice Dowling Questions Alienists. Argument May Open Tomorrow and Case go to Jury Friday or Saturday.

New York, Jan. 27.—The Thaw defense closed its case today with "manic-depressive" insanity as the explanation of the death of Stanford White at the hands of the young Pittsburg millionaire. Tomorrow the prosecution will begin its evidence in rebuttal, and the case should go to the jury by Wednesday night or Thursday noon. District Attorney Jerome tomorrow morning will apply for the appointment of a commission to take the testimony of Abram Hummel, the disbarred and convicted lawyer, who is confined in the penitentiary on Blackwells Island, and who is said to be too ill to appear in court. Mr. Littleton said he would oppose any such action, whereupon Justice Dowling announced that if necessary he would go to the island himself tomorrow night in company with the defendant and his counsel, to preside at the taking of Hummel's testimony. The jury, it was stated, wouldn't be compelled to take the night trip across the river. Thaw seemed delighted at the prospects of the outing.

Mrs. Fifer at K. D. H.

Mrs. John B. Fifer was taken to the King's Daughters' Hospital late yesterday afternoon and submitted to a surgical operation for appendicitis. She stood the ordeal well and is reported to be getting along nicely this afternoon. She grew ill early yesterday morning and was sick only a short time before the operation was performed.

Mr. Burke Dead

News was received here last night bearing information of the death of Mr. Edward Burke which occurred Sunday in Parkersburg, W. Va. Mr. Burke was formerly a citizen of Staunton but had made his home in West Virginia for some years past.

Mr. Witz's Funeral

Funeral rites over the remains of Mr. Isaac Witz, who died yesterday afternoon will be held Thursday morning at 11 o'clock from the family residence on east Main street.

Funeral Held Today

An impressive funeral service took place this afternoon at 4 o'clock at Emmanuel Episcopal church when the family and friends of the late Mr. Churchman Geiger gathered to do homage to his memory. The service was conducted by the rector, Rev. R. C. Jett. The pallbearers were—Messrs. T. D. Ranson, Jacob Yost, Marshall White, George Blackley, R. H. Bell, Jr., Jesse McKay, Walter Danner and William Abney.

Florence Davis

The gowns worn by Florence Davis in her representation of the drama, "A Question of Husbands" are artistic illustrations of what can be done in the dress-making field of science. They will be seen here Thursday night

Valuable Farm Sold

The Barabbarger farm on Naked creek near Mt. Sidney was sold at public auction yesterday for Commissioner W. H. Landes by Auctioneer R. E. Tyler. The farm brought in the aggregate nearly $16,000, about 80 acres bringing $80 an acre and the balance of the 207 acres going at over $73 an acre.

Chorus Beauties

Would you believe it? Twelve college men making good looking girls; well they do. Supple, graceful, lithe, quick, and active they make a chorus that any manager would be proud of; their dances are revelations; intricate and difficult to the real girl they go through with ease; they do them with wonderful ease and grace. These girls cannot only sing but they can dance and look as pretty as any chorus that ever graced the stage and pleased an audience. See the Arcadians at the Beverley, Friday night, the Seventh of February.

Miss Lillian King is expected home tomorrow from Louisa county where she spent several weeks.

Tis Leap Year little girl, and this may be your only chance. Send some fellow a post card. It may settle the question for you. Who knows? Buy your cards at THE LITTLE STORE AROUND THE CORNER.

If you are looking for values in underwear call on

TUTWILER & PARRENT.

One of Fire's Victims Was Only 4 Years Old

The two children who met death yesterday in a fire which completely destroyed the home of Magistrate Samuel McKee near Greenville, were children of Mrs. Lizzie Long, who was employed by Mr. McKee. It is said that one of the victims was only 4 years of age and that the other was only a little older. The entire neighborhood is grieved over the great calamity. It is said that the fire had made such headway when discovered that it was impossible to rescue the little children.

Recital at M. B. S.

An interesting program is promised for Friday night at the Mary Baldwin Seminary, when the pupils of Prof. Hamer, assisted by the chorus class under Miss Brewster, will give a recital in the chapel. The program comprises many gems from Liszt, Rubinstein, Wagner, Chopin, Beethoven, Schubert, Mendelssohn and other eminent composers and will undoubtedly be highly entertaining. The recital will begin at 8 o'clock.

Dorsey Tyler Removed To University Hospital

Dorsey Tyler, the young man who lies at death's door from a serious bullet wound sustained one week ago today, was removed to Charlottesville this morning and placed in the University of Virginia Hospital. His father and mother, Mr. and Mrs. John Tyler, of Augusta Springs, and a younger brother accompanied him to the hospital. He was removed to the University to be subjected to a more thorough examination under an X-Ray machine, as his parents do not seem to favor probing for the bullet which still remains hidden in the man's body. It is feared that the ball cannot be located by means of X-Rays as a thorough test was made here without results, the theory being that the leaden bullet is imbedded in the spine, in which case it would be impossible to find it with the machine, as the rays will not penetrate the bone. Tyler seemed very weak this morning and showed signs that the fearful ordeal is steadily sapping out his life.

Ouidas Last Days Pitiful

Florence, Italy, Jan. 25.—Ouida (Louise De Laramie), the novelist, died today at Oviregglo, after an illness extending over a long period. She died in the most distressing poverty, her only attendant being an old servant woman in whose arms she expired. She was completely blind in one eye and the other was badly affected because of exposure and privation.

Yarmouth wants Fortune

Pittsburg Jan. 27.—The Thaw estate has been notified by attorneys for the Earl of Yarmouth that the fortune of the Countess of Yarmouth will not be given up by the family of Hertford without a bitter fight and a court decision. The London barristers say the Earl has a paper signed by Miss Alice Thaw the day before the wedding providing that in case she should die without children the house of Hertford should receive her entire fortune.

The Earl, on the strength of this agreement, it is declared, has received large sums of money from trades people. His attorneys claim that if she withdraws from the family the house of Hertford's good name will be seriously impaired. They will argue that she is leaving the family without issue, and that her fortune should be turned over to the Earl.

The news of the existence of such an agreement comes as a surprise to the public.

A Good Suggestion

During the happy Xmas days when all hearts were tender and the spirit of the Golden Rule held every breast, many and varied gifts were given and received, many wise and useful, and very many that soon lose their value. Those were fortunate ones that received a box of Honey Chunk or Independo Cigars for in them was found that true merit which alone satisfies.

During the year 1908 they will receive the manufacturers scrupulous supervision and will be kept strict

Brace up old man; tis leap year. Send some pretty girl a post card and that may settle the question. Post cards two for five at THE LITTLE STORE AROUND THE CORNER.

Fine Chrysanthemums, Roses, Carnations and Violets.
2-5-tf. JOHN FALLON

Back at old price 36in. Bleach Cotton at 10c. Shreckhise & Benz.

January 28, 1908 : Staunton approves the nation's first city manager. *Microfilm Archives*

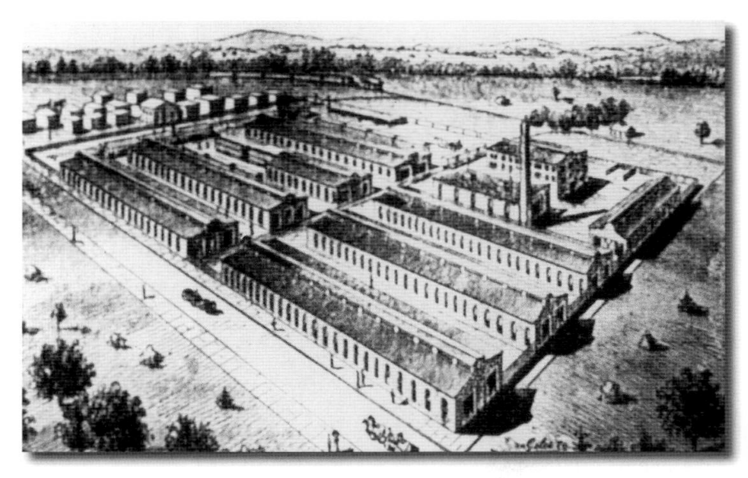

Probably constructed in the 1890s, the Basic City Car Warehouse was expected to produce 57 freight cars per day. This ambitious undertaking was dampened by the financial panic of 1893. This structure was located at the north end of Charlotte Avenue. *Waynesboro Collection*

An 1899 parade moving west on Frederick Street in front of Stuart Hall. The flags and bunting may indicate a Flag Day or Independence Day parade. Interestingly, one of the floats pictured here has on it an oversized, smoking cigar and a sign advertising Buffett Cigars. The float is peopled by small black children dressed up as Indians and wrapped in U.S. flags. *Schwartz Collection*

The Putnam Organ Works was begun in 1894 by W.W. Putnam, a veteran organ builder who moved from his native Vermont to Staunton to manufacture his Little Giant organ in a room in the YMCA Building. He was enormously successful, and by 1896 his large factory – pictured here – was established on the eastern fringe of town. He also sported a three-story showroom at 103 W. Beverley St. in the heart of downtown Staunton. *Schwartz Collection*

Staunton Mutual Telephone Company began operating in 1895 with 10 subscribers. Within a few years, 600 homes, businesses and farms in the city and county paid $15-20 to receive this modern service. Communications needs grew rapidly, and in 1921 city council adopted an ordinance chartering the Augusta-Staunton Mutual Telephone Co. Six years later, on Feb. 15, 1927, the ability to make telephone calls to London came to Staunton but at a whopping price. The first three minutes cost $78, and $26 for each additional minute. *Schwartz Collection*

Attesting to the wide variety of businesses that graced downtown Staunton in the early years of the 20th century was the Beverley Cigar Store, which was located at 112 East Beverley Street. Tobacconists' shops such as this one remained in the downtown area until the early 1980s. *Schwartz Collection*

Photo from the early 20th century showing workers at the White Star Mill, which still stands at the intersection of Johnson and South New streets. This view faces east from Middlebrook Avenue. The concourse of the C&O station and its main tracks are out of camera range just to the right. White Star was established in 1892 and operated until nationally marketed flours forced it to close in 1966. *Schwartz Collection*

Although the Beverley Manor School depicted here was constructed in 1912 and first occupied the following year, the school itself was first incorporated in 1901. Its original quarters were at the corner of New and Academy streets. The structure shown here, which is located on Thornrose Avenue, served in the late 20th century as part of the Statler Brothers Complex. *Schwartz Collection*

The northern Augusta County village of Stokesville flourished in 1900 when the Chesapeake and Western Railway laid tracks from Elkton to North River Gap. The community took its name from the owner of the railroad, W.D. Stokes, and began a short but intense life as a railroad town. A series of calamities such as the chestnut blight, the death of logging in the area and a flood in 1949 wiped out most of Stokesville, which sported such establishments as the Zirkle Hotel. *Schwartz Collection*

Waynesboro's Main Street looking east in the late 19th or very early 20th century. Note the dirt street, gas lamp post and – in the distance – the as-yet unscarred mountain that later would become a Waynesboro landmark. A cow stands in the street near the bottom of the hill. *Schwartz Collection*

Kings Daughter's Hospital was incorporated in 1896 and soon began operations in this two-story house on East Frederick Street near what was then Mary Baldwin Seminary. It served Staunton until 1950 when it moved to a new structure on North Augusta Street. KDH and Waynesboro Community Hospital merged in 1988 under the control of Augusta Hospital Corp. and eventually chose to occupy a regional facility in Fishersville. The original hospital pictured here was demolished by Mary Baldwin College. *Schwartz Collection*

Panoramic photo of Lake Tams in Gypsy Hill Park as it appeared in the earliest years of the 20th century. This view faces south and shows, just to the left of center, Beverley Manor School (later to become part of the Statler Complex). Thornrose Avenue is also shown, as are the tents of a fair or carnival (far right-hand corner).

Lake Tams in Gypsy Hill Park is named in honor of Capt. William Purviance Tams – the man who, in 1890, convinced city government that a municipal park was needed. Tams oversaw much of the landscaping and road building in the park, and the lake named in his honor was the site of many community events, including horseracing, fairs and other civic gatherings. *Schwartz Collection*

Previously unpublished view of the fairgrounds in Gypsy Hill Park, from a glass negative in the collection of David Schwartz of Staunton. This rare photograph shows large numbers of the area's black residents gathering in the park to enjoy the fair. In the days before integration, blacks were not permitted to mingle with whites and had certain days set aside for them to enjoy public events such as this. *Schwartz Collection*

The Augusta County Courthouse pictured here was the fourth of five courthouses to occupy this site at Augusta and Johnson Streets in Staunton. The first two were rude log cabins established during Staunton's days as a frontier outpost; the third was a stone structure constructed in 1789; the fourth courthouse, pictured here, was built in 1835-36; and the fifth and current building was erected in 1901. *Schwartz Collection*

Gallows constructed behind the Augusta County jail in Staunton for a hanging that never took place. Note the noose hanging over the gallows' center beam. *Schwartz Collection*

One of Staunton's most successful businesses – at least until national Prohibition got under way in 1920 – was Harman Brothers Whiskey. The company's headquarters, pictured here, was located at the corner of South New and Johnson streets. The building still stands today *Schwartz Collection*

One of the most aesthetically pleasing aspects of Staunton's downtown is its relatively unchanged Main Street – today's Beverley Street. Most of the buildings shown in these early 20th century photographs are still standing and, thanks to private renovation dollars and governmental protection from demolition, contribute to Staunton's reputation as a center for tourism and historic preservation. *Schwartz Collection*

Photo taken at Main (now Beverley) and South Market Street, facing east toward what is known as Gospel Hill. The large brick structure on the left is the Hardy Carriage Works showroom, one of Staunton's oldest businesses. Founded in 1848 the Hardy Carriage Works produced nearly all the surreys, phaetons, runabouts and other horse-drawn rigs used in Staunton for more than 65 years. This structure burned in 1928. *Schwartz Collection*

The 1910s

City in the Spotlight

The relative tranquility that characterized life in Staunton in the first 10 years of the new century disappeared in the second decade as the city found itself the focal point of a series of newsworthy events.

On Aug. 11, 1910, one of the many caverns over which Staunton is built cracked open near the southeast corner of Baldwin and Lewis streets. Hundreds of spectators gathered to watch the ever-widening hole gulp down a 35-foot maple tree, the front yard of a dilapidated frame house and then, finally, the house itself. As Staunton's telegraph and telephone lines hummed with the news, bringing in reporters from all over the country, two additional holes opened up and consumed even more property, including the foundation of one house and the back yard and kitchen of another.

It took several days for the sinkholes to stop expanding, and about a week for newspaper headlines to return to normal. But work to repair the holes – which included using steel girders and railroad ties to cover them over and brace up the street – was to continue for several months. Despite the severity of the disaster, it claimed only one life – that of a 63-year-old construction worker who fell into one of the chasms and drowned in the waters below. His waterlogged body was recovered the next day, eerily clutching a salvage rope.

Mother Nature wasn't finished with Staunton. On June 4, 1911, at 4:30 p.m., a black, furious wind whipped through the city, snapping the great maples in front of Trinity Church and tossing them like matchsticks through the air. The roof of the United Brethren Church went up like a paper balloon and disappeared into the swirling storm. The air was filled with debris, and the noise from the wind, goose egg-sized hail and thunder "resembled battle, the discharge of artillery mingled with the rattle of musketry," according to an eyewitness.

STAUNTON DISPATCH AND NEWS

GREAT DISASTER VISITS STAUNTON

A Street Caves In Destroying Houses And Threatening Large Public School Building

MINORITY SQUELCHED COUNCIL'S STEAM ROLLER

August 12, 1910: Staunton's famous cave-in received front-page attention. *Microfilm Archives*

When it was over, water stood two feet deep on Main Street. Thousands of windows were broken throughout the city. Damage to buildings and outlying farms was estimated at more than $1 million. Again, the news traveled nationally and put the Queen City in the spotlight once again.

But the hottest and brightest glare of publicity would come to Staunton in the wake of good news, not bad. In November 1912, when native son Woodrow Wilson was elected as the 28th President of the United States, city fathers invited him to a bash the following month to celebrate his birthday on Dec. 28. They and the city were ecstatic when the President-elect accepted.

When Wilson and his wife arrived in Staunton by train on Dec. 27, they were greeted by a sea of spectators and dozens of reporters from all over the country. Staunton decked out in bunting, flags, flowers and banners, and the new First Couple were escorted to Wilson's birthplace on North Coalter Street amid the cheers of thousands.

After spending the night at the former Presbyterian manse, the Wilsons motored through the heavily decorated city and were cheered by as many as 40,000 visitors and residents. Wilson spoke from the steps of Mary Baldwin Seminary and at Staunton Military Academy. A large brass star embedded in the marble floor of the old S.M.A. mess hall marks the spot where Wilson gave his address.

No such earth-shattering events occurred in Waynesboro, which steadily built upon its reputation as the Shenandoah Valley's most important industrial center. Big stories for Staunton's sister city included:

- In 1910 council approved an $8,000 bond issue to finance a tank or standpipe reservoir, and further development of the town water system.
- Mary Channell Stevens created Waynesboro's first public library in 1912.
- Wendy Miller in 1912 was reported to be the last living man to have attended the hanging of John Brown in 1859.
- In 1913 the Brandon Hotel became the coeducational Brandon Institute and in March 1920, became Fairfax Hall, a finishing school for young women.
- A 1915 Fishburne Military School ad in the "Valley Virginian" claimed that Waynesboro had no saloons.
- On July 12, 1915, Mayor Charles Winthrow "stated that he had been approached with reference to having the houses of the town numbered in order that the town might have a free delivery mail service," according to minutes of the council meeting. Council quickly agreed that directions such as "Turn left at the big mud wallow" were unbefitting a progressive community. The measure was unanimously adopted.

Staunton, however, would slip into the national spotlight yet again when, in March 1918, one of its native sons made good. John Greene, serving in France with the 1st Division's 18th Infantry, single-handedly turned back a German attack and drove the enemy from the field. For his action he received the American Distinguished Service Cross and the French Croix de Guerre with Palm and became the first American to receive combat decorations in Europe.

After the Great War, Staunton gradually returned to normal. By August of 1919, the biggest headline of the year announced not disasters or political news or stories of heroic native sons, but something far more indicative that peace, prosperity and the glorious dullness of small-town life were again on the march: "Five Big Days at Staunton Fair."

Swannanoa was originally built around 1911 by James and Sally May Dooley, owners of Maymont in Richmond. After the Dooleys died in the 1920s, there were several attempts to convert the estate to a country club. Later Swannanoa was acquired by Walter and Lao Russell. The restored mansion and gardens were dedicated in 1949 as The Walter Russell Foundation. *Waynesboro Collection*

Rare photograph of two men sitting in a steam-propelled Dawson Auto-Mobile somewhere in the Basic City area, circa the turn of the century. The Dawson, which was manufactured in Basic City, was the first automobile to be built in Virginia and was produced from 1900-1901. The Dawson represented the first of three unsuccessful attempts to manufacture automobiles in competition with the growing industrial giants of the Midwest, which eventually consumed more than 2,000 of their competitors. *Waynesboro Collection*

On Aug. 11, 1910, one of the myriad caverns over which the city is built cracked open near the southwest corner of Baldwin and Lewis streets. Over the next six hours the ever-expanding maw swallowed a 35-foot maple tree, the front yard of a dilapidated frame house and then, finally, the house itself. A second pit opened up in the back yard of C.L. Wilson, who desperately hauled furniture and other belongings out the front door. Nature's rampage continued for two more days, creating a third hole just in front of the fire station at the corner of Baldwin Street and Central Avenue; expanding the first hole to a depth of more than 80 feet; swallowing Wilson's entire back yard and his rear kitchen; and claiming the foundation of a house belonging to James Todd. *Schwartz Collection*

Pictured here are the remains of a March 20 and 21, 1911, fire that raged through the Wharf district destroying more than 10 buildings, killing many animals and threatening the entire downtown. The only thing saving Staunton and what was left of the Wharf was a sudden change in the direction of the wind, and the arrival of the Charlottesville fire company with a modern pumper engine. *Schwartz Collection*

On June 4, 1911, at 4:30 p.m., a black and furious wind whipped through Staunton, snapping the great maples in front of Trinity Episcopal Church and tossing them lightly through the air. The roof of the United Brethren Church on Lewis Street – shown here –went up like a paper balloon and disappeared into the swirling storm. The air was filled with debris, and the noise from the wind, goose egg-sized hail and thunder "resembled battle, the discharge of artillery mingled with the rattle of musketry," according to an eyewitness. *Waynesboro Collection*

STAUNTON DISPATCH AND NEWS

20TH YEAR, NO. 192. STAUNTON, VIRGINIA, TUESDAY MORNING, MARCH 21, 1911. 2 CENTS A COPY

FUNERAL OF JOHN LEWIS

Will be Held From The Residence of His Brother This Morning

John A. Lewis, of Staunton, died early Sunday morning in a hospital at Huntington, W. Va., aged 51. He was a son of the late James A. Lewis, and is survived by four brothers: H. M., W. T., Charles R., and J. H. Lewis, all of Staunton.

The funeral will take place this morning at 10 o'clock from the residence of H. M. Lewis, at 901 West Main Street. Interment will be in Thornrose.

Mr. Lewis had lingered for four months following injuries received on a ride from Richmond to Huntington in a box car. Both of his legs were frozen and amputation was necessary. A second operation was performed and it was believed that the young man stood a chance to recover. One day last week his brothers here received a letter which he had written telling them that his condition was much improved. The change in his condition was unexpected and news of his death came as a great shock.

The active pallbearers at the funeral this morning will be Messrs. R. H. Bell, Jr., Geo. A. Haines, Alex Bickle, Frank Matthews, Geo. C. Fifer and R. A. Fauver. The honorary pall-bearers will be Messrs. Watson Thom, Russell Brown, J. E. Hoover, H. C. Gibson, C. H. Smith and Harry Brynn.

FOR GUARD'S BENEFIT

Special Program to be Presented This Week at The Lyric

Staunton people are always willing to help Staunton organizations especially in a case when their soldiery is concerned. The West Augusta Guards are raising funds to defray expenses by a method which in addition to the small contribution involved, if you could call it a contribution, has the added attraction of giving one something in return. At the Lyric, Monday, Tuesday and Wednesday night a program has been arranged consisting of the usual high-class motion pictures, music by the Beverley orchestra and specialties by Mr. C. M. Hatton, a local entertainer of no mean accomplishments. The proceeds over and above expenses will be devoted to furniture, equipment etc., for the handsome new armory in the Beverley Garage building.

Highland Man Dead

John A. Noel, Confederate veteran, is dead at his home near Dunmore, W. Va., aged 66 years. He was a native of Highland county, Va. He served on the body guard of Jefferson Davis. Surviving him are his wife, who is a daughter of Col. B. F. Jackson, of Rockingham county Va.; seven sons, and one daughter.

His Life Twice Attempted

Roanoke, March 20.—H. P. Eanes, a salesman for a local typewriter exchange, was fired upon through the back door of the office of the company he represents Saturday night while standing at the telephone. The bullet went wild, and the would-be assassin escaped.

About two weeks ago Eanes, who came here four months ago from North Carolina, was fired on from an alley while passing up one of the principal streets. The bullet passed though his clothes under the left arm and he was uninjured.

Fined For Disorder

Charged with disorderly conduct, Lewis Michie, colored, was arraigned in police court yesterday morning and fined $5.80. Michie was alleged to have thrown rocks and to have otherwise misbehaved on Gooch street on Sears Hill on Saturday night.

The Weather

WEATHER CONDITIONS AND GENERAL FORECAST FOR VIRGINIA

Washington, D. C., March 20—Special 9:30 p.m.

Fair Tuesday and Wednesday moderate west winds.

Local U. S. Weather Station E. Rothnagel Observer

8 a. m.	45
12 noon	64
2 p.m.	65
6 p.m.	60

DOUBTFUL AS TO BOND ISSUE

Taxpayer Not Certain as to Wisdom of $1,000,000 For Roads

EDITOR NEWS:

I do not think it is the intention of the writers of the many articles appearing in the county papers on the road question to cast any reflections upon our board of supervisors. We all admit that they are men of wide experience and sound judgment but they are not infallible and may be carried of their feet by the enthusiasm of others.

In your answer to some of the objections is to issuing road bonds it is practically admitted that 15 miles of road might be built each year for 20 years and at the end of that time the county would still be free from debt and be in shape to continue to build roads. Under Captain Kee's plan after building 300 miles of road, which is not one tenth of the mileage of our county roads, and spending the million dollars and interest, there would be no provision for building any more roads for 20 or 25 years, until the debt is paid, unless you issue more bonds. In the meantime your road machinery would be laying idle. If the people have it to pay, why not pay as we go instead of paying interest and adding cost to cost. This is a question for the people of the rural districts to consider; the city people are not in it except with the pen.

If the railroads of the country have been built with borrowed capital it was borrowed by companies organized for the purpose of building railroads. They expected to build the roads and to get their pay from the proceeds of the roads. If a man buys a farm he expects to get his money back from the products of the land, and the same rule does not apply. It is the desire of every right thinking man to have good roads and the most [illegible] the tax-payers is the one to the nearest depot or shipping station. The county now has a macadamized road from Staunton to Middlebrook and Dr. Welland and the people near Middlebrook are asking the county to help build a cross country road from Greenville almost as far as Staunton.

Why should we mortgage the county in the most prosperous of times, the mortgage to be met when times possibly will be less favorable than now. More than this, our force of hands and one crusher like that used on the Greenville road last summer might be run profitably, but start three or four forces in Augusta county and advertise for hands and they will take advantage of the situation and ask fabulous prices. In the rush to get Jamestown fair ready for the opening a laborer told me he got $10 a day or $1 an hour.

The Rockbridge people have had trouble with their railroad bonds ever since they were issued, the Virginia state debt has been a menace to the state for years and it Augusta shoulders this road bond burden she may expect to carry it for generations. The roads of Augusta are being improved now and if the money appropriated for them is properly applied they can be improved more rapidly. This is a question I think should be well considered before it comes to a vote. The question should be, whether the county should increase taxes to build her roads and pay for them as she gets them or whether she should saddle this great debt upon herself for the sake of getting them more quickly.

TAXPAYER.

SACRIFICED LEGS TO LOVE

Refused Wedding Man Stays Abed For Forty Years

Boston, March 20. — Because his father prevented his marriage to the woman of his choice, Joseph Plummer, of Milton, N. H., has remained 40 years in bed. He is now 71 years old.

The girl he loved is dead, but the old man has not been told; in fact, he refused to speak of her from the very day when he said to his father:

"If you will not let me have her, then I will go to bed." He went to bed. The father, thinking that this perversity of youth would pass in a few days, carried him his meals. But he did not get up. He continued in bed day after day, week after week, year after year.

Now he is to weak from his long inactivity that he has lost the use of his legs entirely.

STAUNTON VISITED BY DISASTROUS FIRE

Fire last night raging unconquerable while the department aided by many volunteers fought madly to check it wiped out a whole block in the downtown business section with a probable loss of $75,000.

Originating about 10:30 o'clock in a small structure owned by Thomas J. Hounihan and located in the rear of an eating house on Johnson street the flames spread with lightning like rapidity and at midnight five large business houses with a number of smaller ones had been reduced to ruins. At the hour of going to press the following concerns are known to have been wiped out:

New building nearing completion owned by Mr. Dennis Brown.

W. J. Neff, dealer in buggies, carriages and wagons.

Luther B. Bosserman, feeds and fertilizers.

Staunton Milling Company.

W. E. Tribbett, agricultural supplies.

Edward Dore, wagon yard and stable.

Rissbarger's barber shop.

Wehn's wagon yard and stable.

Trimble's wagon yard.

Dudley Foster, lunch room.

Hounihan's old saloon stand.

Ashby's stable.

Gaybart's Grocery store.

Before 11 o'clock it became evident that the block on Middlebrook avenue, known as the wharf, was in imminent danger of destruction and a force of fire fighters was rushed to the vicinity of the threatened property. Despite their efforts the flames soon attacked the building of the Staunton Milling Company and in a few minutes it was seen that this structure was doomed. The flames next spread to the feed and grain houses of Michael Kivlighan and B. W. Crum and there seemed little hope that these establishments could be saved.

Fanned by a stiff breeze the flames grew to the fury of a furnace and great showers of sparks were sent flying into the air to be carried by the wind to all parts of town. For two hours or more it seemed that the entire section of the city south of Main street was doomed, and there was a demonstration on the part of the people the like of which had never been witnessed here before.

Merchants whose places were three and four blocks from where the fire was raging removed their books to safety and even in the parts of towns farthest away from the conflagration people made preparations to make hasty exists from their dwellings.

The scenes in the streets at this time were beyond description. Men had removed horses from stables in the doomed section and these with vehicles were brought uptown and left standing in the streets. All the while the flames in the burning section lighted up all parts of town being reflected on buildings, on trees, and in the heavens creating a spectacle which struck terror to the hearts of the hundreds who viewed it.

When it was seen that the fire was likely to spread over the entire downtown business section assistance was asked from Harrisonburg, Charlottesville and Clifton Forge.

At half past twelve o'clock all the buildings on Middlebrook avenue seemed likely to go. These were in imminent danger:

R. P. Lankford's, broker.

Baker and Brown's, wholesale grocers.

Humphries and Timberlake's, wholesale fruit and produce.

Blackley's warehouse, unoccupied.

J. H. Bowman and Company's farm implements, seeds etc.

The occupants of all these buildings had ample time to save their books and papers and most to them were taken to places of safety.

Miss Elizabeth Catlett went to Baltimore yesterday.

Mr. R. N. Page has returned from a trip to Kansas.

Prof. and Mrs. F. M. Somerville went to Richmond yesterday to spend several days while Prof. Somerville attends a meeting of all county superintendents of schools in whose counties boys' corn clubs have been organized.

SHOT DOWN BY CONSTABLE

Wesley Fields Filled With Lead When He Attacked Officer

Lynchburg, Va., March 20—While resisting arrest Saturday night at Warminster, 30 miles east of here, in Nelson county, Wesley Fields, a middle aged man with a large family, was shot and mortally wounded by Constable William Hughes. At 2 o'clock today Fields was still in the station waiting-room at Warminster and the attending physician said he could not survive long.

During the day Fields had a difficulty with a neighbor named A. R. Moon, who swore out a warrant for his arrest. In the meantime Fields went [illegible] and when he returned [illegible] took last night the [illegible] and [illegible] he left the [illegible] sentenced to [illegible] to arrest him. [illegible] Penitentiary [illegible] and advanced [illegible] court here. [illegible] the shot disabled [illegible] other evidence [illegible] the knife in [illegible] attack. [illegible] Palmer [illegible] since his [illegible] a married man. The betrayed [illegible] in court with her young [illegible] in her arms.

88,498 Plague Deaths in [illegible] Matron

[illegible] March 20. — [illegible] Here Mr. J. [illegible] February the [illegible] received a telegram yesterday morning announcing the death of Mrs. Susan W. Tidball which occurred in Sewanee Tenn. [illegible] was for some years the matron at the Virginia School for the [illegible] and the Blind and during her [illegible] here made many devoted friends [illegible] a number of relatives [illegible] last November a year ago her [illegible] Mrs. Barton died leaving two young daughters and Mrs. Tidball resigned her position to go and take care of her grandchildren Dr. Barton, their father being a professor in the University of Sewanee. She had not been well this winter but the news of her death is a severe shock to her friends here.

The remains will be taken to Winchester and the funeral will be held there tomorrow.

Circuit Court

In the circuit court yesterday an order was entered allowing E. E. Vint to adopt Golphia Albers and to change her name to Dorothy Sharp Vint.

The case of the Commonwealth vs. Massie Bridge, charged with the larceny of a steer, will come up today.

Mrs. Ed Hoover of Roanoke is visiting her parents Captain and Mrs. W. M. Simpson.

Mr. Malcolm Holliday is over from the University of Virginia for a short stay.

Mr. E. E. Arehart of Middlebrook was a visitor in the city yesterday.

BUSY PEOPLE.

Here's a Writer Who Says They Rarely Accomplish Big Things.

The sun is blazing down on the garden in which lives a saint, so called, whom I visited one day in Bombay. He has not spoken for twenty-three years, and his neighbors look upon him with awe. Some months later I visited at Davos Platz a man who for nearly thirty years has been studying drops of blood under a microscope. He is getting as close to life as he can, but admits that he knows little more than the sage in his hot garden at Bombay. Both the western scientist and the eastern sage smile indulgently at the fussiness of modern life.

My own experience of men in many lands has taught me that the most active are least valuable. It is a notable survival of the simian in man that so many people think that constant mental and physical activity is a measure of value. Busy people seldom accomplish anything. The statue, the poem, the painting, the solution of the economic, financial or social problem, even are all born in seclusion and appear mysteriously from nowhere. Moliere, Cromwell, Washington, Lincoln, Shakespeare, Dante and Cervantes all appear from nowhere and people [illegible] What a crowd of men we all recall who were so busy making themselves remembered that they are already for[gotten] [illegible] Collier in [illegible]

SHOWS APPLE SHIPMENTS

Interesting Statistics Compiled by Secretary Walter Whatley

The following table shows the quantities of apples shipped by the different railroads in Virginia during the movement of the apple crop of the State in the fall of 1910, and also the list, in their order, of the stations from which 20,000 barrels or more were shipped.

STATISTICS OF APPLES SHIPPED FROM VIRGINIA IN 1910

Compiled from information kindly furnished by the general freight agents of the various railroads by Walter Whately, secretary Virginia State Horticultural Society, March 1911.

TOTAL SHIPMENTS 1910

Cumberland Valley Railroad—136,309 barrels.

Baltimore and Ohio Railroad—181,999 barrels.

Chesapeake and Ohio Railroad—265,862 barrels.

Southern Railway—221,751 barrels.

*Norfolk and Western Railroad—250,000 barrels.

Total for 1910—1,061,852 barrels.

*Note—Owing to the failure of the N. & W. Ry. to furnish official statistics of their shipments, I have to insert an estimate of the shipments made by this road, furnished by Mr. E. A. Schubert, traveling agents A. and I. department of the road.

Stations that shipped over 20,000 barrels each, in their order.

Winchester—150,976 barrels.

Staunton—75,110 barrels.

Crozet—42,411 barrels.

Fishersville—34,841 barrels.

Afton—33,324 barrels.

Harrisonburg—25,330 barrels.

Waynesboro—25,180 barrels.

Front Royal—23,639 barrels.

Stephens City—23,630 barrels.

Covesville—23,144 barrels.

Arrington—20,109 barrels.

The above returns were made in boxes, barrels, and loose (bulk); for convenience in tabulation, all have been converted into barrels, at the rate of three boxes and 150 pounds of bulk apples to one barrel respectively.

Full details of shipments from different stations are published in the current annual report of the Society, sent free to all members.

WALTER WHATELY,
Secretary.

DEATH FROM SCRATCH

What Seemed to be Trifling Accident Proves Fatal to Cadet

The funeral of Walter Binford, who died from blood poisoning which resulted from a slight scratch on the hand, was held in Norfolk on Sunday afternoon.

Young Binford's death was peculiarly sad. He was 19 years old and was the only child of Mr. and Mrs. R. Binford of Port Norfolk. He was a student at Blackaburg and in some manner scratched his hand. He thought nothing of the matter until two or three days had elapsed when the pain growing greater, he went to the surgeon of the institution. The surgeon at once recognized the seriousness of the trouble and began a course of treatment, but there seemed to be very little improvement and young Binford was finally brought home and sent to the King's Daughters' Hospital in Norfolk. There every method known to medical science was resorted to in the effort to check the blood poison, but it was of no avail, and the young man died Friday night.

The young man had several relatives in Staunton.

NEW CARS ARE BEAUTIES

Chalmers Roadsters Arrive For Two Well Known Physicians

About the prettiest thing seen here in automobile construction for many a day are the two Chalmers "30's" received Friday at the Beverley Garage. One, a neat little 1911 roadster with double detachable rumble seat is for Dr. M. J. Payne, the well known physician of this city, and the other is touring car of corresponding specifications is for Dr. Carsells of Cave station. The roadster was on the streets yesterday afternoon when it was greatly admired. Chalmers cars have found a ready sale in this section where each year more people are adopting this every ready means of transportation.

ACCUSED OF ABDUCTION

Married Man, 45, And Girl of 16 Arrested in Harrisonburg

Harrisonburg, March 20—This place has a new sensation caused by the arrest here late Saturday night of Jacob Rymel, aged 45, a married man with a wife and two children, and pretty Elizabeth Stocker, the 16-year-old daughter of Chris Stocker, a prominent business man of Martinsburg, W. Va.

Rymel is charged with abduction, a penitentiary offense.

Stocker and Rymel were close friends it seems, and Rymel often visited the home of Stocker, who is a wealthy baker and confectioner, while the other man is a brickmason. Both are sportsmen and often went on hunting and fishing trips together. Through the friendship with her father Rymel had chance to be with the girl and it is alleged that he made efforts to win her affections, apparently being successful.

The couple left Martinsburg for Harrisonburg early Saturday morning, the girl taking some of her clothing with her. Her father soon discovered her absence and instituted search, enlisting the aid of the Martinsburg police. Late in the afternoon they were located and officers came to Harrisonburg in an automobile and returned with Miss Stocker, Rymel remaining in jail here, having announced his intention to resist extradition. Both he and the girl stoutly deny that there was anything wrong in their elopement.

The girl is barely 16 years old and is very pretty. Her mother died several years ago, and for some time she has been assisting her father in conducting his business.

Rymel is a former resident of Harrisonburg.

Personal Mention

Hon. and Mrs. Randolph Harrison and children have returned to Lynchburg after a visit to Mr. Henry Harrison.

Rev. H. T. Hieronimus went to Waynesboro yesterday to officiate at the funeral of Mrs. Sleeth, wife of Rev. W. T. W. Sleeth.

Mr. and Mrs. John Francisco and Miss Genevieve Francisco of Millboro are guests of Mrs. J. N. Ryan.

Rev. B. C. Jett went to Clifton Forge yesterday where he was to preach last night after which there was to be a congregational meeting for the purpose of calling a rector.

Cadet Henry Ransom has returned to the Virginia Military Institute after spending a week at his home here.

Miss Helen Hall of Warren Ohio, who was the guest of Mrs. Fitzhugh Elder has gone to Washington for a few days.

Mr. Fitzhugh Elder went to Washington yesterday on business.

HOLD FAMILY REUNION

Staunton People Attend Pleasant Celebration in Harrisonburg

Mr. and Mrs. Joseph Loewner, of this city, have returned from Harrisonburg where on Sunday they attended a family reunion. The occasion was most enjoyable and at the dinner which was held at night all members of the family with the exception of two brothers were present. Those present were:

Mr. and Mrs. Chas. A. Hammer Mr. and Mrs. Samuel Klingenstein, Mr. and Mrs. Charlie Loewner, Mr. and Mrs. Joe Loewner, of Staunton Mr. and Mrs. Herman Wise and Mrs. Minnie Wise, of St. Louis, Rabbi Jacob Schwanenfeld and Morris Spiro.

Meeting of Camp

Headquarters Stonewall Jackson Camp No. 25, C. V., No. 469 U. C. V.
Staunton, Va., March 21, 1911.

Camp will meet in regular session tonight at 7:30 o'clock. A full attendance is desired.

W. D. ARMSTRONG,
Commander.

F. T. Stribling, Adjutant.

Mrs. Frank Hopkins and children of the Hot Springs are guests of Mrs. J. S. Desarnette.

The Academy and Plunkettsville yesterday afternoon. The kids played a eleven inning game, resulting in a victory for the Academy team by a score of 10 to 8. The batteries were: Academy team: Michael and Lyle; Plunkettsville, Clatterbaugh.

March 21, 1911: This 1911 fire nearly destroyed downtown Staunton. *Microfilm Archives*

Basic City Depot. *Waynesboro Collection*

Three circa 1910s views of Fishburne Military School, all taken from South Wayne Avenue. One view is of the ivy covered main building, another shows several cadets gathered on the school's playing field and the third is of cadets on parade. FMS was founded in 1878 by James A. Fishburne, a student and protégé of Robert E. Lee. It is one of the few military schools in Virginia to continue in operation. *Waynesboro Collection*

Staunton was one of the most progressive towns in the Shenandoah Valley, sporting gas-operated lights as early as 1853. The gas works, which are shown here, were located at the intersection of Johnson and Coalter streets where – today – Columbia Gas has its offices. *Schwartz Collection*

The old Gypsy Hill Park fairgrounds and racetrack – complete with viewing stands and gazebos – graced the Lake Tams area of the fairgrounds and was a popular spot for everything from races and horseshows to picnics and community events. *Schwartz Collection*

STAUNTON DAILY LEADER

VOLUME 17, NO. 122. STAUNTON, VIRGINIA, WEDNESDAY AFTERNOON, NOVEMBER 6, 1912. PRICE ONE CENT

WILSON'S PLURALITY 2,000,000

POWERS DIVIDED ON SPOILS OF THE BALKAN WAR

Great Britain, Russia And France Inclined to Let States Take Territory Conquered.

GERMANY, AUSTRIA ENTERTAIN OTHER VIEW

First Sign of Dissention Among Allies Comes From Servia,That Now Appears to Have Designs on Albania.

London, Nov. 6.—In the absence of news of fighting from the Balkan theater of war, Europe is giving attention to the diplomatic situation arising out of the hostilities. Although all the Powers have not yet replied to Turkey's appeal for mediation it is known that it has nowhere received a very warm reception.

Yesterday Sir Edw. Grey, Foreign Secretary, in stating England's attitude in reply to a question in Parliament, said that the Balkan allies should be permitted to dictate their terms of peace.

A more definite request from Turkey to the Powers to put an end to the war, which she is expected to make in view of the French reply to her first application, is likely to receive more consideration.

Even then, however, the Powers will be unable to overlook the oft-repeated demand of the allied Balkan nations that Turkey must deal directly with them. All that the Powers will be able to do, therefore, is to act as intermediary in bringing the belligerents together.

Sharp Lines Divide Allies

As to the future of the Balkans, a very sharp line divides Germany, Austria-Hungary and Italy from France, Russia and Great Britain. Public opinion in Great Britain, France and Russia argues that the allies should have the territory which they have conquered, and Russia particularly has warned Turkey that conditions could only become worse should further disaster occur at Tschatalja.

What Austria Fears

Austria-Hungary, which after all is the most directly interested of the great powers, being the nearest to

(Continued on Page Four.)

"GREAT CAUSE HAS TRIUMPHED," SAYS PRESIDENT--ELECT

"Every Democrat And Every True Progressive Must Lend Enthusiasm to Fulfillment of Hepe.

I ACCEPT RESULT WITH ENTIRE GOOD HUMOR-T.R.

The Colonel Says The American People Have Decided. Vice President-Elect Makes Statement.

New York, Nov. 6.—"A great cause has triumphed," was President-elect Wilson's message to Chairman McCombs last night in a reply to a telegram sent by the man who managed the campaign for the New Jersey Governor.

"A great cause has triumphed. Every Democrat and every true Progressive must now lend his full force and enthusiasm to the fulfillment of the people's hope—the establishment of the people's right."

In his telegram to Governor Wilson Chairman McCombs told him he had won a significant victory, having received the largest electoral vote ever given a presidential candidate.

VICE PRESIDENT-ELECT MAKES STATEMENT

Indianapolis, Ind., Nov. 6.—Thos. R. Marshall, the vice president-elect had the following to say of the election:

"The Democratic victory of Tuesday will result in the restoration of representative government if Democratic officials, both state and nation, will remember that executive duty consists of enforcement of the law, and insistence of legislative compliance with Democratic platforms and principles.

"Such will be the result if Legislative representatives remember that they represent the people and no special interests whatever, and if judicial representatives will give up the perfection of reason in the light of today and not in the light of two centuries ago, and be content to construe and not make statutory laws.

"The principles of Democracy finding their expression in representative government are now upon trial. This is the last chance that will be given the office holder to prove himself the servant and not the master of the people whom he serves.

"The party appreciates the gravity of the situation and the sacred burden that it bears. It approaches reverently on the discharge of its duties.

(Continued on Page Four.)

IS ELECTED PRESIDENT

Born at Staunton, Virginia	Dec. 28, 1856
Graduated from Princeton College	1879
Graduated from the law department of the University of Virginia	1882
Practiced law at Atlanta	1883
Married Helen Louise Axson of Savannah	1885
Became professor of political economy at Bryn Mawr College	1885
Became professor of political economy at Wesleyan University	1888
Became professor of jurisprudence and politics at Princeton	1890
Became President of Princeton University	1902
Elected Governor of New Jersey on the Democratic ticket	1911
Received Democratic nomination for President of the United States	July 2, 1912
Elected President of United States	Nov. 5, 1912
Author of numerous works on political economy and American History.	

STAUNTON'S SON CARRIES ALL BUT SIX THE STATES

Taft Has Plurality in Three, Roosevelt Carrying Only Three, But Beating Taft's Electoral Vote.

WILSON'S ELECTORAL VOTE 469, T. R.'S 49, TAFT'S 15

Pennsylvania Still Doubtful and Vote May Be Against Wilson. Largest Electoral Vote Ever Given a President.

Figures compiled from the latest returns indicate that Wilson has carried 41 States, Taft 3, Roosevelt 3, with one still in doubt, and that Wilson and Marshall will have 469 votes in the electoral college, Roosevelt 49, and Taft 15. This is the most sweeping victory in the history of national elections.

WILSON TAKES THEM ALL

New York, Nov. 6.—From the latest returns coming slowly in from doubtful States like Pennsylvania and Illinois, and even Iowa, which was first apparently safe for Roosevelt, it looks like Wilson will have nearly five hundred votes in the electoral college.

The Democratic landslide has staggered the politicians, though Wilson headquarters and various New York papers had forecasted Wilson would have over four hundred votes in the electoral college.

It is believed that his popular plurality will be fully two and a half million, probably three.

Cincinnati, Ohio, with over half the State heard from, gives Wilson fifty thousand plurality.

Charleston, W. Va.—Wilson carries West Virginia by probably five thousand plurality. Hatfield, Republican, for Governor, by ten thousand.

Des Moines.—Iowa probably for Wilson by eight thousand.

Returns still incomplete, Wilson gaining over Roosevelt.

PENNSYLVANIA DESERTS TEDDY

Pittsburg.—Wilson now leading in

(Continued on Fifth Page.)

Staunton Wilson And Marshall Club Planning BigCelebration Here Friday. Many Organizations to Take Part.

Plans are in the borning for a great Democratic jubilation and torchlight parade such as Staunton has not seen in twenty years. Friday night has been fixed upon for the big event, and a committee has been appointed to further the work of the fete and to invite all city and county organizations to take part.

It is expected that the parade will consist of mounted police, Stonewall band, Staunton's two military companies, Staunton Military Academy and band, Augusta Military Academy and band, Fishburne Military Academy and band, Roman band, Craigsville band, all city and county Democratic clubs, all local organizations, Staunton Fire Department, and other bodies, as well as floats and automobiles of various descriptions.

The parade will march through the principal streets of the city and will then rendezvous at some convenient point for a giant bonfire and fireworks display.

President Cochran of the Staunton Wilson Club has appointed the following committee on arrangements which will meet tonight at 8 o'clock at the General Manager's office: W. E. Tribbett, A. S. Robertson, W. H. Landes, H. L. Opie, S. D. Timberlake, jr., J. M. Brereton, Major T. H. Russell, W. C. Marshall, L W. H. Pelton, W. T. McCue, J. D. Crowle, George Cottrell and Capt. D. L. Porter.

HURT WHEN AUTO STRUCK AN ENGINE

Harrisonburg, Nov. 6.—While returning from Staunton about 7:30 last evening in an automobile, owned and driven by Lynnwood B. Yates, of the firm of P. L. Yates & Son, a party composed of Mr. Yates, Nelson Deck, W. Payne, Joseph Conrad, Allen Bryan and "Pete" Williams, the last two being hunters just picked up a few miles before—had a narrow es-

(Continued on Eighth Page.)

CARRIED AWAY IN HOUSES BY FLOOD

Nashville, Tenn., Nov. 6.—A portion of the east basin of the reservoir from which Nashville gets its water supply gave way yesterday, letting a torrent of water loose down the hill on which the basin is located.

Several houses were washed away. There was no loss of life.

The break came without warning, and caught nearby residents as they slept. Several persons hearing the rush of water hurried to see what had happened and were caught in the torrent, but most of these have been accounted for.

Residents near the reservoir felt the effects of the flood for only a short time, as the water soon had got to lower levels, where it flooded cellars. The water that swept down South Eighth avenue was six feet deep.

T. M. Heffey, wife and child, were washed out of their home, but were saved by climbing into a tree. W. O. Arsinger and wife were awakened by the roar of the waters and felt their house moving down the stream. They escaped when the water began to subside.

WEST VIRGINIA IS SCENE OF DISORDER

Charleston, W. Va., Nov. 6.—Serious trouble is threatening in the coal fields of West Virginia today. Fred Bobbitt a bookkeeper for a coal company at Mucklow, was dragged from a train and severely beaten at East Bank yesterday.

It is said that conditions in the Paint Creek district, where a strike has been in progress for a long time, are such that martial law may be declared again.

After spending many weeks in the coal strike territory the last of the militia companies left a few days ago.

SEEKS TO ANNUL CUBAN ELECTION

Havana, Nov. 6.—Senor Fererra, Speaker of the House of Representatives, has declared that he would attempt to have the election of Mario Menocal, President of Cuba, annulled on the ground that it was illegal.

Liberal leaders blame President Gomez for the election of a Conservative President, declaring that if General Monteagudo had been removed as head of the army that Alfredo Zayas would have been elected. The Liberals claim that the army was used to help the Conservatives. Liberalpapers continue making revolutionary threats, and it isbelieved that the government will proceed against some ofthe most radical in the courts.

THE WEATHER

Washington, Nov. 6.--Local rains tonight and Thursday. Cooler Thursday in extreme northern portion and extreme west portion.

November 6, 1912: The Leader heralds the election of Staunton's native son, Woodrow Wilson, to the Presidency. *Microfilm Archives*

Postcard view of King's Daughters' Hospital in Staunton circa the 1910s. This facility, which was established in 1895, served Staunton until 1950 when a new hospital was constructed on North Augusta Street. *Waynesboro Collection*

Wilson reviews cadets in 1912. *Schwartz Collection*

In November 1912, Staunton native Woodrow Wilson was elected the nation's 28th President. City fathers invited Wilson to a birthday bash the following month, and were ecstatic when he accepted. The city spared no expense to welcome Wilson. When the president-elect and Mrs. Wilson arrived by train on Dec. 27, the city was enveloped in bunting, flags, flowers and banners. The couple were escorted to Wilson's birthplace at Frederick and Coalter streets, and to the new President's surprise were given separate bedrooms. Officials assumed Wilson would want to sleep alone in the room where he was born.

"If you don't mind," said Wilson quietly, "I would rather sleep with my wife."

The next day the Wilsons motored through the heavily decorated city and were cheered by as many as 40,000 visitors and residents. Wilson spoke from the steps of Mary Baldwin Seminary – where years before Miss Baldwin had denied the young Wilson visiting rights to a cousin – and at Staunton Military Academy. *Schwartz Collection*

The original Robert E. Lee High School stood next to what was then the Staunton Fire Department on Baldwin Street. It moved to its new location on Churchville Avenue in 1927 and the old school was demolished for a parking lot. The firehouse also moved, to its current location on North Central Avenue. This photo, which shows the fire station's horse drawn wagons decked out in flags and bunting, may have been taken on Flag Day or the 4th of July. *Schwartz Collection*

In June 1904, William Larner purchased nearly four acres on the southeast side of Middlebrook Road, about one mile from Staunton's corporate limits. The discovery of a cave on the property led Larner to enlarge the entrance and, in 1907, install lights and open Staunton Caverns to the general public. It is unknown when the cave operation was abandoned. The City of Staunton purchased it in 1932 and, for safety purposes, completely sealed its entrance. *Schwartz Collection*

Flags, bunting, welcome signs and booths set up along Main Street marked the city's efforts to open its arms to returning World War I veterans, in this circa 1919 photograph. *Schwartz Collection*

Brick pavement was laid on North Central Avenue from Frederick Street to Churchville Avenue in 1917. The construction crewmen pictured here were employees of the William A. Larner Co., and are working between Frederick and Baldwin streets. *Schwartz Collection*

Never-before-published photograph of a carnival, complete with Ferris wheel, set up on Central Avenue in downtown Staunton. This view looks north from today's Beverley Street. The office of the Staunton Daily News is shown on the left in the background. *Schwartz Collection*

View of the interior of the Bodley Wagon Works, which moved to Staunton from West Virginia in 1891. This view shows five employees and a small dog sitting up on its haunches. Bodley manufactured carts and wagons for agricultural, mining and logging concerns and distributed them internationally. *Schwartz Collection*

STAUNTON DAILY LEADER

VOLUME NO. 18, NO. 11. STAUNTON, VA., SATURDAY AFTERNOON, DECEMBER 28, 1912. PRICE, ONE CENT.

THOUSANDS IN THE CITY TO ATTEND WILSON'S "BIRTHDAY PARTY"

ADDRESS OF WELCOME, WILSON RESPONDING

Thousands Hear Rev. A. M. Fraser Welcome President-elect in Eloquent Words to City of Birth, and Wilson's Feeling Response.

At 3 o'clock in the afternoon in the presence of a vast concourse of enthusiastic listners, variously estimated at from 10,000 to 20,000, Rev. A. M. Fraser, D. D., as the city's official representative, extended to the Hon. Woodrow Wilson greeting of welcome. He spoke from the balcony of the Mary Baldwin Seminary, standing between the massive colonial columns, immediately at the head of the stairs. It took just ten minutes for Dr. Fraser to deliver his remarks, which are given in full below, and the graceful manner in which he discharged the office charmed the audience into a silence that indicated intense interest and profund approval. The silence was broken half a dozen times, however, when a significent sentence or a striking climax impelled the crowd into an emotional outbreak of cheering and applause. Dr. Fraser was in his best form and all who are acquainted with his speaking ability know what that means. He spoke as follows:

Dr. Fraser's Address

FELLOW CITIZENS OF STAUNTON, AND OF VIRGINIA, AND OUR MOST WELCOME AND HONORED GUESTS FROM MANY STATES:

An occasion like this one has never, in all the history of our Government, come a second time to the same community.

On the ever-to-be-remembered afternoon of the second of last July, when the maddening uncertainty of many days was relieved by news from the Baltimore Convention that Gov. Wilson of New Jersey, a native of Staunton, had been nominated for the Presidency of the United States, a large concourse of people gathered around the house in which he was born, filled with a wild, undefined hope that perhaps the time had come for Virginia to resume the role of "Mother of Presidents," and that perhaps it had fallen to the lot of our modest little city to give a Chief Executive to the nation.

And now we meet again, with our enthusiasm chastened, but neither diminished nor daunted by the clash of tremendous forces in a spectacular and significant campaign, and we have called in our neighbors and friends to rejoice with us and to help us celebrate the fulfillment of our hopes and the realization of our most daring dreams.

On the morning after the November election, early risers in the eastern part of the city saw every window on the crest of yonder line of hills aflame with glory reflected from a rising sun, while those living beyond the Manse declared that a perfect rainbow spanned that now historic home. What more beautiful decoration or what more gracious suggestion could we have had than this celestial token of promise and of hope set like an aureole about the house in which Woodrow Wilson was born!

On the following day a committee from the "Woodrow Wilson Club" of Staunton waited on the President-elect in his Princeton home and invited him to visit Staunton. Notwithstanding the exciting preoccupations of the hour, he received them with gracious cordiality and at once accepted the invitation. In all that political campaign through which he had just passed and which had so often sparkled with his acts of knightly courtesy, there was nothing finer than his instant and hearty response to the proud and grateful sentiments of his native place. And yet he did an even finer deed when, on his own initiative, he selected his birthday as the occasion of his visit.

He went out from us as a very little boy, laden with the prayers and benedictions of a small congregation of Christian people. He comes back to us today, by the favor of an overruling Providence, a proven leader of men, wearing the plaudits of the whole civilized world, and chosen to fill the highest civil office ever given to a man by the suffrages of his fellow-men.

Now then, fellow citizens, lend me your hearts, lend me your throats, lend me your silver trumpets, your drums and clanging cymbals, and whatever else can feel delight or make a joyful noise, whilst I attempt to give utterance to the emotions of this hour.

I speak for all of you, men, women and children, visitors and home people, regardless of political affiliation or religious creed, irrespective of occupation or social rank, nationality or color, as the one voice of this multitudinous assembly, when I say to him that we thank him for the honor of his visit; we extend to him a boundless welcome to the place that gave him birth; we join with him in celebrating his birthday and wish him many happy returns; we congratulate him on the honors he has won and the opportunity for world service he has achieved; we accept him, in the language of the Scriptures, as "the Minister of God to us for good"; we assure him of our respectful sympathy and our Christian prayers amidst all the cares and perils of public service; we pledge him a fair-minded and manly interpretation of all his official acts; and we promise him all proper support in every right endeavor to enforce the laws, promote the welfare

(Continued on Second Page)

MAYOR H. H. WAYT

Who received Mr. and Mrs. Wilson on their arrival here.

Dr. Fraser delivered the address of welcome to the President-elect on behalf of the city.

REV. DR. A. M. FRASER

NEWSPAPER MEN ARE WELL PLEASED

Staunton has shown her best front to the men "who put the news in newspapers" and they seem wel pleased with what they have seen and heard and done and what has been done to them. Representatives of the Associated Press, United Press and International News Service, three newspaper organizations serving some several thousand papers. They sent over sixty-five thousand words last night alone. There has not been a thing written but praise so far as can be learned, many newspapermen declaring that they had never seen a city handle a big proposition any better, and that it compared favorably with even the celebrations of the big cities. They also seem well pleased with the facilities extended them for handling their stuff.

BALTIMORE SUN PHOTOGRAPHER BACK

The man who loves to photograph Staunton, Mr. N. R. Henderson, who was here several days ago and took numbers of fine pictures that have been appearing in every issue of the Baltimore Sun, is back on the job, having slipped away and come with Mr. Wilson. A new lot or artistic celebration pictures will appear in his popular paper. This time he wants pictures of all the ladies.

Miss Nettie Bagby has returned from Washington.

WILSON WILL ATTEND BANQUET

Prominent Men Will Respond to Toasts. Elaborate Affair.

The banquet at the Staunton Military Academy begins promptly tonight at 8 oclock, when it will be opened with a prayer by Rt. Rev. D. J. O'Connell of the Diocese of Virginia.

There will be covers for 300, and the banquet will be furnished by Rauscher of Washington, served in courses.

There will be seven toasts, and speakers will be limited to 15 minutes, with the prayer that it may be even shorter, in order to close promptly by or before midnight. The toastmaster is the Honorable Allen Caperton Braxton of this city.

The toasts in order are as follows:

1st.—The next President of the United States: Response, Gov Woodrow Wilson.

2nd.—The City of Staunton, birthplace of Woodrow Wilson: Col. Hampton H. Wayt, mayor.

3rd.—Virginia: the birthplace of free government: Gov. Wm. Hodges Mann.

4th.—The United States: Fatherland of the American nation: Hon. H. D. Flood.

5th.—The Virginia Military Institute: Gen. E. W. Nichols.

6th.—Party Leadership: Speaker Richard Evelyn Byrd.

7th.—The Democratic Party: Wm. F. McCoombs.

Benediction by Rev. A. M. Fraser, D. D.

Toasts to Congress and the Army were planned but those who had expected to respond were called away.

FIVE ECLIPSES TO OCCUR IN 1913

Five eclipses of the sun and moon will take place during the year 1913, but three of these will not be visible in the United States.

The first eclipse of the year will be the total obscuration of the moon March 22. This will be partially visible in this country. A partial eclipse of the sun, visible only on the Pacific coast north of latitude 36 degrees, will take place April 6. Partial eclipses of the sun, invisible in the United States, are scheduled for August 31 and September 30. Fifteen days earlier than the latter date there will be another total eclipse of the moon, visible only in the western part of this country, the moon setting as the eclipse begins.

JAMES HERE

Among the prominent State officials here is E. O. James, the popular Secretary of the Commonwealth. He is visiting Mr. S. M. Donald.

VISITING BANDS ENTERTAIN CROWDS

All day long the visiting brass bands made the air ring with popular music, and greatly enlivened the crowds on the streets. The Harrisonburg Daily News Band marched through the streets in the morning, playing lively airs and the organization won applause and praise wherever it was heard. The Dayton and Roman bands also furnished spirited music during the day. The latter held a concert in the Augusta Hotel. The U. S. Cavalry band was heard at the Mary Baldwin Seminary and also at the reception at Stuart Hall. The V. M. I. band, the Stonewall Brigade Band and the Basic Band also added their full quota towards entertaining the thousands of visitors in the city.

MANY WITNESS CAVALRY DRILL

After the parade and official welcome of Mr. Wilson at the Seminary, the crowds dispersed to various parts of the city, some to Stuart Hall, some to the hotels where music was furnished by visiting bands and others remaining on the streets by the hundreds.

Quite a goodly crowd repaired to Plunkettsville where they witnessed a series of military manuevers by a squadron of United States Cavalry at 4 o'clock. The fine horsemanship of the soldiers, especially that of the officers, delighted the spectators and the troops executed the evolutions with decided skill. They were under the command of Major Woods of his First Squadron, Fifteenth Regiment, United States Army.

EVERY CONDITION FAVORABLE, PROGRAM FULLY CARRIED OUT

President-Elect Having Recovered From Attack of Grip, Enters Into Spirit of Occasion.

SPLENDID MILITARY PARADE AND REVIEW WAS PRINCIPAL FEATURE

Staunton's Greatest Military Spectacle Since The War. Mr. Wilson to Leave at 11:05 Sunday.

Twenty-five thousand people, it is estimated, were on the streets and at the various affairs held during the day for the celebration of Woodrow Wilson's home-coming to the city of his nativity. The weather was most favorable, temperature being very moderate, with a bright sun in a clear sky. Every condition was auspiscious, and the enjoyment of the day was entered into fully by the great concourse of people and the many distinguished visitors from various parts of the country who gathered to greet the President-elect on his 56th birthday anniversary.

Mr. Wilson, entirely recovered from the attack of grip from which he has been suffering, attended every official function, and the program was carried out in full as planned. He received county and city officials, committeemen, prominent visitors, etc., at the manse at 10 a. m., reviewed the military and civic parade shortly after noon, and was officially welcomed to the city in the afternoon at the Mary Baldwin Seminary at 2:30 o'clock.

The President-elect has signified his intention of attending the semi-official banquet at the Staunton Military Academy tonight at 8 o'clock.

He will leave Staunton to return to New Jersey Sunday morning at 11:05, on C. & O. train N. 4.

Staunton's Distinguished Son Cheered on Ride to Review

While the crowd was gathering in the morning, a reception to city officials, committeemen and distinguished guests was held at the manse. Governor Wilson being attended only by Chairman S. D. Timberlake, Jr., of the Central Committee, who introduced the callers. The line of visitors was continuous for nearly an hour, only those wearing official badges and officers in uniform being admitted. An eager throng, kept back by the ropes and a vigorous squad of special policemen, hung around the manse during the entire reception. The ceremonies were conducted with the utmost simplicity. Governor Wilson seemed in good health and the best of spirits. A score or more of camera and moving picture men were busily engaged before the manse "taking" the crowd, individual groups and well-known men.

Presentations From City

What most affected Mr. Wilson in the whole ceremony attending his welcome was the gift presented to him by the city of Staunton. The presentation was made in the course of the morning reception at the manse, by Mr. Charles Catlett on behalf of the whole city. The gift consisted of miniature portraits on ivory medallions, one each of his father and his mother. The portraits were executed by Miss Ellen Douglas Stuart, the well known painter, niece of Gen. J. E. B. Stuart, an dfor a number of years art teacher at Stuart Hall.

Grand Military Spectacle

Not since the Civil War has there been a military spectacle in Staunton of more grandeur than that which was presented to Mr. Wilson as a feature of the celebration of his home-coming. The military and civic parade was reviewed shortly after noon by the President-elect, from his reviewing stand under the magnificent main arch, opposite Trinity Episcopal church. Following the review, Mr. and Mrs. Wilson returned at once to the manse, this being the last of the functions before dinner.

The parade formed with its head resting at the Presbyterian manse, and as the President-elect took his seat with Governor William Hodges Mann in the carriage provided to convey him to the reviewing stand, five automobiles containing city and county officials, prominent members of Mr. Wilson's party, committeemen, etc., took position in his rear, preceding the military organizations.

Occupants of Carriages

In the automobiles were W. F. McCombs, Wilson's manager, Mayor H. H. Wayt, T. M. Smiley, chairman of the county Board of Supervisors, and S. D. Timberlake, Jr., chairman of the Central Committee, in the first; Senator Edward Echols, L. W. H. Peyton, J. H. Worthington, committeemen, Peyton Cochran, committeeman and Pres. of Staunton Woodrow Wilson club, in second; Judge George M. Harrison of the Supreme Court of Appeals, Judge Henry W. Holt of the Circuit Court, Judge R. S. Ker of the Corporation Court, and Hon. A. C. Gordon, in the third; Chas. Catlett, Julius Witz, A. Shultz, A. S. Robertson, committeemen, in the fourth; C. T. Jordan, W. C. Marshall, Edward Woodward, committeemen in the fifth.

Two secret service men rode with Mr. Wilson in his carriage.

An automobile conveyed Mrs. Wilson, Mrs. Mann, their hostesses respectively, Mrs. A. M. Fraser, Mrs. Edward Echols and Dr. Fraser, to the reviewing stand just before the parade left the manse. Another automobile conveyed Mrs. R. H. Catlett, Mrs. Annie Wilson Howe and her daughter, Mrs. Joseph Wilson Howe, to the reviewing stand.

Organizations in Parade

With four mounted policemen clearing the way, the parade took up the march at noon, the first division, consisting of the Stonewall Brigade Band, United States Cavalry and Field Artillery under command of Major C. D. Rhodes, U. S. A.; a provisional regiment of Virginia militia, Companies A, H and B, 2nd. Inf., and Companies B, E and K, 1st Inf., under the command of Lt. Col. Craighill of Lynchburg; the V. M. I. Cadet Corps about three hundred and fifty strong, under command of Col. J. C. Wise, Commandant, the Staunton Boy Scouts. The 2nd division, commanded by Col. J. F. Templeton,

(Continued on Sixth Page.)

December 28, 1912: Woodrow Wilson returns to Staunton for a triumphal visit. *Microfilm Archives*

Although Augusta Military Academy is credited for having gotten its start in 1865 when Charles Roller Sr. returned from the Civil War and tutored Confederate veterans in or around Mt. Sidney, AMA didn't really get off the ground as a first-rate academy until 1879. At that time, Roller – who had served in the Virginia General Assembly from 1871-74 – formally established the Augusta Male Academy at his home in Ft. Defiance. By 1890 the school's name had changed to Augusta Military Academy and was considered one of the country's top-notch institutions. During its heyday it fielded a band and tough, competitive sports teams. Financial troubles forced the school to close in 1983. *Schwartz Collection*

Let The New Year Revive That Spirit of Progression Which Prompted You To Enter The Commercial World—Advertise; It will Put You In The Procession of Prosperity.

MAIL EDITION

Staunton Morning Leader

WEATHER
FAIR

VOLUME NO. 25, NO. 74. International News Service. STAUNTON, VA., SUNDAY, FEBRUARY 4, 1917. PRICE TWO CENTS

UNITED STATES IS ON VERGE OF WAR WITH GERMAN COUNTRIES

WAR OR PEACE UP TO BERLIN TO ANSWER

President Tells Joint Session of Congress That He Does Not Believe Germany Will Deliberately Sacrifice American Lives.

WILL DEMAND REPRISALS IN EVENT OF ACTUAL OVERT ACTS BY GERMANS

Philadelphia, Feb. 3.—An attempt to sink the United States torpedo boat destroyer Jacob Jones, a hundred yards from shore in the Philadelphia navy yard today was frustrated.

According to information one of the machinist mates opened a sea valve which allowed two and half feet of water to enter before discovered. The suspect was arrested.

Washington, Feb. 3.—With diplomatic relations already actually severed, President Wilson this afternoon went before a joint session of Congress and declared that he did not believe that Germany will deliberately sacrifice American lives in a wilful prosecution of her ruthless naval program.

The President assured Congress that only overt acts on Germany's part can make him believe that American rights are to be deliberately violated.

WAR OR PEACE UP TO GERMANY

"But if such action comes," said President Wilson, "I will again come before Congress," and he made it plain that in such an event he will be forced to demand reprisals.

The question of war or peace tonight reposes in Germany. If American lives are sacrificed in the new submarine operations, the President will demand from Congress authority to use any means that may be necessary for the protection of our seamen and our people in the prosecution of their peaceful and legitimate errands on the high seas.

NAVY PREPARES TO PROSECUTE REPRISALS IF THE WORST COMES

The United States has made good her threats of drastic action unless Germany respects American rights to the freedom of the seas, and the severance of relations is President Wilson's answer to Berlin's declaration of a ruthless submarine warfare.

HOPE TO AVERT WAR

A declaration of war is the next step in defending American rights, but such a widening of the breach depends upon the future attitude of Germany and upon the extent to which her uboat operations encroach on American commerce. Some officials still hope that war may be averted, but there is a general belief in administration circles that the die has been cast, and that the United States is definitely alined against Germany in a fight for civilization.

AMBASSADOR GERARD RECALLED

Ambassador Gerard was this afternoon recalled from Berlin.

Ambassador von Bernstorff, who has represented Germany in all of the trying negotiations in which President Wilson has during the last two years and a half labored to maintain American rights without the drastic step to which he has at last been driven, had not up to this afternoon been handed his passports. Official notification of the severance of diplomatic relations, however, con-

(Continued On Page Two)

JAPAN AND U.S. NEAR CRISIS ON ANTI-ALIEN BILL

State Department Sends A Special Plea to Idaho Legislature.

SITUATION LOOKS VERY SERIOUS

Friction Apparently Kept Under Cover For Some Time.

Washington, Feb. 2.—Japan's representations to the United States against the anti-alien land bills pending in the Idaho and Washington legislatures, although made informally through her embassy here, are considered no less serious at this critical juncture of international affairs than her protests against the California laws four years ago.

Absolutely nothing had been permitted by the administration to become public until the protest was disclosed by appeals to the Oregon and Idaho delegations in Congress to use their influence at home to prevent passage of the bills at this time.

The state of feeling in Japan, probably much disturbed by the recent crisis in the government, has

(Continued On Page Three)

"LEAK" ADMITTED BY NEWSPAPER MAN

Washington, Feb. 3.—W. W. Price, the White House correspondent of a Washington paper, admitted to-day that he sent information of the President's peace note on Dec. 20th to Chicago brokers, thirty minutes after it was given to him in confidence.

Price's admission was made to the congressional leak investigators, and the mystery of the leak which was alleged to have netted big profits in Wall street is now cleared up.

Price's admission also clears the President's official family of charges that high administration officials were responsible for the leak.

IMMIGRATION BILL BLOCKED

Washington, Feb. 3.—Immediate reconsideration of the immigration bill, passed over the President's veto by the House, was blocked in the Senate by Senator Reed of Missouri, but agreement was reached to proceed to a vote on repassage of the measure at 4 p. m. next Monday.

AUTO VICTIM RECOVERING

Stuart Thomas Cox, the little son of Mr. and Mrs. Delmar R. Cox, of Stuarts Draft, who was hurt the first of the week in an automobile acident on the Middlebrook road, has been removed to the home of his parents, and is recovering from his injuries.

The accident occurred when an automobile carrying the rural route mail ran into Mr. Cox's car, he having stopped on the side of the road, to see about his machine. The child was the only occupant who suffered severe injuries, and his face was almost cut open, and a number of stitches had to be taken.

AMERICANS IN PRISON CAMPS IN WESTFALEN

Demand Made For 64 Men Taken From Victims Of Raider.

WAR ALWAYS HAS FOLLOWED BREAKS

Severance Of Relations Has Always In Past Led To Hostilities.

New York, Feb. 3.—The Maritime Exchange here today received a cablegram from London stating that the American steamship Housatonic had been sunk off the Scilly islands.

The state department early this evening had received nothing official in confirmation of the cablegram.

Demands Americans.

Washington, Feb. 3.—The United States has formally demanded of Germany the immediate release of the Americans who were taken prisoners on prize ships by the raiders in the south Atlantic.

There were sixty-four Americans taken from the steamers Georgic, Mount Temple and Voltaire. Sixty of the prisoners are con-

(Continued On Page Two)

COVINGTON HAS EXPENSIVE FIRE; 4 STORES BURNED

Covington was swept by a disastrous fire yesterday which wiped out three stores, a bowling alley and did damage amounting to thousands of dollars.

Fire was discovered in a bowling alley and spread to the Iradue Dry Goods store and Hodges jewelry store and a hardware store opposite McAllisters.

Despite the fact that firemen and volunteers of hundreds of citizens worked frantically the blaze consumed the buildings and was stopped only when a brick wall interposed to stay its progress.

One fireman was injured by falling from a window. Later it was found that he was not seriously hurt.

The blaze was discovered about 10 o'clock yesterday morning and the fire did not yield to the firefighters until late yesterday afternoon.

Firemen fought the blaze with inadequate water supply and the men were literally walking cakes of ice in the bitter wind which added to the conflagration.

Last night it was impossible to compute the loss but it was stated that it would not be less then twenty thousand. Quantities of drygoods an other merchandise was saved by firemen. The origin of the fire is unknown.

INSURANCE COMPANIES HIT

Columbus, Ohio, Feb. 3.—By a vote of 28 to 2 the State Senate passed initiated bill No. 1. which excludes private liability insurance companies from competition with the State in writing workingmen's compensation insurance.

GUARDSMEN MAY AGAIN HAVE TO BE MOBILIZED

War Department Has No Plans as Yet For Present Contingency.

MAY BE NEEDED FOR LOCAL TROUBLES

Action Depends on How Wide Breach With Germany May Become.

Washington, Feb. 3.—There is no immediate prospect that the national guardsmen who have been recently mustered out, since their return from the Mexican border will be again called into service in view of the break between the United States and Germany, according to Washington officials today. The war department has made no plans along this line. Whether or not the guardsmen will be remobilized will depend, they declare, upon how wide the breach becomes and whether this country becomes actually involved in the European war. If a declaration of war comes, the opinion here is that the troops will be called out not for actual service in Europe but for emergency that may arise in this country when troops will be needed.

(Continued On Page Three)

SPELLING BEE TO COME NEXT WEEK

The great spelling Bee is to become a reality. The papers, compiled by experts of the state board of education, have arrived. They contain the words which, in the estimation of the board, will test the mental alertness, "preparedness" in spelling, and either win or lose for young Augustans place at the head of Virginia school children.

Tests will be directly by Supt. Somerville and the two school supervisors Misses Cunningham and Murfee.

Under instructions from the board the spelling tests will be conducted in a way to insure a fair average of figures for the county. The examiners will appear without notice at county schools, line up the children, and "fire" the list of words.

It is said the state board has not selected the "hardest" words with an intention of trying to "stump" the youthful spellers but has hit on such arrangement of letters as occur in words of everyday conversation and with which a majority of the children are more or less familiar.

There is much interest among the county teachers because each of the 250 in Augusta wants her class to show up well in the test next week. A friendly rivalry has been engendered among the teachers as well as among the children.

Plans of the examiners are not made public beyond the intention to being the Bee next week. The Superintendent will visit a few schools in one section and then move on to another, keeping, as he goes, a record of the numbers examined and the "score."

AMERICAN VESSEL SUNK OFF BRITAIN

Housatonic From Newport News To London Goes Down Off Scilly Islands—U. S. Navy Takes Over All Wireless Stations—Efforts To Damage Ships In Harbors —Deutschland Cargo Burns On Dock.

COAL SUPPLIES HELD AT DOCK FOR USE OF U. S. WAR VESSELS; NAVY YARDS UNDER HEAVY GUARD

Washington, D. C., Feb. 3.—Tonight the United States verges on war with the Teutonic empires and their allies since it is not to be supposed that Germany acts independently in her determination to use every means in her power to strike at the entente powers.

Swiftly following the cabled recall of Ambassador Gerard from Berlin came the dramatic incident of the day in handing to Ambassador Von Bernstorff his passports. With these momentous events came the formal severance of diplomatic relations with Germany and a tension in every governmental department that indicated official Washington regarded war as an imminent possibility.

Seizes All Wireless Stations.

Not the slightest hint as to the disposition of naval forces or even the whereabouts of the vessels recently ordered south was available at the navy department. While the department absolutely refused to confirm the action by official announcement it was learned that the navy has taken over every charted wireless station in the United States. These include Sayville, Tuckertson and all other great German stations.

Deutschland Cargo Burns On Dock.

New London, Conn., Feb. 3.—Cargo intended for the German merchant submarine Deutschland, expected at this port momentarily, was in flames at 11 o'clock today. Fire broke out in the combustible material at the north end of the state pier where the cargo was tored soon after word was received that diplomatic relations were to be severed with Germany. The cargo is stored about 200 feet from the German steamship Willehad, which had acted as "mother ship" to the submarine. The entire fire department of the city was called out to fight the fire.

Fear Attempt On Shipping.

Norfolk, Va., Feb. 3.—Sentries are guarding all American warships in the navy yard here, holding up everybody except government officials. Railroads have been ordered by the navy department not to supply coal to foreign ships on new contracts. The action, presumably precedes the commandering of coal for the use of United States vessels.

American Ship Sunk Off British Isles.

New York, Feb. 3.—The American steamship Housatonic has been sunk off the Scilly Islands, southwest coast of England. Details are lacking at the state department. The Housatonic left Galveston January 6 and Newport News January 16, for London. The Ship had a displacement of 3000 tons and was owned by the Housatonic Steamship Company of New York.

Liner Wrecked In Newark Bay.

New York, Feb. 3.—The crews of sixteen Hamburg American and North German Lloyd lines ships interned here since the beginning of the war left their vessels on "lave of absence" tonight. The general exodus followed

(Continued On Page Two)

SUPT. STEARNES HERE

J. C. Stearnes, state superintendent of public instruction was in the city during the day, en route to Richmond. Supt. Stearnes has been inspecting public schools in Rockingham county. He left for the State capital on the noon train.

THE SALVATION ARMY

Sunday, Feb. 4th—Sunday School 2:30 p. m.; Salvation meeting 8 p. m. Captain P. W. Archer, Commanding officer.

February 4, 1917: America's involvement in the European war is anticipated. *Microfilm Archives*

While the players for this baseball team from the northern Augusta County village of Spring Hill are unidentified, it is known that they played against teams formed in other communities throughout the county and the Shenandoah Valley in a precursor to the Valley League Baseball of today. *Schwartz Collection*

Peaceful scene in Gypsy Hill Park showing a slide and children's play area. *Schwartz Collection*

One of several "bird's-eye" views of Staunton, taken in the early 20th century. This one, taken from a then-undeveloped Reservoir Hill, shows the city's central business district facing south. Some structures visible in this postcard view are Lee High, St. Francis Catholic Church and the U.S. Post Office. *Schwartz Collection*

The Leader Papers Set the Pace--In Local and Telegraphic News, in Advertising, In Circulation. Morning and Evening Associated Press Services, and Best Possible Telegraphic Market Reports.

THE EVENING LEADER

VOLUME NO. 25, NO. 124. Always Progressing Upward and Onward STAUNTON, VA., TUESDAY, APRIL 3, 1917. Member A. B. C. and Associated Press. PRICE TWO CENTS

U. S. TODAY AT WAR WITH GERMANY; FORMAL DECLARATION PENDS

WHEELS OF WAR PUT IN MOTION

Every Agency Moving Swiftly to Gird Nation For Defense And For Vigorous Prosecution of Hostilities.

CABINET MEETS IN SPECIAL SESSION TO CONSIDER INITIAL WAR STEPS

Washington, April 3.—The United States is today really at war with Germany, only the formal recognition of Congress being awaited.

Every agency is moving to gird the nation against the government which President Wilson, in his address to Congress, characterized as "a natural foe to liberty."

The cabinet has been called for a special war session at which steps to be taken in a vigorous prosecution of the war will be planned among them being:

An extension of credits to the nations already at war against Germany.

The raising of money by taxation for the United States to use in the purchase of war equipment.

The equipment of the navy to the fullest efficiency to cope with the German submarines.

The raising of a great army on the principal of universal liability to service, the first increment of which will be half a million men.

Senator Chamberlain, chairman of the military committee, launched a universal compulsory military service bill in the Senate today, the amended bill providing for the training of half a million men of the age of 20, and providing in the President's discretion many thousands more, to the age of 23. The bill was referred back to the committee.

AUGUSTA BOYS BRAVED U-BOATS; LAND SAFELY

Bridgewater, April .—George J. Hanger, of Bridgewater, and Clarence Johnson, of Mossy Creek, who left Newport News on a horse laden English vessel on February 1 for Bristol, landed at Newport News Saturday on their return home. The boys left the morning of the day that the German unrestricted U-boat warfare went into effect but the boat going over and the one on the return voyage ran the gauntlet safely. Immediately after they landed at the home port they sent a telegram to their parents which lifted a load of anxiety from their minds and brought relief that can only be measured by fathers and mothers whose sons have been exposed to danger.

MOOREFIELD ELECTS DR. HALL PASTOR

At a congregational meeting held on Sunday morning the Presbyterian church of Moorefield, W. Va., unanimously elected Rev. S. O. Hall, pastor, to succeed Rev. C. D. Gilkeson, recently resigned to accept the position of superintendent of home missions for Winchester Presbytery. This is one of the best churches in Winchester Presbytery, contesting for first place with the Winchester church.

Mr. Hall has been in Staunton since the latter part of December filling the pulpit at the First Presbyterian church while Dr. Fraser has been ill or absent on account of his health. Dr. Fraser is expected home about April 12 to 15, when Mr. Hall will be free to serve the Moorefield church if he decides to accept the call.

CITIZENS MOB HEADQUARTERS OF PACIFISTS

Washington, April 3.—Guardsmen of the Third District Infantry, with a party of citizens, today covered the front of the headquarters of the Emergency Peace Federation with a coat of yellow paint, while another party of citizens destroyed pacifist literature and banners inside.

SANK TREVOSE WITHOUT WARNING; 24 ARE MISSING

New York, April 3.—The British freighter Trevose, which Germany reported sunk, was torpedoed without warning on March 18th, and twenty-four members of the crew are unaccounted for, according to officers of the steamer Venesia, arriving here with five members of the Trevose's crew.

JUNIOR NUMBER OF "THE RECORD"

The junior class issued this month's Staunton High School magazine, "The Record," which is just out, and there are a number of contributions of much literary merit.

Among the contributions are The Violet, a poem by Miss Edith Hanger; Extracts from the Journal of Two Juniors, a clever take-off on Dr. Frederick Cook, with local color; "Let us Appreciate our President" —Vivian H. Berry; Juniors of the 3-B Class, a poem by Miss Edith Eye; the story of a Little Common Flower, by Miss Clara Mote; "Classified Ads," by Miss Edith Eye; "Beyond the Alps Lies Italy," an essay by Sidney Morris. The editors have their usual contributions.

4,474 RECRUITS IN MARCH

Washington, April 2.—A total of 4,474 men were recruited for the navy during March, and the net gain for the month was 3,628, against 2,086 last month. The strength of the navy now is 62,667 men.

PRESENT BUDGET TONIGHT; RADICAL CHANGES URGED

The city council at its meeting tonight will consider financial problems both as to disposition of the established revenues of the city, and means of raising more money to meet contemplated expenditures.

The finance committee has concluded the arrangement of the budget report and will place before council tonight a concrete statement of the financial condition of the city with recommendations for expenditures.

In a matter closely allied with the budget report, a special committee composed of Messrs. Heydenreich, Cushing, Bryan and Silling will make recommendations, regular tax collections on license moneys and a further recommendation for a more thorough system of bookkeeping in the office of the commissioner of revenue.

It is understood that the special committee will recommend that the commissioner of revenue keep a set of books carrying an alphabetically arranged list of names, with classified branches, including the occupations, professions etc., for which tax is collected.

It is said the committee will further recommend that license taxes be collected promptly and that the newly installed system of bookkeeping be audited by the finance committee with the aid of an expert accountant from time to time as the committee or council may direct.

FIRE LOSS FOR 1916 A DECREASE

Fire Chief Jesse M. Bratton has just completed his report for the past fiscal year in his department. The report shows a decided decrease in the fire loss in the city, over that of 1916, and Mr. Bratton states that the people of Staunton are now fully aware of the fact that with a little precaution and common sense the fire risk here can be reduced to a minimum.

Two Big Fires

The total fire loss during the past year, according to the report, was $67,875. Of this amount $59,000 covers the loss in the only two big fires during the year. The Miller Wholesale Company's fire on last April the 6th entailed a loss of $48,000. The other big blaze was on December the 25th, when the plant of the Staunton Daily News was damaged to the extent of $11,000.

The remaining loss of $8,875 was distributed between thirteen fires where the loss reached more than an insignificant sum.

Alarms turned in during the year numbered forty-four. The report lists the causes as—fifteen with a loss, eleven chimneys, four burning grass, one tar wagon, two calls to the county, two oil stoves, two from defective electric wiring, and one from a lamp explosion.

Staunton's fire loss for the fiscal year ending last April totaled $86,726, with the fire at the Woodward stores as the largest, damage in that one instance having been $67,155. Sixty-two alarms were turned in last year.

ARE YOU KEEPING POSTED BY WIRE?

If you are reading the Morning Leader regularly, you can answer that question in the affirmative. The Morning Leader carries in each issue all the important world events sent direct to the Leader office by Associated Press wire. This means that the Leader papers enjoy wire connections with all parts of the world.

Compare the Morning Leader day by day with any newspaper published and you will find that all big news features are carried by the Staunton paper and given the Staunton public at exactly the same time the city papers give them to their readers. This means that the news can be received through the Morning Leader hours before it can be received here through any other paper.

DROVE OF ELK EXPECTED SOON

State Game Commissioner John S. Parsons has wired the Evening Leader that the elk he promised Augusta county will arrive here from the West on Thursday or Friday, consigned to County Game Warden H. H. Mish.

It is expected that fifteen or twenty elk will be in the shipment and they will be liberated in the mountains in the western part of Augusta near the Highland county line, so that both counties will be benefitted.

The supervisors of this and neighboring counties will be asked to put a penalty of $200 fine and six months in jail on anyone killing an elk for the next five years and $100 reward will be offered for information leading to the arrest and conviction of anyone violating the ordinance.

The matter of placing elk in the mountains of Augusta was first taken up with the Game Commissioner by the Leader some weeks ago and received immediate attention.

Efforts are being made to replenish both forests and streams with fish and game in the immediate future.

ARE DISPLAYING FLAGS

Staunton's business places and residents are patriotically displaying the flag at this time, and with every hour a new place is seen adorned with the stars and stripes. Bryan's department store and Spitler and Eakle are among the latest to fall in line.

BASEBALL AT A. M. A.

There will be a baseball game at A. M. A. Wednesday afternoon at 4 o'clock, when the cadets will meet the Randolph Macon Academy nine. A swift game is expected.

ASK COUNCIL FOR PUBLIC PHONES TO COUNTY EXCHANGE

Backed by what is claimed to be widespread interest in an immediate settlement of the telephone controversy, members of a committee, acting for the mass meeting of several days ago, are circulating a petition for presentation to council tonight.

The substance of the appeal to council is a request that the Farmers Mutual be given the right as a temporary expedient to string wires to the business section for the installation of three phones in business houses or public places, the service to be free to the public and the phones to be installed by council.

It is understood that the petitioners base their request on the necessity of communication between the city and certain localities in the county which are now completely cut off. The installation of public telephones, it is said, is intended as a public convenience and can only be had by bringing into town a wire from the Mutual exchange in the suburbs. The resolution, embodied in the petition, asks council to appropriate $250.00 or a less sum to install the phones.

28 ARE MISSING FROM THE AZTEC

Washington, April 3.—Ambassador Sharp cabled from Paris today that nineteen survivors of the armed American steamer Aztec, torpedoed by a German submarine without warning, have been landed, but that twenty-eight are missing, with rescue doubtful because of a heavy sea storm.

The Aztec sailed from New York March 18 for Harve. She was commanded by Captain Walter O'Brien.

The Oriental Navigation Company, owners of the Aztec, also owns the Orleans, one of the first American vessels to run Germany's blockade.

The Aztec carried a cargo of foodstuffs and supplies valued at $500,000.

The Aztec was armed with two 5-inch guns. The crew of naval gunners on board was in command of a warrant officer, and were saved.

The Aztec formerly owned by the Pacific Steamship Company, was a ship of 3,727 tons gross, and 2,345 tons net. She was built in New Castle, England in 1894. She was 353 feet long with a beam of 43 feet.

'LADY' CROOK HAD DESIGNS ON BANK

Nell Gordon, a "lady" crook, came to town to inveigle herself into a position where she could rob the national bank, but love finally caused the lady tendencies to overcome the crook in her make-up, though not until after many thrilling developments in "A Girl Like That," tonight's Paramount at the New, featuring Owen Moore and Irene Fenwick.

CONGRESS TO PASS WAR RESOLUTION

Will Have Overwhelming Majorities in Both Houses When Vote is Reached After Usual Procedure Is Gone Through With.

SENATE COMMITTEE REPORTS FAVORABLY, STONE REGISTERING ONLY NEGATIVE VOTE

Washington, April 3.—The administration resolution declaring a state of war and directing prosecution of war against Germany, presented to the Senate this afternoon, went over until tomorrow on the objection of Senator LaFollette, amid a stormy scene. Senator Martin was wildly applauded from crowded galleries when the resolution was reported.

LaFollette said that he expected "quite a little debate" before any action is taken, but other former filibusters said there would be no protracted debate. The House also adjourned until tomorrow when its foreign relations committee postponed consideration of the resolution.

Washington, April 3. Congress met today to act on the President's request to declare that a state of war exists between the United States and Germany. It is taken for granted this afternoon that both Houses will pass a resolution making such a declaration by overwhelming majorities although pacifist members are expected to offer some opposition.

Approved By Committee

The Senate foreign relations committee has this afternoon approved the administration resolution, introduced by Senator Martin, of Virginia, declaring that a state of war exists with the German empire, in practically the same form that it was introduced in both houses last night. The committee vote was unanimous, with the exception of the vote of Senator Stone, while Senator Borah was absent. Stone said that he would not make a minority report, but that he expected to speak against the resolution.

The Senate resolution, as soon as it was acted on by the foreign relations committee, was taken to the House committee to try to get it put in the same form. Following is the resolution:

"Whereas, the recent acts of the Imperial government are acts of war against the government and people of the United States.

"Resolved, by the Senate and House of Representatives of the United States of America, in congress assembled, that the state of war between the United States and the Imperial German government, which has thus been thrust upon the United States, is hereby formally declared, and,

"That the President be, and he is, hereby authorized and directed to take immediate steps, not only to put the country in a thorough state of defense, but also to exert all of its power and employ all of its resources to carry on war against the Imperial German government, and to bring the conflict to a successful termination."

CENTRAL POWERS TALKING PEACE

Berlin, April 3.—It became known here today that the proposal of County Von Czernin, the Austrian foreign minister, that a peace conference be held without requiring a cessation of hostilities, as reported by the Associated Press correspondent several days ago, apparently represents the attitude of all of the Central governments.

There will be a conference at Berlin shortly of representatives of all four of the central powers to approve the proposal.

The Lokal Anzeiger says the conference will stress that central powers are ready to fight if the proposal is not accepted.

April 3, 1917: America enters the war against Germany. *Microfilm Archives*

Previously unpublished photograph of two Staunton men who have fashioned a snowmobile using an Indian motorcycle as its power source. This photo was taken in 1917 at 214 N. Central Avenue outside the Indian motorcycle dealership. A sign in the window reads, "1917 Indian Powerplus Is Here." The office just to the right of the motorcycle dealership is that of the Staunton Daily News. *Schwartz Collection*

Have You A Father, Son, Brother, Uncle, Nephew, Sweetheart Or Friend Overseas Or In Camp At Home? One, Or More, Of The Seven Big War Organizations Is Helping Him. Are You?

WASHINGTON, Nov. 9— Light rains in early morning followed by fair and colder in the afternoon Sunday. Monday partly cloudy and cooler.

Staunton Morning Leader

MEMBER OF ASSOCIATED PRESS LATEST MARKETS BY WIRE

VOLUME NO. 28, NO. 122. Member Of The Associated Press, Morning And Evening. STAUNTON, VA., TUESDAY, NOVEMBER 12, 1918. Circulation Books Open to All Interested. PRICE TWO CENTS.

Everything For Which America Fought Has Been Accomplished, Says Wilson; Armistice Terms Call For Restitution By Germany—For 30-Day Period; Staunton Celebrates Peace With Monster Parade

Staunton whooped 'em up Monday.

From the time the Leader received the Associated Press dispatch at 2:55 a. m. Tuesday 2 o'clock in the afternoon, every minute saw Staunton grow more and more awake and by that time everyone in the city—or almost every one—was down town for the great peace celebration. Hundreds and hundreds were on the streets—a beaming smile on every face.

Staunton—that city which gave to the world its present leader, Woodrow Wilson, President of the United States of America—celebrated before the sun had sank in the golden west the victory which had been so gloriously achieved by Allied arms. Just eleven hours after the joyous news that peace again was to reign over mankind reached Staunton, its citizens were taking part in a monster peace celebration.

All the business district decorated during the morning, as did the owners of residence property outside the business center. Old Glory was seen from almost every door and Red, White and Blue bunting was in evidence. Horns were lustily sounded, fire crackers discharged, revolver reports rent the air and then, but first, came the ringing of the church bells. There was universal thanksgiving and prayer to Him who reigneth in the name of peace and love.

The parade, at almost a moment's notice, formed on east Main street and off-streets and proceeded west along Main street. Headed by Chief-of-Police S. B. Holt and members of the police department, common

Continued On Page Two

DEATH OF E. C. STOVER

The remains of Edgar C. Stover reached the city during the morning from Richmond, where he had been taken to a sanatorium for treatment. Three weeks ago he was taken ill with the influenza, which was followed by spinal meningitis for which affliction he was being treated in Richmond.

Mr. Stover was twenty-eight years of age and was a resident of the county, living on the Spring Hill road, about three miles from the city. The funeral will be Tuesday morning at eleven o'clock from Pleasant View church. Burial will be there. The service will be in charge of Rev. D. F. Glovier, of the United Brethren church.

Mr. Stover leaves the following immediate relatives—his wife, who was Miss Sadie Reeves, of Rolla; parents, Mr. and Mrs. S. J. Stover; two sisters, Mrs. Hulvey, of Weyers Cave, and Mrs. Miley Wine, at home; five brothers, Russell, of Farmington, Ill., Dorsey and Hugh, in the railway service, Eugene, of this city, and Raymond at home.

Accompanying the remains home from Richmond were his brothers, Dorsey and Hugh, his wife and Miss Fannie Lamb.

MASS MEETING AT WAYNESBORO

Tuesday night at 7:30 o'clock at Waynesboro, there will be held a big Mass Meeting in the Presbyterian church. It will be a peace meeting and also one at which the United War Work Campaign will be launched.

Mrs. Claudia Albright Roberts will sing and Judge Richard S. Ker will speak.

Public Speaking

Weyers Cave public speaking, in interest of United War Work Campaign, Thursday evening at 7:30, by Hon. Jos. A. Glasgow.

At Mt. Sidney, Wednesday evening at 7:30, Hon. Jos. A. Glasgow.

Rev. T. O. Keister, D. D., will speak in same behalf, at New Hope Wednesday evening at 7:30 in the Presbyterian chapel.

CITIZENS OF CRIMORA

The people of the Crimora section of the county are specially asked to remember the War Work Campaign this week and be ready to contribute when the canvassers call on them.

(Signed)

B. Y. HARRIS,
DeWITT ROYER,
L. L. COINER,
Committee.

MILLBORO TO CELEBRATE

There will be a celebration at Millboro Tuesday night and all people from the neighborhood are invited. Speakers from a distance, songs, music and a patriotic celebration. Perhaps the home guards of the county will have a part. Among the speakers will be army officers. A thanksgiving service will also be held.

GREENVILLE RED CROSS

There will be a meeting of the Greenville Red Cross Auxiliary Wednesday, Nov. 13, at 2:30 P. M. All who are interested are asked to be present. Call for the Xmas boxes at Dr. Thomas'.

"STICK TO THE BOYS" IS SENTIMENT OF MEETING TO LAUNCH U. W. W. CAMPAIGN

Appealing to the folks to stand by the boys overseas, as well as in the training camps, until the last one had once more been enfolded in the arms of his mother, his sister, his sweetheart or other dear ones, speakers last night at the Y. M. C. A. thrilled a large audience at the opening of the United War Work Campaign to be celebrated here this week.

During the remaining days of the week Staunton and Augusta are asked to contribute $40,000 to this cause and the seven participating organizations, all of which were represented by speakers last evening. Of this apportionment is asked to contribute $12,000.

The workers began their canvass immediately after the meeting adjourned.

It was a great meeting and not one present failed to see that to

Continued On Page Two

BOARD TO ALLOW ONE MONTH'S PAY

The County School Board has decided to pay the salary of teachers for the first month during which the schools suspended operations for Influenza. No action has yet been taken as to the second month.

Superintendent Somerville stated that the school term will not be prolonged, to make up for lost time, but will stop at the time planned, for, and the pupils will have to lose it.

This will be done because to extend the time would bring the end of the session into the season when many of the children are helping on the farm, and it would be impossible, because of the number kept out, to preserve the average attendance.

N. L. SCHAEFFER DEAD

N. L. Schaeffer, aged forty-eight, died at his home near Valley Mills Saturday morning at ten o'clock, death being caused by heart trouble, following a stroke of paralysis a short time before. The funeral will be held from the residence Tuesday afternoon at three o'clock. Rev. J. M. Tise, of the Churchville Lutheran church, of which Mr. Schaeffer was a member. Burial will be in the Lutheran cemetery.

Surviving are his wife, who was Miss Betty Croft; three daughters, Mrs. E. Paul Spitler, of Alexandria, and Misses Nellie and Laura, at home; three sons, Howard D., of Washington, Frank, of Gary, Ind., and Allen at home; one brother, Jacob Schaeffer, of New Market; one sister, Mrs. Sarah Alexander, of New Market.

IN CASE OF A HITCH MEETING MAY BE HERE

The Presbyterian Synod of Virginia was to have held its annual meeting in Harrisonburg beginning today, but owing to the influenza the meeting was for a time abandoned. The congregation of the Harrisonburg church still wishes to entertain the Synod which will meet some time in December.

In case for any reason it is deemed wise not to hold it in Harrisonburg this year the Staunton First church has signified its readiness to come to the relief of Harrisonburg, the householders of the congregation having decided the matter favorably yesterday afternoon, and the session last night.

The session, however, went on record as favoring the granting of the request of the Harrisonburg church to hold the meeting at Harrisonburg, being unwilling to take any steps that may deprive Harrisonburg of the meeting.

NOTICE TO DELINQUENT LEADER SUBSCRIBERS

Again we call attention to the order of the War Industries Board of the Federal Government which forbids the sending of newspapers to subscribers who are delinquent.

There are yet a few subscribers to the Daily Leader who come under the ban of this order and will have to be cut off in a few days unless they send in their renewals at once. We hope each one to whom this order applies will give heed to this notice in time.

(By The Associated Press.)

VICTORY and PEACE.

After more than four years of struggling the rights of mankind are served. The greatest day in the history of nations has dawned.

The German militaristic classes—arrogant beyond expression—are in defeat.

Kaiser and Crown Prince are

Continued On Page Two

SING, HALLELUJAH, AMEN!

(Editorial)

The news of the signing of the armistice was announced at the State Department in Washington at 2:45 a. m. Monday. At 2:55, just ten minutes afterwards, Miss Gussie Hedrick, whom many people think the politest and most efficient telephone operator in the State of Virginia, had received it from the Associated Press and was calling all the telephones connected with the Leader and all those attached to the Leader, and in a short while the linotype was at work, the press oiled and ready for business, every worker on the paper being at his post, and at 5:25 boys were on the streets selling the extra edition of the Leader announcing the most momentous event of modern times, heralding as it does the fall of the last strongholds of feudalism, and the advent of freedom throughout the world.

The Leader felicitates its readers on this happy event which renders the sons, brothers, husbands, sweethearts of all of us measurably safe once more, from bodily harm and will in due course bring them back to us, warriors bold, as winsome knights as ever drew blade in a just cause. The Lord be praised, bless his holy name!

CANCEL CALLS

(By The Associated Press.)

WASHINGTON, Nov. 11.—By order of President Wilson, Provost Marshal General E. H. Crowder today cancelled all outstanding draft calls, stopping the movement during the next five days of 252,000 men and setting aside all November calls for over 300,000.

Calls for the navy and marine corps are not affected and entrainments for these services will continue as ordered. Draft boards will continue the classification of registrants of September the 12th.

Secretary Baker later announced that as far as possible all men called and not yet completed training will be immediately turned back to civilian life.

PLAY TIE CONTEST

Hot and enthusiastic from the very beginning, the football teams representing the Fishburne Military School and the V. M. I. scrubs played to a tie yesterdey afternoon at the former's grounds in Waynesboro. That the Waynesboro lads have done some stiff work during the past several weeks is shown from the fact that then V. M. I. defeated F. M. S., by a count of 19 to 0.

(By The Associated Press)

WASHINGTON, Nov. 11.—President Wilson issued a formal proclamation this morning announcing that the armistice with Germany had been signed. The proclamation follows:

"The armistice was signed this morning. Everything for which America fought has been accomplished. It will now be our fortunate duty to assist by example and by friendly, sober counsel and by material aid in the establishment of a just Democracy throughout the world."

WASHINGTON, Nov. 11.—The terms of the armistice with Germany were read in Congress by President Wilson at one o'clock this afternoon.

The military terms include the evacuation of all invaded territories, the withdrawal of German troops from the left bank of the Rhine and the surrender of all war supplies.

The abandonment by Germany of the treaties of Bucharest and Brest-Litovsk is also provided.

The naval terms provide for the surrender of one hundred and sixty submarines, fifty destroyers, six battle cruisers, ten battleships, eight light cruisers and other miscellaneous ships.

Among the financial terms are restitution for the damage done by the German armies, restitution for the cash taken from the National Bank of Belgium, and the return of the gold taken from Russia and Rumania.

German troops are to retire immediately from any territory held by Russia, Turkey or Rumania before the war.

The armistice is for thirty days, but the President spoke of the war as "coming to an end."

WASHINGTON, Nov. 11.—The world war ended at six o'clock this morning, Washington time, with a revolution in Germany and with William Hohenzollern, the former Emperor, a fugative from his native land.

The announcement that the armistice terms were signed by the German envoys at midnight last night at five o'clock Paris time, and that hostilities would cease six hours later was made at the State Department at two-forty-five o'clock this morning.

The terms of surrender were not made public, coincident with the announcement, but were to be given out later in the day.

Former Emperor Flees To Holland

LONDON, Nov. 11.—The arrival of Emperor William, with his wife and eldest son, has caused excitement and much uneasiness among Dutch authorities and public, says a dispatch to the Telegraph from Rotterdam.

It is said that the Dutch government faces a difficulty as to its treatment of the visitors. Many people contend that Hohenzollern and his eldest son are still German soldiers and must be interned. Others urge that they should be sent back to Germany. Others argue that they cannot be prevented from visiting their old friend Count von Betinck.

AT PUTNAM FACTORY

The Y. M. C. A. shop meetings, which are being conducted at the different manufacturing plants of the city, will be held at the Putnam Organ Factory Tuesday at twelve o'clock, conducted by the Rev. Dr. A. M. Fraser.

November 12, 1918: The end of the "war to end all wars." *Microfilm Archives*

The 1920s

Prosperity and Prohibition

For area residents, the 1920s began with confidence in the economy, enthusiasm for the city's future and – not to everyone's liking – a new national law that forbade the manufacture, sale and distribution of alcoholic beverages. While prosperity manifested itself in the form of road improvements, building projects, new schools and increased personal salaries, Prohibition worked against it by creating an illegal and untaxable underground economy, and by forcing out of business one of Staunton's oldest, most profitable businesses – the whiskey manufacturing firm of Harman Brothers at New and Johnson streets.

Despite the passage of the Eighteenth Amendment to the Constitution, which took effect Jan. 16, 1920, the decade got off to an auspicious start in Staunton when it was announced that the Valley Turnpike Company – one of the oldest toll road concerns in the South – would cease to function. The turnpike (now U.S. 11) would be taken over by the state highway commission, thereby guaranteeing regular, high quality maintenance of one of the main thoroughfares leading into and out of the city.

Two months later, city officials released the news that Staunton's street-paving program, which had begun in 1891 with Main Street, had resulted in 15 miles of paved roads. Most of those roads were paved with brick or cobblestones, both of which would see their demise before the decade was out.

The Staunton News-Leader

35th Year, Vol. No. 31. STAUNTON, VA., TUESDAY MORNING, FEBRUARY 5, 1924 PRICE TWO CENTS

WHOLE WORLD RINGS WITH PRAISE FOR WOODROW WILSON AS PLANS ARE MADE FOR SIMPLE FUNERAL ON WEDNESDAY; NO POMPOUS RITES FOR MAN WHO GAVE LIFE IN SERVICE

SERMON TELLS OF CHARACTER OF MR. WILSON

Club Wants Fruit Men to Get Money; Wilson is Honored

LEGISLATURE AND CONGRESS PAY TRIBUTE

Staunton Asks That Her Greatest Son Be Laid To Rest In Beautiful Thornrose; Washington Appears Probable Choice

News Leaders For Busy Readers

Old Law Seems To Prevent Closing Of The Departments

Bok Peace Prize Winner Announced

Basic Firemen Are Quite Angry

Income Tax Returns must be filed with the Collector of Internal Revenue at Richmond, on or before March 15th, by all persons having net incomes of $1000.00 if single, or $2000.00 if married. The assistance of our Trust Officials is at your service in preparing these returns. Farmers & Merchants Bank

February 14th Is Sweethearts Day. WE HAVE Valentines for all the Sweethearts, Fathers and Mothers, Sisters and Brothers, Husbands and Wives, Kiddies and Friends. BEVERLY BOOK CO.

Cold Nights. WHEN WINTER NIGHTS ARE LONG AND COLD THERE'S A LOT OF COMFORT IN "FAULTLESS" FLANNEL PAJAMAS OR NIGHT SHIRTS. THEY'RE ESPECIALLY FULL CUT AND ROOMY—MOST ATTRACTIVE TOO. $1.50 and up. ATLANTIC WOOLEN CO.

The AUGUSTA NATIONAL BANK has secured this space for a term in order to more conveniently discuss with the public matters of mutual interest

NEW THEATRE TODAY MATINEE AND NIGHT LAST TIMES. The Covered Wagon. THOS. HOGSHEAD.

KODAK OWNER

SAFETY PLUS COMFORT EQUALS SATISFACTION. A safe deposit box in our new, massive vault, equipped with the last word in automatic and electric safety devices. In addition to the usual facilities, five private rooms for the quiet inspection of securities or papers are provided. Equal service and security to all. National Valley Bank

February 5 1924: The Stonewall Jackson Hotel is completed. *Microfilm Archives*

Downtown Staunton's growth moved ahead at breakneck speed, with stores doing a land-office business, particularly on Saturdays when people from all over Augusta County descended upon the city to do their shopping. It was this influx of shoppers, many of which now drove automobiles instead of horse-drawn conveyances, that prompted the city to install its first traffic lights downtown.

Streetscape improvements not unlike those that would take place during Staunton's revitalization in the 1990s were initiated in the 1920s. Several of the city's annual reports during the '20s presented a series of photographs of the downtown showing what New, Augusta and Beverley Streets looked like before overhead utility wires were buried, and after.

Notable building projects in the 1920s included the Stonewall Jackson Hotel, which was completed in 1925. The Stonewall Jackson adjoined the historic Virginia Hotel, which was demolished in 1929 for a planned expansion of the Stonewall Jackson. The expansion never took place, ostensibly due to tight finances caused by the Great Depression.

The 1920s in Staunton also witnessed sin, silliness and salvation.

In the sin category, newspaper accounts of the day were filled with accounts of local people arrested for making, selling or drinking bootleg whiskey. The making of a silent, two-reel comedy titled "Staunton's Hero" in the streets of the city in 1929 registered in the silliness column, and salvation came by way of a 1926 hellfire-and-brimstone campaign in Gypsy Hill Park by world-famous evangelist Billy Sunday.

Some of Waynesboro's landmark events in this rich, prosperous decade included the 1924 merger of Waynesboro and Basic City, a town on the eastern bank of the South River. Basic was named for the "basic process" of making steel.

The 1920s also saw the founding of Valley Airport at Waynesboro by Col. Carl C. Loth. Loth had been a flyer in the First World War and opened the airport in 1927 to give flying lessons. The land remained a field until 1953 when it was purchased by the General Electric Co., which moved its operations from Charlottesville to Waynesboro.

But without a doubt the single largest economic development in Waynesboro occurred in 1929 when the E.I. DuPont de Nemours & Co. settled on what was to become a 400-acre complex near the South River, to begin production as a rayon acetate manufacturing facility. Untold wealth surged and economic stability would flow into Waynesboro thanks to the DuPont plant – wealth that would be sorely needed in the coming days of the Great Depression.

Interestingly, the news of the great Wall Street crash in October of 1929 failed to generate much excitement in the area. Stauntonians in particular barely noticed the crash itself and, to boot, weathered the coming economic storm better than most. Thanks to the conservative banking policies of Staunton and Augusta County, not one bank closed its doors during the Great Depression and relatively few businesses had to shut down.

Like many communities in Augusta County that, today, are quiet residential areas, Mt. Solon – shown here in a 1928 view – in the northern quadrant of the county was once a booming town that sported many businesses and even some industries. At one time it had so many drinking establishments that wags called it “Mt. Saloon.” The advent of the automobile, decline of the railroad and lack of public water and sewer in Mt. Solon contributed to its fall as a boom town. *Schwartz Collection*

Group photo of carriers and employees of the Staunton Daily News posing outside the company’s North Central Avenue offices. *Schwartz Collection*

The intersection of Main Street and Wayne Avenue in Waynesboro, looking east. Some of the businesses populating that portion of downtown can be seen in the photo, including the Light and Power Co., Shenandoah Inn and Waynesboro Laundry. *Waynesboro Collection*

Postcard photograph of snowy Calf Mountain, a landmark north of Waynesboro and visible from many points of the city. The mountain's clearing – which naturally resembles the form of a calf – remained virtually unchanged for years, although workers building the Skyline Drive gave the calf a "collar." *Waynesboro Collection*

Circa 1910s view, looking east from the window of the old Mt. Sidney School, of a portion of the village. Mt. Sidney, originally known as Ten-Mile Stage, is located 10 miles north of Staunton on U.S. 11. Founded as a way-station for travelers, Ten-Mile Stage was renamed Mt. Sidney in the early 1800s to draw attention to the high hill west of town and to commemorate English gentleman Sir Philip Sydney. Although businesses at one time thrived in Mt. Sidney, today it is largely a residential community. *Schwartz Collection*

Early 20th century photos of the fabled Stonewall Brigade Band, which was organized in 1855 as the Mountain Saxhorn Band. In 1861, when local supporters of the Confederacy formed the Fifth Virginia Regiment, the band marched to war with them and earned its new name while serving with Thomas J. "Stonewall" Jackson. The band, one of the most historic in America, still performs in Gypsy Hill Park every Monday evening in the summertime. It is the oldest amateur concert band in the United States. This view looks east on Main Street near its junction with South Market Street. *Schwartz Collection*

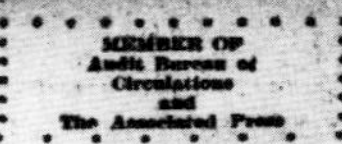

MEMBER OF Audit Bureau of Circulations and The Associated Press

The Staunton News-Leader

Fair and warmer today; unsettled tonight and Monday

35th Year. Vol. No. 118 — DAILY NEWS, EST. 1890 MORNING LEADER, EST. 1900 — STAUNTON, VA., SUNDAY MORNING, MAY 18, 1924 — MEMBER ASSOCIATED PRESS — PRICE TWO CENTS

NEW HOTEL IS A THING OF BEAUTY

Hundreds of Persons Visit and Inspect Handsome Stonewall Jackson Hotel Which Compares Most Favorably With the Finest in Large Cities.

HAS ONE HUNDRED ROOMS BEAUTIFULLY FURNISHED

Lobby, Rest Room, Dining Room, Ball Room and Other Portions Have Exquisite Furnishings; Fashionable Dinner Dance; Detailed Description of Interior.

The Stonewall Jackson hotel, the opening of which Staunton and the county have awaited with eagerness, was visited by a continuous stream of people yesterday afternoon from four to six o'clock, at which time the public had been invited by the management to inspect the building, and was the object of very evident admiration for the beauty of the appointments, for its spaciousness, and general scheme of arrangements.

Pleasure was expressed on every hand as groups passed in and out of the ball room, dining rooms, ladies' rest room, the lobby, and the mezzanine floor at the perfectly charming taste shown in the furniture, draperies, lovely color scheme, and general layout of the different sections, so conveniently and admirably figured out. The striking features in other parts of the structure were commented on, notably the kitchen and other service sections.

(Continued on page 2.)

News Leaders For Busy Readers

New Stonewall Jackson hotel has house warming and smart dinner dance.

House overrides veto on bonus bill and sends measure to senate.

Impeachment bill should be in president's hands first of week.

Old stone church may entertain next General Assembly.

Election for offices in Waynesboro.

Commissioner Lee is exonerated in majority report of committee.

Agent Was Guest Then Made Arrest

Charles D. Fulk, state prohibition agent located at Harrisonburg, arrested H. J. Powell of Centerville, yesterday on a charge of violating the prohibition laws. Mr. Fulk searched the Powell property and found six gallons of "old hen."

SOUTHERN INTER-COLLEGIATE TRACK MEET WON BY SAWNEE

(By The Associated Press.)

STONE CHURCH MAY HAVE THE 1925 ASSEMBLY

Famous Old Church at Fort Defiance Believed to Have Good Chance of Entertaining Great Presbyterian Meeting Because of Desire to Strengthen Country Churches.

(By The Associated Press.)

SAN ANTONIO, May 17.—A little stone church, in the country district of Augusta county, Virginia, may get the next meeting of the General Assembly of the Presbyterian church in the United States.

The church that may be selected is the Augusta church at Fort Defiance, Va., better known as Old Stone church.

Ball Teams Will Be Taken Abroad

(By The Associated Press)

Paris, May 17.—John McGraw, manager of the New York National league baseball team, has cabled to his Paris representatives that he and Charles A. Comiskey, owner of the Chicago White Sox team, have definitely decided to send the Giants and White Sox to Europe this autumn after the world's series.

FROM CHINA COMES ECHO OF DISPUTE

Presbytery of Central Mississippi Makes Overture that Support Be Withdrawn from Missions in Non-Conformance With Doctrine.

(By The Associated Press.)

San Antonio, May 17—From far off China today came an echo of the Fundamentalist-Modernist controversy to the General Assembly of the Presbyterian Church in the United States in session here.

SUPPORTERS OF FORD BID WANT ACTION

Proponents of Detroiter's Muscle Shoals Offer Will Make Move Monday to Close Hearing of Committee; Concentrated Fertilizer Described by Callan.

(By The Associated Press.)

Washington, May 17.—Proponents of Henry Ford's Muscle Shoals bid plan to make a move Monday to have the public hearings of the senate agriculture committee closed to permit consideration of the whole Muscle Shoals question by the committee in executive session.

Majority Report Exonerates Lee; Minority Blames

(By The Associated Press.)

Richmond, May 17.—Commissioner McDonald Lee of the Virginia Game and Inland Fisheries department today was exonerated of charges that he wasted state funds and that state boats were used for improper purposes, in a majority report filed with Governor Trinkle by the special legislative committee which investigated the department.

Taxicab Driver Dies After Dose Given By Doctor

(By The Associated Press.)

12 WIN PLACES

To Wed Premier?

English society circles are expressing surprise at the reported engagement of Prime Minister Ramsey MacDonald and Lady Margaret Sackville, daughter of the Earl de la Warr.

Weyers Cave High School Will Have 19 To Graduate

House Overrides Bonus Veto And Sends To Senate

(By The Associated Press.)

Washington, May 17.—The house today easily overrode President Coolidge's veto of the soldier bonus bill and put to the senate the final word on the legislation.

MANY SHEEP AND CATTLE DIE IN FIRE

Union Stockyards in Chicago Visited by Bad Blaze; Thousands of Animals Are Driven to Safety Zone by Police and Spectators.

BUILDINGS AND GREAT QUANTITY OF HAY LOST

Loss in Building and Pens Will Amount to One Hundred Thousand Dollars; No Estimate Placed on Value of Stock that Perished.

(By The Associated Press.)

Immigration Bill Goes Next To President

WILSON GIRLS PLAY POST SEASON GAME

How Military Academy Teams Ranked In the Shoot for the W. R. Hearst Trophy

Scores in the national competition for the William Randolph Hearst R. O. T. C. trophy (military academies) officially compiled by the United States army and issued today by Lieutenant Colonel Robert H. Sillman, Sixth Corps area, follow:

Headquarters Sixth Corps Area
Office of the Corps Area Commander.
WILLIAM RANDOLPH HEARST RIFLE COMPETITION, 1924

No.	Military Academy, Location.	Team score.	Highest individ'l score
1	St. John's, Delafield, Wis	1,923	388
2	Riverside, Gainesville, Ga.	1,853	374
3	Tennessee, 1st team, Sweet water, Tenn.	1,815	372
4	Tennessee, 2d team, Sweetwater, Tenn.	1,775	365
5	Clason, 1st team, Bronx, N. Y.	1,775	362
6	Staunton, Staunton, Va.	1773	361
7	Harvard, Los Angeles, Calif.	1772	366
8	N. Y. Cornwall-on-the-Hudson, N. Y.	1,718	357
9	Howe school, Howe, Ind.	1,654	347
10	Castle Heights, Lebanon, Tenn.	1,654	341
11	Blackstone, Blackstone, Va.	1,612	360
12	Hill, Portland, Ore.	1,608	338
13	Northwestern, Military and Naval Walworth, Wis.	1,605	351
14	Hitchcock, San Rafael, Calif.	1,599	340
15	Porter, Charleston, S. C.	1,587	337
16	Clason, 2d team, Bronx, N. Y.	1,572	344
17	West Texas, San Antonio, Tex.	1,538	316
18	Bordentown, Bordentown, N. J.	1,519	331
19	Wentworth, Lexington, Mo.	1,471	308
20	Augusta, 2d team, Ft. Defiance, Va.	1,427	337
21	Hitchcock, San Rafael, Calif.	1,374	331
22	Augusta 2d team, Ft. Defiance, Va.	1,269	293
23	Marion Institute, Marion, Ala.	1,196	259
24	Greenbrier, Lewisburg, W. Va.	1,099	253

R. H. SILLMAN,
Lieutenant Colonel Infantry,
In charge Hearst Trophy Competition.

May 18, 1924: The Stonewall Jackson Hotel is completed. *Microfilm Archives*

Built in 1925 at a cost of more than $3 million, the Stonewall Jackson Hotel was once the luxury destination for travelers coming to Staunton. In 1929 a proposed expansion of the hotel led to the demolition of the historic Virginia Hotel adjacent to the Stonewall Jackson, but the Depression killed the plan. In 2004, after many years of decline, the Stonewall Jackson Hotel became the target of an ambitious renovation and revitalization project. *Schwartz Collection*

The cornerstone of Augusta Stone Presbyterian Church was laid in August 1747 in what is present-day Fort Defiance. In the days when Indians presented a threat to settlers, the church served as a garrison with a palisade around it. Today, it is the oldest Presbyterian meeting house in continued use in Virginia. *Schwartz Collection*

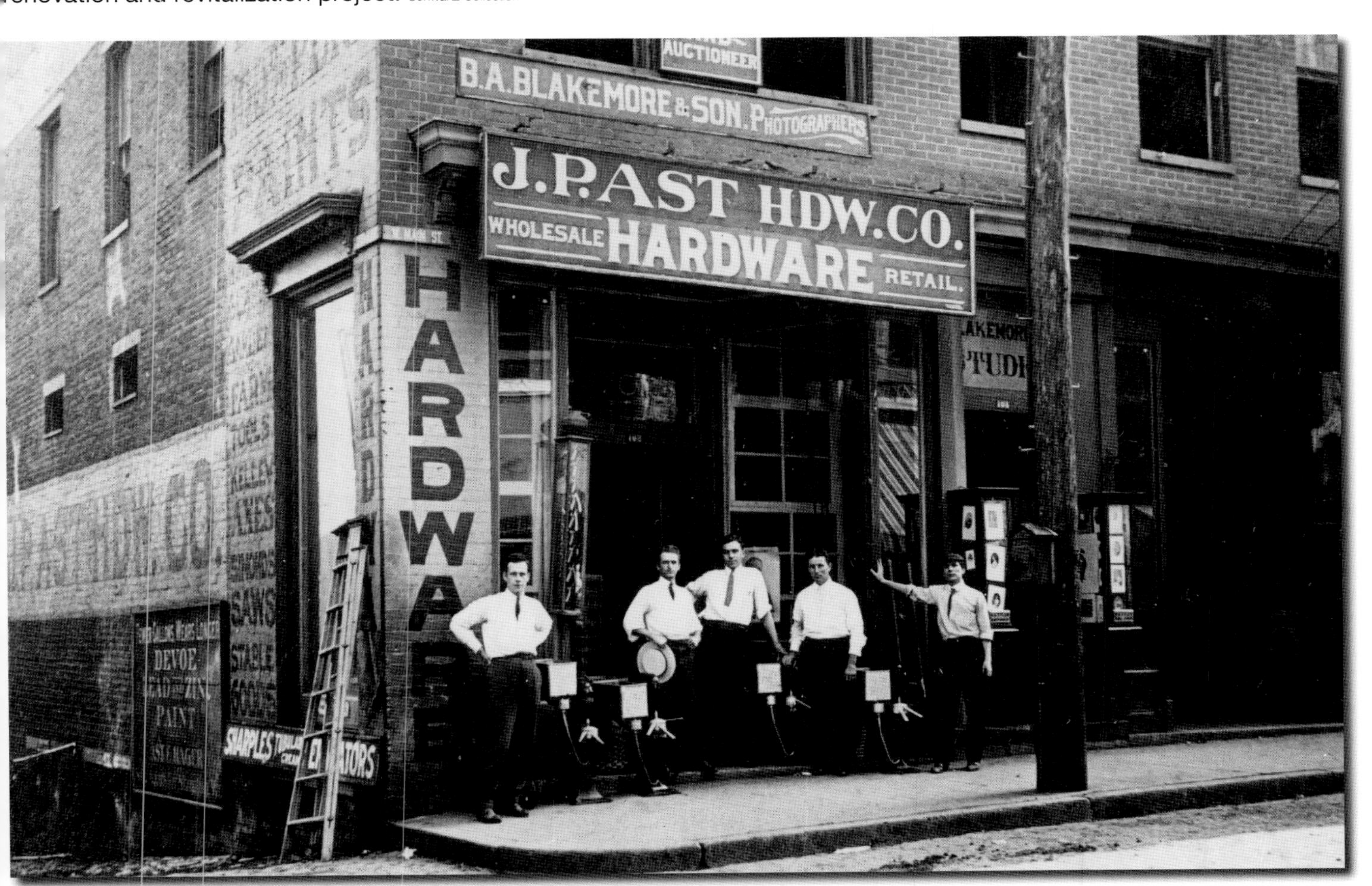

Five employees of Joseph P. Ast's Hardware pose with merchandise in front of the store, which was located at Main Street and Central Avenue. Next door was the studio of photographer Benjamin A. Blakemore, who served as Staunton's premier cameraman for 60 years. A close examination reveals that Blakemore posted a number of local portraits in a street display to entice patrons into his studio. *Schwartz Collection*

A fire in 1928 destroyed the historic Hardy Carriage Works building at East Main and South Market streets. The area was never built upon again and today is a municipal parking lot. *Schwartz Collection*

Staunton Military Academy cadets parading through the streets of the city was a common sight in Staunton for many years. These demonstrations, which sometimes occurred as events unto themselves and at other times helped form larger parades, gave the cadets marching experience and Staunton residents a glimpse of the school in action. The cadets shown here are marching east on Johnson Street. *Schwartz Collection*

The Staunton depot of the Baltimore and Ohio Railroad, shown here, was located at what is now the intersection of Greenville Avenue, Johnson Street and Coalter Street, across from the old Western State Hospital complex at the underpass. *Schwartz Collection*

Member Associated Press and Audit Bureau of Circulations

The Staunton News-Leader

THE WEATHER: Unsettled today and Friday; not much change in temperature.

6th Year. Vol. No. 54 — DAILY NEWS, EST. 1890; MORNING LEADER, EST. 1908 — STAUNTON, VA., THURSDAY MORNING, MARCH 5, 1925 — MEMBER ASSOCIATED PRESS and AUDIT BUREAU CIRCULATIONS — PRICE TWO CENTS

MAN'S GREATEST AUDIENCE HEARS COOLIDGE OUTLINE HIS POLICIES; DAWES DISRUPTS MANY PRECEDENTS

Large Visible Crowd and Millions Unseen Hear President in Inaugural Address, Featuring Simplest Ceremonies of Kind in Many Years; Former President Taft, Now Justice, Gives Oath; Pageant Not Without Color Despite Fact That Plans Had Been Pared to Limit at President's Request; President Reviews an Hour-Long Parade.

INAUGURAL BALL SUBSTITUTE FOUND

Newly Inducted Vice-President Starts Fireworks When He Breaks Honored Customs of Senate; Has New Members Brought to President's Stand "In a Bunch;" One-Man Filibuster Must Pass, He Asserts; Abruptly Dismisses Senators for Inauguration Ceremonies, Without Awaiting Formality of Motion to Recess; Fails to Return.

PRESIDENT SIGNS SALARY RAISE BILL, LAST MEASURE

President Coolidge—Vice-President Dawes

3 Cities Publish Inaugural Photos Relayed By Wire

MAN IN SILK HAT HAD HIS SPEECH READY

New Members For Historic Highway

CONDITION IS WORSE

DEATH OF MISS BYERS

Requisition Papers Sent For Borglum

Woman Dead; Man Dying Following Shooting Affair

Wm. R. Wise, 84, Farmer, Is Dead

DEATH OF J. M. SNELL

TOLL PARLEY BLOCKED BY JURY CASES

Test Case of Commonwealth vs. Harry Hamilton, Self-Appointed Gate-Skipper, Goes Over Till Today; Daniel Awarded $280; Ellinger Acquitted.

CITIZENS' COMMITTEE ORGANIZES

Eight Divisions of Workers to Cover City and County Field in Effort to Raise Fund Pledged to Mary Baldwin College; Judge Pratt Heads Organization.

March 5, 1925: Calvin Coolidge is inaugurated President of the U.S. *Microfilm Archives*

Cars form an impromptu football field for a game involving Staunton Military Academy cadets. The game, which was held at night, would be illuminated when the cars' headlights would be turned on. This field, which was located at Prospect and Tams streets, is the site today of a track belonging to Mary Baldwin College. *Schwartz Collection*

For years a familiar landmark to visitors of Waynesboro was this gateway arch, which stood at the intersection of Main Street and Rosser Avenue (U.S. 250 and U.S. 340). A similar arch was erected at the east entrance to Waynesboro. This western arch was blown down in a storm about 1937 and was never replaced. The eastern arch also has disappeared. *Schwartz Collection*

Three Sections
Eighteen Pages
Section Two

The Staunton News-Leader

Women's Fashions
Men's Fashions
Interior Art

STAUNTON, VA., SUNDAY MORNING, SEPT. 20, 1925.

Autumn Fashion Edition 1925

FASHIONS OF AUTUMN DESIGNED FOR MEN AND WOMEN

THE HOME DONE TO THE TASTE OF THE TIMES

TWO SECTIONS 12 PAGES SECTION I

The Staunton News-Leader

THE WEATHER: Partly cloudy and slightly warmer today; Monday cloudy.

8th Year. No. 122 — STAUNTON, VA., SUNDAY MORNING, MAY 22, 1927 — PRICE TWO CENTS

LINDBERGH ACCLAIMED INTERNATIONAL HERO

Intrepid U. S. Flyer First to Cross Atlantic Without Stop

(By The Associated Press)

Paris, May 21.—Captain Charles A. Lindbergh, the young American aviator, who hopped off from New York yesterday morning all alone in his monoplane, arrived in Paris tonight safe and sound, as everyone hoped he would.

33 1-2 Hours For Trip

The sandy-haired son of the Middle West dropped down out of the darkness at Le Bourget flying field, a few miles from Paris, at 10:21 o'clock tonight (5:21 p. m. New York time) only 33 1-2 hours after leaving Long Island—the first man in history to go from New York to Paris without changing his seat.

Greatest of Heroes

To the young American it was, seemingly, merely the achievement of an ambition. To Paris, to France, to America, to the world, his landing tonight made him the greatest of heroes mankind has produced since the air became a means of travel.

Is Lionized

A crowd of at least 25,000 surrounded his plane, the "Spirit of St. Louis," when it came to earth after its epochal voyage from the New World to the Old. The airman was lifted from the seat, where for two days and a night he sat fixed, guiding his plane over land and sea, and for 40 minutes he was hardly able to talk or do anything else except let himself be carried along by a mass of men, made delirious with joy at his achievement.

Wins Duel With Death

All ties of nationalism were forgotten by the Le Bourget throng. They saw in Lindbergh only a man, who had brilliantly gambled with death and won. There was regret, of course, for Nungesser and Coli and regret, too, that the daring Frenchmen had not been the first. But there was no bitterness in their greeting of the American winner.

It was the common people of France, who first hailed the intrepid Lindbergh as he emerged from what only yesterday morning he had called his "death chamber." Shortly after 10:10, the roar of his motor, for which they had been waiting for hours, came out of the clear night sky to the ears of the multitude. Police lines were swept aside as thousands surged over the field to welcome the man, who had won their hearts and had earned immortal fame.

"There he is," the cry went up as the rays of the searchlight gleamed upon the monoplane gracefully descending from the darkness, which had enveloped all and through which only the sound of the motor gave warning of his approach. At this instant, the crowds began their race across the field.

Smoothly the airplane glided down upon the lighted field. Even before it had come to a pause, a hundred hands caught hold of the wings and scores of feet were trampling upon one another in an effort to reach the side of the fuselage, within which sat a young man, who all alone had succeeded in flying from New York to Paris without a stop.

"Here We Are"

The wheels had scarcely ceased to roll, the propellor had barely come to a stop when Lindbergh, weary-eyed but smiling, got up from the seat where he had so long sat and in a casual voice almost drowned by the cheers of thousands said with charming simplicity, "Well, here we are."

He put his leg over the side of the cockpit and it was grasped by a dozen hands. So was his other leg as soon as he could get it out of the machine. Holding him high and cheering him with cheers that came from the heart as well as the lungs, the crowd took him to itself.

The police did their best to get to the young hero and save him from those to whom he had become a friend, a hero, a sportsman to admire forever; but they were helpless against the common impulse.

For half an hour they pushed one another this way and that trying to take young Lindbergh from his plane to the administration building on the landing field where noted men of his own country and of France had long been waiting to welcome him with due formality. When finally they got him there his tired and trembling fingers were grasped in a handshake by America's ambassador to France, Myron T. Herrick, and by Frenchmen of high position.

But Lindbergh was too weary, seemingly to know what it was all about. He smiled and said "Thank you. I'm awfully happy." And when his fatigue could be fought off no longer, he seemed to go to sleep standing there on his feet.

Outside the crowd was howling for a sight of the hero, who had won the heart of France as no American probably had before. Brilliant searchlights were focused on the balcony of the building into which Lindbergh had been carried. But the crowd had to be disappointed—Lindbergh could do no more.

The American ambassador came to the balcony and waved the aviator's helmet to the crowd, which kept shouting—"The pilot—the pilot. Let us see Lindbergh!"

Lindbergh, asleep on his feet, was lifted up and carried to an automobile and hurried to Paris, a few miles away, to sleep after so many hours when even to close his eyes for a moment might have meant death.

Washington Jubilant

Washington, May 21.—Lindbergh's history-making flight to France today thrilled Washington out of its traditional stolidity.

The thought of this young airman winging his way alone through the darkness of the night over deserted ocean waters, and depending for his life on his own skill and courage, aroused the interest and touched the imagination of the capital as few things have done in the past.

There had been the army's world-circling flight, the hop of the NC-4 across the Atlantic, the trans-Atlantic voyage of the Los Angeles, and other feats of aviation which had brought admiration from Washington, but the adventuresome, solitary attempt of Lindbergh forced the young flyer's personality into the picture and made his flight a test wherein a young sportsman staked everything in the face of the forebodings of experts. That appealed to the popular fancy.

Everybody in Washington "pulled" for Lindbergh steadily and hopefully, and as the day wore along confidently. When the news of his arrival at Paris was flashed over the city there was a spontaneous city-wide expression of gratification, and officials, led by President Coolidge, sent their congratulations and praise speeding over the cables to the daring aviator.

When Lindbergh made his sensational hop-off the word high and low was, "I hope he makes it." Today, as his progress was charted, the admiration and amazement of the city grew in direct ratio to his approach to Paris, and exploded as he landed with the jubilant cry, "He made it!"

MUDDY GURGLE WITHIN FIFTY MILES OF GULF

Flood Waters Cut Path 15 Miles Long and [illegible] Miles Wide; One-Seventh of Louisiana Under Water; Flood Strikes at Weak Levee Points.

(By the Associated Press)

New Orleans, May 21.—The restless gurgle of muddy waters ebbed from the northern boundary of Louisiana tonight to within 50 miles of the Gulf of Mexico after having cut a path 150 miles long and 50 miles wide across the state.

One-seventh of the total area of the state was under water already, and the flood was striking threateningly at weak points along the Atchafalaya, 140 miles northwest of New Orleans on the opposite side of the Mississippi, endangering five other parishes with a total acreage amounting to almost half as much as already has felt the weight of the waters.

A stubborn fight still was being maintained at McCrea on the Atchafalaya, where the fierce current was ripping embankments to pieces. More than 2,000 workers were fighting desperately in the mud and rain to hold the flood waters off fertile sugar plantations of Pointe Coupee, Assumption, Iberville, West Baton Rouge, and Terrebone parishes.

With the situation critical along the western levee line of the Atchafalaya, the evacuation of the Evangeline country was proceeding rapidly. The population of the concentration camp at LaFayette already has sprung to 10,000, passing the total number of inhabitants of the city itself.

CADET MUSICIANS IN WINCHESTER

The 10-piece orchestra of Staunton Military academy was a feature act at the Empire theatre, Winchester, last night. The school musicians will also play there this afternoon and tonight.

"HIGHPOCKET" IN

On a charge of being drunk and disorderly, Ed Strother, colored, known in police circle as "Highpocket," was arrested and lodged in jail early last night by Officer A. W. Holton.

BUCHER TRIAL IS FURTHER DELAYED BY TECHNICALITY

Charges Against Augusta County Magistrate Fall Through Temporarily, At Least, When Three Fellow Magistrates Rule Warrant Defective and Invalid; Local Attorneys Raise Point On Which Action Is Based.

Charges of violation of the prohibition laws against Magistrate M. W. Bucher fell through yesterday, temporarily at least. Bucher is a Confederate veteran. Members of the Staunton bar, believed to be almost solid in their defense of the accused magistrate of Beverley Manor district, raised a point whereby the three magistrates sitting on the case declared the warrant, on which Bucher was arrested, defective and void.

Whether a new warrant will be applied for by G. Frank Baylor, of Swoope, the complaining witness, was a matter of conjecture. It was thought that the matter would be permitted to "die out."

Until Mr. Baylor makes a fresh complaint to the authorities, the hands of Commonwealth's Attorney Hugh H. Kerr are tied, and further prosecution not likely.

Magistrate Bucher was charged with being under the influence of intoxicating liquor which caused him to drive his car into a parked machine in Swoope little less than a month ago.

The three magistrates comprising the tribunal included: J. T. Bear, presiding, of Churchville; I. M. Smith, of Craigsville, and N. A. Arehart, of Middlebrook.

Among those of the Staunton bar present to defend Magistrate Bucher were: J. Wesley Taylor, personally engaged as counsel; Armistead C. Gordon, Col. Rudolph Bumgardner, S. D. Timberlake Jr., J. Harry May, Duncan Curry, H. F. Scheele, W. M. Bass, Curry Carter, and R. A. Fulwiler.

Immediately after the warrant was quashed, Mr. Baylor was approached as to what steps, if any, he might take next. He declined to indicate his attitude.

MAURY CHAMPION

(By The Associated Press)

Abingdon, Va., May 21.—Maury High school, of Norfolk, won the state high school baseball championship here this afternoon in the final contest with the William King high school by a score to 1. Maury High held the Class A championship, and William King the Class B championship. The game was to decide the high school champions of the state of Virginia.

Bellanca Flight Put Off; May Not Fly East at All

(By the Associated Press)

Roosevelt Field, N. Y., May 21.—The Paris flight of Clarence Chamberlain was "indefinitely postponed" tonight when friends persuaded him not to make an immediate attempt.

Chamberlain had announced that he would take off tonight less than two hours after Charles Lindbergh landed in Paris. He had his plane hauled to the runway, and was telephoning officials for permission to use the runway when friends gathered about him to dissuade him.

They showed him that while weather was good tonight, unfavorable conditions were predicted for tomorrow. Also Carl Schory, secretary of the contest committee of the National Aeronautical society, was discovered to have gone to Washington, and it was said that the flight would not be official unless Schory sealed the barograph.

"All right, it's all off," Chamberlain said at length. "It's off indefinitely, and when we do take off it won't be for Paris, in all probability. That has been done. We'll probably fly west instead of east. Perhaps Honolulu."

LINDBERGH WENT TO SLEEP ON WAY ACROSS THE OCEAN

FEARED ONLY SANDMAN; STRUCK ICE AND SNOW

(By the Associated Press)

Paris, May 22 (Sunday).—Before Captain Charles A. Lindbergh went to sleep early this morning, after his New York-to-Paris flight, he asked Ambassador Herrick and others, who have taken charge of him, to let him go back to his plane in order to "show the people how the windows work."

"Never mind your old windows," said the ambassador. "Come and get a rest at the embassy."

Talks of Flight

Just before he retired, Lindbergh had a bracing cup of coffee, which for a few seconds brought him out of his sleepiness enough to talk a little of the flight.

"It was not such a bad trip," he said. "I ran into some snow and ice on the early part of the trip; the rest of it wasn't so bad.

"The biggest trouble was in staying awake. I went to sleep several times, but was lucky enough to wake myself up right away. I was afraid of the sandman all the time."

CONGRATULATED BY PRESIDENT

(By The Associated Press)

Washington, May 21.—President Coolidge, in a congratulatory cablegram to be delivered to Charles A. Lindbergh in Paris, told the trans-Atlantic flyer that the "American people rejoice with me at the brilliant termination of your heroic flight."

POSTMASTER AT MEADOW

Washington, D. C., May 21.—Mrs. Ovlyn F. Westbrook has been appointed postmaster at Meadow, Henrico county, succeeding Robert P. Everhard, resigned.

MAKES NEW RECORD FOR SEAPLANE SPEED

(By the Associated Press)

Washington, May 21.—A new world speed record for seaplanes was claimed tonight by the navy for Lieutenant Rutledge Irvine, who was credited with a speed today of 130.93 miles an hour for 1,000 kilometers over the enclosed triangular course at Hampton Roads, Va.

Poppy Sale Returns Surpass Last Year's

Sales of poppies by the American Legion and its auxiliary in Staunton have passed the mark set last year by sales in both Staunton and Augusta county, it was learned last night from the co-chairman of the committee in charge of sales, Mrs. E. Walton Opie, who reported $582 at the end of the two days.

Included in this was $16 realized at Beverley Manor High school, which school, however, has still some cash to turn in. Fishersville High school's total, $5.57, was not included in the $582. Other schools in the country remain to be heard from.

The sales last year realized $864., for the Clemmer-McGuffin post of the Legion for use in relief work among veterans of the world war. This total, however, was for both city and county. Mrs. Opie said last night that she hopes the final return for city and county for this year, with reports from the remaining county schools will pass the $950. mark. The other co-chairman of the committee is Mrs. J. Hubert Wamsley.

Augustans Tied in Meet for 1st Place; Still Three Events

Information received at Augusta Military academy yesterday at five o'clock was that A. M. A. was then tied with the Asheville School for Boys, of Asheville, N. C., for first place in the All-Southern Preparatory School track meet at Chapel Hill, N. C. The final result was not obtainable last night.

A. M. A.'s last baseball game of the season will be on Monday, afternoon at Ft. Defiance, with Fishburne Military school. On Friday A. M. A. defeated Fishburne, 3 to 2, in a 14-inning game.

MT. SIDNEY HIGH HOLDING OWN IN THE TITLE RACE

Greenville, May 21.—A lead of three runs obtained by Mt. Sidney High school in the initial inning here this afternoon over the local high school baseball team proved just the necessary edge to give the invaders the victory. Mt. Sidney won the game, the fifth in the Augusta county high school championship series, 8 to 5.

The game was unusually clean, Greenville making only two errors and Mt. Sidney but four.

By this win, Mt. Sidney continues to hold the margin of safety in the championship series. The standing of the teams is: Mt. Sidney, won 2, lost 1, percentage .667; Craigsville, won 1, lost 1, percentage .500; Greenville, won 0, lost 1, percentage .000. The next game is Thursday, when Mt. Sidney and Greenville again meet on the local diamond.

RADIO STATION MOVES MONDAY

Fans in city and county, who have enjoyed the radio programs broadcast over The News-Leader's Station WKBG for the past week, will not be deprived of that pleasure during the coming week. The station is being moved from the Strand theatre here to the Wayne theatre in Waynesboro.

Sidney Shepard, announcer, has made arrangements to put excellent programs on the air from Waynesboro and is seeking entertainers from that community. All interested in going on the air are asked to communicate with the radio announcer at the Wayne. A blank for this purpose will be found in this issue.

Reports of the programs and names of performers will be published in this paper, as has been the custom during the past week.

So, starting Monday evening, programs will come from Waynesboro but the dial readings of from 20 down to zero will be the same.

BRIDGE SCENE OF BEAUTY AS LIGHTS GLOW

Illumination of Great Virginia Natural Wonder Is Spectacle of Amazing Grandeur; Current Started by Touch of President Coolidge; Letcher Substitutes for Byrd as Speaker.

(By the Associated Press)

Natural Bridge, Va., May 21.—The pressing of a button by President Coolidge on the Mayflower sent the current through a switch in Washington from the yacht's radio tonight to flood the great Natural Bridge of Virginia with 7,500,000 candlepower of self-made electric light at the first official illumination of this piece of nature's handiwork. Almost 40 giant searchlights played upon the giant span, and a new appearance of grandeur was seen by the official party of 50 which was privileged to view this opening feature.

As skilled operatives manipulated the complicated controls varied spectacles of beauty greeted the observers as they progressed through the bridge and up the gorge of old Cedar creek which is credited with having worn out the giant span which now carries the Shenandoah Valley pike from North to South.

A flood of soft moonlight, rivalled in reality only by nature itself, constituted the first display artifically produced and gave a feeling of ease and wonder to the first group of spectators.

Brilliant Spectacle

Following this brief introduction to the wonders of the artistically applied illumination, the guide and his party progressed through the bridge amid ever-changing effects, visualizing the progress of day from dawn to sunset. One outstanding spectacle and a powerful study in contrast was the change from a one-candlepower illumination to a flood of light thrown from the full battery of lamps headed by a 1,500,000-candlepower beam from an especially constructed light. The picturization of the "divine shaft" was most pleasing, and drew forth a silence and awe second only to that produced by the opening moonlight scene.

Captain Greenlee Letcher, of Lexington, captain of the Rockbridge county artillery unit during the World war and son of Virginia's Civil war governor, substituted for Governor Harry F. Byrd in delivering the chief address of the afternoon program. Briefly tracing the development of Natural Bridge from the time of King George III's original patent grant to Thomas Jefferson, Captain Letcher brought out the growth of the bridge and the state of Virginia as a whole as an attraction to outside tourists, and introduced several interesting anecdotes in connection with the history of the giant arch since the Civil war.

May 22, 1927: Lindbergh is hailed for his solo flight across the Atlantic Ocean. *Microfilm Archives*

Photo showing the circa January 1927 excavation of the site upon which the new Robert E. Lee High School was being built. This new structure, which was located on Churchville Avenue, replaced a smaller high school which stood at the corner of Lewis and Baldwin Streets. It was abandoned in 1983 in favor of a still newer structure on North Coalter Street. *Schwartz Collection*

Photo taken at the fairgrounds in Gypsy Hill Park of "Delegates" of the Women's Federation in Staunton. One woman holds up a sign that reads "Anti-Lynching Division." A notation in the corner notes that this is a "Tribune Photo by Henderson." *Schwartz Collection*

Two Sections
TEN PAGES
Section 1

The Staunton News-Leader

THE WEATHER
Cloudy, light showers today. Friday rain. Not much change in temperature.

9th Year. No. 284 — MORNING LEADER EST. 1904, DAILY NEWS EST. 1890 — STAUNTON, VA., THURSDAY MORNING, NOVEMBER 29, 1928 — MEMBER ASSOCIATED PRESS and AUDIT BUREAU CIRCULATION — PRICE TWO CENTS

COOLIDGES GUESTS OF VA. IN MARBLE MANSION ATOP BLUE RIDGE MOUNTAINS

TO ATTEND CHURCH AND GRID GAME

Charlottesville to Entertain Presidential Party Most of Today; May Visit Monticello; To Be Luncheon Guests; Thanksgiving Dinner at Clubhouse This Evening.

President and Mrs. Coolidge today will turn from their haven of rest atop the Blue Ridge to join with citizens of Charlottesville in Thanksgiving worship.

Back in the kitchen of Swannanoa a fine, big turkey has been put in the broiler to be ready for Mr. and Mrs. Coolidge and whomever they may invite, upon their return from Charlottesville this evening.

The bird was presented to the president by the Charlottesville Chamber of Commerce. It tipped the scales at 30 pounds, a bronze, deep-chested fowl fit to grace the table of any ruler.

The president will motor to Charlottesville in time for the union Thanksgiving services at the First Baptist church. He has accepted an invitation for luncheon directly afterward with Edward Anderson Alderman, president of the University of Virginia, to which Governor McLean, of North Carolina, and Governor Byrd, of Virginia, Mrs. Woodrow Wilson, and a company of 50 guests also have been bidden.

The Monticello guard, a Charlottesville military unit, have donned their uniforms to act as guard of honor for the president during his stay in their city. They accepted the charge of accompanying him to the North Carolina-Virginia football game after the Alderman luncheon and then to escort him to the city limits when he motors back to Swannanoa.

If the opportunity is afforded, Mr. and Mrs. Coolidge may motor to Monticello, home of Thomas Jefferson, before returning to their country residence.

The president and Mrs. Coolidge are spending their week-end at the Swannanoa Country club alone. At the huge white Italian [illegible] country seat, nine servants are caring for the president's comfort. Most of the remaining time before he leaves for Washington Sunday will be spent quietly, a little clay-pigeon shooting probably being the only diversion.

Mrs. Coolidge plans to get the most out of the chance for fresh, country air. With her dogs on leash, she already has indulged in her favorite exercise of walking, for which the lovely countryside provides ample inducement.

Holiday Guests

CALVIN COOLIDGE

MRS. CALVIN COOLIDGE

GIVEN WARM WELCOME AT WAYNESBORO

Arriving on Special Train from Washington at 2 P. M., President and Wife Whisked Away to Mountain Haven Followed by Secret Service Agents and Press Correspondents.

(By the Associated Press)

High upon a lofty summit of the Blue Ridge mountains, surrounded by magnificent vistas of hills and valleys, President and Mrs. Coolidge yesterday began a Thanksgiving holiday in Virginia.

Leaving Washington yesterday morning by special train, the chief executive and his party arrived in Waynesboro, 12 miles east of Staunton, at 2 o'clock, and motored up a steep, winding roadway to the Swannanoa Country club, which was turned over to Mr. Coolidge for his short vacation.

Colorful Welcome

At Waynesboro, Mr. Coolidge was received in true presidential fashion. A long line of cadets from the Fishburne Military school stood at attention while the Waynesboro municipal band played "Hail to the Chief," above which could be heard the booming of a 21-gun salute. Automobiles and an escort of Virginia state police were waiting for the four-mile journey to the country club.

Greeted at Entrance

A group of club officials, headed by the club president, E. M. Crutchfield, of Richmond, received Mr. and Mrs. Coolidge on the steps of the building. After an exchange of greetings, all posed for the photographers and then repaired to the interior of the club house, where the president and Mrs. Coolidge were presented with a 10-pound "old-fashioned" fruit cake.

Mrs. Coolidge later went for a stroll through the expansive club gardens with "Tiny Tim," the reddish-brown White House chow dog, on a leash.

2,400-Foot Elevation

The club house stands at an elevation of [illegible]. To the west spreads the historic Shenandoah Valley, and to the north lies Rockfish gap, the two separated [illegible]

(Continued on Page Two)

Miss Trumbull Is Engaged to John Coolidge

Hartford, Conn., Nov. 28.—(AP)—Coincident with the celebration of their 25th wedding anniversary, Governor and Mrs. John H. Trumbull tonight formally announced the engagement of their eldest daughter, Florence, to John Coolidge, son of President and Mrs. Calvin Coolidge.

BANK TO DISTRIBUTE OVER 650 CHECKS THIS CHRISTMAS

More than 650 Christmas checks will be distributed this year by the Staunton National Bank and Trust company, B. E. Vaughan, president of the institution, said yesterday.

The checks, which amount to more than $54,000.00 will go to the members of the institution's 1928 Christmas club on Dec. 5. Dec. 10 is the date set for opening the 1929 club.

"The first purpose of the Club was to afford members a convenient means of saving up for the buying of their Christmas gifts," Mr. Vaughan said.

"Many of them have found it convenient in other ways, however. Club and lodge dues, installment payments and insurance premiums are some of the items that will be met with Christmas club money this year."

THIEVES GET CAR

A Chevrolet car, bearing state license No. 92-952, was reported to local police last night as stolen from its parking place. The car was owned by Henry Martin, an official of the Staunton Manufacturing company.

The car was parked outside the company's plant on North Augusta street. The theft occurred about 7:45.

To Contest Seat Won by Mrs. Owen

Tallahassee, Fla., Nov. 28.—(AP)—Governor John W. Martin was advised today by a Daytona Beach law firm that William C. Lawson, of Orlando, defeated Republican candidate for congress from the Fourth district, would contest the seating of Mrs. Ruth Bryan Owen, of Miami, elected by a Democratic majority.

DEFECTIVE SAFETY LAMP BLAMED FOR TRAGEDY IN MINE

Williamson, W. Va., Nov. 28.—(AP)—A defective safety lamp tonight was believed by mine experts to have ignited a small pocket of gas, causing a local explosion that killed three officials of the Clogora Coal company in a Himler Coal company mine near Himlerville, Ky., 20 miles from here.

Headquarters of Roll Call Closed; No County Report

Reports of county workers in the annual Red Cross roll call are not in yet, and while roll call headquarters in the Masonic temple were closed yesterday, the roll call will not be considered as concluded until ample time has been given for county reports.

Roll call headquarters were moved, with the closing of the office in the Masonic temple foyer, to the offices of the local chapter in the Knowles building, where chapter officers will be glad to receive further memberships or to furnish information.

Mrs. C. M. Woodbury, executive secretary of the Augusta County chapter, said yesterday that unless the chapter reaches its quota in the roll call, it will not be able to meet its share of obligations when calls for relief come to the Red Cross during the coming year, nor to bear its part in such activities as life-saving, nursing, war veterans' assistance, etc.

"We hope that county reports will bring our total membership well up to the quota," Mrs. Woodbury said, "but all who would like to assist the work of the American Red Cross and have not done so are urged to send their memberships to headquarters in the Knowles building."

Thanksgiving

By BRUCE CATTON

POWER and glory,
Greatness and gold;
That is our story,
Proudly retold.
Let every steeple
Boast with its bell:
We are the people—
We have done well.

Every Thanksgiving
Heightens our pride;
All people living
Envy our stride.
We are the wealthy
Kings of the earth,
Stalwart and healthy,
Knowing our worth.

So we sing, loudly,
In our own praise,
Surveying proudly
All of our days.
Yet, all around us
Shadowy hosts
Rise to confound us—
Pioneer ghosts!

Theirs was the weeping,
Theirs was the pain;
Ours is the reaping,
Ours is the gain;
This is the morrow
Longed-for of old,
Won by their sorrow,
Hunger and cold.

God of Compassion,
Seated on high,
Help us re-fashion
Our haughty cry.
Let us be humble,
Let us be just,
Lest we should stumble
Down to the dust.

For busy cities and peaceful plains,
For shining towers and golden hoard,
For dead men's losses and live men's gains—
Accept our humble thanks, Oh Lord.

Local Churches to Be Centers of Thanksgiving Celebrations Here

Recognition of the purpose for which Thanksgiving day was instituted will be given the holiday today with special services in many of the city churches, notable among which is a jubilee service at St. Francis Catholic church in commemoration of the 50th anniversary of the coming here of the Sisters of Charity. Football, turkey dinners, and hunting will by no means occupy all of the people's time.

Four congregations will hold their annual union Thanksgiving service in Central Methodist church at ten-thirty o'clock this morning — First Baptist, Second Presbyterian, St. Paul's United Brethren, and Central Methodist. The ministers of these churches will participate in the service, the Rev. Brown H. Smith delivering the Thanksgiving message. The public is invited.

Episcopal Churches

At Emmanuel church there will be Holy Communion at 7:30 a. m. and morning prayer and sermon at 10:30 a. m. Music at the morning service will be furnished by the Stuart Hall choir under the direction of Miss Martha Williams.

The service at Trinity will be at 11 o'clock.

Marquis Memorial

The Rev. L. H. Smallwood, pastor, will preach the Thanksgiving sermon at Marquis Memorial church this morning at ten-thirty o'clock. All are invited.

The Thanksgiving service will be held at Christ Lutheran church at 10:30.

Fishersville Hi Is County Champ; Beats New Hope

Championship of Augusta county in high school basketball was won by the Fishersville High school boys' team last evening when that aggregation, undefeated this year, won the second of a three-game series with New Hope, 25 to 12. The game was played at New Hope.

Stone, Coyner and Dudley starred for the Fishersville quint, and the general teamwork of the entire aggregation was excellent. For New Hope Garber and Spitler played a good brand of basketball.

The New Hope team was champion of the "lower" half of the county, and Fishersville of the "upper" half. Fishersville overwhelmed New Hope Monday night in the first of a series of three games to decide the county title.

WANTS MORE FOR SCHOOLS ON SAME TAX

Governor Byrd, Addressing Convention of Virginia Education Association, Promises to Recommend Increased Appropriations for Schools of State; Miss Holt and House in Nomination.

Richmond, Nov. 28.—(AP)—At a business meeting attended by 3,000 delegates and visitors today, Miss Lucy Mason Holt, of the Norwalk City schools, and R. W. House, principal of Prospect High school, of Prince George county, were nominated for president of the Virginia Education association, now in session here.

The School Superintendents' association, affiliated with the Virginia Education association, today elected Superintendent A. L. Bennett, of Albemarle county, to head the organization for another year. David W. Peters, of Henrico county, was elected secretary.

Speaking before the educators, Governor Harry Flood Byrd held the promise for expanded educational facilities in Virginia.

"I stand here tonight as the friend of education," the governor said, "to express my gratification in the progress of our public schools and the development of the higher institutions of learning, both so essential to the progress and welfare of Virginia—and I stand here, too, to justify that faith with a promise to recommend substantial increases in appropriations for public education when I prepare the next budget, without an increase in taxation and made possible by governmental savings and our state development. Increased state appropriations for schools will aid, too, in relief of the burden of local taxation.

"From present indications, the next general assembly will find a substantial surplus in our state treasury, and Virginia can make no better use of her prosperity than to aid the development of education."

The governor reviewed in detail the progress of Virginia in educational work in [illegible] comparing its growth with the national education ideas. He contrasted the amount of the great national income expended for educational purposes—2½ percent, he said, with the huge amount being spent each year by the federal government to pay for wars gone by and to prepare for future wars. The governor explained that he was not intimating that too much was being spent for national preparedness, but he was "suggesting what a delightful world this would be to live in if only the nations could use efficiently a part of their expenditures for war to train men to be trusted not to make war."

Fourth Plant at Hotchkiss Is Announced

Richmond, Nov. 28.—Formal announcement of the textile development at Goshen and other nearby points, involving approximately $3,000,000, was made today by Lee H. Williamson, of Charlottesville, consulting engineer for the Rockbridge company.

In addition to the plants at Goshen, Craigsville and Augusta Springs, previously reported, Mr. Williamson announced that a fourth plant will be located at Hotchkiss, in Bath county. The project is being backed by well-established New England mills, he said, though their identity was not disclosed.

Six hundred operatives, recruited almost exclusively from local labor, will be given employment, while some sheep may be raised in experimental work, though there is no plan for the production of all the raw materials used in the plants.

HOOVER WILL NEXT VISIT S. AMERICA

President-Elect Has Completed Tour of Central American Republics; Holiday Proclaimed Throughout Costa Rica in His Honor; His Purposes Are Praised.

HOOVER MOVES ON AFTER RECEPTION OF UNWONTED FERVOR

San Jose, Costa Rica, Nov. 28.—(AP)—Herbert Hoover brought his good-will visits to Central America to a triumphant close tonight and moved on toward South America. He had received a reception here such as had been accorded previously to only one person, native or foreigner—Col. Charles A. Lindbergh.

This was the first capital visited by the president-elect. Yesterday he had been acclaimed at Corinto, Nicaragua, and on Monday was the guest of La Union, Salvador, and Amapala, Honduras. He is due at Guayaquil, Ecuador, on Sunday for the first of his South American visits.

San Jose, Costa Rica, Nov. 28.—(AP)—Congratulatory expressions of pride in the long and traditional friendship between Costa Rica and the United States were exchanged here today by President Gonzales Viquez and Herbert Hoover, president-elect of the United States. The visit of the distinguished American was made the occasion for a presidential decree declaring him to be the guest of the nation and proclaiming a holiday throughout this republic.

Mr. Hoover landed at Punta Arenas, where he was met by a special government delegation and escorted to a special train which carried him to the capital. Five thousand school children lined the streets of this city and waved flags of the two republics as Mr. Hoover and his escort passed to the [illegible] where President Gonzales Viquez was in waiting.

"Your mission is a very happy inspiration," said the Costa Rican executive in welcoming the nation's guest. "This historic occasion will result in a continuance of the sincere and sound friendship between the United States and Costa Rica, and I believe it will have the safe effect as between the United States and all Latin American countries."

Mr. Hoover in response acknowledged the "glowing tribute to the accomplishment of my country under the stimulus of our common democracy," and added:

"Nowhere do I know of a greater and more proved example of the beneficence to mankind of our common institutions than that which has been accomplished through the hands of the people of Costa Rica. Their advancement of human welfare is well known in my country, and as a student of social and cultural advancement I have long wished to confirm with my own eyes the progress which you have made."

REVIEW OF CADETS

Col. Thos. H. Russell, president of Staunton Military academy, announced yesterday that the cadet corps will be reviewed at the athletic field of the school this morning at 10 o'clock.

November 29, 1928: President and Mrs. Coolidge visit the area. *Microfilm Archives*

SHOPPERS WILL FIND THE ADS A HANDY GUIDE TO PROFITABLE PURCHASING

The Staunton News-Leader

THE WEATHER
Rain today and tonight, probably clearing Friday morning. Mild temperature today. Colder Friday

40th Year. No. 273 — MORNING LEADER EST. 1904 DAILY NEWS EST. 1890 — STAUNTON, VA., THURSDAY MORNING, NOVEMBER 14, 1929 — MEMBER ASSOCIATED PRESS AUDIT BUREAU CIRCULATIONS — PRICE TWO CENTS

TULERAEMIA NOW EXISTS IN AUGUSTA

Presence of "Rabbit Fever" in County Leads City Board of Health to Issue Formal Warning; No Effective Vaccine or Serum Yet Discovered.

HUNDREDS OF STOCK ISSUES CRASH TO A NEW LOW LEVEL

Prize Baby

Third Successive Session of Crumbling Values Leads Stock Exchange Authorities to Seek Source and Character of Relentless Flood of Selling Orders; Drop as High as $80 Share.

ADJOURNMENT NOV. 23 NOW IS EXPECTED

Action Probably to Be Taken Today on Recess Between Terms of Congress; Western Republican Independent Group Opposes Plan; Jones to Offer Resolution.

SLIGHT HOPE FOR RECOVERY OF SEC. GOOD

Cabinet Member in Critical Condition Following Emergency Operation for Appendicitis; Gangrene a Serious Factor in Condition; Colonel Keller Performed Operation.

In Dual Killing

ANDERSON IS NAMED AFTER 15 BALLOTS

Bishop of Chicago Outstanding Figure in Episcopal Church, Elected as Presiding Bishop to Fill Out Term of Late Bishop Murray; Names Assistant.

MELLON TO RECOMMEND BIG SLASH

Treasury Secretary Announces Will Recommend to Congress Reduction of Approximately $160,000,000 in Income Taxes Next Year; Plan Approved by Hoover.

Scheme for Sing Sing Delivery Is Nipped in the Bud

CHICAGO DRYS RAID TEXAS GUINAN CLUB

Governor and Mother to Talk to Commander

Serious Charge Against Alford; Bail is $3,000

SMITH ARRESTED

SMITH INQUIRES OF TOWING CHARGES ON ROAD NEAR STAUNTON

WOMEN'S ELECTION WORK IS COMMENDED BY COMMITTEE

LISKEY-WHETSEL TRIAL TO COME UP AT JANUARY TERM

Baptists Devise a New System for Division of Contributions

County Woman Recovering from Injuries Sustained in Blast Which Wrecked a Wash-House

November 14, 1929: Headlines reflect the continuing decline of stocks in the great Wall Street crash of 1929. *Microfilm Archives*

The 1930s

Survival

While the Great Depression did bring financial losses, unemployment and shortages to the Staunton-Waynesboro-Augusta County area, the suffering here was mild compared with that in other sections of the nation. The area survived the Depression in no small part due to the practicing of conservative banking policies and to the willingness of its citizens to pitch in and help those who were most adversely affected by the economic disaster.

Women established sewing centers in churches and civic halls, manufacturing by hand piles of clothing and bed quilts which were then distributed to the needy by the Welfare Department. Citizens also set up food distribution centers where, once a month, people lined up for the distribution of staple foodstuffs. Undernourished children were the focus of special attention as nutritional camps were established in Augusta County and operated one month of every year.

The Great Depression also brought large numbers of visitors to the area, although not for sightseeing purposes. Freight trains were loaded with transients riding the rails looking for work, many of whom showed up at area homes wanting to exchange odd jobs for food or used clothing. Hobo camps were commonplace.

Not all was bleak, however. Staunton, in particular, had reason to glow with pride as 1930 got underway. In that year, Staunton native William Haines was named Hollywood's number one male film star. Haines had moved from Staunton as a teenager, was discovered by a talent scout on the streets of New York City, and by the 1920s was one of the silent screen's most popular actors.

Also in 1930, one of the nation's most successful companies was founded in Staunton by three brothers – Russell, Raymond and Jake Smith. Their Smith's Transfer Corp. would grow by the 1970s into the 10th largest trucking firm in the United States.

In 1933, overburdened by taxes, 200 Stauntonians descended upon city hall and demanded that council reduce taxes and balance the budget by cutting the pay of city employees by 20 percent. Augusta County that year also was faced with either slashing the length of the school year or cutting teachers' salaries. Like Staunton, the county chose to cut salaries, reducing teachers' base pay to $59 per month.

Anyone wanting to take his mind off the Depression by nipping a little whiskey now and again was simply out of luck – legally, that is. Local police accounts of the day are full of arrests for the possession of booze – and for the busting of at least one still located in a house near the Virginia School for the Deaf and the Blind.

Gold in Your Attic?

The Staunton News-Leader

THE WEATHER

83rd Year. No. 268 — STAUNTON, VA., WEDNESDAY MORNING, NOVEMBER 9, 1932 — PRICE TWO CENTS

ROOSEVELT SWEEPS COUNTRY

VIRGINIA RETURNS TO THE DEMOCRATIC FOLD BY VOTE OF NEARLY THREE TO ONE

Huge Lead Rolled Up in Old Dominion for Roosevelt and Garner; All Nine Democratic Candidates for Congress Also Are Victorious.

THE NATION'S NEW LEADERS

FRANKLIN DELANO ROOSEVELT — JOHN NANCE GARNER

POPULAR AND ELECTORAL PLURALITY OF DEMOCRATS MAY SET NEW HIGH RECORD

People Vote for Change at Washington; Senate and House Both Apparently Placed in Hands of Democrats; Hoover Concedes Defeat and Congratulates Opponent.

EARLY LIFE AND EDUCATION

POLITICAL EXPERIENCE

THE MAN AND HIS FAMILY

MEANS OF REDUCING THE ACCIDENT TOLL STRESSED

Nine Democratic Candidates in State Win Congress Seats

CITY IN LINE WITH RETURNS OVER NATION

Large Audience Gets Newspaper Returns on Vote

Massing of the Colors Ceremony at Victory Ball

COUNTY GOES DEMOCRATIC; BIG MARGIN

BRITISH SHIP RUSHES TO AID DISABLED FREIGHTER

Highland Vote Incomplete But Democrats Win

Cannon Did Not Vote, Paper Says

Youth Suffers Skull Fractures in Auto Crash

November 9, 1932: Franklin D. Roosevelt is elected to the Presidency.

Microfilm Archives

When the vote came, Staunton narrowly voted to repeal Prohibition 1,893 to 1,747. Augusta County narrowly voted to keep it, 1,263 to 1,137. Nationally, however, the vote to repeal Prohibition was overwhelming. Two years later, the Augusta County sheriff reported that bootleg whiskey had dropped in the county by 75 percent.

The area continued to limp through the Depression, wounded but not mortally so. By the early 1930s a number of projects indicated that the area was definitely on the mend, such as the building of a new post office at Frederick and Lewis streets in Staunton and the completion of the Waynesboro DuPont plant that would employ 1,600 new workers.

One of the biggest local stories for 1930s was the August 1939 escape of a circus elephant following a tractor-trailer wreck at Mint Spring in Augusta County. The accident happened when the driver of the vehicle fell asleep at the wheel and crashed into a ditch. In the back of the tractor-trailer were two elephants and a circus employee. The force of the wreck sent one elephant slamming into the employee – killing him – and then on into the wall of the tractor trailer – killing the elephant.

The second elephant, Elsie, walked out the back door of the vehicle, which had sprung open in the crash.

A massive search ensued for the elephant, which disappeared into the Augusta County woods. The Associated Press, United Press International and a host of radio networks converged on the area to broadcast hour-by-hour reports on the unsuccessful hunt.

Finally, after nearly two days, the circus released two of Elsie's elephant companions into the woods where she had escaped, with elephant handlers trailing very close behind. The ploy worked. Elsie sensed the presence of her companions, calmly came out of hiding and walked dutifully back into captivity with her friends and the handlers.

The Second World War got under way on Sept. 1, 1939, when German dictator Adolf Hitler ordered the invasion of Poland. Although the United States would not enter the war for more than two years – the country was deeply isolationist at this time – local headlines reflected a growing national belief that American involvement was inevitable if fascism and the enslavement of the world were to be defeated.

Situated on what is now a 400-acre complex, the E.I. DuPont de Nemours & Co. at Waynesboro began production in 1929 as a rayon acetate manufacturing facility. Pictured here are plant buildings, water tower and smoke stack, with the town of Waynesboro in the background. The plant is still in existence and employs approximately 1,250 people. *Waynewsboro Collection*

The Lambert Barger and Branaman (L.B. & B.) Building, circa 1930, in which was housed the Waynesboro Drug Store, Huwil Five Cents to One Dollar Store, and the real estate firm of E.W. Barger and Co. *Waynewsboro Collection*

In 1936, the ornate interior and third story of the New Theater were gutted by fire. The featured film at the New at that time was “So Red the Rose,” starring Margaret Sullavan and Randolph Scott. Ironically, in the movie a large plantation house burns to the ground. Part of the building’s original Renaissance Revival façade still exists in the ornate terra cotta theater masks and other decorations. *Schwartz Collection*

Gas station on U.S. 11 near Staunton, circa the 1930s. Note the sign that advertises the Beverley Hotel in downtown Staunton. This north-south highway – also known as the Valley Turnpike – was in pre-Interstate years one of two major thoroughfares connecting Staunton with the outside world. The other was the east-west-running U.S. 250. *Schwartz Collection*

FORTY-SIX YEARS IN THE PUBLIC SERVICE
Oldest Virginia Daily West of the Blue Ridge

The Staunton News-Leader

THE WEATHER
Fair today. Saturday mostly cloudy. Slowly rising temperature Saturday and in extreme north portion this afternoon.

47th Year. No. 21 — MEMBER ASSOCIATED PRESS AUDIT BUREAU CIRCULATIONS — STAUNTON, Va., FRIDAY MORNING, JANUARY 24, 1936 — DAILY NEWS EST. 1890 MORNING LEADER EST. 1904 — PRICE TWO CENTS

THREE-TWO COUNCIL VOTE APPROPRIATES $6,500 MORE TO HIGH SCHOOL BUILDING

Two Members of Council Point to Possibility Federal Fund May Be Lost; Hall Appointed Manager at $2,800; Numerous Items of Business Before Meeting.

Members of city council split last night on the question of appropriating $6,500 to the city school board to satisfy an estimated increase in the cost of construction of the Negro school building for which the city has allocated $37,500 to the board for its share in the cost of the construction of the building, which is a PWA project, and the purchase of land, equipment, etc.

Carries, 3 to 2

After a heated discussion of the matter, which was placed before council by Mayor William A. Grubert, Councilman George B. Tullidge offered a motion to grant the appropriation. The motion was seconded by Councilman J. M. Bratton, and was put to a vote and carried, three to two. Grubert, Bratton, and Tullidge, yea; C. K. Brown and Curry Carter, nay.

Members of council said they had not seen the contract for the building, which was negotiated by the school board and the PWA, and decided to ask Superintendent L. F. Shelburne to submit the document to the body for examination at its next meeting.

In Middle of River

Suggestion was made that there was a possibility that the federal government, for some reason, may not come through with its part of the agreement and leave the city "in the middle of the river" and necessitate a huge outlay of cash or the abandonment of the project after thousands had been spent on it.

Hall Gets Appointment

Acting City Manager W. L. Hall was excused from the session while the city fathers unanimously voted to appoint him city manager at a salary of $2,800 per annum. The motion was Mr. Hall's appointment was made by Curry Carter and seconded by J. M. Bratton.

J. Earl Jones, commander of Staunton-Augusta post No. 2216, Veterans of Foreign Wars, appeared before the council and asked for a contribution of $250 from the city to match subscriptions pledged by three hotels and various restaurants and merchants in the city to raise $500 necessary to submit a bid for the 1936 state convention of the V. F. W. The body, on a motion by Mr. Bratton, seconded by Mr. Brown, voted unanimously to pledge $250 if the post was successful in bidding for the convention. The mayor agreed to write

(Continued on Page 2, Column 5)

COMMONWEALTH HAS ARTICLE ON M. B. C.

A familiar view of the main entrance of Mary Baldwin college adorns a page of the January number of the Commonwealth, the magazine of Virginia.

It is used as an illustration for an informative article on the college from the pen of Mary Swan Carroll, of the faculty.

In part, the article says: "Mary Baldwin college, the oldest Southern Presbyterian woman's college in continuous operation and the second oldest Presbyterian woman's college, represents the best educational ideals of both the old and the new south. It has experienced many vicissitudes and changes in its transition from a seminary for young ladies to a recognized four-year liberal arts college. Its requirements of scholarship and personal worth have always been high. Due to its policy of limited enrollment, it can command high standards in its students. For several years it has had more applicants than it could accept."

Much of the article is devoted to historical facts in connection with the institution while mention is also made of honors recently won by college publications in competition with those of other schools, on both a statewide and national basis.

CONTINUANCE OF DOG LAW IS ORDERED

Supervisors Vote Unanimously to Reenact Dog Regulation Until Such Time as There May Be Reason to Rescind It; Sheriff Given Small Salary Boost.

After devoting the morning session to hearing county delegations urgently request that the dog law, which expired Dec. 31, be reenacted, the Augusta county board of supervisors reassembled after lunch and unanimously voted to reenact the dog regulation to be effective until the board may have reasons to rescind it.

Sheriff G. M. Glikeson, who appeared before the body in the morning to request a salary increase, was allowed a boost of $60 per year.

The board turned down a suggestion of the Home Owners' Loan corporation that the county body pay $3 per month on a home loan secured by Richard Gallimore, legless Negro, who resides near the C. and O. tracks in the vicinity of the cemetery. The corporation is threatening to foreclose on the property of the colored man and it was a question in the discussion of the board as to whether or not the property was worth what they would have to put into it if the suggestion were adopted.

No Final Action

No final action was taken in the matter of recommending to the state highway commission that two short stretches of road, one in South River district and the other in Riverheads district, be included in the secondary system. A committee

(Continued on Page 2, Column 6)

Body of George V Lies in State in Westminster Hall

London, Jan. 23.—(AP)—Britain's King Edward VIII stood in silent prayer today before the body of his father George V, borne in death to lie in a catafalque of state in medieval Westminster Hall.

Haggard and apparently weary, he prayed with all of England as the body of King George was placed in its black and gold resting place amid simple ceremonies, at the end of a 100-mile journey from rustic Sandringham where the Monarch died peacefully Monday night.

Atop the royal standard, at one end of the bier, the jewelled crown of empire glistened. At the other end, above the head, lay the floral crosses of Edward and the Queen Mother Mary.

The body will remain until Tuesday in the cold and ancient hall, beneath the high wooden ceiling placed there 500 years ago.

Then it will be taken for the last time through the streets of the empire's capital to the rain, which

(Continued on Page 2, Column 7)

Midnight Blaze Reduces Theatre Building to Ruins

Staunton's Most Disastrous Fire in Years Guts New Theatre With Loss Estimated at About $150,000; Origin Undetermined; Nightly Check by Employees at 11:20 O'clock Revealed No Sign of Fire; Harrisonburg and Waynesboro Companies Rush to Assistance of Local Firemen.

Fire of undetermined origin, that at one time threatened to spread into a block-long conflagration, early this morning destroyed the New theatre, corner Beverley and Market streets, together with all its contents. The loss was unofficially estimated at about $150,000, largely covered by insurance. The building was the property of Warner Brothers.

Flames broke out shortly before midnight. Firemen were hurriedly summoned, but by the time they arrived on the scene, the fire had gained such headway that it was impossible to save the building.

Nothing definite is known concerning the origin of the destructive flames. A check by theatre employees at eleven-twenty p. m., after the crowd attending the last show of the night had vacated the house, revealed nothing to indicate that in a matter of minutes the building would be a mass of smouldering ruins.

Worst in Years

The fire, which was the worst conflagration Staunton has seen since the burning of the Hardy apartments across the street from the theatre, six years ago, was thought to have started in the rear of the stage of the picture house. In a few minutes, flames ate through the tin roofing and spread over the entire upper section of the building.

The flames defied the icy streams from the fire hoses for over an hour and a half and spread onto the roof of the adjoining building which houses the post office and the Arcadia restaurant. At twenty minutes of two, Postmaster R. E. Fifer stated that the flames had not yet eaten through the double brick wall into the postal quarters.

One Harrisonburg firemen suffered a frozen hand. He was C. W. Trenary of Company 4.

Hundreds of men and women backed further away from the theatre building as flames leaped high into the air from the front of the roof of the blazing structure. Heavy coals and sparks poured from the roof and were blown over homes for several blocks beyond Coer street. The home of Mrs. Jane McFarland, in the rear of the theater, was saved from destruction.

Crowds were driven back on the scene several times by bursts of water from busted hose on several streets.

Company No. 4, of Harrisonburg, responded to the call, leaving Rockingham city at fifteen minutes after midnight and arriving at the scene at twenty minutes afterward. There are fifteen men in this unit.

Manager Jack Forney stated that the theatre had been close as usual about twenty minutes after eleven and his first knowledge of the fire was a call from a watchman from Woodward's dry cleaning works, across the street from the burning building. Forney said the theatre had recently been remodeled with about $5,000 worth of new chairs having been installed, in addition to new office quarters and rest rooms.

Lights in the adjoining restaurant went out at ten minutes after twelve and the crowds inside a hurried exit in orderly fashion. Hundreds of onlookers came and out of Woodward's cleaning and office while several thousand people along Beverley and New streets braving the six above temperature.

Fire trucks skidded about the streets as they swung around for positions. Firemen's rubber coats were covered with solid sheets of ice as they fought the spreading flames.

A near-tragedy was averted as three Staunton firemen jumped back from the lower floor of the theatre building just before a lot of flaming timbers and debris crashed from the upper floors of the building. Sergeant R. A. Lynn and two other volunteers were feared to have perished for a while unless several hasty re-checks had been made.

Guests at the city hotels, including

(Continued on Page 2, Column 8)

COLD WAVE EXTENDS TO EAST COAST

New York Experiences Coldest Jan. 23 in Its History; Seventy-seven Deaths Attributed to Severe Winter Weather; South's Citrus Crops Threatened

_____, Jan. 23.—(AP)—Cold kept its capital in the frostbound Mid-west tonight, but extended its subzero sweep to the Atlantic ocean.

As the mercury climbed from lows that set new all-time marks in many sections of the plains and northern border states, readings started a dip in the East with New York experiencing the most frigid Jan 23 in its history and preparing for ten below during the night.

Fourteen states counted one or more fatalities from exposure or causes directly attributable to the most rigorous cold wave in years. The total from the country mounted to seventy-seven.

The sub-zero temperatures ranged from minus 56 on the bridge over the Rainy river between International Falls, Minn., and Fort Frances, Ont.—for the second successive day coldest spot on the weather map and one degree more frigid than yesterday—to New York's two below.

In the Arctic belt's twenty-five to fifty-two-degree below range were Minnesota, Wisconsin, and parts of Ohio, Pennsylvania, and West Virginia. Parts of New York state, Indiana, Illinois, Iowa, Missouri, eastern Kansas, Nebraska, and the Dakotas saw readings of ten to twenty under zero.

Crops Threatened

Wings of the cold wave penetrated the Southland, bringing threats of damage to Florida's citrus fruits with a low of twenty-seven forecast during the night and scattering snow flurries over Tennessee.

(Continued on Page 2, Column 5)

PATTERSON GETS 75 YEARS; PREVIOUSLY SENTENCED TO DEATH ON THREE OCCASIONS

Seven of Family Found Murdered in Blazing Home

Danville, Ill., Jan. 23.—(AP)—The seven members of the William A. Albers family were found shot and bludgeoned to death today in a flaming farm home.

A posse of Edgar county officials and residents who trudged to the snow-bound house in twenty-below zero weather made the gruesome discovery. A hasty reconstruction of the tragedy led them to believe Alberts had killed his wife and five children in a demented rampage a week or ten days ago, and had lived in the grisly household until investigators approached today. They reasoned he then made pyres for each of his victims—mattresses soaked in kerosene—set them afire and slew himself.

Apparently the children, four boys and a girl—all clad in nightgowns—had been slain in their sleep.

Posse leaders asserted the belief John, seventeen; Wilford, fourteen, and Forrest, ten, had been beaten to death. A blood-stained baseball bat was found in their room. Rifle bullets had ended the lives of Mrs. Augusta Alberts, forty-five; Gene, four; Shirley Anne, two, and Albers, fifty-four. All had been shot through the head.

Albers' body was sprawled on the dining room floor. The others lay in their beds—the two oldest sons together—in various parts of the six-room house.

It was the absence of John and Wilford from Sidell High school that led to the formation of the posse. Principal W. J. Gorehan and three other men traveled to the home, twenty-five miles southwest of Danville and six miles south of Sidell, through yesterday's blizzard. Albers opened the door a bare inch. Asked why the boys had not returned from Christmas vacation, he muttered:

"The whole family is quarantined in Champaign."

Gorehan said Albers appeared "wild-eyed and haggard." The quarantine story could not be substantiated. So the investigating party bucked back through the snowdrifts today.

Albers raced into his house as they approached. He apparently saturated the bodies with coal oil, covered them with torn mattresses soaked in the same fuel, and set the blazes. A shot was heard as officials broke in through boarded windows.

After gaining entrance, the investigators stamped out the fires.

Is First of Nine Scottsboro Case Defendants to Stand Trial; Leibowitz Announces Appeal Will be Made.

Decatur, Ala., Jan. 23.—(AP)—Heywood Patterson, first of the nine Negro defendants in the Scottsboro case to face retrial, was convicted today and sentenced to seventy-five years' imprisonment.

Accused of attacking Mrs. Victoria Price, a white woman, aboard a freight train approximately five years ago, Patterson thrice had heard himself sentenced to death, but each time he won a new trial.

The jury that heard his case the fourth time deliberated eight hours, but the verdict was delayed while another panel was struck to try Clarence Norris, a second of the defendants, tomorrow on the same charge.

Mrs. Price, victim of the alleged attack on March 25, 1931, said, "I don't think it was enough punishment."

Samuel S. Leibowitz, of New York, chief of defense counsel, announced that an appeal from the verdict would be taken. Leibowitz said Patterson remarked on the verdict: "I had rather die than spend another day in jail for something I didn't do."

Patterson was stoical, as he has been in the past, while the verdict was being read by John Green, clerk of the court.

New York, Jan. 23.—(AP)—Norman Thomas, former Socialist candidate for president and one of the leaders of the Scottsboro defense movement, tonight said the seventy-five-year sentence given Heywood Patterson at Decatur, Ala., "is still a decision growing out of popular hysteria."

"It is better than death," he said. "It is better than death," he said, "because it gives us more time to work on the defense, but it is still a decision growing out of popular hysteria. It is not supported by evidence."

Rinehart Freed in Wreck Case

Charles Rinehart, twenty-seven, who had been held in the county jail since Jan. 2 on a charge of involuntary manslaughter growing out of an auto-truck collision on the previous day which resulted in the death of Mrs. Robert F. Barry walked out of trial justice court late yesterday afternoon a free man after Justice W. T. Sheehan dismissed the warrant on the grounds of lack of sufficient evidence to carry the case further.

Rinehart was the driver of the truck which collided with the light coupe in which Mr. and Mrs. Barry were returning to their home in Nashville, Tenn., from their wedding trip. The accident occurred on the Lee highway near Verona and Mrs. Barry died the following day in King's Daughters' hospital.

Extended Hearing

The decision of Justice Sheehan climaxed a long, drawn-out hearing in which a number of witnesses were called, including the husband of the victim, the defendant, Sergeant Robert A. Lynn, of the state highway police, who investigated the collision, and several people who arrived at the scene soon after the fatal accident. The hearing was opened about ten o'clock in the morning and proceeded without interruption until five-thirty in the afternoon with the exception of an hour's recess at noon.

Mrs. W. H. Campbell, who resides near the scene of the accident, was called to the stand after the court resumed following the recess and testified that she was in her

(Continued on Page 2, Column 4)

Debt Boost? More Taxes? Inflation?

Three Questions Arise in Wake of Passage of Bonus Bill; Veto Strongly Hinted

Washington, Jan. 23.—(AP)—With a $2,491,000,000 soldiers' bonus bill on President Roosevelt's desk, the administration tonight faced a political dilemma of choosing between a big boost in the national debt, new taxes, or inflation.

Reports circulated widely that the Chief Executive would deliver a sharp veto of the bonus, possibly in person, but so guarded was the silence at the White House that neither a confirming nor denying hint was forthcoming.

In any event, congressional leaders stuck by their predictions that a veto would be overridden, leaving the method of raising the necessary money a moot question.

Demand New Taxes

Some within the administration who have followed the President's thoughts closely contended in private conversations today that if the bonus measure becomes law, Mr. Roosevelt will demand the enactment of new taxes to foot the bill. He mentioned this even when vetoing the inflationary Patman bonus bill last session. Further, he placed in his recent message to congress a pointed reference that no new taxes would be necessary under "existing legislation."

Disclosure that a new tax plan was "in process" to finance the farm program intended to replace the AAA was made today by Attorney General Cummings, further strengthening this line of argument in the bonus case.

More than one congressional leader in off-the-record conversations during the day argued, however, that the financing of the hefty bonus item through regular treasury channels, with a resultant increase in the public debt, might carry less political dynamite in an election year than new taxes.

Republicans already have picked the debt as a big talking point.

Talk of using the fund by inflation was heard in several quarters at the Capitol.

Rome and Addis Ababa Report Thousands Dead

ROBERTSON TO TALK ON WILD LIFE PROGRAM

Washington, Jan. 23.—(AP)—Representative A. Willis Robertson of Lexington, will discuss the national wild life conservation program over the radio tomorrow afternoon.

Robertson formerly Virginia game commissioner, now is chairman of the house special committee on wild life conservation. His address will deal largely with the purposes of the national wild life conference to be held here at the call of President Roosevelt, Feb. 3 to 7.

MEETING AT BETHEL CHURCH POSTPONED

On account of the severe winter weather, the meeting at Bethel church tonight, at which Claude Pritchard, secretary of home missions of the Southern Presbyterian church, was scheduled to speak, has been postponed until a later date.

Each Capital Claims, However, That Victims of Fierce Fighting in Northern Ethiopia Were the Enemy.

By the Associated Press

Thousands slain in a savage battle in northern Ethiopia were reported Thursday in both Rome and Addis Ababa.

But each capital said the victims were the enemy, their claims conflicting.

Complete Success

Rome, Jan. 23.—The Stefani (Italian) news agency said "several thousand" Ethiopians were killed in a battle in the Tembien area of northern Ethiopia Tuesday.

A dispatch from Asmara to the agency said:

"A general engagement in the Tembien extending to the whole northern front was engaged in

(Continued on Page 2, Column 5)

AMENDING OF FARM BILL IS HELD CERTAIN

New Taxes to Finance Continued Federal Payments to Farmers Definitely Projected as Fresh Congressional Storm Breaks Over AAA Substitute Bill.

Washington, Jan. 23.—(AP)—New taxes to finance continued federal payments to farmers were definitely projected today as a fresh congressional storm stent the administration's AAA substitute bill to drydock for repairs.

Sharply conflicting reports over what happened at a secret meeting of Secretary Wallace with a senate agriculture sub-committee left in doubt the extent to which the bill—introduced only yesterday—will be amended.

Everyone agreed, however, that there would be immediate changes, including one suggested by Wallace to provide that subsidies after two years would be granted only to states which cooperate in a permanent program not yet worked out, but based on the idea of "little AAA's" in the forty-eight states.

New Tax Legislation

As Wallace left the committee with instructions to prepare tentative amendments, Attorney-General Cummings told his press conference that new tax legislation was "in process of formation by the justice department and the treasury."

Asked if this would include retroactive re-enactment of the invalidated AAA processing levies, Cummings said "You might, of course, take that as your conclusion." He declined to comment on whether this would be done or whether he believed such a law would be constitutional.

Attempts to ascertain definitely what happened at the meeting of Wallace and Chester Davis, AAA administrator, with the senate group disclosed a difference of opinion among senators on the conclusions reached.

Wallace's Comment

Wallace made only this comment:

"While there had been some preliminary differences on emphasis on various phases of the bill, I was much pleased to discover that there was a meeting of minds in committee. The committee was unanimous in agreeing on changes to be made and requested the department to work with drafting clerks to prepare the necessary amendments."

Refuse to Serve

Senator Smith (D-SC) who earlier in the day reluctantly accepted chairmanship of the five-member sub-committee on which

(Continued on Page 2, Column 7)

Former Police Chief Is Held in Kidnaping

Tampa, Fla., Jan. 23.—(AP)—Police Chief R. G. Tittsworth, relieved Dec. 17, was arrested late today as an accessory before the fact to the kidnaping of three men and the second-degree murder of one of them. He was later released on $7,500 bond.

The arrest was made on a capias issued by Circuit Court Judge Harry Sandler. It was issued after a special grand jury returned two indictments charging Tittsworth with being an accessory to the kidnaping which preceded the beating, tarring, and feathering of three men more than a month ago. He also was charged with being an accessory to the second-degree murder of Joseph Shoemaker, who died from the effects of the flogging and exposure.

Tittsworth was the tenth man to be indicted in the case. The others were: Patrolman Sam E. Crosby, John Bridges, F. W. Switzer, Sergeant C. A. Brown, Special Policemen Robert Chappell, and C. W. Carlisle, all of Tampa, and Arlie Gillian, Ed Spivey, and James Dean, of Orlando, special policemen in the September primaries here.

TO ARRAIGN 3 MEMBERS OF ALLEGED HOLDUP GANG TODAY

Bristol, Va., Jan. 22.—(AP)—John Johnson and Gillis and Virgil Denny, alleged members of a gang of highwaymen who preyed upon Virginia, Kentucky, and Tennessee, will be arraigned before United States Commissioner A. M. Vicars at Wise tomorrow afternoon.

The three men have been held in the Bristol, Va., jail since their arrest recently, and Deputy United States Marshal B. L. Skeen will come here tomorrow morning and take the prisoners to Wise.

Important witnesses at the hearing are expected to be Mrs. Gillis Denny, Sheriff Robert Giles, of Lee county, and Officer Charles Redmond, of St. Charles.

J. K. Collins, from the department of justice at Washington, is expected to be present at the hearing. Collins aided Lee county officers in the capture of the men, who crossed the path of government agents through the alleged hi-jacking of liquor trucks near Louisville, Ky. Lee county officers say that several cars in the possession of the three men and C. D. Richards have been identified as stolen.

Richards, captured with Johnson and the Denny brothers, was removed recently from Bristol to Knoxville, Tenn., and convicted in federal court there of stealing an automobile, his punishment being fixed at three years in federal prison.

FORMER WAYNESBORO MAN TO BE QUESTIONED IN KILLING OF HIS WIFE, TEN YEARS AGO

Police yesterday returned to Huntington, W. Va., Frank Lester Foster, aged forty-nine years, of Chicago—a former Waynesboro man—for questioning about the death of his wife in Huntington ten years ago.

Foster was taken into custody by Detectives Ed Spencer and Roy Hagley, of Indiana Harbor, a Chicago suburb, where they said Foster had lived for five years under the name of Frank Lester.

Detective Lieutenant Leslie J. Swann said he would summon three daughters of Foster to testify as to a quarrel which the officer said preceded the shooting of Mrs. Foster on May 8, 1926.

Swann asserted that Foster accosted her on the porch of their home in Huntington four days after she obtained a partial divorce decree and slapped her and fired as she dropped what she carried and ran down the street.

No formal charge had been lodged against Foster last night, the detective said.

Waynesboro, Jan. 23. — Police here have been informed of the arrest in Chicago of Bud Foster, a former resident of this city, wanted since 1926 in connection with the death of his wife in Huntington, W. Va., where the couple resided at the time.

Mrs. Foster was a Miss Pleasants, of Waynesboro.

Details of the alleged crime and circumstances of Foster's arrest were unknown to police today.

It is said that Mr. and Mrs. Foster had domestic difficulties in Huntington; that she went to court for redress, which she obtained in the form of maintenance, and that in an argument later the woman was fatally shot.

Foster disappeared and had not been heard from until his arrest in Chicago.

Legion Conference of Tenth District to Be Held in City

Clemmer-McGuffin post will be host to the Tenth district American Legion conference on the afternoon of Feb. 22, an event that will bring to the city a number of prominent Legion officials and will have as its climax a banquet starting at seven p. m. The place of the conference has not yet been definitely selected.

The banquet will be attended by legionnaires, friends of the service organization, and members of its auxiliary. The principal address will be delivered by a speaker of national reputation but those in charge of arrangements have not progressed with their negotiations to the point that they are able to reveal the speaker's identity at this time.

Attending the conference and

(Continued on Page 2, Column 4)

Teachers Ask Retirement Legislation Involving a State Fund of $676,209.00

State Capitol, Richmond, Jan. 23.—(AP)—Organized teachers of Virginia, through the Virginia Education association, made their request for teachers' retirement legislation, involving a state appropriation of $676,209 annually, as senate finance and house appropriations began detailed hearings on the budget tonight.

Fred M. Alexander, of Newport News, was chief spokesman for the teachers' organization, and explained in great detail the pamphlet distributed to the legislators at the capitol during the day.

He said the state's appropriation would be gradually reduced through death and removal of 1,000 teachers now retired and through liquidation of accrued liability for teachers now about to retire, until the appropriation would reach $270,484 annually.

Wasn't it understood when the teachers' retirement law was passed in 1908 that the state would not

(Continued on Page 2, Column 3)

LEGISLATURE RUNS INTO CONTROVERSIAL MATTERS; DELAYS ARE THREATENED

Richmond, Jan. 23.—(AP)—Committees driving hard to clear their files and place legislation before the senate and house ran into controversial matters to delay action today on school, liquor, road, and other legislation.

A storm of opposition from Roanoke, Norfolk, and Richmond greeted the school code before the senate public institutions and education committee, the urban representatives construing an amendment as enabling fifty or more voters in a city to force an election on adoption of school budgets in unlimited amounts.

They asked the committee to "let up alone" although former Governor E. Lee Trinkle, chairman of the board of education, and Superintendent of Public Instruction Sidney B. Hall, protested that their interpretation was not the meaning of the proposed change.

Action Postponed

Senator Leonard G. Muse, of Roanoke, City Attorney James E. Cannon, of Richmond, Senator Vivian Page, of Norfolk, and City Attorney John Sebrell, of Norfolk were the chief spokesmen against the proposed school code change. Action was postponed until next Tuesday.

Opposition equally as vigorous met the bill carrying out the legislative advisory council's recommendations for strengthening the liquor board's power to make rules and regulations with the force and effect of law.

"The principle that a single administrative agency may make a law, administer it, enforce it and judge violations cannot be defended," Gordon Ambler senator from Richmond and member of the general laws sub-committee studying the bill, said. Senator Aubrey Weaver, of Front Royal joined with the Richmond senator in saying he could not reconcile

(Continued on Page 2, Column 5)

January 24, 1936: The New Theater in downtown Staunton is ravaged by fire. *Microfilm Archives*

Main Street (U.S. 250) in Waynesboro, looking west, from the vicinity of today's Waynesboro High School. The pedestrians shown in this photograph, particularly those on the left, may be students of the school on their way home. Note the absence of sidewalks. *Waynewsboro Collection*

Photo dating from the 1930s showing the "Eatwell Lunch" room on the northwest corner of Johnson and South New streets. The building, which in earlier times had served as headquarters for Harman Brothers Whiskey, also housed the Greyhound Bus depot. *Schwartz Collection*

In August 1939, a circus elephant escaped into Augusta County following a tractor-trailer wreck at Mint Spring. The accident occurred when the driver of the vehicle fell asleep at the wheel and crashed into a ditch. In the back of the tractor-trailer were two elephants and a circus employee. The force of the wreck sent one elephant slamming into the employee – killing him – and on into the wall of the tractor trailer – killing the elephant. The second elephant, Elsie, walked out the back door of the vehicle, which had sprung open in the crash.

A massive search ensued for Elsie, who disappeared into the Augusta County woods. The Associated Press, United Press International and a bevy of radio networks converged on the area and gave hour-by-hour reports on the frustratingly unsuccessful hunt. Elsie eluded all attempts to locate her.

Finally, after nearly two fruitless days, the circus released two of Elsie's elephant companions into the woods where she had escaped, with elephant handlers trailing very close behind. The ploy worked. Elsie sensed the presence of her companions, calmly came out of hiding and walked dutifully back into captivity with her friends and the handlers. *Schwartz Collection*

On July 23, 1932, the swimming pool in Gypsy Hill Park was formally opened in a ceremony that featured four speakers, the blare of bugles and swimming and diving exhibitions. Two years later, Staunton City Manager W.F. Day reported that the swimming pool, which was operated by the fire department, had not cost the taxpayers a nickel in outlay costs. Interest on the original $11,900 for construction of the pool, plus reductions in the principal, had been paid by the fire department. The pool is today still a central attraction in Gypsy Hill Park. *Schwartz Collection*

The 1940s

War and Peace

Shortly after Hitler ordered the invasion of Poland in 1939, the Staunton News-Leader reported that the 116th Infantry Regiment – Staunton's Virginia National Guard unit – was combat-ready should it be required in the new war. This statement indicated, at least locally, that the nation's long-standing policy of isolationism was drawing to a close. Little did anyone suspect as the new decade dawned just how pivotal a role in the defeat of Nazi Germany the local military unit would play.

Few doubted the certainty of American involvement in World War II after a May 4, 1941 speech in Staunton by the President of the United States, Franklin D. Roosevelt. The President visited Staunton to help dedicate the Woodrow Wilson Birthplace as a national monument, and in a speech from the Coalter Street entrance of the manse Roosevelt claimed that democracy cannot survive in isolationism. Our "simple faith in the freedom of democracy," he said, is worth fighting for.

Nearly every newspaper in the country, including the Leader, latched onto Roosevelt's comment and endlessly speculated what he meant by it. Was he forecasting a declaration of war?

FIFTY-ONE YEARS IN THE PUBLIC SERVICE

The Staunton News-Leader

STATE LIBRARY

THE WEATHER

52nd YEAR. No. 107 — STAUNTON, Va., SUNDAY MORNING, MAY 4, 1941 — PRICE TWO CENTS

WELCOME, PRESIDENT ROOSEVELT!

HAIL TO THE CHIEF!

FRANKLIN DELANO ROOSEVELT

President Will Speak From a Prepared Text

Chief Executive Decided Saturday at Charlottesville to Abandon Original Plan to Speak Extemporaneously; Stirs Speculation as to Possible Major Statement; Halifax Forced to Curtail Stay; Finishing Touches Put Upon Arrangements.

In an atmosphere charged with expectancy, ... night awaited one of the most outstanding events in ... long history—the arrival of President Roosevelt this morning to dedicate the birthplace of Woodrow Wilson as a national shrine.

Months of preparation by local groups and national figures associated with them in restoring the birthplace will be climaxed when the President delivers his address at noon.

Prepared Address

While the Chief Executive had been expected to speak extemporaneously, the Associated Press announced last night that he had decided to deliver a prepared address. Whether he would have a major statement to make, White House officials in Charlottesville were unwilling to predict. But the birthplace of the man who led the United States through the World war, it was pointed out, would offer a fitting forum for a discussion of international affairs.

SHIP LOSS WAS ALMOST A MIRACLE

Iraq Soldiers Are Reported Driven Back by British

Vichy Sources Say Twenty-six American Ships Carrying War Material Have Arrived at Suez, Convoyed by United States Warships; Navy Department Says Bluntly That No U. S. Navy Ships Are Employed in Convoy Duty.

NEW BOMBER IS CALLED A WORLD BEATER

TO DEFER MEDICAL STUDENTS

Davis Succeeds Sproul on Board

REICHSTAG TO MEET AT ELEVEN A. M.

Say 11 German Planes Downed

John F. Brooke, Aged 102, Pays Shrine a Visit

SOME MEMBERS SEE REMARKS OF PRESIDENT AS MANDATE FOR HIGHER INCOME TAXES

Willkie Asserts Administration's Existing Sea Patrol Not Adequate

No Flying Order To Be in Effect For Three Hours

BRITISH NEED A SWING OF U. S. PUBLIC OPINION TOWARD BETTER CONVOY COOPERATION

May 4, 1941: FDR visits Staunton to dedicate the Woodrow Wilson Birthplace. *Microfilm Archives*

War came on Dec. 7, 1941, when Japan launched a sneak attack on the U.S. fleet at Pearl Harbor. When news of the attack reached Staunton, people reacted angrily. One man speaking to a reporter suggested the United States "go down there and wipe the Japs off the face of the earth." Others noted that "while they are at it, they should declare war on Germany, too."

Teletype messages received at police headquarters in Staunton and Waynesboro urged all soldiers, sailors and Marines to report to their bases immediately. All leaves and furloughs were cancelled, and by the next day few servicemen could be found in the area.

At least two local men were killed in the Pearl Harbor attack – John Hildebrand of Fordwick and Raymond E. Powell of Waynesboro.

War for the residents of Staunton, Waynesboro and Augusta County meant rationing, bond drives, blackouts, air raid drills and conservation. By August of 1942, Augusta County ranked first in the state in recovering scrap metal, and in less than two months Waynesboro residents bought $199,475 in war bonds.

Right in the middle of World War II, Waynesboro found itself in a war all its own – with Mother Nature. On Oct. 15, 1942, a 72-hour rainstorm resulted in massive flooding in the downtown area, submerging businesses, stranding motorists and isolating people in the upper floors of their residences. The flood, which resulted in extensive damage and loss of property, provided the impetus for the building of a storm sewer that helped lessen flooding in Waynesboro.

Bright spots in the war for Stauntonians came in the form of native sons and former residents doing well. Jacob "Jack" Manch, son of one of Staunton's music professors, attained instant hero status when he participated in the April 18, 1942 bombing of Tokyo with Lt. Col. Jimmy Doolittle. And Gen. Alexander M. Patch, a former superintendent at Staunton Military Academy, led the southern invasion of France in 1944.

But it was the Normandy invasion – D-Day, June 6, 1944 – that would give Staunton its greatest connection with heroism during the war. On that day, Staunton's 116th Infantry Regiment spearheaded the bloody first-wave attack at Omaha Beach. Among local men decorated with the Distinguished Service Cross were Capt. Archibald Sproul of Middlebook, Tech. Sgt. L.M. Armstrong of Staunton and Staff Sgt. Ralph Coffman of Mt. Sidney.

Staunton collectively mourned the death of one of the 116th's officers, Maj. Thomas D. Howie. A former teacher at SMA, Howie was mortally wounded on July 18, 1944 in Normandy. Just before his death, he ordered the attack at Martinsville Ridge which led to the liberation of the city of St. Lo, where to this day he is celebrated as the "Major of St. Lo."

After the war, life in the Central Shenandoah Valley returned to normal with the gradual lifting of rationing. In 1946, Augusta County contemplated buying the Woodrow Wilson General Hospital site in Fishersville on which it would would establish a new high school, and in Staunton plans were formulated for the construction of a new hospital.

Despite the onset of the Cold War, peace and prosperity were the orders of the day in the Staunton-Waynesboro-Augusta County region. In 1947 Mary Baldwin College's "Campus Comments" was judged the best student newspaper in the state; John Wayne had two big hits with "Angel and the Badman" and "In Old California;" local broadcaster Charles Blackley described to Rotarians the phenomenon of television – a phenomenon expected to reach the Valley in January 1948; and the cost of a U.S. 11 bypass (now Commerce Road) was estimated at $258,000. And on Dec. 30, 1949, the cornerstone was laid on North Augusta Street for a new $2.2 million King's Daughters' Hospital.

Nothing, it seemed, could now interfere with the area's enjoyment of the good life.

Rose Hall in Waynesboro was an elegant example of a Southern home and, during the Civil War, became a favorite rendezvous point for Confederates. It was often referred to by Southern soldiers as "headquarters of the Army of Northern Virginia." Federal Gen. Philip Sheridan reportedly had at least one meal at Rose Hall following the March 2, 1865, skirmish, at Waynesboro, and dispatched a guard to protect the home from plundering and destruction. Historic Rose Hall was demolished by the city of Waynesboro in the 1960s to make way for a shopping center. *Waynewsboro Collection*

Republicans in Staunton strung up this banner across South Augusta Street near its intersection with what is now Beverley Street (at the Visulite Theater), in support of Wendell Wilke. Wilke lost the 1940 presidential election to Franklin D. Roosevelt. The Visulite was showing, at the time, "Waterloo Bridge" with Vivien Leigh and Robert Taylor. *Schwartz Collection*

Circa 1940s photograph of Nelson County native Nelson Durrett who began his life as a preacher at the age of 16. Durrett, shown here holding a small bugle, reportedly preached free to "white and colored" with "any donation" welcome. He is shown here at the age of 86. *Waynewsboro Collection*

In 1927, Col. Carl C. "Rip" Loth, a flyer in World War I, opened the Valley Airport at Waynesboro and gave flying lessons. The General Electric Co. bought the land in 1953 to build their plant and, when G.E. moved to Charlottesville, the site was occupied by Genicom in 1983. Pictured here in a series of photos from a 1940s air show are (1) a Bellanca Cruise-air single engine plane with hanger in the background and (2) an aerial view of the airfield under construction. *Waynewsboro Collection*

Photo of President Franklin D. Roosevelt delivering the dedication speech at the Woodrow Wilson Birthplace on May 4, 1941. Roosevelt's remark that our "simple faith in the freedom of democracy" is worth fighting for sparked a national debate over whether he was forecasting a declaration of war. *Schwartz Collection*

Waynesboro's great flood of September 1945 wreaked havoc on the city, as is evidenced in this series of photographs. Pictured here are; An aerial view of the South River swollen with floodwaters, a swamped Gulf station with several men standing knee-deep in water, a flooded Ford dealership (note the sign for gasoline at 18 1/2 cents per gallon), two men, one with an umbrella, wading in the street in front of the Wayne Music Store and a group of teens try to push a friend's car out of floodwaters where it has become stranded. *Waynewsboro Collection*

FIFTY-ONE YEARS IN THE PUBLIC SERVICE
Oldest Virginia Daily West of the Blue Ridge

The Staunton News-Leader

THE WEATHER
Partly cloudy, colder, occasional snow flurries in mountains of northwest portion today. Partly cloudy, moderately cold Wednesday.

52nd YEAR. No. 292 | MEMBER ASSOCIATED PRESS AUDIT BUREAU CIRCULATIONS | STAUNTON, Va., TUESDAY MORNING, DECEMBER 9, 1941 | MORNING LEADER EST. 1904 DAILY NEWS EST. 1890 | PRICE THREE CENTS

Planes Are Driven Away From Golden Gate

Declaration of War on Japan Signed by President

Congress Acts With Unanimity and Great Speed

President Receives Ovation as He Asks for Declaration of War; To Give Public More Complete Information on Progress of Pacific War in Broadcast at Ten O'Clock Tonight; Battleship, Destroyer, Smaller Craft Sunk by Japanese; 3,000 Killed or Wounded by Enemy Raiders; American Assistance to Britain Not to Be Impeded.

By RICHARD L. TURNER

Washington, Dec. 8.—(AP)—America declared war on Japan today after that nation's air bombers had dealt the navy the severest blow in its history and inflicted losses which raised the harsh possibility that the Japanese fleet may now enjoy a temporary superiority in the Pacific.

Some details of the savage Japanese attack—which admittedly cost the navy a battleship, a destroyer, a number of smaller craft, and killed or wounded 3,000—will be given to the nation by President Roosevelt tomorrow night in a ten o'clock radio address.

His speech will supplement the brief message with which he asked congress for a declaration of war today—a request which both houses followed up with action that was breathtakingly swift and, save for one vote, unanimous.

Germany Accused

These developments came at the close of a day which saw this country not only declare war on Japan, but also accuse Germany of doing its utmost to push the Japanese into the conflict, with the purpose of impeding the program of American assistance to Great Britain.

But, a White House statement said, the program of American help to the British "will continue in full operation." The announcement caused some surprise, because a short while before Winston Churchill had said a diminution of such help was to be expected.

"Obviously Germany did all it could to push Japan into the war," the White House said. "It was the German hope that if the United States and Japan could be pushed into war that such a conflict would put an end to the lease-lend program.

"As usual, the wish is father to the thought behind the broadcasts and public announcements emanating from Germany with relation to the war and the lease-lend program.

"That such German broadcasts and announcements are continuously and completely 100 percent inaccurate is shown by the fact that the

(Continued on Page 2, Col. 3)

COURT WILL NOT REVIEW NEGRO CASE

Supreme Court Refuses to Review Case of Joseph R. Mickens, Who Received Death Sentence for Criminal Assault on Female; New Date for His Death to Be Set.

Having failed to obtain a supreme court review of his case, Joseph R. Mickens, fifteen-year-old Waynesboro Negro sentenced to die for a criminal assault on a female, will be referred back to Augusta county circuit court for the fixing of another date on which he will pay the death penalty.

The supreme court yesterday declined to review the case and Judge F. S. Crosby, who sentenced Mickens in circuit court here, will have to decide on the second date.

Justice Murphy dissented in the supreme court ruling, according to an Associated Press report, holding that a petition for review should be granted.

A stay of execution previously granted by Chief Justice Stone was vacated.

The Negro was convicted of as-

(Continued on Page 2, Col. 8)

YMC Club to Hear Willett

H. I. Willett, supervisor of instruction in the county school system, will address the Young Men's Civic club at its meeting tonight at six-thirty.

Mr. Willett's topic, "Educating for Democracy," is one of vital interest to everyone.

President William Morrison requests that all the club's members be present.

BRITAIN FULFILLS PROMISE TO DECLARE WAR UPON JAPAN IN EVENT OF ATTACK ON U. S.

London, Dec. 8. — (AP) — Britain sprang proudly today to the aid of her kinsmen and ancient friends, declaring war upon Japan even before the United States itself had taken formal action.

Winston Churchill rose before an impressively united and cheering parliament to make good without reserve the pledges that he had solemnly delivered a month ago—the pledge that the outbreak of Japanese-American hostilities would put the British instantly at the side of the United States.

Talked With Roosevelt

He had spoken during the night with President Roosevelt over transatlantic telephone, he said, to arrange "the timing of our respective declarations," and he went on:

"The President told me he would this morning send a message to congress which, as is well known, can alone make a declaration of war on behalf of the United States.

"I then answered him that we would follow immediately. However, it soon appeared that British territory in Malaya had also been the object of Japanese attack and later on it was announced from Tokyo that the Japanese high command—a curious form, not the imperial Japanese government, but the Japanese high command—had declared that a state of war existed between them and Great Britain and the United States.

"That being so, there was no need to wait for the declaration of congress. In any case, American time is nearly six hours behind ours. The cabinet, which met at twelve-thirty today, therefore, authorized an immediate declaration of war upon Japan. Instructions to this effect were sent to His Majesty's ambassador in Tokyo. . . ."

Added Patriotic Touch for Event at Fishersville

With the United States at war, an additional patriotic note will be given the meeting in Fishersville school this evening at seven-thirty when members of the VFW auxiliary will conduct the audience in reviewing Allegiance to the Flag. Mrs. Charles R. Bryan will direct the group. Community singing and a concert by the Stonewall Brigade Junior band are other program features.

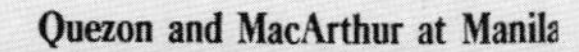

Quezon and MacArthur at Manila

Manuel Quezon, president of the Philippines, is shown with General Douglas MacArthur, recently made commander of all U. S. army forces in the East. Defense of U. S. possessions will be in his hands.

CRITICISM PRIVILEGE IS UPHELD

In Long-awaited Decision Reversing Contempt Citations, Supreme Court Rules Time of Criticism Not Important but Comment Must Not Endanger Justice; Court Split Five to Four.

Washington, Dec. 8.—(AP)—The supreme court today upheld the right of the press and public to criticize the courts at any stage of theri work.

In a long-awaited decision reversing contempt citations against The Los Angeles Times and Harry Bridges, the tribunal ruled that it makes no difference whether the case under criticism is technically pending at the time, so long as the comment does not constitute a "substantial" or a "serious" danger to the impartial functioning of the judge.

(Continued on Page 2, Col. 6)

Japanese Troops Reported To Have Landed on Lubang; Carry Out Widespread Raids

By CLARK LEE

Manila, P. I., Tuesday, Dec. 9.—(AP)—Japanese troops were reported today to have landed with the probable help of "fishermen" fifth-columnists on Lubang island near the entrance to Manila bay as Japanese planes carried out widespread raids on military objectives throughout the Philippines, including moonlit assaults on Manila itself.

The report of the landing on Lubang, some sixty miles southwest of the big American naval base of Cavite, was not confirmed officially, but enough credence was placed in it that defense officers were trying urgently to contact the provincial governor.

Japanese fifth-column activity also was reported unofficially from Davao, on the big southern island of Mindanao, where 25,000 Japanese present a vital threat to Philippine security. One report said 3,000 armed Japanese already were resisting.

Manila, P. I., Tuesday, Dec. 9.—(AP)—A fleet of Japanese warplanes assaulted Manila in the bright moonlight early this morning after a day of almost continuous blasting at U. S. military camps, bases, and ports throughout the islands and an air attack on the U. S. aircraft carrier Langley in Malalag bay, near Davao.

(NBC reporters broadcasting during the Manila raid said Fort McKinley, Nichols Field, and the RCA transmitting station were bombed; that a heavy fire raged for a time "that looks very much as though a gasoline dump or something like that is burning" in the vicinity of Nichols Field. This was between three and three-thirty a. m.—or two to two-thirty p. m. Monday, E. S. T.)

350 Casualties Reported

There were unconfirmed reports of at least 350 casualties at half a dozen points outside Manila.

A series of attacks was made against Clark Field, military airdrome forty miles north of Manila, which adjoins camp Stotsenburg. Unofficial reports said there were 200 casualties.

Still another heavy raid was made on the area of Iba on the Luzon coast, thirty-five miles northwest of Olongapo naval station and seventy miles northwest of Manila. Here there were reports of 100 dead, many injured.

The airfield at Davao was blasted at the same time the Langley was attacked. Twenty-four Japanese raiders struck at this field, hitting hangars and ruining runways.

Fifty persons were reported killed in unconfirmed advices.

Other points raided in the Philippines were Baguio, summer mountain capital in mid-Luzon, where slight damage was caused to the nearby army camp, Fort John Hay; Camp Stotsenburg, where a number of buildings were set afire, and U. S. army phone connections to Manila cut; the Batan islands, northernmost of the Philippines, and Aparri, northernmost port on Luzon.

10,000 Japs Armed

Unconfirmed reports said that 10,000 of the 25,000 Japanese who inhabit the Davao region at the southern end of the Philippines were armed and ready for action, and it

(Continued on Page 2, Col. 7)

GUNS MANNED 24 HOURS DAY

Norfolk, Dec 8.—(AP)—A ray of hope that America's naval forces in Manila were prepared to fire back when attacked by Japanese bombers was contained in a letter dated Nov. 28, and just received here by the wife of a naval officer.

"We have the guns manned twenty-four hours a day because of the fear of what Japan might do," the officer wrote. "I imagine they will be manned until something happens one way or the other."

Say American Plane Mother Ship Sent Down

Berlin, Tuesday, Dec. —(AP)—A DNB dispatch from Tokyo today said Japanese imperial navy headquarters announced an American airplane mother ship had been sunk off Honolulu.

FRUITGROWERS OPEN THEIR SESSIONS TONIGHT

Roanoke, Dec. 8—(AP)—Virginia orchardists, perplexed by a demoralized domestic market that cannot conume the apples and other fruit now cut of ffrom nearly the entire world by war, gather at Hotel Roanoke tomorrow night for the opening of the Virginia State Horticultural society' annual three-day meeting.

CADET CALLS HAWAII TO INQUIRE ABOUT SISTER

Following the Japanese bombing of the Hawaiian Islands Sunday, Cadet John Pennie of Staunton Military academy telephoned Honolulu to inquire about the welfare of his sister, who was visiting there. Cadet Pennie said last night that his sister had already left on a boat before the bombs fell.

Junior Band to Render Concert At Fishersville

Members of the Stonewall Brigade Junior band will meet at the Y. M. C. A. at seven o'clock this evening to board school buses for Fishersville where they are to play at a good will concert begining at seven-thirty under the auspices of the chamber of commerce.

Along with the concert and novelty numbers on the band program there will be an old time community sing in the high school auditorium at Fishersville with C. K. Jones as song leader and William Haines the principal soloist. Dr. Guy R. Fisher will be master of ceremonies and Mrs. R. P. Wall the piano accompanist.

Pearl Harbor, Hawaii Stronghold, Bombed by Japs

The great naval base at Pearl Harbor, on the island of Oahu in Hawaii, is reported officially to have been bombed by a surprise flight of Japanese airmen and widespread damage done, with death toll running high. In the background are units of the Pacific fleet.

Navy Dispatches Three Ships to Learn Source; Wild Night on W. Coast

Brigadier General Ryan of Fourth Interceptor Command Says Large Number of Unidentified Planes Approached San Francisco; Confusion Caused by Series of Air Raid Alarms and Blackouts; First Ones Later Pronounced Surprise Tests; Were Neither Army, Navy, Nor Civilian Planes, Ryan Declares.

San Francisco, Dec. 8.—(AP)—Brigadier General William Ord Ryan of the Fourth interceptor command said tonight that a large number of unidentified planes approached the Golden Gate tonight, but were sighted and driven back to sea.

"They came from the sea, were turned back, and the navy has sent out three vessels to find where they came from," General Ryan said.

'I don't know how many planes there were, but there were a large number.

Headed Southwest

"They got up to the Golden Gate and then turned about and headed southwest."

General Ryan was asked whether he thought they were Japanese bombers.

'Well, they weren't army planes, they weren't navy planes and you can be sure they weren't civilian planes," he answered.

The general was asked if he was willing to be quoted directly. "Certainly," he said.

Three Strange Hours

The general's statement came at the end of three strange hours in which this city of 600,000 population [illegible] from Yokohama—alternately believed it was in peril of immediate air assault and that the blackout ordered by air raid wardens was merely practice.

Police who ordered the blackout at six-twenty p. m. announced at seven-thirty p. m. that lights could be turned on again, but before many were relighted a second blackout was decreed. The interceptor command said it had not lifted the blackout.

Residents along Marina boulevard, fronting the bay near the Golden Gate, said sixty army trucks rushed anti-aircraft guns to the water's edge during the blackout.

Consider Blackout

San Diego, Calif., Dec. 8.—(AP)—Commandant of the Eleventh naval district announced tonight that it might be advisable as a precautionary measure to black out San Diego "at any minute."

The navy announcement urged citizens to stay at home and remain calm and to tune into police broadcasts during the blackout for additional information.

Spokane, Wash., Dec. 8—(AP)—All Spokane radio stations went off the air tonight at seven p. m. (PST) and the signal corps headquarters of the Second air force announced they would not return until eight a. m. tomorrow.

The stations first went off at five p. m., but in a few minutes returned for an additional two hours.

San Francisco, Dec. 8.—(AP)—An "all clear" signal was broadcast throughout the San Francisco bar area at eight-forty-five p. m. after a second report of unidentified planes off the coast had given confusing realism to a test blackout.

(Continued on Page 2, Col. 7)

LABOR GIVES A PLEDGE TO WAR EFFORTS

Heads of Principal Labor Unions Promise Smashing Production Effort to Defeat Japan and Carry On until Final Victory Is Won; Practically No Strikes in Defense Industries.

Washington, Dec. 9.—(AP)—Labor pledged itself tonight to a smashing production effort to defeat Japan and the first day of war found the United States virtually free of strikes in defense industries.

Assurances came from both the CIO and the AFL that every effort would be made to avert work stoppages, while John L. Lewis, head of the CIO United Mine Workers, said in New York that when the nation is attacked "every American must rally to its support."

He asserted in a statement that he joined in the support of the government "to the day of its ultimate triumph over Japan and all other enemies."

William Green, president of the AFL, said American workers would now "produce as the workers of no other nation have ever produced and they will keep steadfastly on the job of supplying our armed forces with the munitions of war until final victory and final peace are won." He asserted also that the AFL no-strike policy must be made 100 per cent effective.

From Philip Murray, president of the CIO, came an appeal for full cooperation of all elements "in the production of the weapons of war and other materials needed for the success of our national effort."

COLOMBIA BREAKS WITH JAPS

Bogota, Colombia, Dec. 8.—(AP)—Colombia broke off diplomatic relations tonight with Japan.

Naval Boss

Admiral Thomas C. Hart, commander-in-chief of the United States Asiatic fleet, is pictured above. He has complete command of the territory in which Japan is moving in its attack on the U. S. and British in the Pacific.

WEST VA. MAN BOMB VICTIM

Wellsburg, W. Va., Dec. 8.—(AP)—A telegram from the war department tonight informed Mrs. George Richey, a widow, that her son had been killed by Japanese bombs in Hawaii.

"Deeply regret official information received your son, First Lieutenant Robert M. Richey, infantry, killed action December 7 at Hawaii," stated the message.

It added that no decision had been reached as to when the body could be returned home.

ALL-OUT VICTORY PROGRAM IS ANNOUNCED BY THE SPAB; OUTLAY OF 150 BILLIONS

Washington, Dec. 8—(AP)—The supply priorities and allocations board, top defense agency, today declared the country was engaged in an "all out victory program," and other defense officials said this called for a $150,000,000,000 outlay.

Such an expenditure would more than double the current armament program for which appropriations and authorizations are nearing seventy billion dollars.

"From this moment we are engaged in a victory program," said a SPAD announcement, issued following a special session in the office of Vice President Henry A. Wallace.

"We can talk and act no longer in terms of a defense program." Victory is our one and only objective and everything else is subordinate to it."

The SPAB announcement itself mentioned no figures for the cot of the victory program.

To Confer With President

It was disclosed that the board had been summoned to the White House for a conference with President Roosevelt tomorrow.

"From now on, every action by this board and by the related civilian agencies of the government must be keyed to one goal—complete victory in this war which has been thrust upon us," SPBA said. "XXX It is clear that a vastly expanded national effort is imperative. Production schedules for all manner of military items must be stepped up at once.

"Every activity of our national life and our civilian economy must be immediately adjusted to that change. To attain victory we aim at the greatest production which is physically possible; we call for the greatest national effort that can possibly be made."

E. S. Garwood Dies in Auto Accident

Word has been received here of an automobile accident near Roanoke Sunday night in which E. Samuel Garwood, thirty-three, of Clifton Forge was instantly killed.

He was a son of E. J. and Mrs. Annie T. Garwood, of Afton, and a brother of Mrs. Homer Thompson of Mint Spring.

Funeral services will be held this afternoon at three o'clock from Lebanon Presbyterian church near Greenwood.

December 9, 1941: The U.S. declares war after the sneak attack on Pearl Harbor by the Japanese. *Microfilm Archives*

Built in 1940 by the Waynesboro Theatres Corp., the Cavalier Bowling alley on Main Street had 16 alleys and was one of the finest facilities of its kind in the Shenandoah Valley. It was destroyed by fire in 1953. *Waynewsboro Collection*

Races in Gypsy Hill Park were a popular pastime throughout the years, as is shown in this 1940s photograph. The races – for both animals and machines – circuses and agricultural shows all came to a halt in the 1960s when Staunton city government demolished the racetracks, grandstands, fairgrounds, historic round barn and other outbuildings, in order to construct a football field. *Schwartz Collection*

1940s view of the Woodrow Wilson General Hospital in Fishersville. The hospital, for which ground was broken on June 26, 1942, originally served to rehabilitate wounded World War II veterans, but evolved into what today is the Woodrow Wilson Rehabilitation Center. *Schwartz Collection*

FIFTY-ONE YEARS IN THE PUBLIC SERVICE
Oldest Virginia Daily West of the Blue Ridge

The Staunton News-Leader

THE WEATHER
...dy, slowly rising temperature, occasional snow in northwest and southwest today. Rain in north today. Saturday rain and warmer.

62nd YEAR. No. 295 | MEMBER ASSOCIATED PRESS AUDIT BUREAU CIRCULATIONS | STAUNTON, Va., FRIDAY MORNING, DECEMBER 12, 1941 | MORNING LEADER EST. 1908 DAILY NEWS EST. 1890 | PRICE THREE CENTS

AMERICA GOES TO WAR WITH ALL OF AXIS

German Peace Feelers Scorned by Russian Officials

No Peace Except by Joint Action Of U. S., Britain

Declaration Cheers Washington, Where There Had Been Some Uneasiness Among Congressmen Because of Long Hours of Silence in Kuibyshev After Japanese Attack on U. S.; Litvinoff Confers With President, Hull, and Hopkins; Is to See Lord Halifax.

Washington, Dec. 11.—(AP)—The declaration of Soviet officials that Russia would never make peace with Germany except by joint agreement with the United States and Britain cheered this capital, though there was no immediate comment from the state department or White House.

Among members of congress there had been indications of some uneasiness over the long hours of silence in Kuibyshev after the Japanese attack on the United States.

Reassuring Statement

However, no such feeling had been evidenced at the state department and only a few hours before the Soviet declaration Secretary of State Hull asserted the United States had "no doubt that the government and people of the Union of Soviet Socialist Republics will do their full part in standing side by side with all liberty-loving people against the common menace."

Hull issued this reassuring statement shortly before a conference with Maxim Litvinoff, the newly arrived Russian ambassador, which was described as for the purpose of a general exchange of information.

After this meeting, Litvinoff declared to reporters that Russia and the United States have "common cause and a common fight" but, despite a barrage of questions on that point, gave no hint of what course the Soviets would adopt with respect to the war in the Pacific.

He disclosed, however, that he had seen President Roosevelt and Harry Hopkins, the President's close friend and adviser, earlier in the day and said he expected to see Lord Halifax, the British ambassador, soon.

As for his talk with Hull, Litvinoff said, "We understand each other." he added:

"Today you have declared war on Germany and Italy and they are the great enemy."

No Action Taken

In response to one specific question as to Russia's attitude toward Japan, Litvinoff replied:

"Japan has taken no action against Russia, and Russia has taken none against Japan."

(Continued on Page 13, Col. 8)

160 ATTEND ANNUAL FETE OF FIREMEN

Turkey Dinner and General Fellowship Meeting Are Followed by Dance; Gifts Are Presented; Firemen Raising Funds to Purchase Emergency Truck.

Approximately 160 persons attended the Staunton fire department's annual banquet at Stonewall Jackson hotel, where they were treated to a turkey dinner, were generally introduced, heard many voice praise for the local firefighters, and ended the program with a dance.

Many present were city officials, members of the police and other city departments, fire department

(Continued on Page 13, Col. 3)

LOCAL RESPONSE TO EMERGENCY RED CROSS APPEAL VERY SLOW; ORGANIZATION WELL UNDER WAY

$650 FIRST DAY

Wm. S. Moffett Jr., treasurer of the local drive to raise $20,000 for the Red Cross, said last night that contributions had come in very well on the first day of the campaign and that approximately $650 had been received.

Despite the fact that a wartime emergency is being faced with the American Red Cross which is calling for $50,000,000 with which to meet the urgent needs of our civilian populations bombed from their homes by the Japanese and of our men in the armed force in the Pacific war zone, contributions are coming in but slowly in this section.

The Leader Papers' office is ready throughout the day to take in contributions in answer to this call, and, that every man, woman, and child may have the opportunity to share in this great work of relief and humanitarianism carried on by the Red Cross, workers are being placed at strategic points throughout the county and the down town district of Staunton to receive donations for this cause.

To Issue Proclamation

Today President Roosevelt will issue a proclamation calling on the American people to rally to the support of this benevolent campaign and Chairman Davis in calling on the 3,700 chapters throughout the country for their allotted quotas states.

"There are millions of our citizens who desire today to demonstrate their will to victory over the enemy. Not all can be in the armed forces, and not all can volunteer their services for humanitarian work, but all can volunteer their dollars to arm the Red Cross

(Continued on Page 2, Col. 7)

Organization of the Augusta County chapter of the American Red Cross is rapidly being put under way and the following additional committee chairmen have been chosen by Lyle G. Weller, Chairman of the drive:

Charles S. Hunter Sr., special bank committee; H. I. Willett, speakers bureau for city and county schools; the Rev. Edgar A. Potts, appeal through churches and Sunday schools; Mrs. Curry Carter, workers; Mrs. Herbert McK. Smith, special gifts; John V. Wise, industries and chain stores; Mrs. R. Morris Armistead, publicity.

In connection with the appeals being made to the various groups in the city and county, Mr. Weller urges through these columns that the head of every business both large and small constitute himself as a committee of one to try and achieve a 100 per cent record for his business. Special recognition will be made to those firms giving the Red Cross one hundred per cent support and Mr. Weller suggests that, if the business is a large one or the head unable to organize his employees in this service, the designate some one in the business to see that all employees are, at least given the chance to do this bit for their country in this time of stress and urgency.

Booths will continue to be established in the Post Office and the local banks, those working these stations yesterday being:

Post Office—Miss Hattie G. Siron; Augusta National bank—Mrs. Charles A. McCray; Farmers and Merchants bank—Mrs. Michael Kivlighan Jr.; National Valley bank—Mrs. R. C. Swanstrom; Planters bank—Mrs. J. M. Uffinger Jr.; Staunton Industrial Loan—Mrs. Clarence M. Elder, and the Staunton National bank — Miss Adele Gooch.

...feline of the U. S.

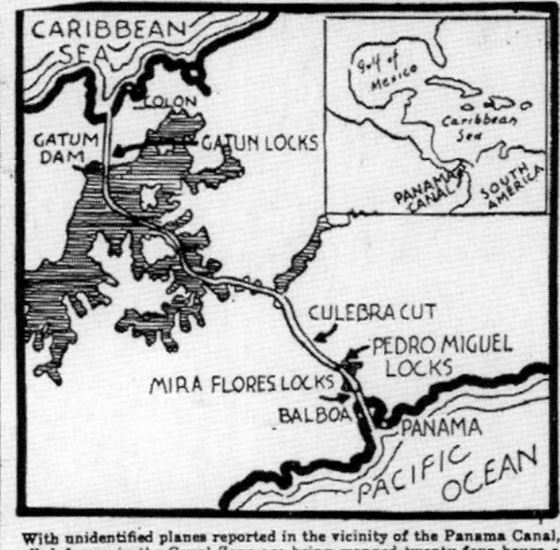

With unidentified planes reported in the vicinity of the Panama Canal, all defenses in the Canal Zone are being manned twenty-four hours a day. The best of America's pursuit planes are continuously flying patrol over the vital waterway that connects the Atlantic and the Pacific Oceans. Map shows course of the Canal. Small map shows relative location of the Canal.

TREE BURSTS INTO FLAMES IN BLACKOUT

Two Persons Detained at Police Station as Trees Burn on Cliff During Evacuation of 1,000 Persons from Beach Area in Santa Cruz County, California.

Santa Cruz, Calif., Dec. 11—(AP)—Santa Cruz county was blacked out tonight and a large eucalyptus tree mysteriously burst into flame while more than 1,000 persons were being evacuated from the beach area fronting the Pacific ocean.

The evacuation was reported as a comprehensive test by the army but several trees on a high cliff in an area inhabited by Japanese strawberry growers suddenly burst into flame.

At least two persons were reported detained at the police station.

Women fainted at wild, unverified rumors that planes had been sighted approaching from sea, and

(Continued on Page 13, Col. 6)

Hampden-Sydney Alumni to Elect Officers Tonight

Valley chapter of Hampden-Sydney alumni will hold its annual dinner and business meeting tonight at six-forty-five at the Arcadia. At that time officers for the new year will be elected.

Principal speaker of the evening will be Dr. E. G. Gammon, president of the college. Also to be in attendance and deliver a short address will be Coach Chas. Bernier, who is also alumni secretary.

Army Recruiting Office Re-opened

Sergeant Detrich of Camp Lee arrived here last night to take over his duties in the postoffice as United States army recruiting office, which has been vacant for some weeks.

Applying in response to an advertisement which appeared in The News-Leader Thursday morning, numerous men who wished to enlist in the army found the recruiting office closed.

The Leader Papers wired headquarters at Richmond, informing officials there of the fact, and they immediately responded with a wire that "Sergeant Detrich, our representative, will be at postoffice building Staunton open for business eight a. m. Dec. 12."

The office here has been closed since Sgt. H. P. Halterman was sent from here to Camp Lee. More recently he has been under treatment at the Camp Lee hospital for a fractured pelvis sustained in a two-car collision during the early morning of Nov. 21.

O. T. WISEMAN ABOARD THE U.S.S. OKLAHOMA

Oscar Thomas Wiseman, who has been in the navy since 1936, having enlisted here, has been at Pearl Harbor several years. He is a petty officer aboard the USS Oklahoma, and a son of J. C. Wiseman, Staunton, route two. He has not been at home since Christmas 1937.

Hitler Declares War Against U. S., Tells of New Pact

Berlin, Dec. 11—(Official radio received by AP)—Adolf Hitler declared war against the United States today and announced that Germany, Italy, and Japan were pledged in a new alliance to fight it together to a finish.

In the course of an address to the reichstag which lasted an hour and a half, Hitler repeatedly and violently attacked President Roosevelt, and expressed on behalf of "the German people" relief and satisfaction with the Japanese attack on America.

Before he spoke the declaration of war was handed—at noon, Berlin time (five a. m. E.S.T.)—to U. S. Charge d'Affaires George L. Brandt by Joachim von Ribbentrop, Hitler's foreign minister. This declaration, which was not made public until it was announced by Hitler, did not mention Japan, but accused the United States of acts of war at sea against Germany.

It concluded: "The reich government therefore severs diplomatic relations with the United States of America and declares that under these circumstances, brought about by President Roosevelt, Germany also, commencing today, regards herself in a state of war with the United States of America."

Brandt was handed his passport at four-twenty p. m. (nine-twenty a. m. E.S.T.) after Hitler had started speaking in the Kroll opera house.

Americans Arrested

A number of U. S. citizens in Germany were placed under arrest, a Wilhelmstrasse spokesman declaring that as many were being taken into custody in Germany as German citizens were arrested in the United States. This, by German count, is 400.

A number of Americans, were said to remain at liberty. Most American newspaper correspondents were taken from police stations to a suburban Berlin villa. Their treatment, it was stated, would depend on the treatment of German journalists arrested in America.

The main new fact in Hitler's speech, aside from the announcement of the war declaration, was his disclosure of the new three-power accord which supplements the tripartite pact under which Hitler declared war and pledges Germany, Italy, and Japan to make common war against the U. S. and Britain, to fight "to a victorious end with all available means; to "bring about a just order" later and to refrain from concluding a separate peace "without complete mutual consent."

The war declaration itself cited Mr. Roosevelt's shooting orders to the navy, the cases of the U. S. destroyers Greer, Kearney, and Reuben James, destruction of German submarines, and "illegal" treatment of German merchantmen at sea. Thus, it was charged, the U. S., "first starting with violations of neutrality has finally gone over to overt belligerent acts against Germany. It has thus practically created a state of war."

This, in substance, was Hitler's narrative before the reichstag:

That President Roosevelt has been "systematically sabotaging European peace" since Nov., 1938, and that he finally "practiced instigation" with Japan.

That Japan "has risen against this violation of the rules of decency."

That even if Germany did not have an alliance with Japan "we are convinced that Roosevelt and the Jews would ruin one state after another;" that Germany and Italy possess the insight and the power to realize that this question "will now be decided forever."

That Germany always tried to prevent a break with the U. S., but that when it heard of an

(Continued on Page 13, Col. 1)

REGISTRATION (OF ALL MEN AND WOMEN, 18 TO 65, MAY BE ASKED) BY GOVERNMENT

Washington, Dec. 11—(AP)—Registration of all men and women from eighteen to sixty-five years of age may be asked by the government in an all-out mobilization of the nation's human resources for the war with the Axis.

Brigadier-General Lewis B. Hershey, director of selective service, disclosed today that this plan was under study as the army called for 10,000 volunteer nurses and congress swiftly passed legislation removing prohibitions against service of selectees outside the western hemisphere.

"We undoubtedly are soon going to consider the registration of women," Hershey told a press conference.

He went on to estimate that 20,000,000 could serve by replacing men in factories, enlisting in civilian defense, or with the armed service in non-combatant capacities.

No. 1 Project

The general proposition of registering and classifying all able-bodied men and women aged eighteen to sixty-five was described by Hershey as the "number 1 project at this time."

This would require new legislation. Emphasizing that the idea still was in the study stage. Hershey said he thought congress should enact legislation presenting the people with "a broad liability for registration and a narrower liability for service."

"I don't visualize five or six million men marching off to war,

(Continued on Page 2, Col. 6)

5 More Enlist in Motor Corps

In addition to the five names already listed as having joined the volunteer motor corps of the Staunton chapter, American Red Cross, five more were announced yesterday by Miss Arvid Samuelson, who has been named head of the unit.

They are Mrs. Thomas W. Atkinson, Betty Lambert, Mrs. B. Wayne Erskine, Mrs. Joseph J. Kivlighan, and Mrs. Charles A. Holt.

OFFENSIVE BY CHINESE EFFECTIVE

Attacking All Along Kwantung Front to Relieve Japanese Pressure on Hongkong, They Report Having Inflicted 15,000 Casualties on Japs in Continuing Two-day Offensive.

Chungking, China, Friday, Dec. 12—(AP)—Chinese troops attacking all along the Kwantung front to relieve Japanese pressure on Hongkong have inflicted 15,000 casualties on the Japs in a continuing two-day offensive, the China radio announced today.

Heavy blows were dealt to the Japanese especially on the northern and western anchors of the battle front, the account stated.

The central sector of the front was in the Shiuchow area about 130 miles north of Canton.

Million Still in China

Approximately 1,000,000 Japanese

(Continued on Page 2, Col. 4)

Challenge of Germany And Italy Is Promptly Accepted by Congress

Killed in Hawaii

Sergt. Vincent Horan

Among those killed when the Japanese bombed Honolulu from the air was Sergt. Vincent Horan, of Stamford, Conn. More than 1,000 men were reported killed in the sneak raid on Hawaii.

OAHU RAIDED 5 SEPARATE TIMES DEC. 7

Fifty to 100 Enemy Warplanes Knifed at Hickam Field, Pearl Harbor Naval Base, and Kaneohe Naval Air Base Sunday: 49 Civilians Killed, More than 100 Injured.

Honolulu, Dec. 11—(AP)—Fifty to 100 enemy warplanes knifed at Hickam field, army air base, the Pearl Harbor naval base, and the Kaneohe naval air base and six separate raids on Oahu island Sunday.

Censorship was lifted partially today, permitting disclosure of more details of the Japanese surprise attack.

The first raiders flew over at seven-fifty-five a. m. Sunday and were followed by other waves at eleven - twenty - nine a. m., eleven-fifty-nine a. m., twelve-twenty-two p. m., seven-fifteen

(Continued on Page 2, Col. 4)

VSDB Pupils to Be Transported to Parade Area

Students of the Virginia School for the Deaf and the Blind will be given the opportunity to witness the Santa Claus parade scheduled for Wednesday night, Dec. 17. Car owners are asked to offer the use of their cars to convey the students from V. S. D. B. to the down town district of Staunton.

The committee in charge requests car owners to be at V. S. D. B. by seven p. m. next Wednesday. In all, 100 or more cars are needed, and those volunteering the use of their cars are requested to 'phone the chairman, Edward L. Stauderman, at 1646.

BOATWRIGHT WITH ARMY IN MANILA

Lieutenant-Colonel John R. Boatwright, a brother-in-law of H. C. Loyd of this city, is stationed with the United States army in Manila, it was learned here last night. No word has been received however, regarding his safety.

IS AT MANILA

Pvt. Raymond E. Campbell of Co.L,31st infantry, is at Manila, it was learned here yesterday. He is a son of A. E. Campbell, 224 St. Clair street. The last letter received from him was dated Oct. 20, 1941.

WILLSON IS REPORTED "SAFE IN MANILA"

Mrs. S. I. Davis has received a cablegram from her brother, Wallace Willson, reporting he "is safe in Manila." Mr. Willson is on a return trip from China where he has been located for a number of years.

THREE JAPANESE WARSHIPS ARE SENT TO BOTTOM BY AMERICANS

Fourth, a Battleship, Badly Damaged; Four Japanese Aerial Attacks on Wake Island Outpost and One by Light Naval Forces Beaten Back; Airport Seventy Miles South of Aparri, Luzon Island, Seized by Jap Parachutists; Legislation Declaring War on Germany and Italy Completed in Record Time.

By the Associated Press

The United States went to war yesterday (Thursday) with the whole of the Axis and within a few hours after that great decision was taken it became clear that hard American blows were falling upon the Japanese assailant in the Pacific.

In that vast theatre of early tragedy—where the invader had won initial successes by springing without warning—the news was no longer of American disaster, but of American victory.

The Story

This was the emerging story last night:

Officially confirmed by the American government:

Four Japanese aerial attacks on the Wake island outpost, and one by light naval forces, beaten back in the last forty-eight hours; a Japanese light cruiser and a Japanese destroyer sunk; American losses were an unstated number of planes; Wake island still holding firm, although momentarily expecting renewed assaults and perhaps an attempt at a Japanese landing.

A 29,000-ton Japanese battleship, the Haruna or a vessel of that same class, smashed and sent to the bottom off northern Luzon by the bombs of American army fliers, the most punishing loss yet suffered by the Asiatic Fascists.

A second vessel of the same class—the 29,000-ton Kongo class—bombed effectively by U. S. navy patrol planes, also off the coast of Luzon. A brief announcement by the navy in Washington said the Japanese ship was badly damaged.

Being Mopped Up

The only Japanese forces that had been able to land in force on Luzon—those in the region of Aparri in the north—being mopped up; the situation in hand.

To all this were added unofficial but reliable reports from Manila that the Philippine army had in fact even recaptured the region around Aparri itself and was driving the invader back into the sea.

Only Setback

The only American setback of any sort reported yesterday from Luzon—the key to all the Philippines—was mentioned in unofficial advices which stated that an airport near Ilagan, about seventy miles south of Aparri, had been seized by Jap parachutists. But, it was added, the Philippine constabulary was preparing to assault the presumably small numbers of invaders there.

(Continued on Page 9, Col. 3)

COUNCIL VOTES TO SPEND $17,000 TO EQUIP SPRING; STREET ARGUMENT SETTLED

At the regular meeting of city council last night, the solons decided to spend $17,000 to equip Gardner's spring near Schutterlee mill as an auxiliary water supply, to pay bills totaling $500 for purging the election books, to grant the Greyhound bus lines an additional sixty days to get their vehicles off the street, and received Staunton Military academy's acceptance of council's proposition for a right-of-way through the school's property.

Considerable Debate

Decision to complete the spring project came after considerable debate. The motion was made by Councilman J. Harold Kivlighan and seconded by Councilman Jesse M. Bratton with all members voting in the affirmative except Councilman S. I. Davis, who thought purchase of the pump was a good investment but that expenditure of $17,000 to complete the undertaking is not justified at this time.

City Manager W. L. Hall's figures on the cost of completing this water source included $1,540 for a million-gallon pump and motor, $7,000 for twelve-inch pipe. Other expenses included cleaning the spring, erecting brick pump house, laying pipe, and installing electric lines.

Mayor George A. Cottrell expressed the opinion that the project should be completed and North River dam allowed to fill up, so that the city could then have soft water.

Would Cost $100,000

Councilman Davis brought up the matter of building an auxiliary dam at North river, at a cost of about $100,000, which was taken into consideration when this watershed was developed. He said the present dam was not adequate for growing Staunton, that the auxiliary dam would be a good investment and would provide the city with soft water all the time, but thought it should not be constructed until labor is more plentiful.

Vice-Mayor William A. Grubert suggested that the pump be installed permanently but that only a temporary line he laid if needed.

Councilman Davis saw no water emergency and considered the expense unjustified and the mayor said that the pump at Gypsy Hill park may break down. Councilman Davis thought there would be time enough to repair it, with plenty of water on hand to last a month and the mayor thought the project would be a good thing and would pay for itself. Money to cover the cost could be appropriated in the 1942 budget.

Is Acceptable

Council was informed that its suggestion for a right-of-way along Prospect street through S. M. A. property was acceptable to the school and deeds were at hand conveying the requisite land to the city. In consideration, the city renounces any claims it may have

(Continued on Page 2, Col. 4)

WHEAT JUMPS 5 CENTS

Swoope Milling Co. yesterday announced the price of wheat at $1.20 a bushel. This represented a five-cent increase over the previous price.

December 12, 1941: America goes to war with the Axis powers – Germany, Italy and Japan. *Microfilm Archives*

FIFTY-FOUR YEARS IN THE PUBLIC SERVICE
Oldest Virginia Daily West of the Blue Ridge

The Staunton News-Leader

THE WEATHER
Fair and cooler today; Thursday fair, warmer in afternoon.

55th YEAR, No. 136 — ASSOCIATED PRESS AND (AP) FEATURES — AUDIT BUREAU CIRCULATIONS — STAUNTON, VIRGINIA, WEDNESDAY MORNING, JUNE 7, 1944. — MORNING LEADER ESTABLISHED — DAILY NEWS ESTABLISHED 1890 — PRICE THREE CENTS

Invaders Swarm Over Vaunted Nazi Wall

Nazi Remnants Flee in Disorder Beyond Rome

Fifth Army Troops Swarm Over Tiber River in Hot Pursuit; Enemy Resistance Weak; French Troops Capture Tivoli, 15 Miles Northeast of City; Thousands More of Prisoners Taken in Lightning Drive.

Allied Headquarters, Naples, June 6—(AP)—Remnants of the German army fled in disorder north and west of Rome today, as Fifth Army troops swarming over the historic Tiber in many places and against weak resistance advanced another five miles beyond the river.

"The battle to destroy the enemy continues without pause," the Allied communique said, and it was made clear that as the United Nations mount the great invasion of the west, there is to be no halt to the slugging Italian campaign.

"With the capture of Rome, the Allied armies in Italy have brought another phase of their campaign to a most successful conclusion," said the bulletin.

To the northeast, 15 miles from Rome, French troops have captured Tivoli on the important Avezzano Road (Highway 5), and as the Fifth Army offensive rolled forward, fanning out west and north of the Eternal City on a broad front, additional thousands of prisoners marched to the rear. The momentum of the Fifth's attack and the disorganization of the enemy hourly were becoming more apparent.

Cross En Masse

All the way from Rome to the sea the troops of Lieutenant General Mark W. Clark have crossed or reached the Tiber, and in the Eternal City itself they plunged in a constant stream across the eleven spans still remaining intact, to chase the Germans to the north. Infantry crossed the river in force and was reported driving due west of Vatican City, and Allied armored forces spread out over a wide area.

Whatever hope Nazi Field Marshal General Albert Kesselring might have had of establishing a strong defense line anywhere south of the northern Apennine range guarding the Po Valley undoubtedly suffered a sharp blow when the Allied armies struck in northern France.

Reserves Slowed

The Mediterranean air force's methodical destruction of rail lines in northern Italy and southeastern France has so curtailed the mobility of Nazi reserves that the German command must decide quickly and irrevocably whether to risk any more precious manpower south of the Genoa-Florence limits line.

Enemy divisions still in the flatlands below the city were in desperate straits. Westward from Rome to the sea all the Tiber's bridges have been blown up or have been captured by the Allies, and in the coastal area alone well over 2,000 Nazis apparently will be unable to extricate themselves. Only isolated rear guards offered resistance.

Soviets Hail Second Front, Mass Armies

London, Wednesday, June 7—(AP)—An indication that the Germans are weakening in their savage eight-day battle near Iasi, Romania, was given by Moscow early today.

Also, the Russian Baltic fleet air arm sank three German transports totalling 11,000 tons Monday night and "in fierce air battles shot down 30 German planes," the supplement added.

Moscow, June 6—(AP)—The three-year-long dream of a western land front came true for the Russian people today when they heard by radio that the Allies had invaded France.

At the same time the Red army was understood to be massing for its expected blow from the east following up the assault from the west.

News of the invasion was welcomed with a heart warming reaction—the full import of the action being realized gradually here as successive broadcasts brought the people word of the developments from London.

There was no public shouting and demonstrations, but Russian citizens and officials alike were discussing events with lively enthusiasm while foreign diplomats expected the reaction to the news to grow as operations developed.

Loud speakers had been switched on in the streets and squares of the capital for the announcements.

Berlin Predicts Red Push

(The German commentator von Hammer broadcast from Berlin that with the attack from the west a big Russian offensive would open soon along the lower Dnestr "where a strong Soviet offensive army has taken action stations and where Soviet artillery and mortar fire is gaining in intensity." Other German commentators said multiple assaults could be expected.

(Tonight's broadcast Russian communique, recorded by the Soviet monitor in London, said the Red army had repulsed continuing Nazi attacks north and northwest of Iasi in Romania and that Russian bombers had carried out a mass raid Monday night on Iasi itself.

Tokyo Still on Air, According to OWI

New York, June 6—(AP)—The Tokyo radio left the air suddenly and without explanation, NBC monitors in San Francisco reported late this afternoon.

San Francisco, June 6—(AP)—The National Broadcasting company said today it had not heard Tokyo radio since 11:15 a. m. (Pacific War Time) but the Office of War Information said it had no indication the station was off the air. The OWI said the only station recorded as not broadcasting was Saigon, French Indo China.

COLONEL TITUS SALUTES BOYS 'OVER THERE'

Chaplain of Woodrow Wilson Army Hospital, in Address Before Rotary Club Here, Says Invasion Should Be Time of Rededication.

Invasion should be a time of rededication for every American, Lt. Col. Cliff K. Titus, of Woodrow Wilson General Hospital, told the Rotary Club yesterday in a tribute to "our kids" who are committed to "the divine plan of liberation and restoration of honor, decency, and order under law in the world."

"It is a day of anxiety," said Col. Titus; "not anxiety for the courage of the kids who have the job to do. They know what they're fighting for, they know the cost, but there'll be no quitting until the job is done. Rather it is a day of anxiety for us! Let each American ask himself: 'Have I any right to quibble about how many hours I work? Have I any right to say that I will not buy another war bond?' Let us rededicate ourselves to the task and continue it with the last ounce of our energies."

Confident in Leaders

Col. Titus declared that the leaders responsible for the invasion plan determined to prepare to the last detail, however long the delay, and that the attack was not launched until every item of preparation was ready. He eloquently expressed his confidence in Allied leadership and in the plan which he said would free Europe and the world and restore justice and honor.

Gilpin Willson Jr. was chairman of the Rotary meeting, and presented Duncan Curry as the principal speaker. Mr. Curry delivered an interesting and scholarly address on men of eminence born in Staunton and Augusta as found in the National Dictionary of Biography. Of 738 pre-eminent men born in Virginia, he showed that 14 were born in or near Staunton and 12 in Augusta.

Compares Favorably

"It is true that Washington, Jefferson, Marshall and Lee were not born in the Valley and that it has no family to equal in history the Lee family and the Randolph family," said Mr. Curry, "but I believe that these books (the Dictionary of National Biography) prove that the general average of three Valley counties in the production of men of eminence in American life and history compares at least favorably with the counties of East Virginia."

Mr. Curry's address has previously been published in The Leader Papers.

Two new members were inducted into the club yesterday, President J. E. Healy making the induction talk. They are C. E. Dorsette, head of the Nehi Bottling Co., and Stuart B. Lam, local Chesapeake Western freight representative.

Guests were Rotarians Norman Patterson, Richlands, Va., Mel Wiggins, Lexington, and Nelson Huffman, Bridgewater; C. K. Moran, Staunton, and Charles Huddle, Charleston, W. Va.

'SUPERMEN' CALL IT A WAR

THE FACES OF NAZIS who had enough and quit to rest as prisoners behind our battle lines in Italy, show bewilderment shock at the lesson they've learned—that as Hitler's "supermen" they've met their masters in our Allied fighters. News of the Day Newsreel. (International)

CITY, COUNTY GREET 'BIG NEWS' CALMLY, WITH MIXED EMOTIONS, CHURCHES OPEN FOR WORSHIP

As Augusta and Staunton sought yesterday to carry on so far as possible with man's greatest battle in history in the lap of the gods, the county and the city probably represented an emotional cross section of the nation at large.

Flags lined the downtown streets, some homes were similarly draped, the normal routine went on with grim hope for good news after months of waiting—sometimes distraught, sometimes keenly confident.

Certainly, as a city official observed, there seemed obvious unanimity—the thoughts of all were joined and the suspense of waiting was over.

The churches of the city and their pastors virtually were on a standby basis—spiritually and devotionally. The doors of all churches were open for those who chose to visit and commune therein. Last night there were prayer services in several, with similar services announced for tonight in others.

Copies of The Leader Papers, which gave the general community its first coherent and substantial account of the Great Invasion, were in demand far in excess of the supply. From the staffs there was concerted and conscientious effort to meet the situation to the best of their resources.

Up and down the streets, downtown and residential, radios muted and blaring, told of listening groups within, some following the commentators with an overtone picture of friend or kinsman in the crucible of combat. Many families up late Monday who heard the early radio invasion flash from Berlin shortly after midnight remained at their sets through the greater part of the early morning as the tragic drama went from climax to climax.

Yesterday was a day when nonessentials gave way to introspection, such as moved the major baseball leagues to cancel their games, race tracks to suspend and similar diversionary activities to cease.

Here as elsewhere, presumably, people performed the routine of living but their consciousness was "of the far fields of battle," as one observer phrased it.

Churches Observe Day

All churches represented in the Staunton Ministerial Association were kept open throughout the entire day, in order that people of the community could enter for the purpose of private worship.

Recently the Association took the following official action: "That we encourage our congregations to keep their churches open daily for prayer and meditation by the community."

Sentiment of the Association was that "since the invasion of Western Europe is not a matter of one day but of a prolonged period, therefore the people who are really in earnest about the need for prayer during this war effort, should attend all the regular services of worship in their churches."

Churches represented in the Association are: Central Methodist, Marquis Memorial Methodist, Beverley Street Methodist, Trinity Episcopal, Emmanuel Episcopal, St. Paul's United Brethren, First Baptist, Pilgrim Holiness, Salvation Army, Church of the Brethren, Church of the Nazarene, First Presbyterian, Second Presbyterian, Third Presbyterian, Olivet Presbyterian, Hebron Presbyterian, Ebenezer Baptist, and Augusta Street Methodist.

At Temple House of Israel an hour of service last night was largely attended.

Rough Wind Blows Over Dover Strait

London, Wednesday, June 7—(AP)—The weather which caused a 24-hour postponement of D-Day, still is one of the biggest invasion worrier. At midnight a strong wind blowing from the northeast raised white-caps in the Dover Strait and high waves swept the beaches, and showed no signs of moderating.

U.S.S. NEVADA LEADS FLEET IN HUGE ROLE

Two Rear Admirals, Aboard Cruisers Augusta and Tuscaloosa, Watch Mammoth Landing Operations as 4,000-Ship Armada Storms to French Coast.

London, Wednesday, June 7—(AP)—The United States Navy, with two rear admirals riding in cruisers and paced by the battleship Nevada, was a part of a 4,000 Allied armada which seared and blasted German defenses before the assault troops hit the beaches of France, it was announced today.

In Washington, President Roosevelt announced that up to noon Monday eastern war time U. S. Naval losses were two destroyers and one LST (landing ship, tanks). The entire Allied naval losses were officially described as "very light."

Rear admiral Alan Goodrich Kirk, commander of one of the task forces, watched the mammoth operations from his flagship, the cruiser Augusta, Supreme Headquarters, Allied Expeditionary Force, announced in a communique.

The other cruiser was the Tuscaloosa, commanded by Rear Admiral Morton L. Deyo.

(In addition to the Nevada, the U. S. battleships Texas and Arkansas took part in the bombardment, NBC quoted the BBC as saying, adding that the British battleships Warspite, Nelson and Romelles, the British cruisers Glasgow, Enterprise, and Orion and the Canadian destroyers Sioux and Algonquin also were in the fleet.)

British warships alone loosed a tornado of fire west of Le Havre, pouring 2,000 tons of shells every ten minutes with 600 ships firing everything from 4 to 6 inches, surprising and stunning shore batteries whose return fire was sporadic.

The assaulting troops ran through the gaps torn in the west wall into a countryside which alternated the black of the ploughed land with the green of cultivation. Thick hedges provided plenty of cover.

Derailment Holds Up Train To D. C.

Scores of passengers on the Washington-bound C. and O. train (11:18) last night were stranded here after a westbound freight train had been derailed a quarter of a mile south of Fishersville.

No one was injured, but two loaded box-cars, as result of a coupling breakdown, were driven three-fourths of a mile before the mishap was discovered, bending and ripping track along the way. Work trains from Clifton Forge and Charlottesville were expected to arrive at three a. m., but road repairs were estimated to take four or five hours. The 11:18 was late, and the accident occurred about 11:45 p. m.

Gripsholm Brings Back 131 Aboard

Jersey City, N. J., June 6—(AP)—The sixth diplomatic exchange of repatriates between the United States and Axis countries were completed today when the Swedish liner Gripsholm arrived here with 131 passengers, 51 of them ill or wounded American soldiers who were prisoners of war in Germany.

The liner docked at three-forty p. m. (EWT) after a nine-day voyage from Belfast which navy officials said was without incident. She left here May 2, carrying 700 German prisoners and civilians who were exchanged at Barcelona.

29TH ASSOCIATION WILL HOLD DINNER MEETING

Woodrow Wilson Post 61, 29th Division Association, will hold a dinner meeting at the Arcadia Hotel Friday, June 9, at seven p. m.

This is a very important meeting and Commander Charles R Bryan requests all members to be present. All members who plan to attend are asked to notify Adjutant C. W. Talley by Thursday evening, June 8, phone 340-R.

DEPUTY FINDS PIGEON

Deputy Sheriff Harry Hildebrand brought in to the sheriff's office today a carrier pigeon that he had found at Craigsville. The bird had two leg bands, a rubber one with 428 K on it and a metal tag with notation D. C. 3609 CAU 43.

Drive Inland Nears Rouen; Reserves Land

Allies Sweep 100-mile Front in Cherbourg-Le Havre Area; Eisenhower and Churchill Calm and Assured Over Progress; Wind Kicks Up Choppy Sea in Channel; Airmen Defy Weather; Casualties "Remarkably Light;" Berlin Betrays Uneasiness.

(By Wes Gallagher)

Supreme Headquarters, Allied Expeditionary Force, Wednesday, June 7—(AP)—United States, British and Canadian troops battled inland against Nazi defenses of Normandy across the white-capped English channel today to expand an invasion operation which Prime Minister Churchill said was proceeding "in a thoroughly satisfactory manner" and with unexpectedly light casualties.

Channel weather was adverse, a strong northeaster kicking up the waves. But this was not permitted to halt the stream of reinforcements and supplies for the forces hacking out positions along a 100-mile front between Cherbourg and Le Havre.

New Landing Expected

The German radio expressed fear of further landings. Fresh and strong naval forces were reported sighted this morning off the Dunkerque-Calais area, opposite Dover and some 200 miles airline northeast of Cherbourg.

The Nazi-controlled Paris Radio said "an important American British naval squadron was cruising off Cherbourg two hours after midnight."

Gen. Dwight D. Eisenhower, supreme commander, was serene and confident of success in the great land, sea and air blow, launched before dawn Tuesday under a screen of bombs and shells from 4,000 warships and 11,000 warplanes.

Build Landing Strips

The Allied High Command disclosed that more than 1,000 troop-carrying aircrafe, including gliders, bore fighting specialists on invasion missions and said this phase was executed with "unexpected success." Allied bulldozers slashed out coastal landing strips.

Naval casualties were officially regarded as "very light."

It was disclosed that among the Allied armada was the U.S.S. Nevada, 29,000-ton battleship repaired and restored to duty after she was badly damaged at Pearl Harbor.

The U.S.S. Augusta, 9,050-ton heavy cruiser on which Prime Minister Churchill and President Roosevelt signed the Atlantic Charter, went into the action as the flagship of Rear Admiral Alan G. Kirk, a veteran of the Sicilian campaign who commands "the western naval task force."

Another American cruiser involved was the 9,975-ton Tuscaloosa, commanded by Rear Admiral Morton L. Deyo.

Disregard Wind

Allied air forces maintained their missions despite the wind. The U. S. Ninth Air Force alone flew 4,000 sorties Tuesday. Clearing the way for ground troops, 10,000 tons of explosives creased down on the German positions from the air, among them some described in a field dispatch as "huge bombs of a mysterious type."

A British naval officer, who accompanied the task forces, said the supreme command was "still worried about the weather" and that there had been much seasickness among the invasion forces. The wind over the channel grew stronger during the night.

Le Havre Fighting

The German high command in a special late communique declared that "fighting in the Cherbourg-Le Havre area is in full swing.

South of Le Havre strong airborne units have been annihilated. New enemy operations must be expected but have not taken shape yet. Fighting is extremely fierce everywhere as the Anglo-Americans are putting up a most tenacious resistance."

Reserves Pour In

"It must be admitted," said the Nazi-controlled Vichy radia, "that the Allied beachhead area has been considerably widened and that Allied reinforcements are pouring in."

There were indications that the Germans were losing touch with their battle groups and that they were not sure where the main force of the Allied assault was striking.

At a late hour last night hundreds of Allied planes still were in the air, guarding the convoys and the beachheads and striking beyond the zone of operations to par-

(Continued On Page 5, Col. 1)

Bulletins

Barcelona, Spain, June 6—(AP)—German reports received here today said Allied forces were in full possession of Honfleur at the mouth of the Seine. Honfleur is just across the river mouth from Le Havre.

London, Wednesday, June 7—(AP)—Gen. Eisenhower is directing the invasion of western Europe from an advanced outpost in England, supreme headquarters of the AEF said early today, denying a report broadcast by the Brazzaville radio that the commander had established headquarters on French soil.

Allied Armies Headquarters, June 6—(AP)—Gen. Sir Bernard L. Montgomery, commander of the group of armies invading France, said this afternoon he was pleased with the initial phase of the landing operations.

He listed a five point receipe for victory: (1) Allied solidarity; (2) offensive eagerness; (3) enthusiasm; (4) confidence (5) all-out effort.

Supreme Headquarters Allied Expeditionary Force, Wednesday, June 7—(AP)—Well over 1,000 troop-carrying aircraft, including gliders, participated in the air-borne phase of the invasion, Supreme Headquarters announced early today.

Supreme Headquarters, Allied Expeditionary Force, Wednesday, June 7—(AP)—The American navy, including the cruisers Augusta and Tuscaloosa, and the Battleship Nevada participated in the bombardment supporting the Allied landings, headquarters announced early today.

New York, June 6—(AP)—The German radio said tonight that "in the area south of Cherbourg a British-American airborne division was engaged in heavy fighting with German anti-invasion forces." The broadcast was recorded by CBS.

Ankara, June 6—(AP)—Ankara buzzed tonight with reports of an Allied landing in the Peloponnesus and, although there was no official confirmation, responsible quarters said it could be true now or shortly.

London, June 6—(AP)—A German radio roundup of Berlin military commentary predicted further Allied landings and suggested that there might be a sudden powerful stab at Paris.

Text of President's Invasion Prayer, Written as Troops Landed in France

(By The Associated Press)

Washington, June 6—President Roosevelt led millions of Americans in prayer tonight for divine aid for the great Allied liberation assault on Europe which he said has "come to pass with success thus far."

From the White House, the President read in a solemn, strong voice over all radio networks his plea for God's aid for the men fighting for country and for freedom for humanity, and for those at home. Text of his prayer, written as Allied troops were landing in France, follows:

My fellow Americans:

In this poignant hour, I ask you to join me in prayer:

Almighty God: Our sons, pride of our nation, this day have set upon a mighty endeavor, a struggle to preserve our republic, our religion, and our civilization, and to set free a suffering humanity.

Lead them straight and true; give strength to their arms, stoutness to their hearts, steadfastness to their faith.

They will need Thy blessings. Their road will be long and hard. The enemy is strong. He may hurl back our forces. Success may not come with rushing speed, but we shall return again and again; and we know that by Thy grace and by the righteousness of our cause, our sons will triumph.

They will be sore tried, by night and by day, without rest—till the victory is won. The darkness will be rent by noise and flame. Men's souls will be shaken with the violences of war.

These are men lately drawn from the ways of peace. They fight not for the lust of conquest. They fight to end conquest. They fight to liberate. They fight to let justice arise, and tolerance and goodwill among all Thy people. They yearn but for the end of battle, for their return to the haven of home.

Some will never return. Embrace these, Father, and receive them, Thy heroic servants, into Thy kingdom.

And for us at home—fathers, mothers, children, wives, sisters and brothers of brave men overseas, whose thoughts and prayers are ever with them—help us, Almighty God, to rededicate ourselves in renewed faith in Thee in this hour of great sacrifice.

Many people have urged that I call the nation into a single day of special prayer. But because the road is long and the desire is great, I ask that our people devote themselves in continuance of prayer. As we rise to each new day, and again when each day is spent, let words of prayer be on our lips, invoking Thy help to our efforts.

Give us strength, too—strength in our daily tasks, to redouble the contributions we make in the physical and material support of our armed forces.

And let our hearts be stout, to wait out the long travail, to bear sorrows that may come, to impart our courage unto our sons wheresoever they may be.

And, O Lord, give us faith. Give us faith in Thee; faith in our sons; faith in each other; faith in our united crusade. Let not the keenness of our spirit ever be dulled. Let not the impacts of temporary events, of temporal matters of but fleeting moment — let not these deter us in our unconquerable purpose.

With Thy blessing, we shall prevail over the unholy forces of our enemy. Help us to conquer the apostles of greed and racial arrogances. Lead us to the saving of our country, and with our sister nations into a world unity that will spell a sure peace—a peace invulnerable to the schemings of unworthy men. And a peace that will let all men live in freedom, reaping the just rewards of their honest toil.

Thy will be done, Almighty God. Amen.

News-Leader Scores Scoop With Invasion

No metropolitan newspaper reaching the Staunton area yesterday morning contained news of the invasion of Europe. None even carried news of the German broadcast announcing that invasion had begun, received at one a. m., two and a half hours before confirmation by Allied Supreme Headquarters.

The News-Leader carried news of the German broadcast in its early mail editions. For its rural and city editions, it carried confirmation by General Eisenhower and all details that had passed the censors up to four-thirty a. m.

These facts demonstrate once again that metropolitan newspapers distributed here are "bulldog" editions printed prior to midnight under a morning dateline.

For late, pre-breakfast morning news, The News-Leader has no competitor in the Staunton area.

Draft Boards Tighten Up Deferments on Men 18-26

There will be no deferments in the age group 18 to 26 except for the most critical reason, members of Selective Service Boards of Augusta and Rockingham Counties were told at a district conference yesterday, with Richmond officials who were represented by General Joel D. Griffin.

The conference was in conformity with an announcement made some time ago that local boards would get specific information from state officials following decision at Washington to screen every available man 18 to 26 for direct army service.

Representatives of the county's agricultural and industrial interests were present and were informed that unless a selectee were critically essential local boards would have no alternative other than forwarding recommendations to the state selective service officials. Upwards of fifty persons officials, staff members and others were present.

Tighten Up On Rulings

The conference, according to W. P. Bucher and J. Harry Bryan of the local boards made it plain that there is to be a tightening up all along the line.

"The instructions as we interpret them new," said Mr. Bryan, "boil down to about this:

"Age group 18-26—There are to be no deferments whatsoever save in cases where the selectee is employed in a position so critical for the war effort there can be no question about his classification. All debatable cases must be forwarded to the state board, accompanied with recommendations. Local boards are left almost without discriminatory power.

Replaced by Older Men

"Age group 26-29—In this bracked wherever possible the intention is to replace selectees with men 30 to 37, and make all the 26-29 group available for service in the armed forces. The deferments are to be determined according to this general principle.

"Age group 30 to 37—Selectees in this category who are physically competent must show employment in some necessary occupation or be inducted, after which disposition will be made according to their availability."

James M. Gorsline county agricultural agent and some representative producers were present, since the government is insisting on maximum production and will make selectee exceptions where it is obvious that deferment is critical in a given situation.

The same, according to the new interpretations, is applicable to industry.

June 7, 1944: D-Day! *Microfilm Archives*

The PUBLIC Interests FIRST

THE EVENING LEADER

THE WEATHER
Scattered light showers in the mountains, followed by clearing and slightly cooler by morning; Sunday, pleasant and not quite so warm.

VOLUME NO. 80. NO. 38. MEMBER ASSOCIATED PRESS WIRE AND FEATURE SERVICES STAUNTON, VA., SATURDAY, JULY 29, 1944 MEMBER OF THE AUDIT BUREAU OF CIRCULATIONS PRICE THREE CENTS

Heroic "Major Of St. Lo" Revealed As Staunton's Own Thomas D. Howie

HEROIC MAJOR WITH FORCES—EVEN IN DEATH!

THE STARS AND STRIPES cover the body of Major Thomas D. Howie of Staunton as it "lies in state" on a heap of rubble amidst the ruins of the Church of St. Croix in St. Lo—his shrine flanked by the men he had led in an assault on the town. One of the war's dramatic classics is associated with the strange scene. Before their entry into St. Lo, a unit of the 116th Infantry had been isolated for several days. The Major vowed he would relieve it and lead the march into the Nazi-held stronghold. He was killed during the battle for the town, but even in death he lead them—for his body was placed in an ambulance and, protected by armored cars, was driven into the fighting area. (International).

(By HAL BOYLE)

WITH THE 116TH INFANTRY IN FRANCE, July 23—(Delayed)—(AP)—They passed out presidential citations today to officers and doughboys who cracked St. Lo, the eastern hinge of the German battleline, and it was a sad ceremony to many because the "Major of St. Lo" was not alive to receive his.

The "Major of St. Lo" was Thomas D. Howie of Staunton, Va., one of the best beloved battalion leaders in the American Army. He was killed July 17, the day before the city fell, after he broke through the Nazi wall to relieve another battalion of this regiment which was encircled on the outskirts.

Today the Major lies in honor with other officers and men in the 29th Division's Cemetery—but on the day St. Lo was taken the dead Major was carried through the streets in state in an ambulance and his flag-draped body was placed on a pile of rubble beside the shell-wrecked Church of Ste. Croix. The storming force passed in review through an artillery barrage thrown by the withdrawing Germans.

Howie was bald and in his middle thirties. He formerly taught English literature, coached football, and was athletic director at Staunton Military Academy. He was an athletic star himself at the Citadel, Military Academy in Charleston, S. C.

Paid High Honor

The wiry, muscular officer, a native of Abbeville, S. C., was popular with all ranks in the division from the lowest private to the commanding officer, Major General Charles H. Gerhardt, who personally ordered Howie's body taken into St. Lo by the combat force as a gesture honoring him and his battalion. By taking the high ground dominating the approaches to the city, his men sealed its capture.

"He had given up an operations post at regimental headquarters to take over the battalion only five days before," said Capt. Charles B. Cawthon of Murfreesboro, Tenn., executive officer of the cut-off battalion to whose relief Howie and his troops came after they had been almost three days with no fresh rations or ammunition supplies.

"We have many officers in the army, but you can't say of all that they are gentlemen. Major Howie was the finest gentleman I ever knew."

"He certainly was," added Lt. George E. Bryan of Allendale, S. C. "I would like to have you talk to some of his stonewall buddies so you really can understand the fine type of man he was," Cawthon said. "But there are not so many left. You know we came ashore on the toughest beach and it wasn't any barbecue breaking through the Germans in front of St. Lo. His closest friend, Capt. Sherman V. Burroughs of Roanoke, Va., was killed before he got to the beach invasion day. I declare we have lost a lot of Virginia men."

Just then Lt. Col. Sidney V. Bingham Jr., Dallas, Tex., Cawthon's commanding officer, who himself had served as executive officer for Howie when the latter led a battalion last year before taking up the regimental operations post, returned from the cemetery.

"There never was another man quite like Howie," he said.

Farther down the road was camped Major Howie's battalion, now under command of 27-year old Capt. William H. Puntenney of Phoenix, Ariz., formerly his executive officer.

Recounts Happening

Puntenney, a tall, blond, former cattle rancher, cleared his voice twice as he told what happened in the battalion command post among the hedgerows.

"We had just finished meeting the company commanders to wind up our attack plans," he said. "They had been dismissed and before they could get back to their companies the Germans began dropping a mortar barrage around our ears.

"Before taking cover in one of two foxholes which we were using, Major Howie turned to take a last look to be sure all his men had their heads down," continued Puntenney.

"Without warning one of their mortar shells hit a few yards away and exploded. A fragment struck the Major in the back and apparently pierced his lung. 'My God, I am hit,' he murmured, and I saw he was bleeding at the mouth. As he fell I caught him.

"I called a medic, but nothing could be done. He was dead in two minutes. Before we jumped off that morning he had told some division officers: 'See you in St. Lo.' General Gerhardt knew that if he lived he would have wanted to be one of the first in the city—and he saw that he had his wish."

Four battalion headquarters men in an adjoining fox hole were slightly injured by the burst that killed the Major, but all insisted on sticking to the job.

They were Tech. Sgt. Roland S. White and Sgt. Daniel O. Affleck, buddies from the same home town of Winchester, Va., Sgt. Darrell R. Spicer, Roanoke, Va., and Pvt. Eddie O'Lear, Newton Falls, Ohio.

The obituary of Howie was given by T/4 Clarence Careste of the Bronx, N. Y., who said: "Every one of us enlisted men looked up to him and admired him as a leader. But at the same time he was so kind and considerate you always felt comfortable around him—even if you were a private and he a major."

MAJOR HOWIE ON STAFF AT S. M. A. SINCE FALL OF '29

Confirmation was received here today that the Virginia major who fell so gallantly in the assault on St. Lo in Normandy was Thomas D. Howie of this city.

The Associated Press had previously reported the death of the Virginia officer, but had not included his name.

"Tom" Howie was a member of Staunton Military Academy faculty for years, and prominently identified with athletics there. Fellow faculty members said today that he was one of the most popular members of the faculty that the school has had in many years.

Major Howie was born in Abbeville, S. C., April 12, 1908, a member of a large family. He attended The Citadel, where he was prominent not only in athletics but in intellectual pursuits. He was graduated with a B.A. degree in 1929 and missed getting a Rhodes scholarship by a fraction of a percentage point.

Coming to S.M.A. in the fall of 1929, he held a position in the school's English Department until 1933, when he was made head coach and director of athletics. In February, 1938, he was made alumni secretary, handling the school's publications and publicity and serving as field representative, a position which he held until he was granted a leave of absence Feb. 3, 1941.

Playing for about five years in the old Augusta County Baseball League, he made many acquaintances and friends throughout the county.

He was second lieutenant of Company L, 116th Infantry, Virginia National Guard, and left here with the outfit early in 1941 for intensive training. In the years between that time and the time of his death, he advanced to the rank of major.

He is survived by his wife, the former Miss Elizabeth Payne of this city and a young daughter, Sally, who live on East Beverley Street. Among other survivors is a younger brother, Capt. Franklin Howie, who is also in the armed services.

Major Howie was a member of Trinity Episcopal Church.

MAJOR HOWIE

GLASS NEW PRESIDENT OF PRESS

ROANOKE, July 29.—(AP)—Powell Glass, general manager of Lynchburg News and Advance, was elected president of the Virginia Press Association at the semi-annual business meeting this morning.

The association endorsed the principles of a world free press and freedom of international news exchange in adopting a resolution offered by Richard P. Carter, editor of the Roanoke World News on behalf of the planning committee which he heads.

Stauntonian Speaks

Speaking at the annual luncheon and roundtable conference of the state's daily newspapers, Brigadier General E. W. Opie, publisher of the Staunton newspapers who appeared in the place of Herbert P. Corn, managing editor of the Washington Star, discussed, "Handling Postwar News." Special attention, he said, must be paid to news coverage in countries occupied by Allied troops after the war, in order that the complicated "scrambles for political power" may be accurately reported. He also called for extension of news coverage in Latin-America. Good, accurate reporting of local news will still be the most important phase of the small "home-town" daily's activities, he declared.

WAYNESBORO MAY SPONSOR LOCKER PLANT

At a meeting of Waynesboro Chamber of Commerce Friday night, it was decided to appoint a committee to help make a survey there to determine the extent of the desire of the citizens for a frozen food locker plant.

Present at the meeting were representatives of the Augusta Cooperative Farm Bureau, Inc., which operates the locker plant near Staunton. The chamber's committee is to work with the Farm Bureau committee in making the survey, the results of which will indicate the size of the plant to be built. Property near the intersection of Route 250 and the Stuarts Draft road has been secured for this purpose.

During the discussion, which was largely general, the difficulty of getting materials at this time was pointed out.

Ray S. Cline of the Farm Bureau said that the Waynesboro Chamber of Commerce had shown itself to be "highly cooperative" in regard to the project.

MINUTE MEN WILL DO SOME WATER CROSSING AND CLIFF CLIMBING

For the purpose of specializing in extended order drill, Virginia Reserve Militia Company No. 8 is ordered to arrive at the Roller chicken farm at Verona Monday night, July 31, at seven-thirty. River crossing and cliff scaling tests by squads will be some of the hazards. Men are expected to bring flashlights, gum boots, and dry socks. Captain Charles S. Roller Jr., company commander, announces that all contests will be timed and the results published.

RESTRICTION IS PLACED ON COAL BUYING

Only restriction on the purchase of coal at this time is that householders buy only 75 per cent of their annual requirements before Oct. 1, coal dealers here said today.

After that date, they feel confident that the remaining 25 per cent will be available. In any case, it was urged that buyers place their orders early.

However, Virginians face the prospect of a winter with ten per cent less coal than last year because of under-production in the Southern Appalachian mines, according to C. J. Potter, deputy solid fuels administrator for war.

The deficiency at the mines, running to 148,000 tons each week, cannot be made up because of insufficient manpower, it was said.

SPAW regulations place Virginia in the Southeastern Area which gets first preference in the retail distribution of soft coals. While this assures that dealers will receive for distribution in 1944-45 about 90 per cent of the coal they received last year, Mr. Potter said, they still will be 10 per cent short of full requirements.

BOY SLIGHTLY HURT WHEN HE RAN INTO CAR

Little Charles Ramsey of Craigsville got away from his mother on West Beverley Street at ten-forty-five this morning and received slight bruises on his face when he ran into the side of an automobile.

Driver of the sedan was Earl K. Kirby, 320 du Pont Avenue, who took the two-and-one-half-year old child to a physician's office, where it was determined that he was otherwise unhurt.

Mr. Kirby said the boy ran from the north sidewalk into the car and that he did not see him.

The accident happened near the ration board office.

SCOUT CAMP CONCLUDES FINE SEASON

McGAHEYSVILLE, July 29.—Camp Shenandoah closed its sixth week and 1944 Boy Scout camping season Wednesday. This season holds the record for attendance and the program and advancement was at its best for many years. Events of the sixth week and winners include: treasure hunt was won by a provisional group composed of University, Lexington, and Staunton Scouts, including Walter Wells and Billy Grine of Staunton. The Order of the Arrow initiated several scouts into membership, including Howell Gruver, Waynesboro.

A field meet arranged by Scouts working on athletic merit badge was held, and events and winners included:

50-yard dash won by James Reese, Waynesboro; Bill Quesenbery, second place. Mile Run, won by Bill Quesenbery, Waynesboro. Shot put won by Tommy Jarman, University; Bill Quesenbery, Waynesboro, second. Mile Relay won by Jim Reese, Waynesboro. Crab walk won by Jim Reese, Waynesboro. Backward run, won by Howell Gruver, Waynesboro. Bear crawl won by Fooley Hubert, Lexington; Howell Gruver, Waynesboro, second place.

Events of the waterfront program and the winners included: Two-man canoe race won by Fil Argenbright-Howell Gruver, Waynesboro; Bill Kinder-Milnes Austin, Waynesboro, second place. 50-yard backstroke swimming race won by Howell Gruver, Waynesboro. Obstacle race won by Bobby and Teddy Wood, University; Bill Kinder and Jackie Ryman, Waynesboro, second place. Canoe relay race won by Pooley Hubert, Lexington; Walter Wells, Staunton.

Awards made at the Court of Advancement included: for the rank of First Class Scout: Pete Grine of Staunton.

PLAY HERE TONIGHT

The Boys' Club and Waynesboro Basic-Wita team play tonight at eight o'clock at the Fairground. Newlen will pitch for the locals.

THE ROAD TO BERLIN

(By The Associated Press)
1—Russian Front—337 miles—(measured from Kolbiel).
2—Normandy Front — 630 miles; (measured from Troarn)
3—Italian Front—605 miles—(measured from Senigallia)

RATION OFFICE TO BE CLOSED TUESDAY

Doors of the War Price and Rationing Board office will be closed all day Tuesday, Aug. 1, it is announced, to give the personnel time to get out the reports.

The office is usually closed on the last day of the month, but because the board's meeting is to be held then, the date was shifted.

AUGUSTA CONSIGNEES AT STATE SWINE SALE

WINCHESTER, July 29—(AP)—The Virginia Purebred Swine Breeders' Association will hold its annual summer sale at the Winchester Stockyards Aug. 4. Among those consigning hogs are Grove Brothers, Waynesboro; C. S. Patterson, New Hope; and James Borden, Grottoes.

MINE SWEEPER LOST

WASHINGTON, July 29— (AP) — Loss of the mine sweeper Swerve was announced by the navy today, bringing to 172 the number of American naval vessels lost since the war started.

The 890-ton minesweeper, the navy said, was sunk in the Mediterranean recently as the result of enemy action.

Super American Bombers Strike Into Manchuria

(BY JOHN GROVER)

A SUPERFORTRESS BASE IN WESTERN CHINA, July 29—(AP)—Giant, far-reaching American B-29 Superfortress bombers struck heavily today at the heart of Japan's "Arsenal of Greater East Asia," raining explosives on the heavy industry city of Anshan in the Mukden area of Eastern Manchuria.

Huge columns of smoke sprang up from the bombed works and it was estimated it would take twelve months to rebuild the installations.

Taking off in favorable weather, the great bombers of the world-ranging United States Twentieth Air Force loosed their explosives from high altitude over the targets in a powerful smash at installations important to Japanese munitions manufacture.

It was the first American air attack on Manchuria, the first daylight assault from high-altitude for the new, giant planes, and their third blow against major Japanese installations.

(The Japanese-controlled Hsingking home radio, in a Japanese-language broadcast reported by OWI, declared one B-29 was shot down over Anshan. The broadcast said raiders also had penetrated into the "Dairen area" near port Arthur and were in two groups consisting of several planes each." A United States War Department announcement of the action did not mention any losses.)

The Superfortresses took off from this base in a blazing-red dawn. One diversionary force headed for Chenghsien, bottleneck of the Peiping-Hankow railway in Northern Honon Province, where it bombed the railyards which the Japanese are attempting feverishly to rebuild.

The others headed northward, and hours later the radio silence was broken by a flashed code word disclosing that the explosives had been dropped on the targets area and that the bombers were started on the long journey homeward.

[The Tokyo radio, heard by United States government monitors, said the important industrial city of Penhsihu, site of important coal fields, also had been attacked. The Japanese, as usual, minimized the effectiveness of the raids, saying that "no material damage was suffered by industrial installations, but residential quarters sustained some slight damage."

More than four hours after the War Department announced that American B-29 superfortresses had raided the Mukden area of Manchuria, the Tokyo radio acknowledged today that the important industrial cities of Anshan and Penhsihu had been attacked.

The broadcast in English and beamed to the United States, was reported by the Federal Communications Commission.

Anshan, a city of about 200,000, is a vital iron and steel center while Penhsihu is the site of important coal fields.

As usual, the Japanese minimized the effectiveness of the raids, saying that "no material damage was suffered by industrial installations, but residential quarters sustained some slight damage."

WILLS RECENTLY RECORDED IN AUGUSTA CIRCUIT COURT CARRY VALUE OF $327,112

Twenty-nine wills, with estimated value of estates totaling $327,112.06, have been probated recently in Augusta Circuit Court.

Largest single estate, one of $97,129.76, is represented in the will of S. F. McClure, Spottswood, who left his possessions to three heirs, Mayme Smith McClure, his wife; S. F. McClure Jr., son; Jean McClure Thomas, daughter. The son and daughter qualified as executors of the estate, of which $25,879.76 is personalty and $65,250 real estate. Appraisers named were W. M. Harris, C. P. McClure, Edwin Bumgardner, C. B. Ramsey, and F. A. Ramsey.

W. D. Quesenbery qualified as administrator of the estate of Thomas W. Quesenbery who died intestate leaving $35,000 in personalty and $40,000 in real estate, a total of $75,000. Appraisers were James W. Wright, L. L. Lovegrove, H. J. Franklin, J. E. Drumheller, and Boyd Stombock.

Administratrix of the estate of R. C. Beam who died intestate was Mae V. Beam, his wife. The Beam estate had an estimated value of $45,683.15—$29,638.15 in personalty, $16,000 in real estate. Francis W. Lineweaver, J. Waller Callison, E. Russell Cover, George S. Wigfall, Richard H. Hensel were appraisers.

Lockridge Estate

An estate valued at $21,000—$10,000 in personalty, $11,000 in real estate—was left by W. R. Lockridge, his wife, Jennie Lockridge, qualifying as administratrix c.t.a. Provision that his son, Robert Lockridge, could purchase the Byrd estate for $3,000 was made, but if he did not, it was to be sold, Robert to receive $2,000 and the rest to go into the total. Stephen Lockridge, another son, was given the home place, and his brother, John Lockridge, $4,000. One-half undivided interest in Hodge Hacken was to be retained as a hunting reserve for the benefit of the heirs, to be disposed of on mutual agreement; $2,000 went to each of four daughters, Vivian Bear, Eleanor Wilson, Louise Gardner, Jeanne Valz. Residue of the estate was to be divided equally among the heirs. Appraisers were J. H. Revercomb, Fred Fink, R. E. Christian, L. T. Zimbro, and D. F. Shinabery.

T. D. Whitaker, Waynesboro, left a provision in his will that a home and care be given his wife, Mabel L. Whitaker, during her natural life. At her death a residence was to be purchased for his daughter, Hazel W. Moore, cost not to exceed $4,000. Residue of the estate of which the total value was $11,000—$1,000 personalty, $10,000 real estate—went to a son, C. B. Whitaker, who qualified as executor. Appraisers were C. G. Quesenbery, James W. Wright, L. L. Lovegrove, G. M. [illegible], C. C. Hall.

Administrator of an estate valued at $7,500—$4,500 personalty, $3,000 real estate—left by Nannie Snead Reid, who died intestate, is R. A. Glover. Appraisers were J. E. Zimmerman, Albert Doyle, W. W. Mathews, C. A. Cleveland, C. G. Craig.

An estate valued at $1,000—personalty $750, real estate $250,—was left by George C. Shiflett, his wife, Carlos P. Shiflett, qualifying as administratrix. J. B. Yount, Humes J. Franklin, O. C. Powell, Samuel Heatwole, and James Taylor were named appraisers.

Kirby Estate

Jacob H. Kirby is administrator of the estate of A. W. Shaner valued at $3,600—$1,600 personalty, $2,000 real estate. Appraisers named were Lloyd Coiner, Ervin Wagner, N. C. Hackworth, Howard Crickenberger, and Eva Hopkins.

All property of Mary F. Johnson was willed to her husband, Godwin G. Johnson, and he was appointed executor. Her estate was valued at $3,833—personalty $283, real estate, $3,550. Appraisers included Samuel S. Loewner, F. C. Hamer, Carl Argenbright, J. Ralston Silling, and Mrs. Margaret Mohler.

Charles Newton White, who left $500 personalty and $4,000 real estate, willed his entire estate to his wife, Mrs. Bertie Lee White, with provision that his sister, Mary Susan White, was to have a home with his wife until her demise and a decent burial thereafter.

Heirs of Nellie V. Wallace who left an estimated $2,300, all real estate, are Margaret Wallace Grogg, administratrix, Elizabeth Wallace Glover, and Callie Bell Wallace.

The entire estate of William H Maxwell, Stokesville, valued at $1,700—personalty $200, real estate,

(continued on Page 4, Col 4.)

ROMMEL'S FIRST STRONG TANK COUNTERBLOWS ARE REPULSED BY AMERICANS

NEW BOMBING TYPE

LONDON, July 29—(AP)—A high Air Force authority announced today that the American breakthrough in Normandy was preceded by a new type of saturation bombing which covered an area of ten square miles with 65,951 bombs dropped from 2,423 planes.

The War Today

(By The Associated Press)

INVASION FRONT — United States tanks hurl back German counterattacks and drive to Sienne River, bringing enemy road hub of Brehal within gun range. Breakthrough widens as armored press advantage.

RUSSIAN FRONT—Red Army within sight of Warsaw, capital of Poland, while other forces penetrate Latvian rail center of Jelgava in thrust aimed at bisecting Baltics.

BALKANS—Break in Turkish-German relations believed imminent. Bulgaria reported demanding withdrawal of two German divisions, possibly preliminary to peace effort.

AERIAL FRONT—Force of 1,100 United States heavy bombers hits Leuna synthetic oil plant in Germany for second successive day, and hammers port of Bremen. Britons hit Stuttgart, Hambburg, Frankfort, and robot bomb bases with 1,000 night bombers.

ITALIAN FRONT—New Zealanders crack German defenses south of Florence and knife into last mountain line guarding city.

ASIATIC FRONT—High-flying B-29's bomb Manchurian industrial center of Anshan in first daylight assault of Superfortresses.

PACIFIC FRONT—Japanese island stronghold of Palau hit by 500 United States carrier-based planes. United States land forces press conquest of Guam and Tinian, killing Japs in ratio of 20-to-1.

(By GLADWIN HILL)

SUPREME HEADQUARTERS ALLIED EXPEDITIONARY FORCE, July 29.—(AP)—United States tanks hurled back the first strong enemy armored counterattack east of captured Coutances today and slashed on down the Normandy coast to within gunshot of the next German escape hatch at Brehal, eleven miles to the south.

Even as enemy broadcasts conceded a withdrawal of the Germans' "entire western wing," tank battles broke out on a wide scale as Field Marshal Erwin Rommel sought to stem the offensive imperilling his positions blocking the way to the heart of France.

He threw fresh tanks recklessly into the first real counterattack since the offensive began five days ago, hammering against the American left flank at Tessy-Sur-Vire, but was checked after a fierce engagement.

Simultaneously, Tiger tanks and other armored remnants by-passed by lightning American columns, opened up in an attempt to break out of the woods west of Le Mesnil-Herman. They were repulsed by quickly-summoned Shermans in tank to tank duels among the hedgerows.

Rommel's armor supply was depleted by incessant aerial attack, which in three days has knocked out 250 enemy tanks.

Summoning reinforcements from east and west, Rommel was stiffening the resistance, however, and was trying to keep the tide of Allied armor from the coastal routes over which his battered divisions are withdrawing.

But one American column drove through Lengrone, only six miles from Brehal, where the coastal roads converge, and moved on to bring the town within range of United States guns.

Brehan is eleven miles below Coutances and two and one half miles from the sea.

AIR ACE IS MISSING

OIL CITY, PA., July 29—(AP)—The parents of Lt. Col. Francis S. Grabeski, top scoring ace in the United States Air Force with 31 planes to his credit, were notified by the War Department today that he has been "missing in action" since July 20.

Germans In Northern Baltics Facing Complete Entrapment

LONDON, July 29—(AP)—Berlin announced today a Soviet penetration to the Latvian rail hub of Jelgava which threatens to trap Nazi garrisons in the northern Baltics as Colonel General Mikhail I. Kazakov's heavy artillery shelled Warsaw's distant suburbs in furtherance of the Red Army Polish plains offensive.

A Stockholm dispatch quoted a Wilhelmstrasse spokesman as saying there would be no further German stand east of Warsaw, but great battles "will be fought between the Vistula and the Oder—or perhaps between Warsaw and Berlin."

Russian troops have reached the Vistula, which passes Warsaw, on a wide front below the Polish cipital. The Oder flows through eastern Germany from below Breslau to Stettin, winding at one point to within 25 miles of Berlin.

Dispatches from Moscow told of the opening of artillery fire against the German forces in the outlying settlements before Warsaw and British accounts said the city itself had been sighted.

Associated Press Correspondent Eddy Gilmore said Marshal Konstantin K. Rokossovsky's advance detachments possibly had "reached hill positions where the capital of Poland is in plain view just beyond the Vistula."

The German High Command communique, broadcast from Berlin, disclosed the Soviet penertation to Jelgava, which would practically bisect the Baltics.

Bisecting Baltics

LONDON July 29— (AP) —Red Army spearheads rolling across the Polish plain were reported within sight on Warsaw today and the German communique said other Soviet forces had penetrated the Latvian rail hub of Jelgava, which would practically bisect the Baltics.

The German bulletin said a Nazi counterattack had thrown the Russian vanguard out of Jelgava, 120 miles northwest of Daugavpils (Dvinsk) and about 21 miles southwest of Riga on an arm of the Baltic Sea.

British dispatches from the eastern front said Warsaw could be seen by advance Soviet forces in the Polish offensive, made up of cavalry, scout cars, and tanks.

Fighting apparently raged on in the vicinity of Jelgava as the Russians threatened to pinch off German Baltic divisions by gaining mastery of the rail line from Siauliai to Kaunas. The Russians already held Siauliai, 50 miles south of Jelgava.

The Germans declared they still held Siedlce, 50 miles east of Warsaw, but Russian dispatches said Marshal Konstantin K. Rokossosky's right wing was moving on the city for the purpose of joining forces which were battling Germans in the streets after capturing Brest Litovsk. Dispatches did not locate the Russian spearhead positions.

As Ukrainian Army units to the south seized Jaroslaw and Przemysl, Nazi strongholds on the route to Germany, Rokossovsky's advance units stabbed forward during the night from Kolbiel, 30 miles southeast of Warsaw, and powerful artillery pieces behind them were wheeled into position.

July 29, 1944: Thomas D. Howie of Staunton receives post-mortem tributes for his heroism at Normandy. *Microfilm Archives*

A bust of Major Thomas D Howie that sits in the lobby of the National Guard Armory at Gypsy Hill Park that bears his name. Maj. Howie, known here and in France as "The Major of St. Lo," was a former teacher at Staunton Military Academy. He was mortally wounded just prior to the attack at Martinsville Ridge which liberated the heavily defended stronghold of St. Lo.

FIFTY-FIVE YEARS IN THE PUBLIC SERVICE
Oldest Virginia Daily West of the Blue Ridge

The Staunton News-Leader

THE WEATHER
Cloudy and continued warm Friday and Saturday with scattered showers.

56th YEAR. No. 88 — ASSOCIATED PRESS AND (AP) FEATURES, AUDIT BUREAU CIRCULATIONS — STAUNTON, VIRGINIA, FRIDAY MORNING, APRIL 13, 1945 — MORNING LEADER ESTABLISHED 1904, DAILY NEWS ESTABLISHED 1890 — PRICE THREE CENTS

Cerebral Hemorrhage Fatal to Roosevelt

END COMES TO WORLD LEADER AT 4:35 EASTERN WAR TIME

Warm Springs, Ga., April 12—(AP)—President Franklin Delano Roosevelt died suddenly at 3:35 p. m., Central War Time, today of a massive cerebral hemorrhage.

Commander Howard Bruenn, naval physician, made this announcement to reporters shortly after White House Secretary William D. Hassett called a hurried news conference to announce the death of the nation's only fourth-term chief executive.

Mr. Roosevelt died in the little White House on top of Pine Mountain where he had come for a three-week rest. He was 63 years old.

Saw President Early

Dr. Bruenn said he saw the President this morning and he was in excellent spirits at 9:30 a. m.

"At one o'clock," Bruenn added, "he was sitting in a chair while sketches were being made of him by an architect. He suddenly complained of a very severe occipital headache (back of the head).

"Within a very few minutes he lost consciousness. He was seen by me at 1:30 p. m., fifteen minutes after the episode had started.

"He did not regain consciousness and he died at 3:35 p. m."

Only others present in the cottage were Commander George Fox, White House pharmacist and long an attendant on the President; Hassett, Miss Grace Tully, confidential secretary; and two cousins, Miss Laura Delano and Miss Margaret Suckley.

BRITISH AND NAZIS LOCKED IN BIG BATTLE

Rome, April 12—(AP)—The British Eighth Army hammered westward today from three bridgeheads across the Santerno River and British armor locked in a heavy battle with Nazi Tiger tanks.

North of the new bridgeheads troops which had made amphibious landings from Lake Comacchio behind the enemy's lines captured the villages of Menate and Longastrino and linked up with other units advancing astride the Reno River.

Polish troops of the Eighth Army, smashing along the vital highway nine (via Emilia) which runs from Bologna through Faenza captured Castel Bolognese, an important junction town five miles west of Faenza and 24 miles southeast of Bologna. Their dawn attack routed a strong enemy rear guard.

In the west the American Fifth Army battled within 14 miles of the naval base of La Spezia, seizing the mountain villages of Tornana and Gragnana against only light resistance.

SUPERFORTS STRIKE DEEP INTO JAPAN

Guam, Friday, April 13—(AP)—Superfortresses struck deeper into Japan Thursday—in their longest mission yet from Marianas bases—as they bombed Koriyama and Tokyo targets on Honshu Island by daylight.

Flyers returning from the record 3,800-mile roundtrip to Koriyama, industrial center some 110 miles north of Tokyo, reported they left large fires burning. This was the first raid so far north.

The Tokyo target was the Nakajima Musashino aircraft engine plant, bombed seven times before by B-29s. It was the third raid this month on the important plant.

Seventh Air Force P-51 Mustang fighters, making their second escort mission over Japan from their Iwo Jima base, accompanied the bombers.

Twentieth Air Force Headquarters in Washington said the B-29s flew in "very large" force. Previous raids by 300 and more B-29s have been similarly described.

A 20th Air Force communique issued at Washington later identified the Koriyama targets as chemical plants. The communique reported officially that none of the Superfortresses was lost to enemy action and that three enemy planes were shot down and four others probably destroyed.

MAY HAVE TO POSTPONE 'FRISCO CONFERENCE

Washington, April 12—(AP)—Chairman Connally (D.-Tex.) of the Senate Foreign Relations Committee said tonight the United Nations Conference in San Francisco may have to be postponed because of President Roosevelt's death.

TRUMAN IS SWORN IN AS PRESIDENT

Washington, April 12—(AP)—Harry S. Truman, of Missouri, was sworn in as thirty-second President of the United States tonight at 7:09 p. m. (EWT).

Law Enforcement Officials Meet Here F.B.I. Instruction

Law enforcement officials representing Staunton, Augusta, Harrisonburg, Charlottesville, Waynesboro and Scottsville filled Corporation Courtroom Thursday afternoon to hear addresses by special agents of the Federal Bureau of Investigation and view the motion picture, "Baptism of Fire."

Staunton Chief of Police E. L. Bragg introduced Major William A. Grubert who in turn presented to the assembly Harold Nathan, special agent in charge of the Richmond FBI.

Mr. Nathan lectured to the group on "Public Relations," and J. E. Lawler, also a special agent for the FBI, discussed "Report Writing."

THE GREATEST FRIEND OF COMMON MAN SINCE DAYS OF LOWLY NAZARENE–FLANNAGAN

Bristol, Va., April 12.—(AP)—Congressman John W. Flannagan Jr., of the Ninth Virginia District said at his home here tonight that President Roosevelt would be remembered "as the apostle of freedom and peace and the greatest friend of the common man since the days of the lowly Nazarene."

The full comment of Congressman Flannagan on the death of the President follows:

"He laid down his life in his efforts to bring about world freedom and lasting peace.

"He has not died in vain.

"Inspired by his sacrificial death, his world-wide followers will be fired by a zeal that will insure the ultimate crushing of the dictators and the bringing about of lasting peace.

"He will be remembered as the apostle of freedom and peace and the greatest friend of the common man since the days of the lowly Nazarene."

WEST VIRGINIA GOVERNOR STATEMENT OF ROOSEVELT

By the Associated Press

Governor Clarence W. Meadows of West Virginia, voicing the grief and shock of residents of the Mountain State at the death of President Roosevelt asked last (Thursday) night that the people "even in this sad hour carry on—as he would wish us to carry on."

West Virginia, which for four consecutive times gave Mr. Roosevelt its vote, accepted the word at first with shocked unbelief and then with deepest mourning.

Governor Meadows, enroute for an inspection visit to Babcock State Park in Fayette County, heard of the news by telephone and returned immediately to Charleston.

"The news of the death of our President has struck deep into the heart of every West Virginian," he said in a formal statement.

TYNES PLAN APPROVED BY CITY COUNCIL

City council Thursday night put its stamp of approval on a plan advanced by City Health Officer Dr. A. L. Tynes for bringing to the city a health educator, and requested the Board of Health to pursue the matter further.

Finances for the undertaking would be forthcoming from federal sources, the health officer pointed out, and the city would not be obligated in the least for the plan which could "make Staunton the center from which might radiate throughout the valley the work of public health education."

Councilman Ralston Silling who voiced the motion, declared that the City Fathers "are definitely interested in anything which may improve the health of our people." Second was made by Fred Baylor.

After reading of the accomplishments of such educators in health journals and reflecting that Staunton is in a highly desirable position to serve as a center for such a project, Dr Tynes wrote Dr. J. C. Funk, director of health education in Richmond, for information.

More correspondence and a personal interview with Dr. Funk resulted, he told Council. The health education director in turn presented the matter to the U. S. Public Health Service which indicated its willingness to give financial support.

Dr. Tynes took the matter up with the Board of Health, securing its approval as well as that of Superintendents of Schools A. C. Gilkeson of the County and L. F. Shelburne of Staunton.

Established at strategic points throughout the county, the health educators are usually women with good college backgrounds and specialization in health education who are equipped to work through the home and the school to help insure a better health program for the people, Dr. Tynes related.

To date, he said, the only one in this state is located at Danville and from all indications has had very successful results.

He expressed a desire to secure a person for the job as soon as possible and begin the work which he believes will extend north and south through the valley with other educators being added when expedient and desirable.

Upon motion of Councilman Baylor, seconded by Forest Taylor, the resignation of Mrs. John Shelley, dated April 30, was accepted with "very deep regrets." The group was highly complimentary of the work done by Mrs. Shelley as clerk of the Council for fourteen years and expressed reluctance to release her. City Manager W. L. Hall was instructed to write her a letter of appreviation for her faithful service.

Final adoption was made of the city Department of Public Welfare budget which had received tentative approval at an earlier meeting.

Rental from the government of seven buildings below the North River Dam area at a rate of $25 per year was voted. Conditions for the rental were specified in a letter to the city manager from M. C. Howard, forest supervisor. The buildings will be used by the city as a nutrition camp.

At the request of Mayor William A. Grubert, the city manager was instructed to determine the advisability of replacing a worn brick sidewalk on Prospect Street—from New to Point—with a concrete walk.

The city manager reported that as much repair is being carried out on the city's streets as is possible with limited materials and the help shortage. He said that in almost all cases, the worse places are patched, although no resurfacing has been possible for several years.

Action as to the installation of a new water pump on the property of John D. White in College Park was delayed until Mr. Hall can investagate the matter more fully and determine the city's obligations.

Churchill To Pay Tribute To Late President Today

London, Friday, April 13—(AP)—Prime Minister Churchill received the shocking news of the death of President Roosevelt early this morning and was reported to have decided immediately to pay tribute to him when the House of Commons convenes at 11 a. m. today.

The Prime Minister had not yet gone to bed when word of the President's death was received and associates said Churchill was deeply affected.

U. S. Ambassador John G. Winant, informed of the death, said "the greatest American of our age is dead. I hope every citizen of the United States will stand by his post."

England learned of the President's death in the midnight broadcast of BBC and soldiers and civilians who still roamed Central London seemed stunned by the news, which swept through the city like wildfire.

NEW PRESIDENT

HARRY S. TRUMAN

Harry S. Truman Now President of United States

(By ERNEST B. VACARRO)

(Member of The Associated Press senate staff, who traveled with Vice President Truman during Truman's campaign for the vice-presidency last fall.)

Washington, April 12—(AP)—Harry S. Truman entered the White House tonight in one of the most critical periods in his nation's history with humble confidence that he is big enough to meet the burdens of a war-time presidency.

He entered it with a determination to call upon the best brains of the country to help guide him through the perils of war, peace negotiations and reconversion.

Those of us who travelled with him on a transcontinental speech-making tour for the Vice Presidency last fall and who were in daily conference with him before and after his election, think of him as a man:

1. Whose courage has been demonstrate time and again as a campaigned and as chairman of the Senate War Investigating Committee who never hesitated to lambast those high in administration favor.

2. Whose knowledge of his own limitations is such that he never hesitates to call on others whose qualifications on matters of high importance he may consider superior to his own.

3. Whose ability to "pick the brains" of others raised the Truman committee to a status rarely enjoyed by a Congressional committee.

4. Whose friendliness and modesty is the same as it was when he entered the Vice Presidency and as it probably was when he was a farmboy down in Missouri.

SPECIAL EDITION OF EVENING LEADER AND CHIMES FROM TRINITY EFFECTIVE IN CITY

Within an hour after the first flash telling the world that one of its leaders, President Franklin Delano Roosevelt, had died, the complete story of the momentous calamitous national tragedy was on the streets of Staunton, Woodrow Wilson General Hospital and Waynesboro in the form of an extra edition of The Evening Leader, the first of which was sold at seven-twenty-three p. m.

The Leader Papers were ready to swing into action sooner but there was some delay between the flash and the time details of the story began to tick. The linotype machines started to run. Soon they were grinding in unison.

The story cleared the printer and the linotypes at practically the same time. From that point only minutes elapsed before the massive press was starting the extras on their way to the eager public already attracted to the office by the flash bulletins pasted in the windows.

It was quick work. It was a sad job to perform. It was a duty the management owed the public and the paper's subscribers. It was taken in its stride. It was done.

Adding to Solemnity

Adding to the solemnity of the occasion, and strength to all there came the while the full toned chimes from Trinity Episcopal Church whose impressive tunes brought forth the message that the ways of the Lord are righteous altogether and that through faith in Him there will come forth other leaders to carry to a successful conclusion the blessings to be ours through strengthening and applying the principles Roosevelt so nobly set forth. They reminded, too, that even Moses was only permitted to glimpse the Promise Land. The hymns pealing forth were appropriately selected by Mrs. W. Carroll Brooke.

The chimes and the extra edition of the Evening Leader, the former soothing the hearts and the latter satisfying the minds of a sorrowful, pitiously stricken populace were the only concrete results reflecting the reception of the sad news here.

It was announced last night by the Rev. W. Carroll Brooke that memorial services will be held at Trinity church Saturday one hour after the Washington rites. The service to be conducted by the Rev. Brooke and the Rev. Dr. J. Lewis Gibbs, is for all Staunton people.

Flags at Half Mast

Mayor William A. Grubert indicated last night that the flag on City Hall will be lowered to half mast for the rest of this week.

Dr. L. Wilson Jarman, president of Mary Baldwin College, will speak briefly at a memorial service in Waddell Chapel at ten-twenty-five this morning to which are invited all friends of the college.

Although he did not have opportunity to contact the members of the local Ministerial Association, the Rev. W. J. B. Livingston, president of that organization, said last night that he was certain the other ministers stood behind him in urging the people generally to observe the death of their President throughout the rest of the week in their private devotionals and wherever possible in public church meetings.

Stauntonians are recalling the visit of President Roosevelt here on May 4, 1941, when he addressed an audience of over 7,000 people in dedicatory services making a national shrine out of the birthplace of Woodrow Wilson—a place he termed "a new shrine of freedom."

At that early date he emphasized his position on isolation when he said:

"Wilson fought because democracy could not survive in isolation. We applaud his judgment and his faith. I can think of no more fitting place in all the land for Americans to pledge anew their faith in the democratic way of life than at the birthplace of Woodrow Wilson."

YANKS LAND BOHOL ISLAND IN PHILIPPINES

Manila, Friday, April 13—(AP)—Veteran American Division Yanks landed Wednesday on Bohol Island, last of the Central Philippines still in enemy hands, under cover of naval and air bombardment, Gen. Douglas MacArthur reported today.

STALIN SENDS CONDOLENCE TO UNITED STATES

London, Friday, April 13—(AP)—Premier Marshal Stalin expressed his sorrow at the death of President Roosevelt today in a message to Mrs. Roosevelt in which he characterized the President as "a great organizer of the struggles of the freedom-loving nations against the common enemy."

The text of the note as broadcast by the Moscow radio:

"Mrs. Eleanor Roosevelt, Washington:

"Please accept my sincere condolences on the occasion of the death of your husband and an expression of my sympathy in your great sorrow.

"The Soviet people highly valued President Roosevelt as a great organizer of the struggles of freedom-loving nations against the common enemy and as the leader in the cause of ensuring the security of the whole world. Signed, Joseph Stalin."

Stalin also sent a separate note to Vice President Truman.

"On behalf of the Soviet government and myself personally," the message said, "I express our profound condolence to the government of the United States of America on the occasion of the premature death of President Roosevelt.

"The American people and the United Nations have lost in Franklin Roosevelt a great politician of world significance and a pioneer in the organization of peace and security after the war."

DEATH AND DESTRUCTION IN OKLAHOMA

Oklahoma City, April 12—(AP)—At least 58 Oklahomans were listed as dead tonight in tornadoes which dipped into many communities over the state, leaving hundreds injured and homeless.

Red Cross Chairman Paul Osborn at Antlers in Pushmataha county said 47 bodies had been recovered there from wreckage over one third of the town of 3,000 and added he would not be surprised if the final toll ran as high as "80 or 100."

Red Cross workers from over the state were arriving to aid in caring for the hundreds of injured at Antlers and ambulances from nearby army posts were called into service.

Nine were reported dead at Muskegee and two at Oklahoma City in an afternoon of horror during which twisters struck in at least eight communities.

Osborn said the situation at Antlers was desperate with light and power services suspended and urgent need for more ambulances, doctors and nurses. The army sent eight ambulances from Camp Mixie, Tex.

IMPORTANT MEETING JR. BASKETBALL LEAGUE

Announcement is made by Frank Shaffer, chairman, that there will be an important meeting of the Kiwanis Junior Basketball league, Wednesday night at seven-thirty on the second floor of the YMCA at which time plans will be formulated for the coming sandlot baseball league. It is very important that every member be present, declared Mr. Shaffer. Charles Nooney of the YMCA will be incharge of the program, and Ralph Simmons of SMA and Francis Lineweaver will be in attendance.

To Be Honored At Service Sunday

PFC. MOHLER

Killed in action in Germany Feb. 28, the memory of Private Thomas A. Mohler, 18, son of Mr. and Mrs. Alfred F. Mohler of Mt. Solon, will be honored at special services Sunday, April 15, at three o'clock in the Parnassus Methodist Church. Lieutenant Colonel Cliff K. Titus of Woodrow Wilson General Hospital will be among those on the program.

DEATH NEWS SHAKES NATIONAL CAPITAL TO ITS FOUNDATION

Washington, April 12—(AP)—The death of President Franklin D. Roosevelt shocked Washington to its foundations today.

From the man who now will become President—Vice President Harry Truman—down to the least of the city's people the news was overwhelming.

Mrs. Roosevelt, after dispatching a widowed mother's message of strength to their four sons in service, prepared to fly to Warm Springs.

The capital prepared for a funeral in the east room of the White House Saturday.

The burial of the only man to serve three terms

room of the White House Saturday.

The burial of the only man to serve three terms as President—only to die in the third month of his fourth term—is to be at Hyde Park, N. Y.

That is the home for which he said last year all that was within him cried out for.

A Cabinet meeting was called immediately and Truman was present—10 years ago an obscure county judge in Missouri. He would become the 32nd President.

The President's death was announced by his secretary, Stephen Early, who on Dec. 7, 1941 gave the world the news of the Pearl Harbor attack that plunged this country into war.

The White House called the three major news services at about 5:45 p. m., (EWT), on a conference call. There was a long pause.

Then Early came on the wire and made the electrifying announcement. His voice sounded fairly calm and measured, but he obviously was laboring under intense emotion.

His first words were—

"Here is a flash.

"The President died suddenly early this afternoon—"

There was a sudden flurry among his listeners.

"You mean President Roosevelt," someone shouted over the line.

"Of course," Early replied. "There is only one President."

Although interrupted several times, he continued to recite what he called "notes for the story."

DANCE CANCELLED

Because of the death of President Roosevelt, the Civil Air Patrol dance scheduled to be held at the Veterans' Home tonight, has been cancelled.

TRUMAN FIRST PRESIDENT FROM WEST EXCEPT HOOVER

Independence, Mo., April 12—(AP)—Harry S. Truman, successor to President Roosevelt, is the first native Missourian to become the Nation's Chief Executive, and, except for Herbert Hoover, native of Iowa, and a resident of California, is the only president from west of the Mississippi River.

Now approaching his 61st birthday Truman was born at Lamar, Mo., May 8, 1884. Lamar is a town of 2,300 population.

PRESIDENT DEDICATED PARK IN VA.

Richmond, Va., April 12—(AP)—Nine years ago President Roosevelt spent three days in Virginia—the longest consecutive period he was in the Old Dominion during his twelve years in the White House.

Beginning July 3, 1936, the President spoke at the dedication of the Shenandoah National Park at Big Meadow; moved on to Charlottesville to be introduced by United States Senator Carter Glass of Monticello; was cheered by thousands of Richmonders preliminary to boarding the Presidential Yacht Mayflower at the city wharf; attended services in historic Bruton Parish Church, Williamsburg, visited Carter's Grove and thence returned on his yacht up the Potomac to Washington.

Several times the late Chief Executive made brief journeys into Virginia, to lay wreaths at the tomb of the Unknown Soldier, and to visit Charlottesville, where his son Franklin, Jr. was a law student at the University of Virginia. The President's 1936 [illegible] highlight of his presidency, as far as Virginians seeing him in person was concerned.

In Many Towns

Through every town and village in the rolling Northern Virginia terrain, men, women and children lined the highways and narrow streets to have greetings and display American flags. Luncheon was served on a mountain top. Newspapermen recalled that Mrs. Roosevelt personally served cake to the correspondents.

At Big Meadow, Mr. Roosevelt was introduced by former Governor George C. Peery. Establishment of Shenandoah National Park, he stressed, meant that America intended to conserve its natural as well as human resources. Secretary of the Interior Harold Ickes was another dedication speaker.

Speaking a short distance from the tomb of Thomas Jefferson, President Roosevelt in his Monticello address emphasized that America could relight the fires of freedom.

(Continued on Page 2, Col. 1)

HIMMLER ORDERS TOWNS AND HOUSES HELD TO LAST MAN

Threat of Death Made to Anyone Disobeying Orders; Danger of Capture Hangs Over More Big Cities; Breman, Hamburg, Magdeburg, Leipzig and Berlin; Army High Command Issues Statement Holding Garrison Commanders Personally Responsible For Execution Of Himmler Order.

London, April 12—(AP)—With the threat increasing to more big German cities—Bremen, Hamburg, Magdeburg, Leipzig and Berlin itself—Gestapo Chief Heinrich Himmler decreed today that "every German town and every house must be defended to the last man" and threatened death to anyone disobeying the order.

Himmler's decree was followed by one from the Army High Command declaring that "garrison commanders are held personally responsible for the execution of this order" and warning that "any who deflect from this duty will be condemned to death, together with civilians who may have prevailed on them."

In a swift sequel the German High Command announced the death sentence had been imposed in absentia on General Lasch, who surrendered the East Prussian fortress capital of Koenigsberg to the Russians earlier in the week.

"Reprisals will be taken against Lasch's family," a High Command communique asserted.

This was the first such bald official statement of the Nazi practice of inflicting punishment—possibly death—upon the relatives of those incurring the displeasure of the army or the Nazi party.

Himmler's decree obviously was aimed at combatting the epidemic of white flags on the Western Front. He accused the city populations there of cowardice in surrendering to the Allies on the promise that their cities would be spared destruction. Some cities, he declared, had surrendered to scouting parties riding in armored cars far ahead of tanks and artillery.

Henceforth, the Gestapo chief said, no German town will be declared an open city, but must be "defended to the last man." Every person responsible for the defense of a town or village who disregards the order will lose his honor and his life, he said.

Obviously the Wehrmacht has neither the men or the material to defend every town and village, and the German people do not have the will to do so. Some British observers interpreted Himmler's decree as intended solely for the record, aimed at establishing the legend of united German resistance to the last rather than at actually organizing such resistance.

The fact that the high command was forced to resort to death threats indicated that the army's discipline was weakening, for the pronouncement plainly indicated that some garrison commanders were surrendering towns in defiance of strict orders.

The high command's pronouncement was issued as a supplement to the regular military communique. It was extraordinary in that it bore the signatures not only by Field Marshal Wilhelm Keitel, head of the armed forces, but also of Himmler and Martin Bormann, the latter as "head of the party chancellory."

London observers, who believe Hitler has been superseded, interpreted the several signatures to mean that Hitler no longer was in control of the government at his headquarters, else he would have signed the order.

April 13, 1945: President Roosevelt dies in office; Truman is sworn in as President. *Microfilm Archives*

FIFTY - FIVE YEARS IN THE PUBLIC SERVICE
Oldest Virginia Daily West of the Blue Ridge

The Staunton News-Leader

THE WEATHER
... warm and humid with ... showers Tuesday; Wednesday fair and little cooler

56th YEAR, No. 155 — ASSOCIATED PRESS AND (AP) FEATURES AUDIT BUREAU CIRCULATIONS — STAUNTON, VIRGINIA, TUESDAY MORNING, AUGUST 7, 1945 — MORNING LEADER ESTABLISHED 1890 DAILY NEWS ESTABLISHED 1889 — PRICE THREE CENTS

Atomic Energy Loosed on Japan May Speed War's End

GOVERNMENT MOVES TO SPEED UP PRODUCTION OF MUTTON

Government action designed to increase the supply of lamb and mutton by helping producers meet increased costs through Commodity Credit Corporation Secretary of Agriculture, Clinton P. Anderson. The payments will become effective on sheep and lambs marketed on or after August 5, 1945 and through June 30, 1946, it was stated by the Staunton office of triple A.

The Commodity Credit Corporation payments to the seller of lambs and sheep to legally authorized slaughterers for slaughter will range from $1.50 to $2.50 per hundredweight for lambs weighing 65 to 90 pounds; from $2.15 to $3.15 per hundredweight for lambs weighing over 90 pounds; and $1.00 per hundredweight has been set for all other sheep and lambs.

The variation of payments is designed to increase the returns from heavier lambs and to make feeding more attractive. The highest payments are to be made on lambs weighing over 90 pounds, during the months when fed lambs are usually marketed.

90c Subsidy Withdrawn

At the same time the Reconstruction Finance Corporation announced that the subsidy of 95 cents per hundredweight now paid to slaughters for all sheep and lambs slaughtered in authorized plants will be withdrawn, as to any slaughter performed on and after August 5, 1945.

The program seeks (1) to encourage the raising and feeding of lambs to heavier weights, (2) to bring about a more normal seasonal distribution in the marketing of lambs, (3) to divert more market lambs into legitimate slaughter channels, (4) to help producers meet increased costs without increasing consumer prices on lamb and mutton.

Recommendations Considered

Recommendations of a sheep industry committee composed of representatives of sheep raisers, feeders, and packers were considered in drawing up the program.

In recent months sheep raisers and lamb feeders have been subject to increasing costs and decreasing profits. As a result breeding ewes and relatively light lambs have been sold for slaughter. Stock sheep have decreased from slightly less than 50 million head on January 1, 1942, to approximately 41 million head, January 1, 1945.

To be eligible for payments under the new program, ewes and lambs must be sold to a legally authorized slaughterer who has certified that the animals are purchased for slaughter. Sellers should retain their sales accounts, invoices, and other evidence showing the weights and purchasers of all lambs and sheep sold on or after August 5, 1945.

Payments to sellers are to be made through the offices of the county committees of the Agricultural Adjustment Agency.

COFFMAN IS NOT RESIGNING AS CHAIRMAN

H. D. Coffman declared last night that he has not submitted his resignation as chairman of the Staunton Republican Committee, and does not contemplate doing so in the near future. He said he had not yet received any communication from I. R. Dovel asking that he relinquish the chairmanship.

Dovel, state chairman, said in an Associated Press statement Saturday night, that he was requesting Mr. Coffman's resignation because of an assertion that the local man made following the withdrawal of the two candidates for the House of Delegates named by a special committee of Republicans.

Mr. Coffman had advised a News-Leader reporter that no further activity would be carried on as to the naming of candidates, after C. C. Leap of Waynesboro and Bruce L. Showalter of Weyers Cave had withdrawn. Mr. Leap for health reasons and Mr. Showalter because of his business.

Maj. H. A. Jacob On Terminal Leave From U. S. Army

Major Herbert A. Jacob, who has been in the U. S. Army, stationed in Washington, for several years, is on a terminal leave, and has been visiting Mr. and Mrs. B. A. Jacob at Palcroft.

He expects to be given an honorable discharge early in September and will resume his position as alumni secretary at Virginia Military Institute, which Col. O. L. Denton has been doing, in conjunction with his other duties at the Institute.

Mrs. Jacob will remain in Washington for the present.

Fretwell Hurls Firemen's Victory Over W. S. Hospital

Pvt. Jack Fretwell, on furlough here, hurled an 8 to 3 victory over Western State Hospital for the Firemen last night on the softball diamond at the fairgrounds. Fretwell chalked up 17 straight wins for the Firemen squad last season.

U. S. O. SHOW AT ARMY HOSPITAL OPEN THEATER

Horace McMahon, "Hollywood's favorite gangster," heads the cast of a USO Camp Show scheduled to be staged for patients and personnel at Woodrow Wilson General Hospital's open air theater Wednesday night at eight-fifteen, it is announced by Special Services Officer Lieutenant Fred Ehardt.

Starting in show business 17 years ago, McMahon worked himself up until he was able to secure parts in several Broadway hits including "Sailor Beware" and "Three Men On a Horse."

Unknown and unlisted, McMahon arrived in Hollywood and the next day had a job in "Double Wedding,"—an Ethel Waters picture. From then on he specialized in tough-guy roles, among his most convincing being "Dangerous Blondes," "Timber Queen," and "Navy Blues." One of his most striking parts was said to have been in "Roger Touhy."

Also appearing in the cast is Lorraine Vernon, one of few female jugglers, who comes from a family of jugglers and acrobats. Miss Vernon began her act at the age of three, and has made appearances at points all over the world.

Others with the show who will help entertain the soldiers are the Three Hollywood Steppers, a dance trio, the Continental Trio, a musical act, and Toni Lange, singer.

Civilian Bond Buying At Wilson Wins Recognition

Because 95 per cent of its civilian employees set aside at least 12 per cent of their earnings in war bonds, Woodrow Wilson General Hospital has been placed on the Council Honor Roll established by the Third Service Command's Savings Promotion Council, ASF.

Advice to this effect reached Colonel Haskell L. Conner, post commander, Monday from Third Service Command Headquarters.

"Such better than required attainment," the letter stated "means much to this Service Command's present average of 96.2 per cent and 13.2 per cent as of June 30, 1945."

FIVE WAYNESBORIANS ARE INJURED IN SKYLINE ACCIDENT

Three men and two women all Waynesboro residents, were injured early Monday when the car in which they were riding failed to make a turn on Skyline Drive about one mile from the intersection of Route 250 and plunged over the side of the mountain.

Charles Lavender, son of H. B. Lavender of Highland Avenue, Waynesboro, was driving the 1941 Ford in which Driver R. Lamb 20, Cpl. Glen W. Thompson, 23, Mrs. Margaret Dempsey 37, and Miss Mary Ann Painter, 29, were passengers.

Both women were admitted to Waynesboro Community Hospital at approximately one-thirty a. m. while the men were removed to Woodrow Wilson General Hospital.

Mrs. Dempsey suffered two broken legs, and deep leg lacerations and Miss Painter, also two fractured legs, face and head lacerations and a broken left arm.

Hospital officials said last night that Mrs. Dempsey's condition was "critical" and that of Miss Painter, "fair." Both underwent severe shock. Colonel Cliff K. Titus, public relations officer at the army hospital, said that Lamb and Lavender each had a broken leg and that one of Thompson's hands was broken. They were considered to be seriously but not critically injured. All were operated upon he said, and their condition was satisfactory.

Lamb, son of David E. Lamb of 665 Highland Avenue, received an honorable discharge from the Army Aug. 1. He served in the European theater for about a year, and suffered leg injuries in action.

Cpl. Thompson is a son of Mr. and Mrs. Walter Thompson of Florence Avenue and has been home on a 30-day furlough since July 13. He served with the Eighth Air Force and was overseas since March 1944.

A daughter of Mr. and Mrs. C. E. Painter of Raphine, Miss Painter had been residing on Arch Avenue and working at the du Pont plant in Waynesboro. She is a niece of Mrs. Dempsey whose address was given as 1545 Mulberry, Jefferson Park.

The automobile was almost completely demolished, reports indicate.

TO AUGUSTA ELECTION JUDGES AND CLERKS

Aug. 7 is Election Day and we are again calling on you for an expression of your interest in assisting The Staunton News-Leader to obtain a complete report that night on the election results in the 37 precincts in the county.

Please call, 481 or 511, as soon as possible, after your vote has been tabulated and give us the results. We will pay long distance charges where necessary. If you find our phones busy, please stand by until you do get through to us with your precinct's figures.

Your cooperation in other elections has been excellent; please assist us again Aug. 7.

222 PATIENTS ONLY $40 IS ADDED TO FUND

Forty dollars was subscribed to the First Call Home Fund yesterday, and additional subscriptions will be needed this month to care for arrivals from European hospitals, according to the best information on the progress of evacuation. The re-opened fund stands:

Previously acknowledged	$683.60
Brownsburg Home Demonstration Club	2.00
Mrs. J. S. Lee, Crozet	2.00
Mrs. Margaret Hickman	5.00
29th Division Asso., Woodrow Wilson Post No. 61	5.00
Mr. and Mrs. Chas. R. Bryan	10.00
Sara, Bobby and Joe Gayhart	5.00
Nannie Barkman Class, Central Methodist Church	5.00
Mrs. Grace K. Ramsey	5.00
	$723.60

Two Waynesboro men—Pfc. Morris A. Williams, Box 6, and T/5 Malcolm E. Rhodes, route two—were among 222 patients, including 78 litter cases, admitted to Woodrow Wilson General Hospital on Aug. 4 and 5.

Two of the wounded came from the American theater of operations by air, 37 from the European theater by air and 138 by boat.

Virginians and West Virginians from the European area included:

Pfc. Donald D. Krupp, Pennsboro, W. Va.; S/Sgt. Russell A. Bowles, Narrows; T/5 Reuben H. Wharm Jr., New Canton; Pfc. Henry W. Holt, Lynchburg; Pfc. Walter I. Pratt, Floyd; Pvt. Orville C. Christian, Portsmouth; Pvt. William A. Brislendine, Dunnsville; T/5 Earl Danberg Jr., Glenn, W. Va.; Pfc. Jessie O'Berry, Smithfield; Pfc. John G. Marshall, Pulaski; T/4 Andrew P. Williams, Cereo; T/4 Linwood Worrell, Holland; Pvt. Frank A. Chaney, Danville; Pfc. John T. Haney, Arlington; Pfc. Carroll P. Thoms, Manassas; T/ George A. Parker, Amburg; T/5 Roland P. Senften, Warrenton; T/3 Don W. Cunningham, Crafton, W. Va.; Pfc. Richard P. Clark, Rocky Mount; Pfc. William L. Jenson, Portsmouth; Pfc. Dolly Bryant, Garrisonville; T/3 Albert L. Yolle, Weirton, W. Va.; Sgt. William M. Hager, Fieldale; Pvt. John R. Murphy, Mt. Clare; Cpl. Frank Coleman, Fredericksburg; Pfc. Clyde M. Johnson, Norfolk; Pfc. Hubert C. Jones, Sandyville, W. Va.; S/Sgt. William R. Hutchins, Troutville; Pfc. Robert W. Jenkins, Winchester; Pfc. Wesley R. Bolton, Alexandria; T/5 Robert L. Thomas, Fredericksburg; Pfc. William Wilson, Raphine (direct, casual, pass); Capt. John W. Cake Jr., Lynchburg; Cpl. James N. Mock, Abingdon; Major Phillip W. Hamilton, Gloucester County; Pfc. Hustin F. Cook, Richmond; Pfc. Selam O. Cordell, Nokesville; Pfc. George E. Smith, Portsmouth; Pfc. Walter W. Ingram, Bassett; Pfc. Elisha R. Lewis, Zuni; Cpl. William H. Eades, Petersburg; Pfc. Herman H. Baldwin, Maxie; Pfc. Wendell H. Bloomington, Arlington; Pvt. Carl G. Dewey, Clifton Forge; T/5 Norris J. Brooks, Brokenburg; Pfc. John S. Cells, Hillton Village; Pfc. William T. Jones, Kennig; T/Sgt. Robert E. Allen, Arlington; Pfc. Samuel E. Vick Jr., Richmond; First Lieutenant Frank D. Crews, Roanoke; Second Lieutenant Benjamin W. Nall, Alexandria; T/5 Ernest W. Kidd, Bastin, transferred from Kennedy General Hospital, Memphis, Tenn.;

Pfc. Leonard Whitlock, Winchester; Pvt. Harry W. Bean, Elkton; Pvt. Maynard E. Salyers, Bandy; Sgt. Kenneth A. Eckert, Richmond; Pfc. William F. Grigsby, Amissville; T/5 John P. Hewlett, Richmond; T/5 James E. Compton, Christiansburg; First Lieutenant Robert L. Thomason, Arlington; Capt. Clarence E. Major, Stormont.

Plecker Building Sold At Auction For Over $19,225

As agent for F. C. Hamer, J. Earl Jones, Charlie Crafton and City Manager W. L. Hall, Joseph M. Wayman purchased at public auction yesterday the Plecker Building at 109-117 North Augusta Street for $19,225.

According to Mr. Hall, the men have "absolutely no plans" now as to what they will do with the property.

Owned by the late Emma Plecker Cassell, the building consists of six large four-room apartments and three ground-floor store rooms.

The sale, which began at ten a. m., was cried by Clay McClure.

JAPANESE NOW FACE THREAT UTTER DESTRUCTION, EXISTENCE OF MIGHTY WEAPON NOW KNOWN

Washington, Aug. 6—(AP)—The new atomic bombs are now being turned on the islands of Japan by United States bombers. The Japanese face a threat of utter desolation, and their capitulation may be greatly speeded up.

Existence of the great new weapon was announced personally by President Truman in a statement issued through the White House at 11 a. m., Eastern War Time. He said the first atomic bomb, invented and perfected in the United States, had been dropped on the Japanese army base of Hiroshima.

That one bomb alone carried a wallop more violent than 2,000 B-29 Superfortresses normally could hand an enemy city, using old type TNT bombs.

Secretary of War Stimson followed through with a statement that the blast stirred a cloud of smoke and dust so impenetrable as to make immediate, accurate observation of results impossible. The power of the bomb, Stimson said, is such as to "stagger the imagination" and he asserted it would "prove a tremendous aid" in shortening the Japanese war.

Stimson's emphasis on this point renewed speculation all over again as to whether Japan may be completely crushed by air attack without invasion.

Mr. Truman noted that the Japanese rejected the Big Three surrender ultimatum from Potsdam, and that this had been intended to spare the Japanese people from "utter destruction."

Now, he said, with the new bomb, the Japanese "may expect a rain of ruin from the air, the like of which has never been seen on this earth."

The announcement heralded an Anglo-American victory at a cost of $2,000,000,000 in one of the grimmest battles of the war—the battle of the laboratories—to unlock the secrets of the atom and yoke its energies to military use.

The Germans were striving desperately to win this highly secret contest in the closing months of the European struggle.

Scientists agreed that a new epoch in both war and peace is probably at hand. Although much experimenting remains to be done, this newly controlled energy can doubtless also be used to drive rockets, planes, ships and trains for constructive as well as destructive purposes.

President Truman said the new bomb, which draws its energy from the same sources as the sun, had more power than 20,000 tons of TNT, itself a tremendously powerful explosive.

By another standard, Mr. Truman declared the bomb has 2,000 times the blast power of the British "grand slam" bomb—the most concentrated bundle of destruction previously known on earth.

In fact, in evaluating the enormous power involved in this new weapon, the President had to reach beyond the limits of the earth for comparison.

"It is a harnessing of the basic power of the universe," he said. "The force from which the sun draws its power has been loosed against those who brought war to the Far East."

This line appeared to hold dramatic possibilities for propaganda against the Japanese. They regard their Emperor Hirohito as a direct descendant of the sun god now they can be told that the very power of the sun itself is being turned to their destruction.

President Truman, as he was nearing American shores on the Cruiser Augusta, homeward bound from the Potsdam Conference, and Secretary Stimpson worked together to tell all that can be told at this time of the revolutionary new weapon.

Still thick secrecy shoruds much of the atomic bomb work despite the intense excitement in the usually staid government offices, which attended today's startling announcement. Its size has not been revealed, beyond the statement that the size of the explosive charge is exceedingly small. Nor was it told how the atoms are stored for the moment of explosion.

Escaped Convicts Caught On Hunch In Baltimore

Baltimore police last night notified R. G. Holt, superintendent of the State Limegrinding Plant, that two convicts who escaped from the plant Saturday afternoon were apprehended in Baltimore yesterday.

Mr. Holt said that he wired Baltimore on a hunch that the escapees had fled there, and received a wire at approximately seven p. m. that they had been found.

The men, Leo Major and Oliver Richards, will be returned to the plant as soon as arrangements can be made, the superintendent said. They made their get-away Saturday in a load-lugger truck used in the plant quarry.

COL. JOHN MINOR MEDICAL CONSULTANT VISITS ARMY HOSPITAL

Colonel John Minor, medical consultant of the Third Service Command, paid an official visit to Woodrow Wilson General Hospital yesterday. He was formerly chief of medical service at the local institution.

MUST PRESENT MILEAGE RATIONING RECORD WITH APPLICATION, SAYS BOARD

... rations, War Price and Rationing Board officials would like to call the attention of those under the jurisdiction of the Staunton Board to the fact that it is absolutely necessary to present a mileage rationing record with each application before gasoline rations can be approved.

This is true of furlough gas rations and rations for discharged veterans, it was stated. If relatives and friends of soldiers and veterans will pass the information on, it will help to prevent needless trips to the board.

It requires about ten days to process a gasoline application, so applicants are asked to anticipate their needs and give the board ample time to put the application through the regular channels.

FIRST TEST OF ATOMIC BOMB OPERATED BY ROBOT AMAZES, STARTLES BLIND 120 MI. AWAY

Los Alamos, N. M., Aug. 6—(AP)—A blinding flash followed within 40 seconds by a shuddering explosion that sent a huge multicolored cloud roaring upward to an altitude of 40,000 feet and caused reverberations felt for a 25-mile radius across New Mexico and Arizona marked the first test of the new destructive atomic bomb, conducted July 16 at a remote location on the Alamogordo, N. M., army air base.

The steel tower which held the bomb was melted and turned into vapor by the blast, and in the earth of the remote New Mexico desert test ground a deep crater was gouged.

As winds dispersed the mass that had shot into the stratosphere in five minutes, and the tremendous pressure wave that knocked down two men standing five miles away passed over, the scientists and military authorities whispered, "this is it." They said the test of their $2,000,000,000 experiment was successful beyond all hope.

They had observed the test from ten miles. In disclosing details of the bomb which hit Japan for the first time today, the army quoted them today as seeing a ball of fire "many times brighter than the mid-day sun."

The brilliant flash startled a blind girl, Miss Georgia Green, 120 miles away, and she asked "what's that?" Windows rattled at Gallup, N. M., 250 miles northwest.

"It was just like the sun had come up and then suddenly gone down again," one witness 150 miles west remarked.

In the control center, Dr. James B. Conant, president of Harvard University, and J. R. Oppenheimer, director of the atomic laboratory, stared ahead in the long seconds just before the blast.

When the announcer shouted "now!" and there came a burst of light followed shortly by a deep growling roar, Oppenheimer's face relaxed in tremendous relief.

What Observers Saw

The test had been delayed an hour and a half by a thunderstorm which prevented aerial observation.

So terrific was the blast that the Associated Press in New Mexico and Arizona received numerous inquiries, some an airline distance of 250 miles from the blast scene, regarding an earthquake.

Maj. Gen. Leslie R. Groves, head of the atomic bomb project for the War Department, said the shock wave reached the observers about 40 seconds after the flash of light, then came the sound itself.

"A massive cloud was formed which surged and billowed upward with tremendous power, reaching the substratosphere in about five minutes," Major Groves said.

Two supplementary explosions of minor effect other than the lighting occurred in the cloud shortly after the main explosion.

"The cloud traveled to a great height first in the form of a ball, then mushroomed, then changed into a long trailing chimney-shaped column and finally was sent in several directions by the variable winds."

Brig. Gen. Thomas F. Farrell, Groves' assistant, said "no man-made phenomenon of such tremendous power had ever occurred before.

"The whole country was lighted by a searing light with an intensity many times that of the mid-day sun," he continued. "It was golden, purple, violet, gray and blue. It lighted every peak, crevasse, and ridge of the nearby mountains with a clarity and beauty that cannot be described. xxx"

Farrell expressed the belief the discovery would bring speedy conclusion of the war with Japan and predicted that it would prove to be "immeasurably more important than the discovery of electricity or any other great discoveries which so affected our existence."

Other witnesses of the test were J. R. Oppenheimer, director of the atomic bomb laboratory here; Dr. Vannevar Bush, head of the office of scientific research and development; Dr. James B. Conant, president of Harvard University. The detonation was in charge of Dr. K. T. Brainbridge, of Massachusetts Institute of Technology.

The test bomb was assembled in a deserted ranch house the night of July 12, its parts having been shipped in from different plants.

Only one hitch came during the assembly when one of the machine-tooled parts wedged. After a delay of only three minutes the bomb was completed.

It was mounted to the top of the steel tower July 14 and two days were spent in preparation for the detonation.

The several observation points were tied into the control by radio with 20 minutes to go. At "minus 45 seconds" a robot took over "the complicated mass of intricate mechanism."

AFTER 3 MONTHS CAMPAIGNING CANDIDATES AWAIT TODAY'S VOTE

Richmond, Va., Aug. 6—(AP)—For months candidates for the Democratic nomination for Governor and Lieutenant Governor have endeavored to get the attention of war-minded Virginians. The primary tomorrow will show how successful they were and by whom the voters were impressed.

Lieutenant Governor William M. Tuck, who has the backing of the State Democratic Organization headed by United States Senator Harry F. Byrd, ended his campaign here today with a statement predicting he would be nominated by a big majority, and left for his home at South Boston. His opponent, Moss A. Plunkett, of Roanoke, who has campaigned against what he termed "machine mis-rule" in Virginia, finished his campaign with a radio address over station WOPI at Bristol tonight.

Radio Addresses

All three of the candidates for the nomination for Lieutenant Governor made election eve addresses. Senator Leonard Muse, of Roanoke, who has not been aligned with the dominant state Democratic organization, spoke today at Rocky Mount in Franklin County. Charles R. Fenwick, of Arlington, finished his campaign with a radio address broadcast over radio stations WRVA and WMBG here tonight. Lewis Preston Collins, of Smyth, spoke from Lynchburg over radio station WLVA and his talk was rebroadcast by station WRVA at Richmond, WDBJ at Roanoke, WBTM at Danville, WOPI at Bristol and WGH at Newport News. Both Fenwick and Collins are Byrd organization stalwarts.

No one expected that tomorrow's vote would even approximate the record vote of 388,000 cast in the general election for President last fall, but all expected the vote to go above the 85,000 who participated in the referendum on a Constitutional Convention on March 6. All candidates appealed to Democrats to participate, But I. R. Dovel, Republican state chairman, urged voters of "independent thought" to stay out of the primary and remain free to vote for Republican nominee in the fall.

Organization Working

It is generally conceded that the Democratic organization will get a good number of voters to the polls, and that a small total vote will favor the organization.

Organization wheelhorses were taking nothing for granted, however, and were seeking to get out the vote for Tuck in view of the strenuous campaign waged by Plunkett for what he has called his "progressive program," and against what he has termed "a handpicked candidate."

Tuck has praised the Democratic administration in Virginia, and has promised to keep the state free of debt, but has committed himself to keep the state free of debt, but has committed himself to greater state support for and further expansion of education, health, welfare and farm service and to an expanded building and highway program. He said he saw no need for increased taxes now.

Plunkett has denounced the Denny School Commission report and its six-year program and announced himself for a state appropriation of $100 er child in average daily school attendance now. He has criticised the "machine" for "penny pinching" and has asserted that its policies have brought Virginia near the bottom of the states in education, health and welfare services.

VANDENBERG TO GUARANTEE FREE PRESS

Washington, Aug. 6—(AP)—Senator Vandenberg (R-Mich) demanded today that the Big Three specifically guarantee the free access of an uncensored American press into Poland and other "blacked-out areas of Europe."

He asserted in a statement that what he called "rhetorical reference" in the Potsdam communique by President Truman, Prime Minister Attlee and Generalissimo Stalin to "free elections" and a "free press" is not a sufficient guarantee.

With Mr. Truman expected to return to the White House soon, Vandenberg expressed hope that the President "will shortly give us definite word that uncensored American correspondent actually have been admitted" to Poland, Romania, Bulgaria, Hungary and Finland.

FIRE DESTROYS LARGE BARN ELLISON FARM

Spontaneous combustion, caused by green hay is believed to have been the origin of a fire which swept the Ellison Farm, three miles west of Waynesboro on White Bridge Road, Sunday afternoon, destroying property valued at between $10,000 and $12,000.

County firemen reported last night that they were called out Sunday at three-fifty, and again Monday morning at ten-twenty when the still-smouldering grain alarmed the farm residents. The Waynesboro Fire Department was also summoned, and neighbors assisted by forming a bucket brigade.

Flames consumed a feed mill and grain drill as well as hay, straw, wheat, barley, and an unestimated number of chickens and turkeys.

W. G. Ellison, who leases the property from his sister, Miss Eva Ellison of Waynesboro, said all damages were covered by insurance.

Central Club To Sponsor Picnic At Harper's Camp

The Men's Club of Central Methodist Church will sponsor a basket picnic at the Harpers' Camp, on Wednesday evening, August 8. A cordial invitation is extended to all men of the church and their families to be present. This will take the place of the regular August meeting of the club.

Weyers Cave To Open Cannery Today And Friday

The Weyers Cave community cannery will be open on Tuesday, Aug. 7 and Friday, Aug. 10 from 8 a. m. until 2 p. m.; also on Wednesday, Aug. 8 from 1 until 4:30 p. m. Beginning Tuesday, Aug. 14, the cannery will be open each Tuesday, Wednesday and Friday from 8 until 2 p. m. until further notice.

Easy to See How Atomic Power Could Destroy Most Mankind, Says Scientist

New York, Aug. 6—(AP)—The atomic bomb, by official description, is probably just a beginning of a new science, and not the terrific thing the size of a football or maybe a stove, that could wipe New York off the map in one explosion.

But is the opening wedge, and the terrifying aspect at present is that no man can know how far its destructive effects may be developed.

The President said this bomb is 2000 times more powerful than the British "earthquake" bomb. But that does not mean it can spread its destruction 2000 times farther. Air and earth cushion explosions, so that their effects fall off rapidly in distance.

The British bomb, for example, was unofficially given a radius of utter destruction of 100 yards, meaning a circle 200 yards in diameter. A bomb 2000 times more powerful would probably cause equal destruction over a diameter of a mile or a little more.

The air waves would carry secondary destructive effects, like bowling over unstable walls and smash-windows for many miles.

The official reports say that uranium is the basic atomic material.

This uranium drama began in the early thirties, in Italy, as something quite different. There Enrico Fermi, physicist, now a Columbia University professor and one of the scientists who developed the atomic bomb principles, was using powerful electronic and atomic rays to bombard solid matter. He got what he reported to be a new chemical element, which he called uranium 93. The Italian Senate in Rome broadcast this discovery.

Work in Laboratories

In other world-famous laboratories physicists went to work and for nearly 10 years got nowhere. They could not verify the new element. They got, out of their experiments a lot of chemical elements of a mass, or weight, about half way between hydrogen, lightest element, and uranium the most massive.

Then just as the present world-war was starting Lize Meitner, a German jewess, a mathematician, made a clever guess. She said, if your experiments are splitting an atom of uranium about in two equal parts, then all the puzzles can be explained. She made mathematical calculations to prove the point.

Dr. Neils Bohr, Danish physicist, who afterward escaped the Nazis to England and the United States, learned of Dr. Meitner's calculations. He brodcast them.

Inside two weeks the physicists of Columbia University, Carnegie Institute, of Washington, Johns Hopkins and other places, and of England and France had made the test and proved the German woman right.

Incredible Shock

But what an incredible shock they got. They split uranium easily with Neutron particule rays. And when one single uranium atom split, it released 200,000,000 (two hundred million) electron volts of energy.

One pound of T. N. T. releases five electron volts energy for each molecule of the explosive. And there are usually millions of atoms in one molecule.

All the scientists of all countries saw the result. There wasn't anything secret about it. Germany, England, France and the United States went to work. Japan may have done so too.

Considerably more of this story, about how to cause a chain reaction so that a piece of uranium would blow up all at once was published before censorship clamped a world wide blackout on atomic bombs.

There are three kinds of uranium and the explosion occurred in the atoms of only one. The three are uranium 235, 238 and 234. The only known differences are in atomic weight. Only 235 exploded atomically. In one ton of commercial uranium there are 14 pounds of 235 and two ounces of 234.

May Be 235

The huge size of the American atomic bomb plants and the official descriptions of the great quantities of materials shipped into them indicate that 235 probably has been the main source of the new bomb.

It may not be the only one, for Secretary Stimpson said another chemical element is giving off atomic power in the form of heat, which is still too meagre to run a steam engine. And Winston Churchill told of raids on a Norwegian heavy water plant. Heavy water is deuterium, or heavy hydrogen, which means hydrogen atoms of twice ordinary weight.

It is easy to see how atomic power could be used to destroy most of mankind. In principle it is not yet easy to see how the earth could be destroyed, as was suggested to Ambassador Winant recently by Commander Herbert Agar, an officer who had learned the atomic bomb secrets.

The principle under which the earth ought to stay put is that when it explodes one kind of atom does not necessarily explode any other kind, and there are 92 kinds. Uranium is a comparatively rare chemical element. The 235 variety is more rare. If all the uranium were to blow up, it still would not be likely to start the atomic ... that would disintegrate the rest of the earth.

August 8, 1945: The U.S. drops an atom bomb on Japan in an effort to bring the war to a quick conclusion. *Microfilm Archives*

View of the interior of a barn at the Gypsy Hill Park fairgrounds during an agricultural show. In addition to this display of implements and vehicles for Wards Farm Store, some entrepreneurial recruiter has posted a sign that reads, "Volunteers Needed for the United States Army. Enlist now, Don't wait." *Schwartz Collection*

This Staunton Evening Leader photograph of 18-year-old Shirley Selby holding up a copy of the paper announcing Japan's surrender gained nationwide fame at the time. The photo was wired all over the country and, since World War II, has been duplicated in many publications. Selby typified the euphoria most Americans felt when Japan gave up in the wake of two atomic bomb attacks at Hiroshima and Nagasaki. This picture was taken in the middle of Beverley Street in front of Hogshead's pharmacy. *Schwartz Collection*

PEACE!

FIFTY - FIVE YEARS IN THE PUBLIC SERVICE
Oldest Virginia Daily West of the Blue Ridge

The Staunton News-Leader

THE WEATHER
Wednesday, showers. Thursday fair and cooler and less humid.

56th YEAR. NO. 162 | ASSOCIATED PRESS AND (AP) FEATURES AUDIT BUREAU CIRCULATIONS | STAUNTON, VIRGINIA, WEDNESDAY MORNING, AUGUST 15, 1945 | MORNING LEADER ESTABLISHED 1905 DAILY NEWS ESTABLISHED 1890 | PRICE THREE CENTS

History's Most Destructive War Comes to End by Surrender

COUNTY FUND FOR VISUAL EDUCATION

To discuss selection and use of film projectors and films for use in classrooms and auditoriums of Waynesboro and Augusta County Schools, Martin L. Hogan, supervisor of the Bureau of Teaching Materials, State Department of Education, met with school officials at two-fifteen here yesterday.

At its last special session, the Legislature made available over a million dollars for the purchase of projectors and films and other teaching materials, Superintendent of County Schools A. C. Gilkeson pointed out.

$17,462 Is Allocated

Allocations for the county and Waynesboro, made on the basis of $2 per pupil on enrollment, total $17,462. This was evidently allotted on the basis of 8,741 original entries in the schools of the county and Waynesboro for the 1943-1944, the superintendent said. Waynesboro schools had 1,818 original entries and would be entitled to $3,636. Other schools in the county had 6923 originals and the amount given them would be $13,846.

Already county school officials have bought over $2,000 worth of films and a few projectors, but because their purchase came near the close of the last school session, they have not been used, Mr. Gilkeson said that additional equipment may be available by the first of next year.

Present at Discussion

Present at the discussion yesterday were Superintendent Gilkeson; Miss R. Alice Keane, rural elementary supervisor; D. C. Berry, county director of instruction; Robert T. McElhaney, principal of Fishersville; C. W. Swartz, New Hope principal; R. C. Jennings, supervising principal of Waynesboro schools; Lloyd Chew, principal of Thomas Jefferson Grammar School, Staunton; Colin E. Smither, principal of Robert E. Lee High School, Staunton; Miss Kate E. Drake, teacher at Lee High.

Mr. Hogan, who has visited Staunton once previously, was scheduled to lead a similar discussion at Madison College yesterday afternoon at four-thirty. He will visit various other schools in this section within the next few days.

MAYOR WILLIAM A. GRUBERT'S VICTORY DAY PROCLAMATION ISSUED

"I hereby declare this V-J Day and a legal holiday.

In accordance with the suggestion made by the several committees on the city's V-J Day celebration, I request that the day be celebrated in a spirit of thanksgiving that all the churches in the community be opened to the public. I urge that there be no riotous celebration, but rather one of devout thanksgiving that hostilities have ceased, remembering in our jubilation the thousands of boys who have given their lives and the families of these boys. How nobly they fulfilled their duties and bore their responsibilities is forever settled.

"The purpose of the day should be to thank God for the great victory of principle. The divine glory of justice, and righteous war triumph.

The sounding of fire alarm 99 signified that the end of the war. All merchants are requested to display the national emblem and close their places of business in accordance with the announcement made by the Retail Merchants and Business Men's Association of our city.

"The ABC store has ceased selling alcoholic beverages as well as all stores having beer and wine license."

ROBERTSON IS SPEAKER AT BROADWAY

Broadway, Va., Aug. 14— (AP) — Rep. Robertson (D-Va.) said tonight the United States must take four more steps to do its part in preserving world peace. He urged:

1. Enactment of legislation outlining powers of this nation's delegate to the United Nations Security Council.

2. Formulation at a conference next autumn, and approval by the Senate, of a treaty for western hemisphere defense.

Approval by the Senate of a treaty establishing the U. S. quota of forces and facilities for use by the United Nations Security Council.

Approval by the Senate of the treaty ending the war.

FARM BUREAU PICNIC AUG. 16 AT A. M. A.

Major C. S. Roller Jr. has invited the Augusta Cooperative Farm Bureau Association to hold their annual picnic at A. M. A. starting at ten a. m. Aug. 16. Moving pictures will be shown at ten followed at ten-forty-five by group singing. At ten-fifty-five invocation will be pronounced by the Rev. H. Ruffner Lowman. At eleven o'clock the business meeting will be held at which time the state auditors report will be read, a general report read by the manager giving the general report of the services of the cooperative, and outline of plans of development. Half of the board of directors will be elected at this time too.

At 12:30 the meeting will adjourn for a picnic basket lunch.

Afternoon of Recreation

The afternoon will be devoted to recreation of which Ernest B. Craun will be chairman. There will be four softball teams organized the captains of which are: Fairfield, Red Runkle; Staunton, Cecil Bowman; Weyers Cave, P. M. Dice; and Waynesboro, Elwood Shifflett. H. D. Hawkins will be umpire. The captains are urged to meet Mr. Hawkins at 1:45 to draw for first round. D. L. Glick and J. C. Layman are to be in charge of the swimmnig pool. Richard Coffey will be in charge of the horseshoe throwing contest, and J. M. Gorsline will police the tug of war.

It is hoped that music may be arranged for the large auditorium where the children and ladies can go.

The Farm Bureau wishes to thank Major Roller for his kindness and trouble in arranging the picnic.

The program for the day is as follows:

Forenoon

10:00 Moving pictures, Office of War Information.
10:45 Group singing.
10:55 Invocation, H. Ruffner Lowman, pastor, Olivet Presbyterian Church. Song, America.
11:00 Business meeting, Secretary report, election of officers, annual reports, general discussion.
12:25 Announcements.
12:30 Adjourn with picnic lunch.

Afternoon

2:00 Recreation, Softball, Tug o' war, horseshoe pitching, swimming.

"The directors have arranged this meeting hoping that you will have a most educational and pleasant day," states Ray S. Cline, general manager

(Continued on Page 3, Col 6)

GREAT CROWDS FLOCK TO LAWN OF WHITE HOUSE TO LISTEN AS PRESIDENT OF U. S. SPEAKS

Washington, Aug. 14—(AP)—Britain, Russia and China today agreed with the United States to accept Japan's surrender note—without ever seeing it.

The agreement was worked out verbally by Secretary of State Byrnes in a worldwide telephone call which he made from the Pentagon Building late this afternoon. He talked with officials in London, Moscow and Chungking, told them of a report on the enemy message which he had received by telephone from American Minister Leland Harrison in Bern, Switzerland.

He assured them that he considered the note a complete acceptance of the Potsdam ultimatum for unconditional surrender, and they agreed.

This dramatic incident in a historic day was revealed tonight by an assistant to Byrnes, Walter Bown, who told the inside story of the day-long activities by which the secretary handled details of the surrender agreement.

Washington, Aug. 14—(AP)—The Second World War, history's greatest flood of death and destruction, ended tonight with Japan's unconditional surrender.

Formalities still remained—the official signing of surrender terms and a proclamation of V-J Day.

But from the moment President Truman announced at 7 p. m., Eastern War Time, that the enemy of the Pacific had agreed to Allied terms, the world put aside for a time woeful thoughts of the cost in death and dollars and celebrated in wild frenzy. Formalities meant nothing to people freed at last of war.

To reporters crammed into his office shoving now-useless war maps against a marble mantle, the President disclosed that:

Japan, without ever being invaded, had accepted completely and without reservation an Allied declaration of Potsdam dictating unconditional surrender.

General Douglas MacArthur had been designed Supreme Allied commander, the man to receive surrender.

There is to be no power for the Japanese Emperor—although Allies will let him remain their tool. No longer will the war lords reign, through him. Hirohito—or any successor—will take orders from MacArthur.

Allied forces were ordered to "suspend offensive action" everywhere.

From now on, only men under 26 will be drafted. Army draft calls will be cut from 80,000 a month to 50,000. Mr. Truman forecast that five to five and a half million soldiers may be released within 12 to 18 months.

The surrender announcement set in motion a whole chain of events. Among them:

To a Japanese government which once had boasted it would dictate peace terms in the White House, Mr. Truman dispatched orders to "direct prompt cessation of hostilities," tell MacArthur of the effective date and hour, and send emissaries to the general to arrange formal surrender.

Manpower Controls End

The War Manpower Commission terminated all manpower controls.

The navy piled a $6,000,000,000 cancellation of contracts on top of a previous $1,200,000,000 cut in its shipbuilding program.

Congress was summoned back to work on Sept. 5, more than a month ahead of schedule, to get busy on unemployment compensation, surplus property disposal, full employment, government reorganization and the continuation or abolition of war agencies.

The office of censorship said it was getting ready to fold up. News, radio and mail censorship are due to end on V-J Day.

Washington, Aug. 14— (AP) — President Truman tonight proclaimed August 15 and 16 as legal holidays with the stipulation that war workers who work on those days would be paid overtime.

SON OF SUN NOW IS TO TAKE ORDERS FROM GEN. DOUG. M'ARTHUR

Washington, Aug. 14—(AP)—Now Emperor Hirohito — whom the Japanese believe descended from the sun — becomes a mouthpiece for the Allies.

General Douglas MacArthur, appointed Supreme Allied Commander to receive the Japanese surrender, will tell Hirohito what to do.

The Japanese understood this when they accepted the surrender terms. Nothing like this—taking orders from a white man or any foreigner—has ever before happened to a Japanese Emperor.

Hirohito has no choice. He has agreed to carry out whatever orders given him by the Allies.

WEDNESDAY IS MADE HOLIDAY BY DARDEN

Richmond, Aug. 14—A few minutes after President Truman announced the Japanese acceptance of surrender terms, Governor Darden issued a proclamation designating Wednesday as a state holiday. Concurrently, Mayor Herbert declared Wednesday and Thursday holidays for the city of Richmond.

The Governor in his first proclamation set both Wednesday and Thursday as legal holidays, but later retracted his statement, limiting the legal holiday to Wednesday, because he feared that the closing of banks would result in serious inconvenience to business firms and depositors.

Asked if he had heard that the war was over, Governor Darden exclaimed, "Yes, thank God!"

The text of the statement accompanying the Governor's proclamation follows:

Text of Message

"By the mercy of God we have escaped the incalcuable disaster that has overhung Western Civilization these recent years. The bloody tide of Conquest, embracing within its violent and turbulent sweep, enslavement, and unspeakable degradation, has been beaten back by the incredible exertions and courage of men and women determined to be free. We have destroyed the shackles forged for us in the arsenals of tyranny and have overthrown those who fashioned them for the thralldom of humanity. The guns have ceased to thunder around the world. Thank God we are at peace again.

"In honor of those Virginians who constitute Virginia's contribution to the fighting forces of our nation, I proclaim Wednesday, Aug. 15, a state holiday. I urge our people to observe it in prayer and thanksgiving for our deliverance and I ask them to rededicate themselves to those principles of humanity and justice without which a free society cannot exist."

MARSHAL HENRI PETAIN CONVICTED AND SENTENCED TO DIE BY FRENCH COURT

Paris, Wednesday, Aug. 15—(AP)—Marshal Henri Philippe Petain was convicted and sentenced to death early today by three judges and a 24-man jury who deliberated almost seven hours.

STAUNTONIANS GO WILD OVER NEWS THAT JAPANESE FOLD UP, LAUGHTER AND SONG REIGN

The war is over!

That stupendous news thrilled all Staunton to the depths last night, producing wild jubilation in some quarters, and wringing tearful prayers of thanksgiving in others.

Reserve flew to the wind as hundreds of merrymakers thronged the city streets for several hours, church bells rang, car horns tooted incessantly, children and grownups alike shouted and sang. Fire engines sailed down the street at intervals with bells clanging and sirens screaming.

Chief of Police E. L. Bragg roped off a block on New Street above the Strand theater, and gala crowds danced to tunes furnished by jeep and radio.

Numerous Queries

As The Leader Office went to press with an extra edition, telephones rang constantly and quaries of "Can it really be true?", "Does it mean the war is actually over?", and "Is it official?" greeted staff members. Upon confirmation, there were cries of happiness, and not a few reverent "Thank Gods."

Fire signal 99 signified the war's end here, and was followed at first by small commotion which grew until the streets were in near-bedlam. As many Police Department members as possible were called to duty as were 8 extra military policemen from Woodrow Wilson General Hospital. The crowd generally was orderly but enthusiastic.

After they had received official word, policemen toured restaurants and other places with ABC licenses, asking that they close.

Through all the noise and exhilliration ran a note of sadness as there came the thought of the many who have paid the supreme sacrifice that this victory might be achieved. Some residents gathered in the city churches to worship and offer thankful prayers that the grim holacaust is ended.

Stores To Close

All places of business will be closed today in accordance with action taken by the Retail Merchants Association.

Firemen were called out five times on false alarms. The first call was sounded at eight o'clock from Box 25, the second at eight-fourteen from Box 39, the third at ten-fifty-eight from Box 57, the fourth from Box 64 at 11:54 and the fifth at twelve-fifteen from Box 44.

Du Pont plant officials in Waynesboro announced that that plant will continue in operation throughout the official holiday.

At eleven this morning, brief services are scheduled to be held at the open air theater at Woodrow Wilson General Hospital to which Staunton people have been cordially invited. Colonel Haskett L. Conner, post commander, will open the assembly with the reading of the proclamation of the commanding general, Third Service Command, and a few brief remarks.

Lieut. Col. Cliff K. Titus, post chaplain will deliver a short address to the group, and will be followed by Major John I. Kane, Catholic chaplain, who will offer a prayer of benediction. The service will conclude with the singing of the Star Spangled Banner.

Colonel Titus has also been asked to make the main address at memorial services, sponsored by the American Legion, to be held in the Courthouse at two-thirty p. m. today.

Mayor William A. Grubert and all City Councilmen have been extended a special invitation to attend this program which will consist of several brief talks and several musical selections.

Thanksgiving Services

Two thanksgiving services will be held in the city tonight.

One is to be held at Ebenezer Baptist Church, the other at Central Methodist church. The services will be held at eight o'clock, and an identical form of worship will be used in each church.

Ministers participating in the service to be held at Ebenezer Church are: the Revs. R. C. Pannell D. D., Melvin Law, J. P. Dabney, and T. J. Jemison.

Ministers to take part in the service at Central Church are: the Revs. H. Ruffner Lowman Jr., Edwin W. Moffitt, J. Lewis Gibbs, D. D., D. N. Welford, and Melvin S. Lange.

The order of worship will consist of four parts: thanksgiving for

(Continued on Page 3, Col 6)

Captain Archie Sproul, Staunton, Tells How Little French Boy Saved Virginians

Richmond, Aug. 14.—(AP)—A Staunton, Virginian told today of a bright-eyed French lad, 16, credited with saving the lives of countless Virginians when the famous 29th Division made its historic landing in Normandy on D-Day, June 6, 1944.

Captain Archie Sproul, here visiting his sister, Mrs. Frank E. Taylor Jr., of 1102 Seminary Place, said: 'I shall never forget him. You know something of what the Twenty-Ninth faced; they said later our regiment caught it worse than other outfits, and I guess they're right. You perhaps remember we had some bad luck, such as running smack into a German division that was on maneuvers.

Hit the Beach

"Well, we hit the beach and our losses were running heavy. We were under fire of all descriptions. But, we fought our way slowly on through the fields and hedgerows.

"In the middle of it all, up popped this little French boy, right out of nowhere. He said he had been forced to work on the beach defenses by the Germans. He said he was anxious to help the Americans. Naturally, we shoved him aside."

However, when a battery of German 155's began a "particularly hellish bombardment," Sproul said, "up popped Jean again," and started to find out where the battery was located. He dodged through Allied lines and then through the German lines, found out where the 155's were grouped and reported. "We had radio contact with our heavy ships offshore, so we called for naval shelling, and we told them the exact point to hit."

Capt. Sproul said: "Jean did it—Jean and the navy, but the navy wouldn't have had a chance without him. And we wouldn't either."

Sproul Rifle Company

Captain Sproul commanded a rifle company in the assault. Young, dark-haired and square-jawed, he is himself one of the war's heroes. Willing to talk about others but not himself, his own family doesn't know the circumstances that brought him the Distinguished Service Cross. In addition, he has the Purple Heart with Oak Leaf Cluster.

He went with the Twenty-Ninth all the way, except for two short "vacations" when he was wounded.

Back to Jean.

To get back to Jean, Captain Sproul said: "The Twenty-Ninth took that kid to its heart. We got him an American uniform, a piece here and a piece there. Not a very good fit, but he didn't seem to mind. He was so anxious to help; he ran every errand to be run. He went out under terrific fire, time after time, and brought in wounded men.

"He stayed right with us until the commanding general came around. The men would always hide him. He went with us and he was there when I had to leave, after being wounded the second time. I don't know where he is now but I can tell you where he'll always stay—that's right in the hearts of the Twenty-Ninth Division."

STAUNTON MFG. CO. PLANT ONE DONATES TO FIRST CALL FUND

Over one thousand dollars has been subscribed to the First Call Home Fund, by generous persons so that soldiers at WWGH may call their parents, wives or sweethearts, upon their arrival here.

A bill for $239.61, however, has just been received representing almost two hundred calls from July 30 to Aug. 11. This leaves a balance of a ebtter over $500 on hand, so it may readily be seen that the money is paid out almost as fast as it came in, and only one call is allowed each patient.

An outstanding contribution today is $30.75, from employees of Plant One, Staunton Mfg. Co. These men and women invariably help on nay worthy cause and are to be commended for their splendid cooperation. Another is one from the Worthwhile Bible Class of Central Church.

Here is how the contributions stand:

Woman's Missionary Society, Pleasant View Lutheran Church	$ 5.00
Mr. and Mrs. Geo. B. Powers	10.00
Worthwhile Bible Class	25.00
Miss Nettie M. Kanost	2.00
Virginia Campbell	2.00
Alanna Critzer	1.00
Fairfield Ruritan Club	5.00
Employees, Plant 1, Staunton Mfg. Co.	30.75
	$ 80.75
Previously acknowledged	953.00
Total	$1033.75

Leader Linotype Operator's Sister Has Polio Attack

Mrs. L. M. Crotts, daughter of Mr. and Mrs. B. C. Kincely Sr. of Port Defiance, was stricken Aug. 3 with a mild case of poliomyelitis, according to word received here by her family. It was necessary to place her under quarantine in her home at Tacoma Park, Md. because of the lack of facilities to handle such cases in hospitals of that vicinity.

Her condition was believed to be better, and at last communications to her family, no paralysis had set in.

She is the former Miss Rosebud Knicely, a sister of Carroll Knicely, a Leader Papers' linotype operator.

BAPTISTS AND UNITED BRETHREN CONGREGATIONS TO HOLD JOINT SERVICE

There will be a special prayer, praise and thanksgiving services at the United Brethren Church, Wednesday night at 7:45.

This will be a union service of the Baptist and the United Brethren, and all who wish to attend will be welcome.

Come let us give thanks to God, for bringing this war to an end and express to him our gratitude for his loving kindness. And let us pray for a permanent peace.

Newspaper Carrier Has Bicycle Stolen Waiting For Extras

Victory celebration brought a measure of unhappiness to a small Negro boy, Walter Hart, 146 Straigth Street, one of The Leader Papers delivery boys. While he waited in front of the office for extras to come off the press, someone removed his bicycle from the alley beside the office.

The bicycle was described as a "streamlined" black and white model, bearing squirrel tails on the handlebars. Anyone having any information as to the whereabouts of the cycle are asked to contact this office.

SHENANDOAH VALLEY ELECTRIC CO-OPERATIVE RE-ELECTS ITS OLD BOARD AT DAYTON MEETING

Dayton, Va. August 14—Following one of the most enthusiastic meetings yet held the Shenandoah Valley Electric Co-Operative membership expressed its faith in the management of the organization by re-electing the full slate of board of directors.

The board is made up as follows: W. W. Trimble, W. M. Harris, J. C. Horn, E. A. Jordan, A. E. Krause, Howard May, W. H. Wright, J. H. Burner, D. W. Burress, H. L. Garber and M. S. Swartz.

Considerable interest centered in the address delivered by officers of the co-operative, the principal one being that of President D. W. Burruss, who spoke in part as follows:

"It gives me a great deal of pleasure to welcome all of you to our annual meeting. Some of you have traveled quite a distance at considerable inconvenience just to be on hand to take part in running your cooperative.

"This co operative is one of the largest business organizations in this region. It is operated by and for the rural people who make their living from the soil. It became a big business because its members weren't afraid to apply age-old principles to modern-day problems, in order to accomplish results. It is strictly a private business enterprise which grew out of the initiative of the members.

"Many people would have said a few years ago, that bunch of farmers had no business trying to do something they knew nothing about, like running a rural electric system. Back in the old days we were told that electricity was just something the farmers couldn't afford to have unless they lived on the edge of town.

"It was just about nine years when the first little group of men in this territory got together to see if they couldn't do something about organizing their own rural electric system. They believed that if the power companies couldn't supply electric service at a reasonable cost, they themselves could do so on a cooperative basis. I am glad to see that most of those men are here with us today.

"We applied for and obtained an REA loan of $125,000.00 to cover costs of building 125 miles of line to serve three hundred consumers. It was a happy day for all of us in January 1936 when the switch was thrown to energize the first one hundred miles of line in Rockingham, Augusta and Shenandoah Counties.

"Our cooperative hasn't been afraid to expand whenever possible. From the start, as a mere idea in the minds of a few farmers, the system has grown to the point where there are now 1285 miles of lines in Virginia and 750 miles in West Virginia, serving 6316 members in Augusta, Rockingham and Shenandoah Counties and [illegible] in West Virginia, Counties. Plans for further expansion call for [illegible] to about 2,900 additional [illegible]. We don't know just how [illegible] of line that will take. [illegible] a minor item. We [illegible] the line and [illegible] ever mileage [illegible]. [illegible]

August 15, 1945: Japan surrenders unconditionally. *Microfilm Archives*

Carriers of the Staunton News-Leader and Evening Leader react wildly to the surrender of Japan on Aug. 15, 1945. The words "Japan Surrenders" has been written on the plate-glass window of the Leader offices just behind the children. *Schwartz Collection*

Photo taken circa 1949 that shows a group of boys from Olivet Presbyterian Church gathered in a car for their Sunday School class. Cars were used as classrooms for a period while the congregation was in transition from one building to another. Two of the boys shown here – Harold Reid and Phil Balsley – would become founding members of The Statler Brothers, the most awarded act in country music history. Pictured, from left, are Bob Craun, Billy Hiner, Francis Halterman (partially hidden), Harold Reid, Freddie Stone and Phil Balsley. *Schwartz Collection*

Maj. Gen. Alexander M. Patch, a former commandant of cadets at Staunton Military Academy. Gen. Patch commanded the land campaign at Guadalcanal and two years later the forces that spearheaded the Allied drive into France from the south.

Officers of the 11th Bomb Squadron while the unit was a part of the China Air Task Force in Kunming, China. Jack E. "Shorty" Manch is standing in the back directly in front of the propeller. Manch, of Staunton, co-piloted one of the B-25's on Doolittle's gutsy raid on Tokyo in 1942.

The 1950s

The Good Life

The Staunton News-Leader

62 YEARS In Public Service

STAUNTON, VIRGINIA, WEDNESDAY MORNING, NOVEMBER 5, 1952

PRICE FIVE CENTS

WEATHER

EISENHOWER WINS

General Swe... County; Harrison Wins

Ike Cracks South, Carries New York, Has Big Plurality

Area Gives Eisenhower Big Margin

Virginia In GOP Line First Time Since 1928

General In Front From First Count

Burr Harrison Expresses Thanks

Tidal Wave From Mighty Earthquake Hits Hawaii

Water Wall Is 13 Feet High

Highland Stays With Republicans

WeyersCave P-TA To Meet Thursday

Queen Wants Closer Ties With U.S.

Dwight D. Eisenhower

Highland County

BURR P. HARRISON

November 5, 1952: Gen. Dwight D. Eisenhower wins the Presidential race of 1952. *Microfilm Archives*

Years after the 1950s ended, four of Staunton's native sons immortalized the decade and its cultural icons with songs like "Whatever Happened to Randolph Scott?," "The Movies" and "Do You Remember These?" But this nostalgic look at a simpler, sweeter time in America wasn't just wishful thinking on the part of The Statler Brothers; their songs truly served as musical historical markers, for the 1950s – segregation, the Korean War and the advance of communism notwithstanding – truly represented good times for residents of Staunton, Waynesboro and Augusta County.

Statistics highlighting the economic prosperity of the 1950s include:

- Gross wages from 1950 to 1957 rose more than 100 percent in Staunton, and employment increased by nearly 50 percent.
- Unemployment in Staunton and Waynesboro was no more than 2 percent throughout the decade, and 44 percent of employed residents in the two cities had white-collar jobs.
- The median income in Augusta County by the end of the decade was $4,352. Fully 10 percent of the population earned more than $10,000.
- Waynesboro's population in the 1950s grew a whopping 27 percent, reaching 15,694 souls by 1960.
- Staunton's population grew at a slower pace in the 1950s – 12 percent – with its headcount reaching 22,232 by 1960. The median income in Staunton was $5,395, with 13 percent of Stauntonians pulling in $10,000 or more a year.
- Augusta County's population by the end of the decade was 37,363. Less than one-fourth of these people lived on farms.

The availability of both personal and governmental cash generated a spending and construction boom not seen since the 1920s. In 1951 a new King's Daughters' Hospital was dedicated in Staunton, and the decade saw the erection of several new schools, including Bessie Weller, Westside and Northside, and a $1.1 million addition to Robert E. Lee High School.

With an eye toward moving its plant from Charlottesville, General Electric in 1953 took an option of the Valley Airport, which was located just north of Waynesboro. Ground was broken for the new plant on March 29, 1954 – the same year that Waynesboro annexed 100 acres from Augusta County in order to bring the GE site into the city.

Waynesboro then embarked on a growth spurt of unprecedented proportions.

It went into annexation proceedings again two years later and succeeded in gobbling up 200 acres that included the 125-acre Brandon Farms tracts, 20 acres adjoining the Hillcrest subdivision and 45 acres from Union Apple. In December of 1956, Waynesboro City Council sought and got authorization to annex another 300 acres from the county.

Meanwhile, new industries and businesses were springing up in Waynesboro. In 1950, for example, Dunlop and Lennox Dawbarn founded Dawbarn Brothers – a company that made automobile seat covers from polypropylene. The company started out in a warehouse with 15 employees and by 1955 had 160 employees and a new plant and offices. The firm expanded again in 1957 and 1959.

Staunton, while not an industrial center in the mold of Waynesboro, experienced not a penny's worth reduction in affluence than its sister city on the South River. Staunton's downtown teemed with businesses that included clothing stores, barber shops, news stands, department stores, furniture stores, soda shops, pool halls, restaurants, photography studios, book shops, movie theaters, banks, jewelers, car dealerships, hardware stores, electrical contractors – and more.

Patrons from all three localities – Staunton, Waynesboro and Augusta County – jammed its sidewalks six days a week, and the bulky cars of the period narrowly missed one another on Staunton's narrow, two-way streets. And while Waynesboro began to knock down its old buildings in the 1950s – a move the city would live to regret – Staunton merely covered over its old facades with modern facings.

In 1956, the 100th anniversary of the birth of the late Woodrow Wilson, Staunton kicked off a yearlong centennial celebration that included as guests Wilson's widow, Edith Bolling Wilson; former Virginia Gov. Colgate Darden; U.S. Sen. Alben Barkley; and many other notables. Staunton's post office held first day of issue sales of a new Woodrow Wilson stamp, and the Wilson Birthplace announced gifts of more than $100,000 for renovations to the manse.

But trouble lay on the horizon for Staunton. In 1959, a master plan for the city's future called for the demolition of buildings that were antiquated or substandard – and while that plan didn't come to fruition immediately, it did plant the seeds of destruction that would grow into the ill-fated "urban renewal" craze of the 1960s.

Photo taken in the 1950s of a horse and wagon driven by an elderly black man with a child beside him. The wagon has halted in front of the editorial offices of the Staunton News-Leader and The Evening Leader on North Central Avenue.
Waynewsboro Collection

Photo by the Beverley Studio in Staunton of Fairfax Hall, which for many years was a nationally known preparatory school and junior college for girls in Waynesboro. The school's graduates were known to successfully transfer to all leading four year colleges and universities. Declining enrollment forced the school to close in 1975.
Schwartz Collection

April 15, 1951 photo of the dedication of the new King's Daughters' Hospital on North Augusta Street.
Schwartz Collection

When Wright's Dairy Rite was established at 346 Greenville Avenue in 1952, it was one of only a few eateries on the road – joining Anderson's Frozen Custard, The Parkette and the all-night Valley Diner. Today, all of Greenville Avenue's early 1950s eateries are gone – with the exception of Wright's Dairy Rite, which in 2004 celebrated its 52nd birthday. *Schwartz Collection*

One of the city's most successful auto repair shops was Central Garage, located at 115 N. Central Ave. Owned and operated in its latter days by the Knowles family, Central Garage – shown here in a 1950s photograph – fell victim in the 1960s to the city's ill-advised "urban renewal" project and was demolished along with 25 other businesses. *Schwartz Collection*

66 YEARS
in Public Service
Oldest Virginia Daily West of the Blue Ridge

The Staunton News-Leader

WEATHER
Mostly sunny and colder Sunday. Monday, fair, a little warmer.

67TH YEAR, NO. 48 | ASSOCIATED PRESS AUDIT BUREAU CIRCULATION | STAUNTON, VIRGINIA, SUNDAY, FEBRUARY 26, 1956 | MORNING NEWS ESTABLISHED 1906 DAILY NEWS ESTABLISHED 1890 | PRICE FIVE CENTS

13 Dead, Hundreds Homeless As Tornadoes Cut Across U.S. Damage Runs Into Millions

By THE ASSOCIATED PRESS

A violent storm rolled eastward from Texas to New York Saturday leaving at least 13 dead, dozens injured, hundreds homeless and property damage in the millions.

The storm caused the season's worst dust clouds in the Southwest. Tornadoes knifed through parts of the Midwest. Hurricane-force winds pounded areas in the East.

Hardest hit was an area in southern Illinois near St. Louis. Tornadoes, striking in predawn blackness, killed 6 and injured 10. About half the 196 businesses or residences in the town of Summerfield, a community of 500, were destroyed or damaged.

Mayor Eldon Loehring, a rescue worker himself, estimated Summerfield's damage at around one million dollars.

Another Illinois man was killed when his truck skid off the highway during a gusty snowstorm near Galesburg, in central Illinois.

Ohio counted three dead, Texas two and Oklahoma, one.

The storm, spawned by a cold front, hit Texas first and roared eastward.

At the storm's height, winds with gusts up to 95 miles an hour, lashed western Texas, eastern New Mexico, Oklahoma and parts of Kansas.

It became a black blizzard—so dense that fire fighters coping with two major prairie fires in Texas were unable to find the flames until they were right upon them.

The wind blew a man from an oil rig near Ada, Okla., killing him. Visibility was blotted out by the dust and traffic virtually stalled.

The storm churned eastward and shortly after midnight Friday became laced with tornadoes.

Millstadt, a small Illinois town along the Mississippi River just south of St. Louis, was the first victim of the deadly twisters. A man and woman perished in their splintered home.

But Summerfield bore the brunt of the destruction. The wind hit one end of the community like a giant fist, knocking buildings helter-skelter.

The victims were a 16-year-old student who died in his bed under a pile of bricks, a 64-year-old bartender whose body was found in a field 50 feet from his house and an 83-year-old woman.

The wind did strange tricks. One side of a two-story building was peeled off clean. The contents appeared undisturbed.

AGED VETERAN SUFFERS COLD

GATE CITY, Va., Feb. 25 (AP) — John Salling, one of three surviving veterans of the Confederate Army, was confined to his home here today with a "deep chest cold."

Doctors told the 109-year-old Salling to drop plans to attend the 9th District Democratic convention at Bristol today to aid recovery.

Salling, who was laughing, talking and chewing tobacco today, was reported "in fine spirits." He has been confined to a wheel chair since he fractured a leg about two years ago.

The other two living Confederate veterans are William A. Lundy, 107, of Laurel Hill, Fla., and Walter W. Williams, 109, of Franklin, Tex.

Westinghouse Strike Still On

WASHINGTON, Feb. 25 (AP)—Several sessions of mediation talks were held today but there were no outward indications of major progress toward a settlement of the 132-day Westinghouse strike.

A three-member mediation panel first met with representatives of the International Union of Electric Workers (IUE). Later the mediators met with the IEU representatives only.

Joseph F. Finnegan, director of the Federal Mediation and Conciliation Service, was in on the discussions for a time. He declined to comment afterward concerning any progress or lack of it.

"We've agreed not to talk for the time being," he said.

THE HARDEST WINTER that Europe has experienced in a century carved out these picturesque ice formations on the Rhine River. The scene is near the town of Lorch, Germany, in the background. The extreme cold has claimed 737 lives and may have a disastrous effect on some of the area's vineyards.

851 Perish In European Storm As Bitter Cold Wave Subsides

LONDON, Feb. 25 (AP)—Sunshine today brought Europe's first real promise of a break in the 26-day disastrous cold wave. With hopes of a thaw, however came fears of floods.

NATO headquarters in Paris readied plans, troops and relief supplies for any new disaster area. The big danger was that melting snows might overload river already piled high with pack ice.

Deaths in the Continent's worst freeze in 50 years reached 851. Holland, Belgium and parts of Germany still shivered in bitter cold. New blizzards hit Spain and Portugal. Elsewhere things looked brighter.

Springlike sunshine sent London temperatures above freezing for the first time in 163 hours. France was warming up though still far from normal. Berlin forecasters claimed the cold spell was finally broken.

Army trucks tried to reach a snowed-in passenger train in northern Portugal. Giant drifts forced them back.

A 13-ton stone, undermined by the weather, crashed from the battlements of a castle into the streets at Leiria, Portugal. People evacuated houses under the castle walls, fearing more masonry might fall.

Hundreds of Portuguese villages and farmsteads were isolated and unable to get food. Three houses collapsed in Rebordoes.

A blizzard raged over Spain's Guadarrama Mountains where a U. S. Air Force transport crashed with six men aboard.

Snow two to seven feet deep covered north and central Spain. Six villages have been isolated for 24 days.

Spanish officials called the crop losses a "national disaster" and said this was the "worst winter in Spanish history."

Trains from northern Spain reaching Madrid had taken 48 hours for trips that usually take 6.

Temperatures rose slowly across France, reaching 50 above zero at Pertignan and Nice in the south.

Water from melting snow covered the streets in Bordeaux. Northern France had fog.

Bright sunshine came to north Germany and weathermen predicted a slow thaw. But night temperatures were still way down.

Rome, just over one of the worst snowstorms in memory was hit by a 10-minute hailstorm. Fog covered Venice bringing about a collision between a tanker and a 120-ton fishing boat. The fishing boat sank but the crew was saved.

The CARE mission to Yugoslavia made available to cold wave victims there more than 25,000 food packages. The packages were distributed by the Yugoslav Red Cross.

Block ice pierced a small tug in Antwerp. Belgium's biggest port. The tug sank but the crew was rescued. Seagoing ships could leave port only in daytime because of danger from floating ice.

Some Dutch farmers reported finding sparrows nestling under chickens' wings for warmth.

This was the latest known death toll: France 230, Italy 105, Turkey 72, Yugoslavia 70, Holland 63, Britain 59, Denmark 42, Germany 41, Greece 30, Austria 22, Spain 25, Sweden 21, Belgium 20, Portugal 18, Norway 15, Switzerland 14, Poland 4.

Landslide Ballot Is For Ike In Mary Baldwin Test Vote

An upset-minded group of girls threatened to throw an already turbulent political situation into further turmoil yesterday.

The girls were the 275 students of Mary Baldwin College; The event was a mock Republican Nominating Convention.

Pre-convention sentiment indicated an easy first ballot victory for Eisenhower. That was not the case, however.

Forces supporting the candidacy of Sen. William F. Knowland (Calif.) caused the greatest difficulty as they mustered 380 votes on the first ballot.

Sen. John W. Bricker (Ohio) commanded 195; Henry Cabot Lodge Jr. got 91 and Goodwin J. Knight (Calif) was far back with 52. The President polled 604 votes, falling short of the nomination by 59.

Between the first and second ballots considerable activity was detected by both the Knowland and Eisenhower forces as they endeavored to sew up the nomination for their candidate.

Though Knowland gained some strength on the second ballot it was not nearly enough and Eisenhower got the nomination with a total of 921 votes.

More surprises were in store as the Convention went about the business of nominating a vice-presidential candidate.

As many as five nominations had been anticipated but only the names of Ambassador Clare Booth Luce and Vice-President Richard M. Nixon were placed before the convention.

As the vote began it became obvious that backers of other vice-presidential hopefuls had realized they could not hope to muster enough support for their favorite candidates and had agreed to support Mrs. Luce.

Delegations which had been pledged to Everett M. Dirksen (Ill.), Christian Herter (Mass.), and Clifford Case (N.J.), joined with the Luce forces and came within a breath of gaining for her the nomination.

Until almost the last vote it appeared that the move was going to be successful and that Mrs. Luce would be the students' choice as the first woman vice-presidential candidate. She led through most of the ballot but a last minute surge of strength by Nixon backers carried him through to victory by the slender margin of 687 to 636.

Theme of the convention was set by Keynote Speaker Robert S. Carter, Executive Assistant to Leonard W. Hall, Chairman of the Republican National Committee, who told the delegates, "The Republican Administration has brought this nation Prosperity based on Peace; a bold and dynamic policy of building and maintaining the strength and unity of the free world; and has been responsible for the soundest period of economic activity in our history."

He cited record employment of 65½ million, higher take-home pay for all workers, tax relief, a sounder dollar, and a balanced budget as adequate proof that the Republican Administration should be returned to office in 1956.

Student delegates represented every state in the union and the territories of Alaska, Hawaii, Puerto Rico, and the Virgin Islands plus the District of Columbia.

Each delegation chairman had been in contact with either an elected representative from the state or territory she represented, or with the Republican committee for that state. As nearly as could be, the convention expressed feelings and sentiments of the Republican leaders of the country at this time.

Evidence of the satisfaction the student delegates felt came during the many demonstrations which were staged for each candidate nominated. A Pennsylvania group, dressed as Quakers, presented a song, favoring the candidacy of Eisenhower, especially written for the occasion.

Ohio delegates serenaded the

(See MBC, Page 2)

$17 Million Stake In Senate Debate Of Local Farm Bill

WASHINGTON, Feb. 25 (AP)—Virginia farmers have an estimated 17-million-dollar stake in the farm bill being debated in the Senate.

William V. Rawlings of Capron Va., executive secretary of the Assn. of Virginia Peanut and Hog Growers, said about 12 million dollars of this estimated state total involves Virginia peanut growers.

Others involved are growers of wheat, corn and cotton.

Rawlings said tobacco growers are not affected since that crop has 90 per cent parity support.

The interest of Virginia's peanut producing area, he said in an interview, is centered primarily on two provisions contained in the farm bill as reported by the Senate Agriculture Committee.

These provisions, favored by the growers, call for an extension of dual parity and a restoration of a 90 per cent of parity program in 1956 and 1957 for the basic commodities.

Parity is a formula designed to give farmers a fair return for basic crops as compared to prices farmers must pay.

Indications are efforts will be made on the Senate floor to eliminate these provisions.

Elimination of one or both, Rawlings said "would be a severe jolt to peanut growers and to the economy of the producing areas."

The bill as approved by the committee provides that both the old and "modernized" formula be applied to each of the basic commodities, using for price support purposes the higher of the two. This is termed dual parity.

The "modernized" parity formula which became effective Jan. 1 "served to reduce the support level of peanuts by approximately 20 per cent, the severest cut in price dealt to any of the six basic commodities by virtue of the new formula for computing parity," Rawlings said.

This cut alone, he added, amounts to about 9 million dollars for Virginia growers, "already in a tight cost-price squeeze."

Rawlings said the "moderized" formula has not worked "as the experts who recommended its adoption predicted, and it is completely contrary to the established and accepted concept of parity."

Extension of a 90 per cent of parity support program for the basic commodities, he said is considered essential if any real progress is to be made in bolstering farm income.

"History has consistently shown that lower supports do not decrease production, but on the contrary only result in farmers receiving lower prices for what they produce," he added.

"Further, the basic commodities are either under strict acreage controls or they are not eligible for 90 per cent supports."

THE WINNER! Eisenhower banner is raised by cheering Mary Baldwin students as President emerges victorious in mock Republican convention here. (Staff Photo)

Heavy Gains For Ike, State Survey Reveals

RICHMOND, Feb. 25 (AP)—President Eisenhower not only holds the 1952 strength that won him the state of Virginia but also may have increased it slightly, the Times-Dipatch reported tonight in disclosing results of a recent presidential poll among its readers.

The poll indicated that if Virginians voted this month on an Eisenhower-Adlai Stevenson race for president, they would give Eisenhower at least the 56.5 per cent majority he took in his first run.

Answers to the poll questions were returned to the Times-Dispatch prior to the report by Eisenhower's doctors the President was physically fit to serve another term.

The poll was conducted by the Times-Dispatch research department. It took a random sampling of the newspaper's readers in counties and cities. Results were analyzed to give an accurate reflection of economic, social and other variable factors, the newspaper said.

Persons polled were asked not to return their ballots unless they were qualified voters and expected to vote in the 1956 presidential election.

The basic question was: "If the presidential election were held tomorrow, for whom would you vote?"

Between Stevenson and Eisenhower the results showed 55 per cent for Eisenhower, 40 per cent for Stevenson and 5 per cent undecided.

A normal breakage of the undecided vote, the Times-Dispatch said, would give Eisenhower something over 57 per cent. That's a figure better than his 1952 percentage of 56.5.

Against either Sen. Estes Kefauver (D-Tenn) or Gov. Averell Harriman of New York, the Times-Dispatch poll indicates Eisenhower would take two-thirds or more of the Virginia vote.

Virginians prefer Stevenson over Vice President Nixon by 49 per cent to 34 per cent, with 17 per cent undecided. Stevenson also holds a 50-28 edge over Sen. Knowland (R-Calif), with 22 per cent undecided.

The percentage lineups in other trial runs:

Nixon 38, Harriman 34, undecided 28; Nixon 34, Kefauver 39, undecided 27; Knowland 34, Harriman 32, undecided 34; Knowland 31, Kefauver 36, undecided 33.

STATE DEATH TOLL

By THE ASSOCIATED PRESS

A Newport News man was killed and his companion injured Saturday when their car left State Rt. 609 east of Prince George Courthouse and struck a tree.

Death of Thomas Junior Hall, 30, raised Virginia's highway toll for the year to 98 compared with 102 at the same time in 1955.

ONTARIO TO HIRE TEACHERS FROM ENGLAND

TORONTO, Feb. 25 (AP)—Ontario will try to hire teachers from England to meet a scarcity. The Education Department reports the province is barely able to hold its own in teacher-training to keep up with increased elementary school enrollment. About 3,500 teachers were graduated last year, but 2,000 others left the profession.

NEW NAME FOR WEST GERMAN FORCES

BONN, Feb. 25 (AP)—A new name for the West German armed forces is being recommended to Parliament. In World War II the forces were called the Wehrmacht —defence might. Germans want to avoid that name now, so a parliamentary committee came up with Bundeswehr—Federal forces.

5 Killed In Head-On Crash Near Allentown

ALLENTOWN, Pa., Feb. 25 (AP)—Five employes of the Bethlehem Steel Co. plant at Bethlehem, were killed today when their automobile crashed headon with an oil truck on Route 309, about 1 miles northwest of here.

The victims were identified by State Police as:

William A. Soduskas, Robert Yiengst, Nicholas Copper, all of Mahony City; Peter Soper of McAdoo, and Walter Medalis of Keylares.

Police said all were killed instantly in the tragedy which occurred about 8:30 a.m. as the men were on their way home from working the night shift.

It took more than an hour to extricate the bodies from the twisted automobile.

The driver of the truck, owned by the Lehigh Farm Bureau Cooperative, was identified as Raymond E. Hausman of New Tripoli.

FRENCH SMASH REBEL STRONGHOLD

ALGIERS, Algeria, Feb. 25 (AP)—French military headquarters today reported smashing a rebel stronghold in the Kabylie Mountains with a sudden raid by mobile troops and helicopters. The commando-style raiders killed 27 nationalists and rounded up another 47 in a short but violent clash. Sizable stores of arms were taken.

Air Force Now Boasts Great Striking Power

WASHINGTON, Feb. 25 (AP)—The Air Force may substantially increase the number of heavy, nuclear weapon bombers in each strategic wing to give them even greater striking power.

Under this plan, the Strategic Air Force would have upwards of 160 more B52s under the 137-wing Air Force program scheduled for attainment in mid-1957.

How fast the big long-range B52s are being turned out is a matter of controversy among critics of administration defense policy. Sen. Symington (D-Mo) said yesterday it will be "a great many months" before the B52 production rate reaches as many as 17 a month.

Air Force officials have formed in recent months that while the 137-wing total unit strength now appears adequate, further expansion of the numbers of modern aircraft in the Soviet air force might call for reconsideration of the program.

The present 137-wing program provides for 54 wings of Strategic Air Command planes. Included in this total are several jet fighter wings, assigned the mission of protecting SAC bases and escorting bombers.

The Air Force may reduce SAC's total strength by three fighter wings, but this would be offset by the increase of unit strength in the Tactical Air Command, which will increase from a present 34 to 41 wings under the program. This increase will be in day fighter planes used for both defense and ground attack missions. Virtually all TAC combat aircraft are capable of carrying at least the smaller size atomic bombs.

There also has been talk, so far of the B47 medium range jet bombers now in SAC could be used for tactical missions, to augment the light bombers and fighter-bombers of TAC.

Gen. Nathan F. Twining, air chief of staff, told a Senate Committee recently that the flexibility and range of the Tactical Air Force is being augmented by aerial refueling.

The approaching advent of the intermediate and intercontinental ballistic missile is bringing a new problem in reconnaissance.

In present-day operations, planes make preliminary studies of a target, then return after the bombing strike to survey the results.

But what will be done when unmanned missiles are used as strategic bombers?

Some experts say missiles themselves may become reconnaissance craft.

Sen. Byrd Appeals To South For Massive Resistance Against U.S. Court Ruling

WASHINGTON, Feb. 25 (AP)—Sen. Byrd (D-Va) called today for "massive resistance" in the South to challenge the Supreme Court's order for racial integration in the public schools.

Byrd made it clear in an interview he is not advocating or condoning violence in opposing enforcement of the order but said he wants Southern states to stick together in declaring the court's opinion unconstitutional.

"If we can organize the Southern states for massive resistance to this order I think that in time the rest of the country will realize that racial integration is not going to be accepted in the South," he said.

"In interposition, the South has a perfectly legal means of appeal from the Supreme Court's order."

Interposition is a doctrine under which some students of constitutional law contend the states could refuse to implement within their own confines a Supreme Court decision they felt did not comply with the Constitution. Legislatures of some of the Southern states already have passed resolutions of this type.

While Byrd did not cast it in that light, his call for Southern unity on the school issue apparently was akin to the "passive resistance" urged by some proponents of racial integration.

Rep. Adam Clayton Powell (D-NY) has urged a one-hour period of nationwide nonactivity by Negroes for boycotting segregated city buses.

Byrd's call for unified Southern support of interposition was in line with the study being given to the question by a group of 13 Southern senators who met recently under the leadership of Sen. George (D-Ga).

The group named Sens. Russell (D-Ga), Stennis (D-Miss) and Ervin (D-NC) as a subcommittee to draft a manifesto the 18 might sign setting forth their opposition to carrying out the Supreme Court order.

U. S. Helicopter Finds Survivors Of Transport Crash

MADRID, Spain, Feb. 25 (AP)—A Medical Corps helicopter found three survivors tonight where a U. S. Air Force transport crashed in a snowstorm 50 miles north of Madrid. They were flying from Chateauroux, France.

Three men aboard perished in the crash, an Air Force spokesman said, but did not identify personnel as survivor or dead.

Announcement of the finding of three survivors was made by the Air Force after the wreckage had been spotted in the snow-covered Guadarrama Mountains by another transport piloted by CD-Ft. Robert L. Hess of the U. S. Air Force in Spain. Ten Spanish and American planes had searched for the wreckage since dawn.

POLICE ARREST THREE CHARGED WITH LYONS ROBBERY

Staunton police report the arrest of three men charged with the robbery of $686 from Mrs. Joseph Lyons, proprietor of Lyons' Store, Greene St., on Feb. 12.

Briscoe B. Marshall, 21, George Washington Marshall, 29, and Paul Edward Clements, 28, all of Rt. 5, Staunton, were arrested in Frankfort Ky., early this week and held for Staunton authorities.

Capt. R. R. Cline, Lt. J. M. Boyers, and Officer W. F. Reed of the Staunton Police Department went to Frankfort this week and returned the trio to Staunton where they were placed in jail and charged with grand larceny, pending trial.

General Assembly Is Set To Argue Discordant Items

RICHMOND, Feb. 25 (AP)—The Virginia General Assembly gets the biggest threat to its honeymoon compatibility next week on the major item of discord — the Moore resolution on school operations.

Moving Monday into the final two weeks of a session that hasn't produced any first rate floor fracas to date, the House will tackle the resolution that could convert the aura of sweet agreement into a free-for-all family spat.

The House has divested itself already of its biggest assignment of this or any other regular session—getting out a record budget bill appropriating the revenue to keep the state operating for the two years beginning July 1. The appropirations bill is now in the Senate Finance Committee, which doubtless will write in some of its own fiscal ideas and ask the House to agree.

Sen. J. D. Hagood of Halifax, Finance chairman, said he didn't expect Senate changes to be too extensive. His committee will probably work on the bill for a week or more and get it to the Senate floor during the last few days of the session which winds up March 10.

Another money matter, the sales tax package which was wrecked on a 9 to 8 adverse vote in the House Finance Committee, still showed backers were expected to try to resurrect the measure and do all possible to get it to the floor for a vote.

The resurrection process may take two forms. Backers may move on the floor to discharge the Finance Committee — a move virtually never crowded with success and unlikely to be successful this time in spite of the fact the sales tax measures had 43 backers.

Or they may seek to have the committee agree to reconsider the vote by which the committee throttled the 2 per cent levy for teacher pay.

The sales taxers would have to enlist the aid of someone who voted against them in committee Wednesday since such a move must be made by someone who voted on the prevailing side in the first instance. Until a move to reconsider has been defeated, a bill killed in committee is not irrevocably and officially dead.

But even if the sales tax is sprung out for a House vote, the Senate almost certainly will block the rather spirited drive of Del Sam Pope and associates for action now on the tax to relieve localities of their share of the teacher pay burden.

Moore has opposed reported plans of a group in the Senate to amend his resolution—possibly to write in the time for a special session. He has sought to put his critics on the defensive by saying he can't see why anyone would want to speed up mixing the races in the schools by a single day.

Against critics who said inaction would leave the state with no defense against federal court orders to proceed and desegregate with all "deliberate speed," he said he felt the Gray Commission study, the referendum on the constitutional convention and the convention, itself, set for March 5, were evidences of "deliberate speed."

He added he thought more emphasis should be on "deliberate"

(See ASSEMBLY, Page 2)

Lee Senior Class Play Draws Standing Room

A standing room only audience apparently enjoyed the fast-paced series of skits and musical interludes that constituted the Robert E. Lee High School's senior class variety show Saturday night in the high school auditorium.

Cleverly woven around the central theme of a typical graduating class banquet, it used the banquet scene as the springboard for its vaudeville-style sequences. Each was representative of an item of the traditional class prophecy.

And the sequences ran the gamut from army careers through nursing, medicine, business activities, teaching, music, both vocal and instrumental, up to space exploration.

Continuity attention was centered on the off-stage, orchestra level banquet scene chairmanned by Joe Alexander. Life in military service for a select circle of seniors was depicted as the opening skit and a quick switch to the women's ward of a hospital promised misery and pain for some seniors, nursing careers for several, a medical role for one, and a bewildered existence for another.

A musical show-stopper was provided by Sara Collins and her presentation of variations on the piano of "Pop Goes the Weasel."

A clever concoction, all in verse, by Judy Doering, which featured the booming voice of Bobby Bowman, was a takeoff on a busy office day for a group of secretaries.

A colorful western scene, featuring folk dancing, a recitation by Wayne Clements, and a neatly performed rendition of "Whispering Sands" by James Harris and Charles Whisman, provided a refreshing change of pace.

The football scene featured the cheerleaders and senior grid stars who appeared in the Rose Bowl, as peanut vendors.

Appearing in trio were Joyce Fleshood, Dana Wilson, and the show director, Nancy MacGregor.

A takeoff on the faculty in the students' conception of a teachers' meeting met with an appreciative reception particularly by pupils in the audience.

The space visitation was completed in three scenes, under the able command of Mason Sproul.

And the show swung into a talent search skit under the direction of Wayne Clements which produced a variety show of its own within the overall program.

Featured in a ballet number was Dianne Tucker while five senior boys, billed as "The Hopeless Five," combined their voices well to present "Faith, Hope, and Charity."

An advertising break on a ghoulish side preceded a Dixie-

(See LEE, Page 2)

LENTEN GUIDEPOSTS

Personal Messages Of Inspiration And Faith

Time In For A Lift

By Raymond Thornburg
A report, from across the U.S.A., On religion in the work-a-day world.

Irwin W. Tucker runs a filling station on Highway 77 at Wynnewood, Oklahoma.

One night Tucker and his wife, Thelma, watched Ruth Hussey playing the Virgin Mary on a television program. They were impressed by one scene showing a family group around an altar. The next day Tucker and his wife built a family altar of their own.

Two days later he told his employees at the filling station about the family altar.

"We could use a little meditation right here in the filling station, Mr. Tucker," one employee replied.

Tucker and his six employees (four white and two Negro) cleaned and repainted a small room in the filling station.

Other Places, Too

Today when a driver stops by Tucker's station, he finds the sanctuary with a Star of David, a statue of Christ, and a crucifix side by side. No one disturbs him. If business is brisk, an attendant will move his car.

Travelers can find other such oases scattered about the country.

Logan International Airport in Boston has a chapel where passengers can stop before a flight for a moment of prayer and meditation. Sunday morning services are now held in a chapel at Idlewild Airport in New York.

A "Chapel of the Highways" is under construction outside of Rocky Mount, North Carolina. The Biltmore Hotel in New York City has a chapel for transients, while the people of Shreveport, Louisiana, financed a prayer sanctuary in the new Texas Eastern skyscraper.

Chapel at Solar

Several years ago, Edmund T. Price, president of Solar Aircraft of San Diego, called his employees together. "I would like to see a chapel, representing the great religious faiths, here on company property. If you employees would like such a chapel, Solar will donate the space, the architect and the building materials, but you'll have to build it with your own hands and hearts—and I'll help you."

Price had one specification: if the employees wanted the chapel, at least 50 must express the desire in writing. Hundreds wrote in to say they did. "Perhaps the chapel will generate a renewal of spiritual faith, productive honesty and pride of workmanship," wrote one worker.

On Christmas Eve, 1952 the land was dedicated. Since then scores of employees, on their time, have wielded picks, shovels and hammers. The first service in the new chapel was held on Christmas, 1953.

A Laundry Firm

In other industries the move is on. Recently, several large laundry firms throughout the country gathered in Crestview, Florida.

It wasn't a business convention, services of the Webb Chapel, a modern sanctuary constructed for employees of Charles Webb's Laundry in Crestview. Today the chapel is used for morning devotions, held by 20 women employees.

Another man who believes in this idea is Bill Blumert, who opened his new Pacific Painting

(See LENTEN, Page 3)

February 26, 1956: "Massive Resistance" is urged in Virginia to combat integration. *Microfilm Archives*

The PUBLIC Interest FIRST

THE STAUNTON LEADER

and

The Staunton News-Leader

Weather: ...tonight, lowest 25-32 ... east. Saturday ... planes, rain likely western portion by afternoon or evening.

VOL. 109, NO. 13 MEMBER OF THE AUDIT BUREAU OF CIRCULATIONS STAUNTON, VIRGINIA, FRIDAY, JANUARY 2 1959 MEMBER ASSOCIATED PRESS WIRE AND FEATURE SERVICE PRICE FIVE CENTS

Five Persons Injured in Wreck Scene at Right, Icy Roads Caused Rt. 250 Turnovers

Eleven Injured, Three Critically, In Series of Highway Traffic Accidents

The New Year's holiday, combined with icy highway conditions Thursday and early today, caused dozens of crashes in Augusta County, Staunton, and Waynesboro.

Injuries to the following were reported:

Francis Waters VanFossen, 157 Bellview St., Staunton, in "poor" condition at the University of Virginia Hospital, Charlottesville, suffering from severe head injuries, scalp lacerations, and a foot laceration.

George Bethel Powers, of 509 McMahon St., Staunton, in "critical" condition at King's Daughters' Hospital suffering from chest and internal injuries.

SECOND FATALITY

Edward M. Barger Jr., 22, of Natural Bridge Station died in a single car accident early Thursday morning. He was the second Virginia fatality. The accident occurred on U. S. Rt. 11, about four miles north of Lexington, at 4:30 a. m.

State Trooper J. R. Carter said Barger was thrown from his car when it crashed. He was trapped in the wreckage when the auto rolled over on him.

Eugene Floyd Bishop, Rt. 5, Staunton, treated and released at King's Daughters' Hospital for lacerations of the face.

Louise Leach Gum, 25, Rt. 1, Churchville, treated and released at King's Daughters' Hospital for lacerations of the forehead and sprained neck muscles.

Frederick Paul Brown, 2200 Mt. Vernon St., Waynesboro, admitted to the Waynesboro Community Hospital suffering from a broken left shoulder and hip.

Willis Calvin Gregory, of Fordwick, treated by a Craigsville physician for a deep gash above the eye and a bruised hand.

Betty Stone, 335 Poplar Ave., Waynesboro, in "fair" condition at UVA Hospital suffering from dislocation and fracture of the left hip, and lacerations of the forehead.

Mary Ellen Miller, Stuarts Draft, in "fair" condition at UVA Hospital suffering from a cerebral concussion.

Doris Craig, of Rt. 2, Waynesboro, in "fair" condition at UVA Hospital suffering from a fractured skull, broken right leg.

Douglas Sidney Perry, Rt. 3, Staunton, admitted to the Waynesboro Community Hospital suffering from a fractured jaw and lacerations of the face.

Hiram Lee Phillips, Rt. 1, Raphine, treated and released at Waynesboro Community Hospital for a scalp laceration and abrasion of the legs.

Motorists Blamed

State Police today blamed most of the crashes on motorists not taking precautions and not driving according to demands of road conditions. In many wrecks, car after car slid off the roadway and into other wrecks because drivers could not stop.

VanFossen, the most seriously injured, Powers, and Bishop were injured on Rt. 252 about two miles north of Middlebrook at 8:30 a.m. Thursday while going hunting.

A 1949 Ford driven by Bishop skidded on the icy roadway, went sideways, and crashed into a tree about 10 feet off the road. The vehicle was demolished. The injured were rushed to King's Daughters' Hospital by Voorhees ambulance. VanFossen was later transferred to Charlottesville.

State Trooper E. J. Good, who investigated, said the crash is still under investigation.

HIGHWAY CREWS BUSY

The State Highway Department has had road crews out scattering chemicals and abrasives on the highway which have been dangerous due to freezing rain since yesterday morning at four o'clock.

All of the roads have been treated.

The three girls and Perry and Phillips were injured in a single-car crash about 1:15 a. m. Thursday on N. Delphine Ave. in Waynesboro, about 150 feet south of B St.

Waynesboro Police Chief C. H. Benson and Officers O. M. Allsworth and R. W. Wright said a 1957 Chevrolet driven by Perry left the roadway and struck a tree. The vehicle was a total loss.

All five of the injured were rushed to the hospital by the Waynesboro First Aid Crew, and the three

(See ELEVEN, Page 8)

Furnace to Left Overheated, Caused Blaze

Rt. 742 Residence Damaged By Flames on New Year's Day

The home of John G. Lightner Jr. on Rt. 742, the Huckleberry Hill Road, was heavily damaged by fire Thursday morning at 9:52. The seven-room frame dwelling was damaged in amount estimated at $3,000.

Mr. Lightner, his wife, and two children were visiting relatives in Highland County at the time of the fire and could not be notified until about two p. m. yesterday afternoon.

But Mr. Lightner was unable to return until this morning due to icy driving conditions.

According to Augusta County firemen, the fire started from an overheated furnace in the basement. It burned the first story flooring, ate its way up the partitions into the second floor.

The living room was destroyed. The fire continued up a partition in the wall, damaging the floors on the second story. There also was heavy smoke and water damage.

The first firemen at the scene had little hope of saving the building because at first sight smoke was pouring out of every window, door and the roof.

However, through the combined efforts of Augusta County and Staunuton fire departments the house was saved. Two of the county trucks were sent to the scene. When they ran short of water at 10:20, Staunton firemen were called. One city truck arrived shortly.

No damage was done to the outside of the home. The home was owned by Brooks Rexrode.

One hour and 47 minutes after the new year came in, the county fire department received a fire call on Rt. 250 near the Farm Bureau where a rear axle on the car of S. W. Maupin broke and the tire of the car caught fire. The fire was out on arrival.

Last night the department was called to a chimney fire in Churchville at 9:40. It was also out on arrival. The home was occupied by C. B. Davis and owned by Lyle Jordan.

In addition to helping the Augusta County fire department, the Staunton fire department was called yesterday morning to the Dairy Kite on Greenville Ave. at 2:15 to extinguish a fire in an electric motor which had shorted.

Icy Nightmare For Va. Trooper

A state trooper's nightmare caused by icy road conditions was reported to have occurred just after seven a. m. Thursday on Rt. 340 about five miles south of Stuarts Draft.

State Trooper E. J. Good said six vehicles became involved in sliding accidents, causing damage well over $1,000, as drivers found it impossible to stop for the road tie-up caused by the first accident.

It all went like this:

A 1953 Ford driven by John H. Funk of RFD Crimora was the first to leave the roadway — smashing headon into a tree. Damage to the car was about $300.

A short time later, near the same spot, a 1953 Ford driven by Andrew Jackson Johnson of Greenville skidded crossways in the road and was struck by a following 1953 Buick driven by Melvin Hall Humphries of Rt. 1, Vesuvius. Damage to each car was estimated at $300.

Just a few minutes later, a 1954 Ford driven by Bobby Lee Painter of Rt. 1, Greenville, skidded on the ice and hit a parked car at the wreck scene, a 1950 Ford owned by John Thomas Campbell of Rt. 2, Staunton, and then continued to skid until it also ran into the already damaged Humphries Buick. Damage to the Painter car was estimated at $250 and to the Campbell car $75.

Finally, to top it off, a 1958 Studebaker driven by Garfield Charles Gamble of Silver Springs, Md., tried to stop for the wreck scene, skidded, and ran into a fence. Damage to the Gamble car was $25.

After all of the tangle was straightened out, it was found that no one had been injured, although damage totaled an estimated $1,250.

No charges were placed in any of the crashes.

No Easy Answer To School Issue Seen

By THE ASSOCIATED PRESS

RICHMOND (AP) — One high state official suggests that 1959 well might be tagged the Groundhog Year.

"Find a good hole and crawl into it" is his bit of New Year's advice to Virginia citizens and officials alike.

This is his way of saying the new year will be a good one to miss if you are looking for a simple solution to Virginia's school problem. He sums up what many others are saying privately: 1958 was hectic but nothing like what 1959 is certain to be.

All have in mind the overriding problem of schools. The problem, of course, has to do with federal court decrees ordering integration of races in the public schools and the state's policy of resisting race mixing in the classrooms.

Reduced to its simplest terms, the question appears to be whether the state can continue a system of public schools in the face of these court orders and this policy.

As the New Year started, the state administration awaited decisions of a three -judge Federal District Court at Norfolk and the Virginia Supreme Court of Appeals on the massive resistance laws which thus far have been used to stave off integration.

The federal decision generally is expected to knock down the school closing law under which nine white schools in Norfolk, Charlottesville and Front Royal have been closed.

This law and other key ones in the massive resistance package are involved in the friendly test suit the state administration brought in the State Supreme Court.

The administration asked the Supreme Court to hold that the U. S. Supreme Court knocked out the state's obligation to operate a public free school system when it killed the constitutional section requiring segregation.

This was the chief argument made by Atty. Gen. A. S. Harrison Jr., before the State Court.

Schools dominated the first year of J. Lindsay Almond Jr.'s term as governor of Virginia. There seemed little likelihood the emotional issue would b erelegated to any lesser spot during the remaining three years of his administration.

Almond said he felt like a man caught "in the jaws of a vise" during the period of waiting for the courts to act on the laws' legality. He insisted he would stay with the state's statutes "as long as they are vital."

If these laws are knocked down, he said, he will appoint a commission from the General Assembly to advise him and get his own suggestions.

An extra session of the General Assembly probably would come shortly after the commission concluded its work. Soe persons guess this might be in the late winter or spring.

If the State Supreme Court goes along with the argument the constitutional provision for a public school system is dead, the way would be opened for localities to operate or abandon public schools as they see fit.

Few state officials or legislators care to speculate publicly on what may develop.

The governor himself has kept his official plans under wraps and has steered away from press conference discussions of the subject.

Some viewed the state's arguments in the Supreme Court case as indicative of new thinkin gat the top level—as the groundwork for a new course in the fight against school integration.

Advocates of massive resistance

(See SCHOOL ISSUE, Page 8)

Eight Boys Charged In Breakin Spree

The Augusta County sheriff's department has cited eight Stuarts Draft area juvenile boys for a recent splurge of breaking and vandalism.

A hearing has been set for the youths for Jan. 14.

Two of the juveniles have been charged with breaking and entering the cannery at the Stuarts Draft School, the Stuarts Draft Fire Department, Weaver's Hatchery, Williams' Store, and a camp owned by Stuart Coiner of Waynesboro. Sheriff John E. Kent said larceny committed in each of those five-breakins.

All eight of the youths have been charged with breaking and entering a camp owned by Mrs. Pearl Dodge of Washington, D. C., and wrecking the building. Reports said the youths broke dishes, windows, furniture, and did damage which will amount to several hundred dollars.

Investigations and arrests were made by Deputy Sheriffs W. L. Lucas and M. T. Sours who said 18 warrants have been issued in the string of breakins — ten against the two youths involved in the five breakins, and one each against all eight for the breakin and vandalism at the Dodge camp.

Willie and his Pop

News, Inside

Victory Proclaimed By Castro in Santiago

BULLETIN

HAVANA (AP) — Advance spearheads of Fidel Castro's revolutionary forces entered Havana today.

HAVANA (AP) — With all Cuba virtually in his hands, rebel leader Fidel Castro today triumphantly proclaimed his native Santiago as the nation's provisional capital and named Manuel Urrutia as provisional president.

While Castro's success in his 25-month-old rebellion seemed close to complete, he still must bring his oft-proclaimed choice to Havana and install him in the presidential palace from which dictator Fulgencio Batista fled Thursday.

To install Urrutia in the capital, Castro ordered a mass public demonstration in Havana's Central Park at 4 p.m. today.

The country will remain in a state of paralysis from a general strike ordered by Castro until Urrutia takes over in Havana.

Castro spoke just before dawn to a huge crowd in Santiago, the capital of easternmost Oriente province, after a parade of orators had hailed his leadership and his selection of Urrutia.

Castro said the road to Santiago, occupied Thursday after the defending garrison surrendered, had been a long and hard one. He called Santiago "the strongest fortress of the revolution" and said its triumph was being crowned by making it the provisional capital for some 2 hours, until he and Urrutia go to Havana.

Castro's supporters controlled all communications and every radio broadcast referred to Urrutia as "provisional president of Cuba."

Former President Carlos Prio Socarras, an exile in Miami since Batista ousted him by military coup in 1952, arrived meanwhile in Havana. Prio has supported Castro's revolt from exile. He and all other revolutionary organizations recently agreed to accept Urrutia as provisional president.

There was little doubt that this island republic would accept Urrutia, a former judge about 56 years old who long has been Castro's choice to succeed Batista until free elections can be held.

Castro called a general strike across Cuba until Urrutia was installed. The strike seemed 100 per cent effective, thus removing any question of remnants from the Batista regime trying to run the country.

Castro was still in Santiago, the capital of easternmost Oriente province and birthplace of his battle against Batista. Celebrations of his victory continued there all night.

Until Urrutia takes over in Havana, Castro's announcements from Santiago provided the only framework of government. Men he designated were giving orders to Cuba's armed forces and police. Castro supporters held Havana under tight control — virtually martial law — today after victory celebrations Thursday led to violence.

Castro, a lawyer who has been a rebel for more than a third of his 32 years, outlined his platform in 1955.

It included nationalization of U. S. financed and operated utilities, splitting up American - owned sugar estates among the peasants, confiscation of all properties acquired through corrupt government and breaking the hold of some big businessmen on Cuba's economy.

The bearded guerrilla warrior has denied Batista's charges that he is a Communist or is Communist-influenced. Castro says his goal is to end corruption, establish decency and help the small man among the 6,410,000 people of this Pennsylvania-sized island.

Castro and Urrutia were expected to make a triumphal entry into Havana.

The capital quieted down Thursday night after an orgy of celebration, looting and retaliation against supporters of Batista. Three policemen and 10 looters were reported killed.

There was no indication that any of the 12,000 Americans in Havana had been harmed. The State Department said in Washington it had no plans for evacuating U.S. citizens.

With the Havana International Airport closed and cruise ships avoiding the city, however, the U. S. Embassy announced a ship was on the way from Key West to take home stranded tourists.

Batista gave up the presidency and fled to the Dominican Republic early Thursday. His family and scores of his top officials departed hastily with him or in planes and boats for the United States.

Batista said he was quitting to save Cuba from further bloodshed.

Castro sought to restore order as soon as possible, both to stop bloodshed and to protect Cuba's normally prosperous economy. Sugar and sugar products make up 75 per cent of national exports and the cane grinding season is at hand.

To head the armed forces, Castro appointed Col. Ramon Barquin, who had just been released from a Batista prison with 700 other political prisoners. Barquin broadcast an appeal from the military headquarters at nearby Camp Columbia for the people of Havana and the nation to remain peaceful in their homes.

There were reports that some army units might resist Castro's advance to Havana from Santiago. Prospects for resistance seemed to be dimming hourly, however.

There was no indication of continued fighting anywhere in Cuba between Batista's 37,000 troops and the rebels.

The sudden collapse of Batista apparently resulted from the first major battle of the rebellion. Three columns of rebels who previously had raked only hit-and-run raids and small battles launched an attack last weekend on Santa Clara. Batista had to protect vital road and rail center in the middle of Cuba to maintain ground contact with the eastern end of the island.

The president threw tanks, warplanes, artillery and reinforced infantrymen into the battle against rebel foot soldiers. By New Year's Eve rebel casualties were estimated by Batista's regime at 3,000 dead and wounded. The government said it had suffered 1,000 or more casualties.

These losses caused Batista to decide to give up. He was in danger of having the army turn on him rather than continue to suffer such casualties.

While continuing to claim publicly that the rebels were losing and would be stamped out, Batista had a plane standing by.

The dictator gathered his top henchmen around him at Camp Columbia on New Year's Eve. He broke off a toast to peace and prosperity to announce that he was giving up the presidency and leaving.

About 3:30 a.m. he flew off in his personal DC3 to Ciudad Trujillo, capital of friendly fellow dictator Rafael Trujillo of the Dominican Republic. Batista' swife,

(See CUBAN, Page 8)

An Around the World Glance At Cuban Situation Reaction

B THE ASSOCIATED PRESS

HAVANA — Fidel Castro rebels control Cuba as President Batista flees into exile. Castro-called general strike appears 100 per cent effective. Havana calms down after orgy of looting and revenge. All Americans apparently safe. Castro names new army chief who begins negotiations for cease-fire. But fighting apparently is stopped.

SANTIAGO DE CUBA — Thousands cheer Castro leaders at park rally far into night. Rebel leader expected to proclaim ex-Judge Manuel Urrutia as provisional president.

CIUDAD TRUJILLO, Dominican Republic — Batista, wife, three children and leaders of his regime take refuge in Dominican Republic.

NEW YORK — Leading Batista supporters come by plane to New York, New Orleans, Jacksonville, Key West, Daytona Beach and West Palm Beach. Some flee by boat. Batista's other five children among refugees.

WASHINGTON — State Department in close touch with Havana embassy but says has no plans to remove U.S. citizens. President Eisenhower kept advised of events at Gettysburg farm. Castro representatives expect United States to recognize his government.

PARIS — Cuban Ambassador Hectore de Ayala switches to Castro, says he will propose French government recognize Urrutia government.

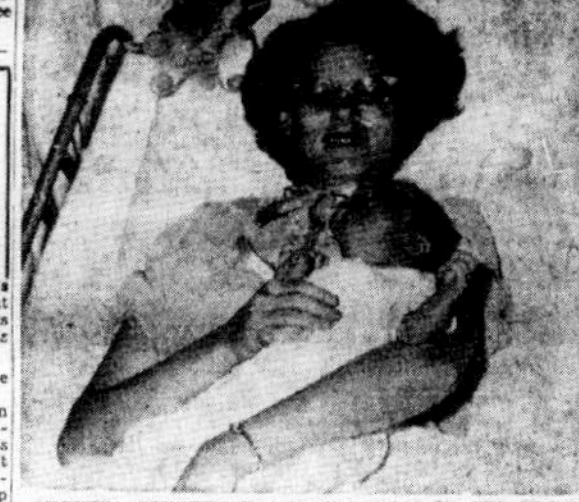

AUGUSTA COUNTY'S first hospital arrival for 1959, Michele Alene, arrived at the Waynesboro Community Hospital New Year's Day at 12:55 a.m. Michele is the daughter of Mr. and Mrs. Fred Bowlin, 131 James Ave., Waynesboro, and weighed eight pounds, 10 ounces at birth. Dr. J. L. Davis was the attending physician for the Bowlins' fifth child. Mr. Bowlin is employed as an auto battery repairman. (Staff Photo by Rife)

No New Year's Day Baby For Staunton, First Arrival Today

The stork failed to make a delivery in Staunton New Year's Day — but did bring the firstborn of 1959 this morning at 9:25.

The first baby of the year to be born at King's Daughters' Hospital is the son of Mr. and Mrs. Gilbert Durette of 8 C Street. The boy weighed six pounds, eleven and one-half ounces.

Mr. Durette is a janitor at the Virginia School for the Deaf and the Blind.

This is Mr. and Mrs. Durette's second child. The first was a girl.

State Police Office Has Auto Stickers

A State Police spokesman said today that automobile inspection stations that have not yet received an adequate supply of new inspection stickers can obtain a small number at the State Police office in the Courthouse, Staunton.

Staunton in 1959

Municipally speaking, what's in the cards for Staunton in 1959? Some of the largest financial commitments for the coming twelve months are outlined and discussed in today's Follow the Leader column. To page four, if you please.

Salaries of City Sergeants, County Sheriffs Posted

Salaries and expense allowances for county sheriffs and city sergeants throughout the state will be $264,585 higher in 1959 than last year according to the Associated Press report of the State Compensation Board's announcement of the total for the new year of $3,353,759.

The figure released for the Augusta County sheriff's office is $6,200 salary, $40,282 expenses; Bath County, $3,900, $3,041; Highland County $3,600; $542; Rockingham $6,500; $37,660; Rockbridge, $6,000; $29,601.

Allowances for the city sergeant's office in Staunton is $5,500 salary and $3,640 expenses; Waynesboro, $5,350 salary and $2,575 expenses.

Five-Day Weather

RICHMOND (AP) — Extended five - day forecast for Virginia, Saturday through Wednesday, Jan. 3-7: Temperatures will average three to five degrees below normal, much colder over the weekend and again about Wednesday.

Batista Bewails His Lack of Manpower

CIUDAD TRUJILLO, Dominican Republic (AP) Fulgencio Batista figures his army fought a lost cause in Cuba partly because it had an insufficient edge in manpower over Fidel Castro's rebels.

The dictator who fled into exile here Thursday told newsmen it has been calculated that an army would need 100 men for each guerrilla it fought.

"That was the case of Tito in Yugoslavia and the Chinese Communists," Batista said, referring to Tito's World War II campaign against the Germans and Mao Tze-tung's drive against Chiang Kai-shek's Nationalists.

Batista's 37,000-strong armed forces were estimated to outnumber Castro's men perhaps 6-1 even in the last states of the bloody warfare that finally caused Batista to flee.

He gave left - handed praise to Castro's bushwhacking tactics, saying the rebel chieftain got the jump on the government by restricting his activities at first to guerrilla warfare against rural soldiers not trained for that type of fighting.

He also credited Castro with superior armament, though Batista's forces had tanks and warplanes the rebels lacked. He said the rebels received a continuous flow of weapons while government troops could not be supplied.

The deposed President contended that Castro had dominated rural populations by terror.

"Before this revolt, Castro's life was in my hands three times and thee times I pardoned him," Batista said. "I did the same for other revolutionaries."

Asked about the future prospects of Cuban politics he said:

"I am not a prophet. I see much confusion."

With Batista are his second wife and three of his eight children. The other children are refugees in the United States.

COINWORD No. 23 Explanation Today

EXPLANATIONS ACROSS

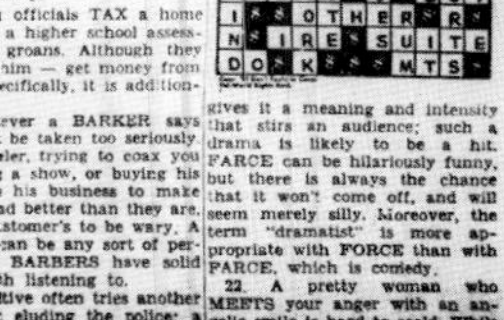

1. While their ship is HEAVING through the waves, passengers had best stay inside. The ship rises and falls alternately, and there is some danger of passengers' being thrown across the deck, or even overboard. HEADING through the waves describes the pitching and tossing less accurately.

6. When officials TAX a home owner for a higher school assessment, he groans. Although they also TAP him — get money from him — specifically, it is additional TAX.

8. Whatever a BARKER says should not be taken too seriously. He's a spieler, trying to coax you into seeing a show, or buying his wares; it's his business to make things sound better than they are, and the customer's to be wary. A BARBER can be any sort of person; some BARBERS have solid views worth listening to.

9. A fugitive often tries another CRIME in eluding the police; a frequent one is stealing a car for a getaway, sometimes kidnaping the driver. CLIME is a poetic word for a country or region, and does not fit so well with the prosy wording of the clue.

18. A lot of FORCE in a play gives it a meaning and intensity that stirs an audience; such a drama is likely to be a hit. FARCE can be hilariously funny, but there is always the chance that it won't come off, and will seem merely silly. Moreover, the term "dramatist" is more appropriate with FORCE than with FARCE, which is comedy.

22. A pretty woman who MEETS your anger with an angelic smile is hard to scold. While you rage, she smiles sweetly till you're the one who looks foolish. The way she MEETS your anger is what finally MELTS it.

24. Some OTHER brown tone

(See COINWORD, Page 8)

January 2, 1959: Fidel Castro claims victories in Cuba. *Microfilm Archives*

The PUBLIC Interest FIRST

THE STAUNTON LEADER

and The Staunton News-Leader

VOL. 109, NO. 34 — STAUNTON, VIRGINIA, MONDAY, FEBRUARY 2, 1959 — MEMBER ASSOCIATED PRESS WIRE AND FEATURE SERVICE — PRICE FIVE CENTS

Weather: Clear and quite cold tonight, lowest about 18 degrees. Tuesday mostly sunny, cold in morning but temperatures rising in afternoon.

Smooth Transition on First Integrated Day

Grudgingly, But Peacefully At Outset, Historic Change Made

RICHMOND, Va. (AP) — Virginia calmly thrust aside the color barrier today and for the first time in her history put Negro and white pupils together in public schools.

Grudgingly, but peacefully at the outset, the Old Dominion made the transition from segregation to integration in a fraction of her public schools, in Arlington County and the city of Norfolk.

No Disorders

No violence, no rowdy incidents occurred as four Negro pupils filed quietly into Stratford Junior High School in Arlington, across the Potomac from Washington.

Two hundred miles down the state in Norfolk, Negro children began showing up to enroll for the first time in six junior and senior high schools. Again, there were no disorders.

Police with riot gear stood by at Arlington. None was in sight at Norfolk.

The quartet of Negro children at Arlington — three boys and a girl—marched onto the school grounds from a seldom used roadway and through the doors shortly before 9 a.m. They were alone. They didn't look alarmed or worried.

Nobody tried to stop them; there was an absence of picketing and demonstrations.

Something like 100 police, equipped with white helmets, portable loud speakers and radios, canteens, and the customary night sticks and guns, converged on Stratford long before the school opening hour.

Only pupils and school employees were allowed on grounds. Even parents were kept out.

In Norfolk, a Negro, Lewis Cousins, and his mother calmly paraded past a cluster of white children on the steps of Maury High School to become the first of his race to shatter the color line in the city.

There was the usual chatter of school kids, but no trouble of any kind.

Again there was no disturbance a few moments later when Betty Jean Read, another of 17 Negroes assigned to previously all white schools, turned up unescorted at Granby High.

The six Norfolk schools, closed since September under Virginia's now dead massive resistance program, were holding no classes today—only enrolling pupils and assigning them to classes.

At Norview High School, two pairs of Negro girls turned up. White students watched curiously and quietly. By that time, police were on hand and cleared a path for the Negroes.

One white girl was heard to say:

"Here they are. . .I hope they're satisfied."

Others said they were glad to get back to school.

Some remarked that they didn't think there would be any trouble, although one white lad said be had heard "rough kids" might cause some later in the day.

At least 14 of the 17 Negroes had entered the Norfolk schools by 9:20.

In both Norfolk and Arlington, police, community and school authorities and student leaders had predicted and said they hoped there would be no violence.

But extra precautions and extra police were used, because officials were well aware of the riots over integration at Little Rock, Ark.

The absence of disorder in Virginia brought word from Gov. J.

(See Change Made, page 2)

EXPECTED NO TROUBLE — Ray E. Reid, Arlington County (Va.) School Superintendent, told reporters that he expected no violence or incidents when four Negro children came to the Stratford Junior High School in Arlington.

Legislature In Session Again This Afternoon

RICHMOND (AP) — The Virginia General Assembly after taking action last week to keep children from being forced to attend integrated schools, meets at noon today to take up a bill which would go further.

A measure introduced by Sen. Joe Hutcheson and approved for floor action by the Senate Education Committee would give the governor authority to close any school termed inefficient.

The measure outlines conditions under which a school is inefficient, and gives the governor authority after closing the school, to transfer pupils, hire teachers and use any appropriations other than that for public schools to reopen it on an efficient basis.

Before a Senate committee were identical bills tossed in Saturday by Sens. J. D. Hagood of Clover and Charles T. Moses of Appomattox.

These bills would allow localities to make tuition grants over and above the state tuition grants approved by the General Assembly. Authority would be given to the localities to levy any taxes necessary to raise funds for these tuition grants.

Both houses completed action Saturday on Gov. J. Lindsay Almond Jr's. program to hold school integration to a minimum. Under the program, the state's compulsory school attendance law was repealed and children who don't want to attend an integrated school were guaranteed tuition grants of up to $250 to pay for private schooling.

Little Truancy Foreseen Here

It is the opinion of school officials in this area that the repeal of the state's compulsory school attendance law will have no great effect on school attendance here.

L. F. Shelburne, city schools' superintendent, stated that "We hope that the people of this city will see that the schools are important and will continue to send their children, regardless of any laws but we'll just have to wait and see."

S. Gordon Stewart, director of instruction of county schools, said that some of the students will take advantage of it. Mostly those who have been waiting to become 16 so they might drop out.

He foresees no great number of dropouts.

No Coinword Solution Yet

Approximately 1,650 entries failed to solve Coinword No. 27 last week. So somewhat like the cat with nine lives, the grand prize —$350 for subscribers and $300 for non-subscribers — still survives.

Why not turn to Page 8 of this issue, read all the contest rules carefully, and then do your utmost this week to win the big award? If perchance you owe some income tax, that cash prize would certainly help to get it paid.

Equalization Board Opens Public Session

North River First District On Schedule

FREIGHTER HITS ICEBERG WITH 95 ABOARD—The "unsinkable" Danish freighter Hans Hedtoft (above) carrying 55 passengers and a crew of 40 struck an iceberg in heavy seas, 40 miles south of Greenland. The ship sent out the first S.O.S. of its kind since the sinking of the Titanic in 1912, with a loss of 1,517 lives.

Faint Signals Spur Search For Lost Danish Vessel in Atlantic

Threesome Apologizes For Incident

Charged With Beer Throwing

Goshen Man Cut In Altercation

Youths Find $10,000 Cash

Sunstruck

Cold Wave Holding Tight

State Leaders Reflect Calm Of First Day

John L. Lewis 'Quite Ill'

Fatter Social Security Checks

Six Injured In Accidents Over Weekend

Burr Harrison Assails Policies Of SBA, Labor Department

Exchange Club Begins Week Of Crime Prevention Observance

Break-ins Over Weekend in Area

Staunton Man Accidentally Shot While Working on Rifle

To Be Held Sunday — Cost $640,000

KDH Wing Dedication To Climax Expansion Project

By MRS. W. J. PERRY

Police Seeking Stolen Auto

Five-Day Weather

Missionary To Speak at Zetta

Willie and His Pop

News Inside

February 2, 1959: Integration of Staunton schools goes smoothly. *Microfilm Archives*

Sutton Collection

Sutton Collection

Twenty-six of 27 people aboard a Piedmont Airlines flight died when the airplane slammed into the Blue Ridge Mountains about 10 miles east of Waynesboro on Oct. 30, 1959. The lone survivor, a Clifton Forge man who sustained a dislocated hip, sat calmly in the forest for three days until rescue workers found him. *Sutton Collection*

The PUBLIC Interest FIRST

THE STAUNTON LEADER

and

The Staunton News-Leader

VOL. 110, NO. 100 — STAUNTON, VIRGINIA, MONDAY, NOVEMBER 2, 1959 — MEMBER ASSOCIATED PRESS WIRE AND FEATURE SERVICE — PRICE FIVE CENTS

Weather: [east and central] ... Fair and colder Tuesday.

Probe Begun to Determine Cause of Friday Air Crash

Area Units Played Role In Search

By FRANK REESE
Leader Staff Writer

Death rode the skyways Friday night, but it was 8:33 a.m. Sunday before the wreckage of the Piedmont Airliner DC-3 was spotted on Bucks Elbow Mountain, some 10 miles east of Waynesboro, by an Air Force helicopter. Immediately a large number of rescue workers, arriving by air and on foot, converged on the scene.

The plane carrying 27 persons, including three crew members, disappeared Friday night on a flight from Washington to Roanoke via Charlottesville.

The first persons to arrive at the scene were confronted by a grim sight, as 33-year-old E. Phil Bradley of Clifton Forge was found to be the sole survivor. Some bodies had been thrown from the plane and were strewn about the area, but the majority were found in a portion of the cabin which had crashed into the side of the mountain.

Not Badly Hurt

Miraculously, Bradley, who received only a dislocated hip and numerous abrasions and contusions, was thrown from the wreckage, still strapped to the seat he had occupied in the plane. Through the use of a pole, found in the heavily wooded area.

(See Area Units, page 6)

MUTE EVIDENCE of disaster. Luggage of crash victims stacked on top of Blue Ridge Mountain peak. (Staff Photos)

Piedmont Line Had Flown 667 Million Safe Passenger Miles

From Wire Dispatches

Thomas H. David, president of Piedmont Airlines, which, until Friday, had flown 667 million passenger miles without a crash fatality, says "several weeks will perhaps be required" to finish an exhaustive investigation of the Friday crash of the Piedmont airliner just east of Waynesboro.

"Things were all quiet, no moans, no groans."

This was the way a 33-year-old union official described the aftermath of a crunching impact against a Virginia mountainside in which 26 persons aboard the twin-engine airliner lost their lives. He alone survived.

"I yelled to see if anyone else was alive, but no one answered," said E. Phil Bradley of Clifton Forge, Va., as he told of his 36-hour ordeal in the wilderness following the crash of the Piedmont Airlines DC3 Friday night.

He suffered a dislocated hip and minor cuts.

Within a few hours after Bradley was taken to a Charlottesville hospital Sunday, 26 bodies, wrapped in tarpaulins, were laboriously carried to the summit of Bucks Elbow Mountain near Skyline Drive.

Bradley, who said he noticed his watch showed 8:40 p.m. moments after the crash, was first reached at the wreck scene by Air Force Sgt. John Weis of Pittsburgh.

"I was damned glad to see him," Bradley said.

The plane, en route from Washington to Roanoke, Va., was last heard from at 8:24 p.m. Friday, when the pilot requested landing instructions at Charlottesville.

The wreckage 18 miles west of Charlottesville was not sighted until 8:30 a.m. Sunday.

Bradley said the pilot never gave any indication there was anything wrong.

Of the actual crash, it "sounded like the roaring of an ocean," he said. "The only sensation was the wings cutting the tops of trees."

Bradley, who was seated near the rear of the plane was thrown from the cabin still strapped in his seat. Because of his dislocated hip, he remained upright in the seat some five feet from the wreckage until rescuers arrived.

With a pole he managed to fish for a coat and blankets to warm him in the chilly mountain air.

Weis reported Bradley's first words were:

"I'm all right, go on up and see if anybody else is alive."

Asked when he realized he was the only survivor, he said:

"I can't say I ever really knew."

He is a district representative of the International Assn. of Machinists.

An Air Force helicopter spotted the wreckage on a steep, heavily wooded section of the mountain. The plane was an estimated 500-700 feet from the top, its front half disintegrated and the fuselage mangled. The craft apparently did not burn.

Bradley, who was returning from a business trip to Oklahoma City, Okla., is married but has no children. All the time he was waiting for help, he said he was "constantly thinking of my wife Evelyn in Clifton Forge."

Mrs. Bradley, a quiet, pleasant young woman, was brought to Charlottesville in a state police car while her husband was being

(See Crash, page 6)

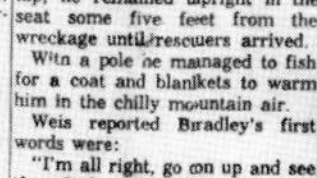

IN DENSE WOODS, this is the scene that greeted rescue teams as they first sighted the plane's wreckage.

STRETCHERS BEAR the bodies of some of the victims of the crash.

RESCUE WORKERS carry one of the bodies up the mountainside.

'Trading Post' Opens Tuesday

The Trading Post, a new division of the Augusta Furniture Co., of this city, will be opened for business tomorrow morning at 19 S. Central Ave., halfway between Beverley St. and the Johnson St. parking lot.

All aspects of a celebration will be present, it was stated, with $1,000 in door prizes and free gifts to the first 200 visitors. Registration for the door prizes will continue until Saturday at five p.m. when awards will be made.

The new furniture store will specialize in budget priced merchandise, such as closeouts or discontinued suites offered from time to time by various manufacturers, damaged floor samples from the stock of the parent store, special buys, and used furniture obtained as trade-ins or repossessions. Vinyl linoleum and coal and wood heaters are also shown.

Over 3,000 square feet of display space has been created in the new store. It is located in a warehouse section, which was decided according to S. Wilson Sterrett, manager of the Augusta, "because this enables us to further cut prices with the reduced overhead of being out of the high rent district."

Weather Wise

WEATHER OBSERVATIONS
By R. L. CASON
VSDB Observer

From 8 a.m. Sunday until 8 a.m. today.
Maximum — 65
Minimum — 45
Precipitation — None
Wind Direction — Northwest
For today's forecast see upper right hand corner of page.

FIVE DAY WEATHER

RICHMOND (AP) — Extended Virginia forecast for the period from Tuesday through Saturday:

Temperatures will average from 3 to 6 degrees below normal throughout the period.

It will be cold Tuesday and Wednesday, not as cold Thursday and Friday and cooler again Saturday.

Mostly fair skies are expected throughout the period with little or no rain.

REIGNING AS MISS WESTINGHOUSE-Staunton this week is five-year old Debra Smith of Staunton, Rt. 6. Miss Smith will reign as queen of the anniversary week at the Verona Westinghouse plant. She was crowned at noon today by Harold L. Goehring, manager of industrial relations at the plant. (Staff Photo by Stephenson)

Westinghouse Crowns Queen

Blond, blue-eyed Debra Smith today was crowned "Miss Westinghouse - Staunton" for the fifth anniversary celebration this week at the Westinghouse Electric Corp. air conditioning division here.

Known as Debbie, she was selected for the honorary title because she is the daughter of an employee and because she will be celebrating a kind of anniversary herself this week — she will be exactly five years old on Wednesday.

In recognition of her new title and her birthday, Debbie received two appropriate gifts from the air conditioning division; a new dress that she was wearing for the occasion today and a brand new tricycle that she was eager to take on a trial run.

Her mother is Mrs. Shirley B. Smith of Staunton who is a stenographer in the division's manufacturing department. According to Mrs. Smith, Debbie right now has her heart set on becoming a nurse for a career.

In the meantime, though, she spends a good deal of her time with Dale K. Smith, 4, her brother, and also keeps occupied with dolls, hide-and-seek, jumping rope, and play involving both cooking and housekeeping.

Also honored at today's luncheon were six original employees of the Westinghouse Verona division.

Those assisting with the cutting of the 20-pound birthday cake were William J. Lawrence, works engineer; John H. Fyock, industrial relations; Robert Thacker, production planning; Mrs. Betty Van Fossen, purchasing department, and E. Elwood Hensley, foreman of the receiving department.

Dedication For New Oak Grove

Dedication services for the Oak Grove Elementary School which opened were held Sunday afternoon at four o'clock.

The fireproof structure, located near Waynesboro, cost approximately $46,000, including the establishment of a water system and furnishings.

Speaker for the occasion was Hugh K. Cassell, superintendent of Augusta County Schools. Speaking briefly also were G. Dayton Hodges, chairman of the school board, and S. Gordon Stewart, director of instruction.

Following the services, open house was held.

News Inside

VanDoren Admits To Trickery

WASHINGTON (AP) — Charles Van Doren told House investigators today he "was involved, deeply involved, in a deception," when he appeared on a television quiz show three years ago.

Van Doren, the most famous of the big money quiz show winners, also swore under oath that his testimony before a New York grand jury last year "was not in accord with the facts."

Contrary to advance predictions, Van Doren made no request to tell his story behind closed doors.

Appearing before a House subcommittee under subpoena, Van Doren said he had "learned a lot in the last three years, especially in the last three weeks."

"I learned a lot about good and evil," he declared, "and I learned things are not always the way they appear to be."

His face appeared drawn and his eyes bloodshot.

Van Doren entered the hearing room by a side elevator and side door, eluding a throng of reporters awaiting at the main entrance to the chamber.

The wavy-haired big winner on the defunct "Twenty-One" program looked youthful and grave as he shook hands with committeemen and went to the stand.

In advance of the testimony before House subcommittee, there was some uncertainty whether he would do his telling in public or behind closed doors.

Crowds of spectators jammed the hearing room to capacity and were lined up outside.

One of the early arrivals was Mark Van Doren, white-haired poet father of the witness.

"We'll announce that when the time comes," he said.

However, subcommittee sources already have acknowledged that at least two other shows — The "$64,000 Question" and the "$64,000 Challenge"—will be looked into.

Charles Revlon, president of Revlon, Inc., which once sponsored both the $64,000 shows, volunteered Sunday to appear.

The Columbia Broadcasting System scuttled both programs last year in the wake of the rigging allegations.

LEADER'S REQUEST TO ELECTION OFFICIALS

Tuesday is an important day in Augusta's election to fill all county offices. One election official in each precinct is asked to assume the responsibility for communicating that precinct's vote to The Staunton Leader as soon as possible after the polls are close. We will have a full staff on hand to compile results, and three telephone lines are available. Our number is TU 6-6266. If all three lines should be busy when you call, please stand by until you can get through to us.

Record Turnout of Voters Expected in County Tuesday

A record number of voters may visit Augusta County's 29 precincts Tuesday in what has been termed one of the liveliest campaigns for county officials in many years.

The polls will open at 6 a.m. and close at 7 p.m., giving the voters a full 13 hours to cast their votes.

Staunton voting is expected to be light, as there is no opposition. The city ballots will include the names of State Senator Curry Carter and Delegates George M. Cochran and Felix E. Edmunds. Write-in votes may be cast.

On November 9, 1955 approximately 2,743 voters turned out in Staunton. At this time Senator Carter was opposed by Joseph R. Nutt Jr.

The 1955 election in Augusta County, at which only county office one contest was featured, that of the office of commissioner of revenue, some 2,325 persons visited the polls. At least this many are predicted tomorrow.

In the 1955 election J. Hunter Shomo defeated two write-in candidates, Harold Armstrong and Frank C. Hanger. Tomorrow's election will renew a battle between Mr. Shomo and Mr. Armstrong. Mr. Hanger is seeking the office of county treasurer.

New Polling Places

In Staunton the voting places will be the same as in the past for Ward II (West) and Ward II (East), but the Ward I voting place, heretofore located in the Farley building, will be at the Strand Theater lobby.

Locations of three Augusta County voting precincts have been changed.

At Burnett the voting place has been moved from the school building to the Boy Scout hut. At Weyers Cave the voting place has been moved from the school building to the firehouse and at Parnassus, the location has been changed from the school building to the office building at E. E. May's residence.

Parents of SMA Cadet Killed In Crash of Piedmont Plane

The parents of a Staunton Military Academy cadet were killed in the Piedmont airliner crash. They were en route to this city to spend the weekend with their son.

Marvin J. Silberman and his wife of Scarsdale, N. Y., were among the 26 victims.

Mr. Silberman, 46, was chairman of the executive committee and former board chairman of the Consolidated Cigar Corp.

He was associate general chairman of the combined campaign for American Reform Judaism, vice chairman of the board of governors of the Hebrew Union College-Jewish Institute of Religion, and a trustee of the Jewish Community Center in White Plains, N. Y.

The son, John P. Silberman, 14, is in school here for his third session. He took the seventh and eighth grades in SMA's junior department, and this session is a freshman at the high school level.

Receiving word of the death of the couple, the boy's uncle chartered a private plane in New York and flew to Charlottesville Sunday, but the pilot did not land there because of search and rescue activities at the Albemarle-Charlottesville airport. The plane was flown to Waynesboro airport, where it was landed. Cadet Silberman was taken to that point by school officials and from there was flown to Scarsdale Sunday afternoon.

The Silbermans had been visitors in Staunton six or eight times since their son had been at SMA. They always used Piedmont to come from Washington to Charlottesville, and there rented an automobile for the trip to Staunton and return to Charlottesville.

This weekend they had a reservation at Ingleside, where they had been guests on numerous occasions.

Highland County Plane Crash Victim Well Known in Dramatics

CHARLOTTESVILLE — James S. Helms, 32, of the University of Virginia was widely known for his work in drama productions at high schools and community theaters throughout Virginia.

Mr. Helms was one of the 26 persons killed in the crash of a Piedmont Airlines plane in the Blue Ridge mountains Friday.

He was returning to Charlottesville from Detroit, where he had attended a conference of broadcasters and telecasters.

Mr. Helms was director of the University's bureau of school and community drama, a part of the extension division program. The bureau helped with the production and staging of plays in scores of Virginia localities.

Its director also was active in the University's drama group, the Virginia Players, and had served as its president. He was the author of several plays for the group.

Mr. Helms, unmarried, lived near Charlottesville. He was a native of Highland County and lived at McDowell. He received

(See Mr. Helms, page 6)

New Series Advises You To Relax And Live Every Hour of the Day

Are you tense and nervous? Do you have an inferiority complex?

Do you have trouble getting along with people?

Do you find it hard to stand your wife, or husband, or children?

Do you find your boss, or your fellow workers, or your neighbors impossible?

If such questions sound trite and familiar, it's because problems of the kind they indicate have been around for so long, and affect so many people, that nearly everybody has put them to himself at one time or another.

That's the reason we think you will find "Master Your Tensions and Enjoy Living Again" very helpful, and very interesting too.

It's the serialization of the new book by Dr. George S. Stevenson, internationally known mental health expert, and by Harry Milt, a widely read writer on the subject, which starts in this paper Monday.

It gives practical, down-to-earth advice. It tells you how to decide whether your own tensions are just normal or potentially dangerous. And it gives you nine easy-to-follow suggestions on how to ease those tensions.

This is something that every adult will want to read carefully. And, dealing frequently in case histories as it does, it's as fascinating as it is helpful.

Watch for it in Monday, Nov. 9 and daily thereafter.

The Authors, Dr. Stevenson, (left), and Harry Milt.

November 2, 1959: Piedmont airline crash in the Blue Ridge Mountains. Only one person survived the crash. *Microfilm Archives*

The PUBLIC Interest FIRST

THE STAUNTON LEADER

and

The Staunton News-Leader

VOL. 110, NO. 50 — STAUNTON, VIRGINIA, FRIDAY, AUGUST 21, 1959 — MEMBER ASSOCIATED PRESS WIRE AND FEATURE SERVICE — PRICE FIVE CENTS

Weather

Generally fair tonight, low in the ..s. Tomorrow mostly fair and continued hot.

Low Bid For MBC Project Under Study

$668,340 Figure For Dining Hall, Heating Plant

A low bid of $668,340 for the construction of a dining hall and central heating plant for Mary Baldwin College was submitted by J. M. Turner and Company of Roanoke as bids were opened before trustees and architects here Thursday.

The Turner bid was among nine submitted. Next lowest was for $671,671 by the English Construction Company of Altavista.

An executive committee of the Mary Baldwin trustees is now studying the bids and hopes to let a contract within the next 30 days, it was stated today by President Samuel R. Spencer Jr.

Other Bids

The base bids, other than those of the Turner and English companies, were as follows: Fred B. Fuqua, of Lynchburg, $735,000; S. T. Gay & Company, Lynchburg, $712,000; C. L. Lewis & Co., Lynchburg, $648,000; Nielsen Construction Company, Harrisonburg, $686,897; B. J. Parrott & Company, Roanoke, $694,840; John P. Pettyjohn Company, Lynchburg, $707,262; F. N. Thompson, $631,900.

Working drawings and specifications on still another building, a dormitory for 134 students, are to be put out to bids in September. It is expected that the heating plant and service center will be completed by next summer and the dormitory and dining hall by January, 1961.

The dormitory and dining hall are to be located almost on a line with the Memorial and Hilltop dormitores and the Student Activities Building. The central heating plant and maintenance shops to serve the expanded campus will be an one-story building just east of Bailey dormitory and behind the Nannie Tate Building now used for a nursery school.

The dining hall for a planned future enrollment of 600 students has bee given in memory of Lyda Bunker Hunt, trustee of Mary Baldwin from 1939 until her death in 1955.

Architects for the Mary Baldwin development plan are Clark, Nexsen and Owen, of Lynchburg.

ROCKING ALONG TO A WEDDING—Steven Rockefeller (bottom, left) and his fiancee, Anne Marie Rasmussen, take time out from last minute wedding arrangements to meet an usher, Robert Waldron of Boston, and his wife as they arrived in Kristiansand, Norway. They were followed a few planes later by Steven's brothers, Michael (top, right), 21, and Rodman Rockefeller, 26, and the latter's wife, Barbara. Steven, 23, and Anne Marie, 21, chose the flowers for the Lutheran ceremony.

Gov. Rockefeller Arrives In Norway Today for Wedding

KRISTIANSAND, Norway (AP) — Gov. Nelson A. Rockefeller comes to Norway today for the wedding of his son Steven to Anne Marie Rasmussen and with his arrival the rosy atmosphere of romance turns even more political.

The New York governor was due late this afternoon with his two daughters, Mary and Ann Pierson. They left New York aboard a KLM airliner Thursday night.

Rockefeller, a potential candidate for the Republican presidential nomination next year, probably will be confronted with more questions about politics in the United States than love in the fjords.

Steven himself said Thursday his father's position in the American political picture is the reason for the great attention his romance is receiving. Nearly 100 reporters and photographers from a dozen nations have swarmed into this little south Norway town to cover the wedding Saturday.

To many Norwegians the excitement doesn't stem from the fact that the 23-year-old bridegroom is an heir to one of the greatest fortunes in the world or that the 21-year-old bride was a maid in the Rockefeller home when she met Steven.

When Steven and Anne Marie announced their engagement Aug. 2, a Norwegian newspaper editorialized that "the people on the south coast of Norway will follow next year's nomination and presidential election in the United States with special interest."

A number of European newsmen here think the engagement furor, the disappearance of Steven and Annie Marie with her parents for a week of private travel, and all the fanfare attending the wedding were carefully planned to give the governor publicity as a presidential possibility.

Meanwhile, crowds gather daily in front of the Kristiansand hotel whenever another member of the Rockefeller family files in.

Steven's mother, who arrived here Monday, has become a familiar figure. She took a tray and ate hamburgers in a local cafeteria Thursday. Later she went to a government liquor store, but clerks there said it was against the law to disclose what she bought.

Steven's two brothers, Michael and Rodman, and Rodman's wife, attracted another crowd when they arrived Thursday.

Thursday night the brothers and the other four ushers for the wedding — Jerry Rigg of Omaha, Neb., David Montgomery of Niagara Falls, N.Y., Harold Talbot of New York City and Robert Waldron of Rockford, Ill.—gave Steven the traditional bachelor's dinner at the local hotel.

Byrd Orchard Picnic Aug. 29

Senator Harry F. Byrd's 26th annual orchard picnic will honor Dr. J. R. Magness of the U. S. Dept. of Agriculture, who will be the principal speaker.

Dr. Magness is retiring this year as chief of the fruit and nut crops research branch of the Department of Agriculture.

The picnic will be held at Rosemont Orchard near Berryville on Saturday, Aug. 29. In the event of rain the picnic will be held at the Byrd canning plant.

Also speaking at the gathering of fruit growers from throughout the United States will be Everett Severe, promotion director of the National Apple Institute, and L. A. Putnam of the Lake Ontario Fruit Growers Co-op.

Attending will be apple brokers and wholesale buyers from Alabama, Florida, Georgia, Louisiana, Maryland, North Carolina, New York, Pennsylvania, South Carolina, Tennessee, Texas, and West Virginia.

A picnic lunch will be served at noon with a menu of butter broiled turkey, ham sandwiches, Byrd apple sauce, cup cakes, potato chips, and iced tea.

Speaking will begin at one p.m.

Review Saturday For 29th Division

INDIANTOWN GAP, Pa. (AP) — Gov. Millard Tawes of Maryland is scheduled to review the 29th Infantry Division, comprising Maryland and Virginia National Guardsmen, at this military installation tomorrow.

The governor will be among a number of dignitaries on hand to see the troops march in review at the windup of the first week of their annual two-week summer encampment.

Other visitors will include: Lt. Gen. George W. Read, commander of the 2nd Army, and the adjutant generals of Maryland Virginia Maj. Gen. Milton Reckord and Maj. Gen. Sheppard Crump.

North River Fair Set Sept. 17-19

MT. SOLON — The 25th annual North River Fair will be held at North River High School on Sept. 17, 18, and 19, with the horse show on Saturday Sept. 19.

E. M. Reeves was elected president of the North River Fair Association at a meeting of the group recently. Harry N. Arey was elected first vice-president; Edward C. Burtner, second vice-president; and Dudley Rexrode, secretary-treasurer. Executive officers named were Eugene Smith, Ernest Craun, William L. Simmons, and Mrs. Phyllis Smith.

Aside from the regular fair attractions, the horse show with afternoon and evening classes is usually one of the final ones of the summer circuit in this area. Anyone desiring to compete in the horse show is directed to contact Douglas Withers at Mt. Solon.

The North River Parent-Teachers Association will serve a country ham and oyster supper Saturday, Sept. 19, from five to 8:30 p.m.

Family Weekly

Nixon's Mother Reveals Unknown Story Of Her Son

THE MOTHER of one of the most likely Presidential prospects reveals her memories of Vice-President Nixon's childhood and youth in an exclusive Family Weekly feature. She also shows for the first time snapshots of Richard and his brothers from her private photo album.

LIKE MOST MOTHERS, Mrs. Nixon thinks the world of her son, and here she tells why. She describes the incident that first turned his imagination to the study of law, how he courted his wife, and how he desciplines his children.

AS A PUBLIC FIGURE, the Vice-President must hide many of his feelings, but his mother takes the reader behind the scenes and recalls how he reacted at family crises, and of his dvotion to her. Read Mrs. Nixon's exclusive story, "What People Don't Know About My Son," in Family Weekly appearing with Sunday's Staunton News-Leader.

IN THE SAME ISSUE, read about Alex Omedo, credited with winning back the Davis Cup, tennis' greatest prize, for the United States, and now rated the world's top amateur player. Plus the regular Family Weekly features: Cookbook Section, "Quips and Quotes" and the "Junior Treasure Chest" page.

Arlington Votes Against Appeal

ARLINGTON (AP) — The Arlington School Board voted 2-1 last night against appealing a federal court order directing the admission of 12 Negro pupils to white schools.

The action confirmed a vote taken by the board in a secret meeting two weeks ago.

Board Chairman L. Lee Bean, and member James G. Stockard supported the motion. Member Helen S. Lane opposed it. Robert A. Peck, abstained. The fifth member, Barnard Joy, was absent.

British Jet Lost

LONDON (AP) — Ships and planes searched the coasts of England today for a clue to the baffling disappearance of Britain's newest top-secret jet bomber.

POP UP UNEXPECTEDLY

Kennedy Facing Troubling Issues

WASHINGTON (AP) — Labor leaders and Roman Catholic governors—who some might assume would be his best rooters — are proving troublesome to the presidential aspirations of Sen. John F. Kennedy (D-Mass).

The three governors are threatening to prevent Kennedy, also a Roman Catholic, from contesting for about 200 presidential nominating ballots he may need badly at next year's Los Angeles convention. These votes add up to nearly one-third of the 680-odd likely to be required to win the nomination.

The labor leaders, who loved him in April when he was fighting their battles against what they regarded as punitive labor control legislation, are cooling on him in August as the prospects increase for congressional approval of a strong labor bill.

The political blockade presented to Kennedy by the three Catholic governors, Edmund G. (Pat) Brown of California, Michael V. DiSalle of Ohio and David L. Lawrence of Pennsylvania, may not be entirely insurmountable, in the view of Kennedy's friends.

Much as he would like to test his popularity in California, Kennedy obviously isn't going to cross Brown in the later's determination to become at least a favorite son — and possibly a national candidate for the party's No. 1 nomination.

But the story may be different in the case of DiSalle and Lawrence. Unless his present intentions change, Kennedy is likely to challenge in the May 3 Ohio primary DiSall's plan to control an commitd delegation as a favorite son.

It is no secret that Kennedy is miffed at what he regards as Lawrence's desire to hold a publicly uncommitted Pennsylvania delegation in reserve to support Adlai E. Stevenson if the latter's name comes up for the third time in the presidential nomination contest.

Kennedy is toying with the idea of entering the state's April 26 primary, despite the obvious drawbacks of such a move.

BY VERONA MERCHANTS

Town Status Study Begun

The subject of incorporation as a town again is being discussed by merchants in Verona.

At a meeting of the merchants' association board there last night it was agreed that an investigation would be made of the advantages and disadvantages of incorporation.

Members of the board will serve as a committee to make the study, or assign the task to the special activities committee, said President Clarence W. Switzer.

To Investigate

"The question is whether it would be to our advantage to incorporate," said Mr. Switzer, "and at least we have decided to look into it."

Some investigation will be made between now and the association's next dinner meeting Sept. 10. There is a possibility that the Verona merchants will invite the mayor of one of the nearby incorporated towns in Rockingham County to be its guest then and discuss the pros and cons of incorporation.

The Verona group also may evaluate Craigsville's recent experience in trying to incorporate. The move there was defeated at the polls, but a final decision has not been made in Circuit Court, which ordered the election.

Augusta County has not had an incorporated town in the past half century with the exception of Waynesboro which, on Jan. 1, 1948, became a city of the first class. Since then only Craigsville seriously has considered incorporation. The issue has been raised before in Verona.

In Rockingham, however, there are numerous incorporated towns, including Bridgewater, Dayton, Mt. Crawford, Timberville, Broadway, and Elkton.

Hot, Humid Again Over Wide Area

By THE ASSOCIATED PRESS

It's going to be hot and humid again today in most areas from the Rockies to the Atlantic Coast.

No early general break in the long spell of muggy weather appeared. Temperatures in the 80-90 degree range were indicated again in most of the sweltering belt. A sticky weekend appeared in store for most areas.

Temperatures during the night in the warm-humid air were mostly in the 70s except for parts of the Dakotas. Readings were in the 50s and 60s from the Pacific Coast to the Rockies.

The mercury climbed to 101 degrees at Pickstown, S.D., Thursday. The 90 mark at Buffalo, N.Y., was a record for the date while Pikeville, in eastern Kentucky, baked in a reading of 98.

Precipitation during the night was widely scattered and generally light.

Jailed After Hitting Policeman

Richard T. Wiseman of 221 Kalorama St. was jailed shortly after four p.m. Thursday on charges of disorderly conduct, resisting arrest, and assault on a police officer following an incident on S. New St.

Wiseman's arrest came after he reportedly struck Capt. Martin E. Miller in the face while being questioned concerning a complaint. He will be heard in court Monday.

She's 29 Today

LONDON (AP) — Princess Margaret became 29 today. Queen Elizabeth's younger sister spent her birthday at Balmoral Castle, in Scotland, where the Queen and her family are vacationing.

No Secretary Yet for Valley Travel Group

Shenandoah Valley, Inc., valley promotional organization, is still without a secretary.

James A. Payne, president of the group, told the executive committee at a meeting in Staunton Thursday, he expects to have a satisfactory applicant within the next 10 days. SVI has been without permanent office secretary since the resignation of Mrs. George McComb on July 21.

Mrs. Mae Ralston of Staunton has been serving as temporary secretary of the organization. Mr. Payne, James S. Simmons Jr. of Staunton, and Miss Gladys Fellow of Grottoes, are a commitee to operate the organization until a new secretary is obtained.

In other business conducted at the meetng Thursday, it was announced that Mr. Simmons would epresent Virginia and the Shenandoah Valley at the Canadian National Exposition in Torono Sept. 5-12. Mr. Simmons, accompanied by Mrs. Simmons, wil be on hand to pass out folers and attempt to attract Canadian tourists to this area.

His Boyhood Church

Dr. Gibbs to Speak At Lynwood Homecoming

LYNWOOD — The Rev. J. Lewis Gibbs, D.D. retired Staunton Episcopal rector, returns to this Rockingham County village Sunday to participate in homecoming services commemorating the 75th anniversary of a church he attended in his boyhood.

Grace Memorial Episcopal Church of the Lynwood Parish will observe its 75th anniversary and at the same time dedicate recent additions to the church.

Boyhood Haunts

The morning service will begin at 10 o'clock, with Dr. Gibbs, who roamed the hills of "Lynwood Farm" when he was a boy, delivering the sermon. Lunch will be served on the grounds at 12 noon.

At 2:30 p.m. a service of dedication will be conducted by Arch-Deacon S. B. Chilton, D.D., of the Diocese of Virginia and the Right Rev. W. Roy Mason, D.D., of Charlottesville.

Grace Memerial Church, together with St. Stephen's Mission at Elkton and Good Shepherd Mission at Rocy Bar, constitute the Lynwood Parish in the Diocese of Virgina.

In 1884 Grac Church was erected on "Still House Run," on land donated b Mrs. Samuel H. Lewis, a relative of Dr. Gibbs. Mrs. Lewis has other descendants who still ive in this area. During the 75 years since then it has been in ontinuous service, ministering to he people in the surrounding vlley and mountains.

The Rev. Joh C. Wheat, onetime vice prinipal of the Virginia Female Istitute at Staunton, was the fist minister of the parish. He maried Miss Elizabeth Lewis andoccupied the original "Lewistor" home, which is located across Rt. 340 from the present church.

Dr. Wheat's only daughter, Miss Ellen Wheat, was for years the Sunday School superintendent and often the only teacher. She worked in both church and secular schools, teaching mountain and farm children. She was known to have been afraid of nothing, from the occasional bears to teen-agers who would "show-off" with their squirrel guns. After dark, visits back and forth between mountain homes were made by the girls with Miss Wheat accompanying them as both chaperone and guard.

Another early minister, the Rev. Joshua Ellis, was a familiar figure on his mule, traveling between the missions in East Rockingham County as a man of strong and outspoken convictions. His reputation was widespread for handling the toughest customer.

It was not until the fall of

(See DR. GIBBS, Page 9)

Hawaii Joins Union Officially

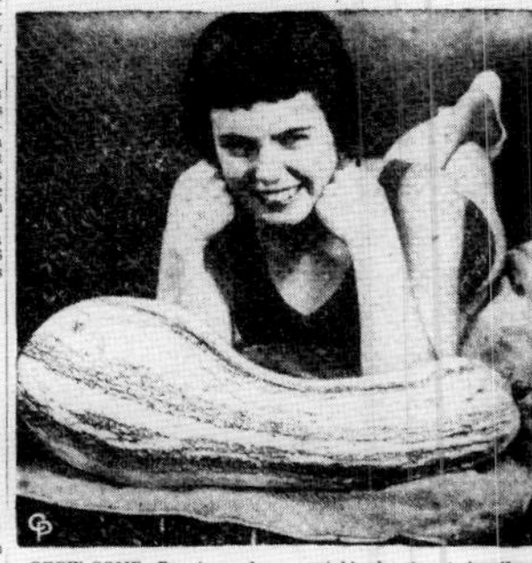

GREW-SOME—Beauty and a vegetable beast get together at Ft. Leavenworth, Kan., as Lily Ann Hoge, 16, checks the size of a monstrous squash. The king-size specimen weighs 17 pounds, is nearly two-feet long and grew from a small seed.

Joins As 50th State Of Union

WASHINGTON (AP) — Hawaii, a group of volcanic and coral islands 2,400 miles west of San Francisco, officially joins the Union today as the nation's 50th state.

President Eisenhower arranged a 4 p.m. (EDT) ceremony at the White House to proclaim statehood for the territory after a 56-year effort by Hawaiian citizens, now numbering 585,000.

Besides signing the statehood proclamation today, the President issues an order designating a new 50-star flag to become officially effective next July 4.

The new banner will take the place of the 49-star flag which became official only last July 4. The 49-star emblem, to provide for Alaska, has a blue field of seven staggered rows of seven stars each. It supplanted the 47-year old, 48-star flag which had six even rows of eight stars each.

Soon after the Hawaiian proclamation, the government will put on sale a special 7-cent air mail stamp commemorating the event.

The signing also will be the signal for Gov. William F. Quinn, a Republican elected as the state's first governor last July 28, to take the oath in Honolulu, capital of the new state.

Quinn will then notify Washington of his certification of the election last month of Hawaii's first congressional delegation in time for the two senators and one representative to take their oaths here Monday.

The two senators are Hiram L. Fong, 52-year-old Republican of Chinese descent, and Oren E. Long, 70-year-old Democrat and former territorial governor. The House member is Daniel K. Inouye, 34-yearold Democrat of Japanese parentage who lost an arm fighting with the 442nd Regimental Combat Team in Italy in World War II.

Southern States, Petroleum Co-Op Session Here on Sept. 1

"Will Farmers Control Agriculture in the Future?"

A discussion of this question and elections of board members will highlight the Staunton area Southern States annual membership meeting at the Beverley Manor School on Sept. 1 at 7:45 p.m. The session is being sponsored by Augusta Petroleum Cooperative, Staunton, and Southern States Cooperative.

Another highlight of the session will be a "What Do You Think?" discussion period by members attending the meeting. The basis for the discussion will be 15 thought-provoking questions dealing with Southern States Cooperative, its operations and local services.

The problem, "Will Farmers Control Agriculture in the Future?" will be presented by Forrest L. Yeakley, Southern States District Manager, of Richmond. Since today's farmers are caught in the increasing squeeze between production costs and prices received for goods produced, they are vitally interested in whether they will continue to control their own destiny.

S. N. Karicofe of Churchville will serve as chairman of the local meeting. The Rev. Robert S. Crutchfield of Fishersville will give the invocation.

A report on local operations and services will be given by Charles W. Switzer, manager of the Augusta Petroleum Cooperative, Staunton.

Nominees for the Southern States board posts for the Staunton area are Vernon L. Garber of Mt. Sidney, Mervin L. Pence of Weyers Cave, Cooper E. Lotts of Spottswood, and D. Graham McCray of Middlebrook.

Other nominations may be made from the floor.

Members of the board whose terms expire this year are Thomas J. Lotts and Paul Wright.

Overtures Made for Withdrawal of 18 Negroes From Warren County High School This Term

WASHINGTON (AP) — It was unofficially disclosed here yesterday that overtures were made at a secretive meeting for the withdrawal of 18 Negroes from Warren County High School in the coming school term.

Warren County Commonwealth's Atty. William J. Phillips and representatives of the American Viscose Corp. reportedly hinted that at least some of the Negro youngsters would be admitted to the public high school in 1960-61 if they would agree to attend new Ressie Jeffries School for Negroes this year.

The 18, plus only 330 white pupils of a normal enrollment of 1,000, have registered to attend the Front Royal school.

It was reported no commitments were made either by the officials or Negro representatives.

One conferee said Phillips mentioned the idea of submitting a plan to solve the Warren school problem to Federal District Judge John Paul.

County, town, labor and industrial leaders planned to meet behind closed doors late today at Front Royal for a report on Thursday's conference here between white and Negro leaders. The Warren schools are scheduled to reopen Aug. 31.

Yesterday's session here was held in a hotel suite rented by the American Viscose Corp. The company is Front Royal's largest employer. It's now actively trying to unravel the county's school troubles.

Among those attending were George C. Horst, director of industrial relations for the company; Ray Gott, personnel director of the Front Royal plant; William J. Phillips, attorney for the Warren County School Board; and Oliver W. Hill, NAACP lawyer representing 18 Negroes ordered into the public high school by federal court.

Earlier, Hill had said he would agree to any reasonable offer to avoid further court action except recommending the withdrawal of the pupils already in the high school.

One possible compromise includes the adoption of a districting plan by the school board that would eliminate 12 of the 18 Negroes now enrolled at Warren High and place them in the new Negro school, Ressie Jeffries.

Also present at yesterday's meeting were George O. Butler of Washington, a staff member of the president's Committee on Government Contracts, and Frank D. Reeves of Washington, an NAACP attorney.

A report on yesterday's three-hour session was expected to be made today in Front Royal before a group that would include representatives from the private Warren Country Educational Foundation and Loal 371, Textile Workers Union of America.

The foundation is to decide Monday whether to operate a private school this year. The plant union gave financial support to the foundation last year through voluntary payroll deductions.

But American Viscose reportedly has ruled out any more deductions this year. The company is said to be faced with a short-because of the school problem.

Five Day Weather

RICHMOND (AP)—The extended forecast for Virginia for the period from Saturday through Wednesday:

Temperatures throughout the period should average 6 to 8 degrees above normal. It'll be warmest over the weekend with a chance of occasional widely scattered thundershowers.

Guardsmen Move Into Quake Sector

WEST YELLOWSTONE PARK, Mont. (AP)—National Guardsmen moved into this earthquake-ravaged area today to prevent possible looting.

The quakes' death toll, meanwhile, reached nine. Mrs. Ray Painter, 42, of Ogden, Utah died Thursday in a Bozeman, Mont., hospital. She was hurt when the quake split a mountain and sent it thundering down on Rock Creek campground and into the Madison River.

Search officials fear other campers may be entombed in that massive landslide. Army engineers are expected to determine soon whether to attempt to move the 50 million tons of rock, earth and debris.

Special Services At Finley Memorial

Sunday, Aug. 23, will be observed at Finley Memorial Presbyterian Church, Stuarts Draft, with special services at 11 a.m. and 7:30 p.m.

Dr. John Bright, professor of the Old Testament at Union Theological Seminary, Richmond, and a noted preacher will be heard at both services.

The public cordially invited, said the pastor, the Rev. Thomas E. Grafton, D.D.

Rt. 250 Group Considering Fund Raising

HARRISONBURG—Members of the executive group of the Committee for the Retention of Interstate 64 in the Route US 250 Corridor met here Thursday with their counsel, J. Sloan Kuykendall, of Winchester.

There was a full representation of localities in the Northern area, it was announced.

The following statement was authorized by the Committee of which Randolph Perry of Charlottesville, is chairman.

"J. Sloan Kuykendall, of Winchester, counsel for the committee was present and discussed certain phases of the problem involved.

"After discussion, a steering committee of five members was appointed but it was deemed inadvisable to announce the names at this time.

"Following the adjournment of the full committee, the steering committee concerned itself with the matter of raising funds to enable the area group to present its case in support of Interstate 64 in the Northern Corridor.

"The proper allocations of an area fund raising program was considered by the steering committee."

The Corridor 250 Committee is seeking to have the State Highway Commission's decision in favor of the Southern Route reversed by the U.S. Bureau of Public Roads, citing the $37 million additional cost of the Southern route and the lack of any engineering recommendations for that route.

Weather Wise

News Inside

August 21, 1959: Hawaii becomes the 50th state. *Microfilm Archives*

The 1960s

Cities in Transition

In the early 1960s, Staunton's proponents of "urban renewal" – a federal program which centered on the government's power of eminent domain – focused on three blocks between Augusta Street and Central Avenue just north of Frederick Street and insisted that this area was "blighted" beyond redemption. Opponents – which included owners of the 26 businesses and 17 households that would be wiped out by demolition – argued that only bankruptcy and homelessness would result.

The fight was prodigious and took several years, but in the end the proponents of "urban renewal" won and the demolitions took place. Central Avenue, which once had sported a row of thriving businesses, lay devastated. The western side of Augusta Street, which sported many beautiful mid-nineteenth century homes – including the home of Staunton's Civil War mayor, Nicholas Trout – was also gutted. And when plans for an inner-city shopping center failed in 1967, the demolished area sat like an open, seeping wound.

Other important events in Staunton in the 1960s included the October 1960 visit of President Dwight D. Eisenhower, who came at the invitation of the Woodrow Wilson Birthplace Foundation; a $2 million expansion in 1961 of the Westinghouse plant; the opening of Shelburne Junior High School in 1963 with its first 297 seventh-graders; and, also in 1963, the arrival of the new five-digit ZIP code.

The Public Interest First

THE STAUNTON LEADER

The Staunton News-Leader

Weather

VOL. 112, NO. 95 — STAUNTON, VIRGINIA, THURSDAY, OCTOBER 27, 1960 — PRICE FIVE CENTS

President Eisenhower Arrives for Rainswept Visit to Mother's Birthplace, MBC Speech

Ike Stresses Wilson Ideals In His Speech

Tours Vicinity And Stops At Wilson Shrine

Trustees Of Birthplace Session Here

Governor Almond, President Eisenhower, Senator Byrd, and Senator Robertson at Airport

Prayer Of Invocation At MBC

Political Figures Dimmed By Hollywood Celebrities at Rally

Pastor Is Guest At Ceremony

Of Ike's Administration

Sen. Byrd Cites 'Peace' Record

On Monastery Issue

Zoning Board To Meet on Nov. 3

News Inside

The President Steps Off for Visit Here

October 27, 1960: President Eisenhower visits Staunton and is greeted by

The 1960s also saw Staunton City Council purchase an additional 33 acres to expand Gypsy Hill Park and, at the same time, demolish the historic "round" barn at the park's fairgrounds. The city in 1965 pursued a sales tax and, after the U.S. commissioner of education rejected Staunton's blueprint for the integration of city schools, undertook a reworking of the plan.

One of the biggest stories for Staunton residents in the 1960s was the April 11, 1967 murder of two High's Ice Cream Store clerks at Terry Court Shopping Center. The young women were shot execution style in a back room of the store near closing time. Despite an energetic manhunt by lawmen from Staunton, Waynesboro, Augusta County and the Virginia State Police, the killer was never caught.

In 1968, four young Staunton men who had made a name for themselves in the field of country music – The Statler Brothers – recorded a song about the city called "Staunton, V-A." The song was written by country music legend Carl Perkins. The next year, plans got under way for the city to host a free, July 4 musical concert featuring the Statlers.

In the 1960s, Waynesboro continued the rapid business and industrial growth begun the decade before. In 1963 an entire neighborhood, including its street, was wiped out to accommodate construction of Willow Oak Plaza. One of the structures razed in this project was historic Rose Hall mansion – referred to by Confederate soldiers during the Civil War as "headquarters of the Army of Northern Virginia" and used once as a stopover by Federal Gen. Philip Sheridan, who personally saw that the house did not come to harm.

In January 1964, Waynesboro's new Kate Collins Junior High School opened for grades 7, 8 and 9.

Augusta County concerned itself with matters small and large, which included the decision in 1961 to reject daylight savings time and a 1961 bank robbery in the previously sleepy village of New Hope. The county also watched as two great ribbons of asphalt – Interstates 81 and 64 – began to snake their way along north-south and east-west corridors, and in 1965 county officials announced that Weyers Cave would be the site for a new educational institution (which would become Blue Ridge Community College).

The final year of the 1960s proved to be a big one for area residents. In Staunton, a fire destroyed the J.C. Penney building on West Beverley Street. On April 24, just south of Staunton on U.S. 11, hundreds gathered for the grand opening of a new shopping center. Even though it was called the Staunton Plaza, the shopping center was firmly situated in Augusta County, which added a bit of salt to Staunton's "urban renewal" wound.

And in August 1969, the rain-drenched remnants of Hurricane Camille hammered the area, causing millions of dollars of damage. While Staunton, Waynesboro and Augusta County experienced flooding from the torrential downpour, it was neighboring Nelson County that took the brunt of the storm's fury. Twenty-seven inches of rain triggered massive flash floods and landslides, and an estimated 114 people died. Another 37 were reported missing and 100 were injured. Some 900 buildings were either damaged or completely destroyed, and more than 17,000 acres of cropland was damaged.

The recently completed Interstate 81 at the U.S. 250 interchange lacks only one thing – traffic. View looks north.

The DeJarnette State Sanitorium just east of Staunton that treated, according to one promotional write-up, "nervous and mental diseases, drug addicts, inebriates and those who need rest." The facility, which was conceived and organized by Dr. Joseph DeJarnette in 1932, was financially self-supporting, which made it unique in the United States. In 1972, now known as the DeJarnette Center for Human Development, it became a hospital for children with behavioral problems. The buildings pictured here were abandoned in 1996 when the hospital moved to a new facility and, in 2001, the name was changed to the Commonwealth Center for Children and Adolescents. *Waynesboro Collection*

William E. Warden photograph of Norfolk and Western diesel number 509 pulling into Waynesboro on Feb. 2, 1963. This was the last regularly scheduled passenger train on the Shenandoah Division. *Waynesboro Collection*

South Augusta Street, depicted in this 1960s photo, sported an impressive array of late 19th century buildings, including the John Burns Building, which housed the popular Mary's Restaurant. This building – which occupied lot number 1 of the 13 original lots laid out in 1747 – was built in 1874 and demolished in 1972. The city tore it down in an effort to provide additional space for the Augusta County seat, despite objections by a fledgling preservationist movement. *Schwartz Collection*

View of Augusta Street facing south. The First and Merchants National Bank to the right was demolished and replaced with a newer structure, and further south on Augusta the second oldest building in the Wharf district – the Burns Building – was torn down to make way for a parking lot for the county office complex. *Schwartz Collection*

The PUBLIC Interest FIRST

THE STAUNTON LEADER

and

The Staunton News-Leader

Weather Warmer tonight with occasional rain, low 45 to 50. Cloudy, occasional rain, mild Thursday.

VOL. 112, NO. 104 — STAUNTON, VIRGINIA, WEDNESDAY, NOVEMBER 9, 1960 — MEMBER ASSOCIATED PRESS WIRE AND FEATURE SERVICE — PRICE FIVE CENTS

Sen. Kennedy Clinches Victory; City Votes for Redevelopment

Record-Smashing Turnout In City Rolls Up Nixon Margin

Staunton voters in a record-smashing turnout Tuesday indicated approval of establishment of a redevelopment and housing authority here and voted the city into the Republican side of the presidential picture for the fourth consecutive time.

The positive reaction to the redevelopment and housing authority question was counted at 2,230 to 1,681 against the creation of the agency as a means of implementing the city's master plan for future municipal development.

Nixon Two-to-One

Vice President Nixon proved to be the city's choice by better than a two-to-one margin. Mr. Nixon won handily at all three polling places with a total of 2,789 votes to Sen. Kennedy's 1,233. C. Benton Coiner found favor with only seven Staunton voters. The Socialist-Labor ticket garnered three votes.

The record turnout at the polls totalled 4,066, somewhat short of the 4,700 to 4,800 prediction on election eve by a Staunton Electoral Board official. But there are those who contend an even higher vote would have been recorded had there not been the day-long jam at some of the polling places.

The crush of voters, particularly at the Fire House voting booths, is said to have discouraged many persons who turned away rather than wait in line for more than one hour.

Party leaders on both sides, along with election officials, pointed to the bottlenecked polling place as proof of need for an additional precinct to serve the northwestern city area.

The Fire House location topped the three city polling places with a total vote of 1,629. At the Y.M.C.A. there were 1,336 votes cast while the total at the Beverley Hotel was 1,101.

Sen. A. Willis Robertson rolled up 3,233 votes in Staunton, proving to be the number one attraction in the whole fistful of ballots thrust upon those who voted here yesterday. His opponents, Stuart [illegible] and Clarke T. Robb, received 412 and 38 votes respectively.

Rep. Burr P. Harrison, unopposed for his Seventh District House seat, received 2,615 votes.

Amendments

The two proposed state Constitutional amendments, one dealing with voting privileges for service men and the other permitting election of joint officers for adjoining political subdivisions, were approved. The first was agreed by a 2,582-1,018 count and the second, 1,832 to 1,257.

The referendum on the redevelopment and housing authority met approval across the board at the three polling places. It carried 566 to 483 in the First Ward, 774-509 in the Second Ward West (Fire House), and 896 to 689 in the Second Ward East (Y.M.C.A.).

In the presidential balloting it was Vice President Nixon all the way, too. He won 709 to 378 in the First Ward, 986 to 340 in Second Ward East and 1,094 to 515 in Second Ward West. Mr. Coiner picked up three votes in the First Ward and four votes at the Y.M.C.A. The Socialist-Labor ticket garnered one vote in the First Ward and two votes at the Fire House.

Sen. Robertson in the respective polling places 932, 1,092 and 1,309

(See City Vote, Page 2)

Augusta In Column For Nixon

Vice President Nixon carried all but four precincts in Augusta County Tuesday.

The Republican candidate collected 4,633 votes to Senator John F. Kennedy's 1,916 votes. The only precincts not going for the Republican candidate were Augusta Springs and Craigsville in Pastures District and Greenville and Spottswood in Riverheads District.

All magisterial districts went for Vice President Nixon with Riverheads having the closest count. Sen. Kennedy had 293 votes to Mr. Nixon's 321 in Riverheads.

Heavy Turnout

It was the heaviest presidential election turnout in the history of the county. Some 6,153 voters cast their ballots, while in the 1956 election, [illegible] count was [illegible].

Middle River District gave Mr. Nixon the greatest edge, with the Vice President gathering 1,117 votes to his opponent's 379. The count was also lopsided in Mr. Nixon's favor in South River District. The Republican candidate collected 1,032 votes to Sen. Kennedy's [illegible].

In the 1956 election President Eisenhower carried 27 of the county's 29 precincts, with only Crimora and Greenville going to Adlai Stevenson by slim margins.

Augusta Springs and Craigsville, both manufacturing areas, favored Sen. Kennedy. Augusta Springs gave the Democrat 40 votes to his Republican opponent's 26. Craigsville handed Sen. Kennedy a 41-vote margin.

Greenville for Kennedy

Greenville, which usually goes Democratic, gave Sen. Kennedy 138 votes to Vice President Nixon's 114. Spottswood favored the Massachusetts senator by two votes, 90-88.

Senator A. Willis Robertson totaled 4,650 votes in the county. His opponents, Stuart Baker and Clarke T. Robb, scored 921 and 115 respectively.

Rep. Burr P. Harrison polled a total of 4,021 votes in the 29 precincts.

County residents voted for the

(See County Vote, Page 2)

Redevelopment Vote Reaction

Yesterday's vote favoring a redevelopment and housing authority for the City of Staunton was greeted with expressions of satisfaction today from city officials who are active in promoting urban renewal.

Councilman and former Mayor Richard W. Smith said:

"I am gratified with the outcome, especially in view of the fact that there was a very representative vote, the largest ever cast in Staunton. I hope we can go forward carefully and make some constructive improvements in the core area of Staunton."

Mr. Smith pointed out that the next step will be the City Council's appointment of five commissioners to serve as a redevelopment and housing authority.

'Very Happy'

"I do hope that whoever is contacted will agree to serve. It will require a real sense of civic duty on the parts of prospective commissioners to agree to serve," Mr. Smith added.

C. M. Moyer Jr., city engineer and assistant city manager, said: "Naturally I am very happy that the proposal to create a redevelopment and housing authority carried. I think Staunton took a step in the right direction. One thing I am not so happy about is that it did not carry by a bigger majority." However, he also observed that there is no doubt that the vote is representative, in view of the large turnout at the polls.

It is understood that the authority will be chosen for staggered terms under provisions [illegible] 1954 Housing Act of 1954 as amended. It is to serve without compensation, but probably will employ an executive secretary. One of the first acts of the authority probably will be to apply to the federal government for a planning grant to be used in studying the downtown area to determine the best ways to implement the master plan.

It Was Ring-Around-Rosy at Fire House Polling Place

Nixon Victory in Virginia Narrow by Ike Standards

RICHMOND (AP) — Virginia, out of step with the national presidential trend for the first time since 1924, put its 12 electoral votes in the losing Republican column in yesterday's election.

It was the third time in a row the Old Dominion sided with the GOP—twice for President Eisenhower and this time for Vice President Richard M. Nixon.

But the Nixon victory was narrow compared to the one-sided margins of Eisenhower.

He emerged with a winning cushion of about 40,000 of the record turnout of three-quarters of a million votes.

Returns from 1,915 of the state's 1,947 voting precincts gave Nixon 394,519 to 354,485 for President-elect John F. Kennedy. Nixon took 52.4 per cent of the total vote to 47.1 for Kennedy. C. Benton Coiner who headed the Conservative party ticket was no factor and his 3,000-plus votes accounted only for one half of one per cent of the total.

The closeness of the Virginia race was post-mortem proof of the aggressive campaigns waged by the Democrats, even without the aid of top organization party leaders, and the Republicans and the allies that overshadowed them, the Democrats for Nixon-Lodge.

Sen. Harry F. Byrd, still perhaps the most potent individual on the state political scene, declined as he has in the past several presidential elections to endorse the national Democratic ticket and maintained an attitude of "silence is golden." Rep. Howard W. Smith, miffed at Robert Kennedy's criticism of the House Rules committee he heads, kept quiet. Rep. William M. Tuck, who pushed through the nation's first right to work law when he was governor of Virginia, did likewise.

The Democratic platform, as it has in the past, calls for repeal of state authority to enact such legislation.

Both Reelected

Both Smith and Tuck were reelected with the entire 10-member Virginia congressional delegation, Tuck without opposition. In addition Sen. A. Willis Robertson, D, with no Republican opponent won handily over Independent Stuart D. Baker, an Arlington machinery salesman. Incomplete returns from 1,608 precincts gave Robertson 353,193 to Baker's 65,491.

The Virginia lineup in the House of Representatives was left unchanged at 8 Democrats and two Republicans.

Republican campaign leaders and the Democrats for Nixon-Lodge took a degree of solace from their Virginia victory but it didn't make up for the gloom that rolled in with the rising tide of Kennedy votes on the national scene. A victory celebration set for a hotel ballroom withered and died.

Democratic campaigners suffered mixed emotions, too, if for reverse reasons.

Democratic campaign director William C. Battle called the presidential election in the state a good, hard fight that was much

(See State Vote, Page 2)

Nixon Tops Ballots In Waynesboro

Waynesboro gave Vice President Nixon a better than 2-1 edge in the presidential race Tuesday. Approximately 700 more voters turned out than did for the 1956 race between President Eisenhower and Adlai Stevenson.

Vice President Nixon captured 2,444 votes to Sen. John F. Kennedy's 1,047 votes, a margin of 1,397 votes. C. Benton Coiner, a conservative of near Waynesboro, drew only 22 votes from his native city.

In the 1956 election President Eisenhower drew 2,049 of the city's votes to his opponent's 748 votes.

Vice President Nixon carried all four voting precincts in Tuesday's election. His biggest lead was in the Second Ward, where he polled 702 votes to Sen. Kennedy's 213.

Sen. A. Willis Robertson captured 2,875 votes to Stuart Baker's 374 votes. Clarke T. Robb had 98 votes.

Rep. Burr P. Harrison tallied 2,504 votes. The city voted for the poll tax amendment by 2,557 to 671. The office consolidation amendment passed by a 1,804 to 1,304 vote.

Write-in votes for the House of Representatives included one vote each for H. D. Dawbarn, C. Benton Coiner, Fred Bowman and J. L. Moore. Three votes were cast for Louis Spilman.

Election Tables On Page 3 Today

For a complete precinct-by-precinct account of the area elections turn to page 3 where you will find tabulated results of Staunton, Augusta County, Waynesboro, Bath County, and Highland County.

News Inside

Democrat Holds Hairline Edge of Vote

BULLETIN

MINNEAPOLIS (AP) — Minnesota gave its 11 electoral votes to Sen. John F. Kennedy today and clinched the U.S. presidency for the Massachusetts Democrat.

It stretched Kennedy's nailed-down electoral vote to 272, three more than the minimum needed.

WASHINGTON (AP) — Democratic Sen. John F. Kennedy inched close to the presidency today with only a tantalizing handful of electoral votes lacking for victory over Vice President Richard M. Nixon.

In a neck-and-neck popular vote race with his Republican opponent, the 43-year-old Massachusetts senator rolled up 261 electoral votes—only eight short of the needed 269—in his bid to become the youngest man and the only Roman Catholic ever elected to the nation's highest office. Nixon's count was 168.

Nearly 70 Million

Nearly 70 million Americans took part in the decision.

Kennedy amassed his impressive total by taking the electoral vote of 19 states and winning the support of five of Alabama's 11 electors. The other six were uncommitted.

But the Democratic candidate was finding Nixon a difficult man to down finally, despite the fact that the vice president all but conceded defeat in an early morning television appearance from Los Angeles.

Nixon in fact was cutting steadily into Kennedy's lead in Illinois, throwing that state's 27 electoral votes into doubt. At that point the Democratic nominee still could win with either Minnesota's 11 or California's 32. But Nixon, who was polling about 49.5 per cent of the national popular vote, was pushing Kennedy in those states, too.

President Eisenhower's first official caller today reported the President looked fine, "but he's not happy about the results of the election."

White House Call

C. Burke Elbrick, U.S. ambassador to Portugal, called at the White House before departing for his post in Lisbon.

Nixon had all but conceded de-

(See National, Page 2)

President-Elect John F. Kennedy

Kennedy Told He Is President-Elect

HYANNIS PORT, Mass. (AP)—Sen. John F. Kennedy is aware that he is the president-elect, his press secretary said today. Pierre Salinger said the senator was told by a campaign aide that he has carried California and therefore has won the election.

The word was given to Kennedy shortly after he awoke at 9:30 a.m. EST today, Salinger said.

He said Kennedy would not have anything to say, however, until he hears from Vice President Richard M. Nixon.

Salinger said he understood from a statement made by Nixon's press secretary, Herbert G. Klein, in Los Angeles, that Nixon would not have anything to say until 9 a.m. Pacific time—noon Eastern time.

Therefore, Salinger said he doubted Kennedy would have anything to say before noon.

California has 32 electoral votes which, if he won it, would give Kennedy 293. It takes 269 to win.

The senator, wearing striped pajamas, could be seen in the house. He waved through a window.

Salinger joshed that he knew that Kennedy had "made it" when he found Secret Service agents at the senator's home today.

Kennedy was having breakfast with his wife, Jacqueline, at the time.

Kennedy went to bed at 3:50 a.m.—not knowing if he were president-elect — and slept until 9:30, Salinger told newsmen.

A bevy of Secret Service men was on duty at Sen. Kennedy's house this morning, a symbol that at least—protective-wise—he was considered the next president.

At 9:35 a.m. daughter Caroline made an appearance with Kennedy's cousin, Ann Gargan, and two playful Kennedy dogs. They walked across the rear lawn and disappeared in the direction of neighboring houses.

Not long afterwards, Senator Kennedy waved from an upstairs window.

And at 9:50 a.m., Salinger and Ted Sorenson, a campaign aide, went into the Kennedy house, presumably to confer with the Democratic candidate.

Highland Voted For The GOP

Contrary to the record breaking vote in the nation Tuesday, Highland County fell behind the 1956 election by some 137 votes.

Vice President Richard M. Nixon carried the small, mountainous county, 527 to 401. He had a 126 vote margin in the presidential race.

In the 1956 election President Eisenhower polled a total of 633 votes to Adlai Stevenson's 432 votes. There were 1,065 votes cast in the 1956 election.

Eight of the county's 12 precincts went for Vice President Nixon. Sen. John F. Kennedy carried Wilson's Mill, Doe Hill, Pullin's School House, and Patna precincts.

In the 1956 election President Eisenhower carried seven of the 12 precincts, dropping Blue Grass, Wilson's Mill, Doe Hill, Pullin's School House and Patna.

In the Senate race Sen. A. Willis Robertson polled 645 votes. Stuart Baker gathered 104 votes and Clarke T. Robb got 29 votes. Rep. Burr P. Harrison, who was unopposed, collected 573 votes.

The poll tax amendment was defeated, 419 votes to 313 votes. The other state amendment, dealing with consolidated government for counties, was also defeated, 442-102.

Hawaii Switches

HONOLULU (AP) — The Hawaii lieutenant governor's office announced early today that a recheck of Hawaii's 240 precincts gave this state's 3 electoral votes to Sen. John F. Kennedy by a margin of 102 ballots.

The total announced were: Vice President Richard M. Nixon 92,091; Kennedy 92,193.

Previous unofficial totals had given the state to Nixon by 141 votes.

The switch, giving it to Kennedy, is still not final, although listed as official.

It was announced that, in view of the closeness of the totals, a recount would be made some time in the next several days.

Democrats in Solid Control of Congress

WASHINGTON (AP) — Solid Democratic majorities will control the Senate and the House when the 87th Congress convenes Jan. 3.

The Democrats quickly nailed down control of the Senate in Tuesday's election. And by 3 o'clock this morning, they had captured more than half the 437 House seats.

Nonetheless, with returns still incomplete, it appeared the Republicans had dented the top-heavy margins the Democrats held in the out-going 86th Congress. In the Senate the old line-up was 66-34 and in the House 283-154.

Two GOP Seats

With all of the Senate races settled except for a tight battle in Montana, the Republicans had picked up one seat in Delaware and another in Wyoming.

Sen. Karl Mundt, veteran South Dakota Republican, squeaked to victory over Rep. George McGovern, a Democrat who decided to give up his House seat to make the race for the Senate.

In Montana, Democratic Rep. Lee Metcalf and Republican former Rep. Owen B. Fjare were in a mid-and-tuck contest for the Senate seat being vacated by Sen. James E. Murray, D-Mont.

In the House, Republicans had gobbled up 18 seats held by Democrats but had lost 5 for a net gain of 13. In races still undecided, Democrats were ahead in 30 and Republicans in 27.

Over-all, however, the outlook was for Congress similar in makeup and key figures to the one President Eisenhower had to deal with in the last two years of his administration.

Southern Democrats, most of whom supported Sen. John F. Kennedy even though strongly opposed to parts of the party platform, would continue to hold many of the committee chairmanships and be in position to team up with Republicans against legislation they dislike.

Senate Democratic Leader Lyndon B. Johnson of Texas won re-election to the Senate, but was prepared to resign to assume the vice presidency.

The Big Three in the House, Speaker Sam Rayburn, D-Tex.; the majority leader, Rep. John W. McCormack, D-Mass., and the Republican leader, Rep. Charles A. Halleck of Indiana, all won re-election.

Another long familiar figure in the House, former Republican Speaker Joseph W. Martin of Massachusetts, won re-election after a tussle with his Democratic foe, Edward F. Doolan. Martin trailed in the early returns.

Most of the overturns in the House were at the expense of freshman Democrats swept into office in the 1958 Democratic landslide from normally Republican areas.

Republican gains were chalked up in Connecticut, Vermont, Indiana, Maryland, Colorado, Ohio, Pennsylvania and Maine. The GOP lost seats in New York, New Jersey and Idaho.

In New York, the Democrats picked up three House seats and for the first time in 10 years won control of the state's 43-member delegation.

With 34 of the 100 Senate seats at stake in th[illegible] Democrats had wo[illegible] [illegible]licans 12 by the ea[illegible] hours. Only one incum[illegible]t, Sen. J. Allen Frear Jr., D-Del., had been toppled.

Turned Back

Frear's bid for a third term was turned back by Republican Gov. J. Caleb Boggs even as Kennedy captured Delaware's three electoral votes and the Democrats won the governorship.

The Republicans picked up a second Senate seat with the election of Rep. Keith Thomson to replace veteran Democratic Sen. Joseph C. O'Mahoney, retiring at the age of 76. Thomson's Democratic opponent was Raymond B. Whitaker.

The election of Maurine B. Neuberger, an Oregon Democrat, will give the Senate two women mem-

(See Congress, Page 2)

Post Office To Close Friday

The Staunton Post Office will be closed all day, Friday, Nov. 11, 1960. There will be no deliveries by city or rural carriers. All windows will be closed all day.

Mail deposited in the main post office will be dispatched as usual except there will be no service on the Charlottesville, Monterey, and Middlebrook star routes due to the holiday. Special delivery mail will be delivered between the hours of seven a.m. and 11 p.m.

Named Editor Of C. of C. Magazine

RICHMOND — James S. Wamsley, 36, an Associated Press staff writer, was named managing editor of the Commonwealth Magazine, monthly publication of the Virginia State Chamber of Commerce, according to an announcement made today by Verbon E. Kemp, State Chamber executive director.

William S. Lacy Jr., editor of the Commonwealth for the last 15 years, died of a heart attack on Oct. 17.

A native of Staunton and a graduate of Washington and Lee University, Mr. Wamsley has been with the Associated Press in its Richmond bureau almost four years. Prior to joining the AP he was associated with the Life Insurance Co. of Virginia.

The new Commonwealth managing editor is a veteran of four years' service with the U. S. Air Force. He served as a public information specialist in the United Kingdom and France during the Korean conflict.

Mr. Wamsley is married to the former Gwen Cooper of Clarksville. They have two children, Robin 4, and Cooper 2. They reside on Woodcroft Road in Bon Air.

He will assume the duties of his new position with the State Chamber of Commerce on Nov. 21.

MR. WAMSLEY

November 9, 1960: John F. Kennedy defeats Vice President Richard Nixon in the Presidential race. *Microfilm Archives*

Another early 1960s view of Central Avenue before the wrecking ball started to swing. This picture shows the Leader offices and, beyond, the buildings that would soon be demolished in the name of "urban renewal." *Schwartz Collection*

Planters Bank demolished Joe's Restaurant and Steele's Lunch on the corner to expand its operations, and the buildings shown at the corner of Johnson and Lewis would be knocked down to construct the city's first parking garage. *Schwartz Collection*

Photograph of Central Avenue from Johnson Street, showing how the area looked before it was developed to accommodate Staunton's first parking garage. *Schwartz Collection*

View from Reservoir Hill showing the empty lots left on Central Avenue by the "urban renewal" demolitions of the 1960's. *Schwartz Collection*

Looking west on Frederick Street, this view shows the rubble of a building just demolished as part of the city's poorly thought-out "urban renewal" plan. A sign reads, "Renewal of this area is being carried out with financial aid from the Urban Renewal Administration United States Housing & Home Finance Agency." The other buildings shown on the left would also fall to the wrecking ball, as would three entire blocks in the city's central business district. *Schwartz Collection*

February 10, 1962 photograph of the Staunton Fire Department responding to a blaze at Vames Candyland, which was located at the intersection of West Beverley and Lewis streets. The fire began in the upper floors of the building, known as the Dixie Hotel, and was so intense that it also damaged Bennie's Shoe Store, Cline Furniture and Piedmont Loans. The 1937 ladder truck pictured here was sold in 1978 for $1,101 to a museum in Arizona. *Schwartz Collection*

ASTRONAUT JOHN GLENN GOES INTO ORBIT

Off Into Orbit He Went

Cleared for Full 3-Orbit Mission

CAPE CANAVERAL, Fla. (AP) — Astronaut John H. Glenn Jr. reported that despite minor difficulties with his capsule control system, he was in good condition to complete his full three-orbit mission around the world.

While officials were considering the possibility of terminating the flight after two orbits, the astronaut told the Kauai tracking station in Hawaii that he was in good shape and having no trouble controlling his craft.

The Hawaii station confirmed Glenn's judgment, advised the Mercury control center at Cape Canaveral, and Glenn was given the green light to continue.

CAPE CANAVERAL, Fla. (AP) —Astronaut John H. Glenn Jr. rocketed into orbit today in his spacecraft "Friendship 7" at 9:47 a.m. Eastern Standard Time, and scientists planned to bring him down after he circled the earth three times in four hours, 50 minutes.

As Glenn soared toward his rendezvous with the stars, he reported by radio to Mercury control center at Cape Canaveral that "I feel fine and the view is tremendous."

He said he could see the Atlas booster rocket falling away behind him and that he had a clear view of much of the earth stretching back to the Cape from his vantage point about 100 miles in space.

"It's a beautiful sight," Glenn exclaimed.

The reports came from the control center here, where officials monitored the historic flight of the first American to be fired into orbit.

Glenn's space capsule was blasted skyward by a powerful Atlas booster.

The massive rocket, generating 360,000 pounds thrust, performed perfectly and with pinpoint precision, boosted the spacecraft to the proper speed and altitude for the mission.

Officials reported the capsule was in an orbit ranging from a high point of 160 miles to a low of 100 miles and the speed was 17,545 miles an hour. Estimated time of each circuit of the globe was 89 minutes.

Like True Test Pilot

As the rocket rose skyward, Glenn, acting like a true test pilot, reported on the condition of his instruments and of himself. He said forces of eight times the pull of gravity worked on him during the peak acceleration.

After reporting the fallaway of the booster, he radioed that his spacecraft had successfully turned around 180 degrees as planned so that he was riding upright and backwards, with the craft's heat shield leading the way.

Almost immediately, the Mercury tracking station at Bermuda picked up signals from the swiftly moving vehicle and reported Glenn's voice coming in clearly.

At this point, the National Aeronautics and Space Administration confirmed that orbit had been attained.

It was planned to bring Glenn down to a landing 800 miles southeast of Cape Canaveral at approximately 2:37 p.m.

The launching came after several frustrating postponements dating back to Dec. 20. Several technical delays today slipped the scheduled 7:30 a.m. launching for more than two hours and almost forced reduction of the flight to two orbits.

Officials had said that if the liftoff occurred too much past 9:30 a.m. they might cut the number of orbits.

The gravity forces which gripped Glenn on liftoff, making his lean, trim body feel eight times heavier than its normal 165 pounds, vanished suddenly when the capsule entered orbit.

The pressure was gone and Glenn became weightless — the buoyant feeling that results when a delicate balance is achieved between the outward pull of centrifugal force and the downward pull of the earth's gravity.

Glenn was to be in this mysterious weightless condition for most of the remainder of his flight, until Friendship 7 re-entered the atmosphere en route back to earth. A major goal of today's flight was to determine man's capabilities and limitations in that weightless environment.

It is a sensation future space travelers must learn to cope with for days and weeks at a time.

Putting Glenn into orbit does not necessarily make the mission a success, however.

Critical Period

Still ahead lay a critical period of re-entry at completion of the three orbits. A trio of reverse rockets at the base of the capsule were to be fired by a signal from an automatic clock aboard the craft as it approached the West Coast of the United States near the end of the third circuit.

If all fire properly, speed will be reduced enough to take the capsule out of orbit and enable it to descend gradually to a landing near Grand Turk Island in the Bahamas.

Because Friendship 7 was traveling five miles a second, it would miss the intended impact zone by five miles every second of error in the clock. Or, if only one or two of the rockets fired, he would miss the area by hundreds of miles and recovery would be more difficult.

After firing of the retros, Glenn then had to rely on the complex spacecraft control parachute and landing systems and the far-flung recovery forces for his salvation.

Or, as in the case of the orbital flight of Enos, the chimpanzee, last November trouble could develop in the capsule and the flight be terminated early.

Torrent of Flame

The huge missile spilled a torrent of flame over the launching pad.

Ponderously, the 125-ton monster rose slowly from the earth to start Glenn toward his intended rendezvous with the stars.

This first attempt to put an American astronaut into orbit came after a series of frustrating postponements dating back to Dec. 20.

Technical troubles involving the Atlas guidance system, a faulty respiration sensor in Glenn's helmet, a broken bolt on the capsule hatch cover and a fueling problem today delayed the launching past its intended 7:30 a.m. time.

As the rocket was ignited, great billows of smoke poured out of the bottom of the tall Atlas shot through with flashes of brilliant light.

Jetting from the bottom was a long tongue of bright orange flame, looking much like a Fourth of July fireworks flare.

Two small rocket engines, used for minor course corrections, blazed brightly on either side of the long, pencil-like silver rocket.

In seconds, a great roar barreled across the Cape and struck the ears of reporters and other observers nearly two miles away.

Less than two minutes after blastoff, which was 9:47 a.m., Eastern Standard Time, systems in the spaceship were "go." He confirmed booster engine cutoff about two minutes after liftoff and was reading his instruments, reporting back on cabin pressure and the gradual buildup of the pressures of gravity that were forcing him back into his contour seat.

Climbing Well

Shortly before three minutes he reported the escape tower separation and the space ship was reported climbing well on its trajectory.

Below, a high-altitude observation plane traced a lazy "S" contrail to the south of the climbing missile.

As the rocket soared on toward orbit, Glenn reported "I feel fine" and that his view was tremendous.

Mercury control center, receiving a steady stream of reports, said that when the Atlas separated from the capsule about five minutes after launch.

Glenn reported it was a "beautiful sight to see."

At 9:56 a.m., Glenn was reported in contact with Mercury tracking station at Bermuda.

Glenn reported from his space ship that he saw a very large cloud pattern near the Cape Canaveral area.

The space ship was tilted into its proper attitude.

Glenn was described as primed and confident before he retired early Monday night. He had done the same last Tuesday, Wednesday and Thursday nights only to be disappointed by the weather delays—marking a total of 10 postponements of scheduled firing dates since last Dec. 20.

Newsmen discovered the astronaut in a Cocoa Beach barber shop Monday and he told them he was ready and eager to go and that he was not the least disturbed by the numerous delays. He said they "are of no consequence because I have been training and waiting for three years, and a few more days won't matter."

He said he had been passing the time "running through simulated missions and boning up on the stars" he might see as he whirls about the earth.

Before retiring, he phoned his wife, Annie and two children at their Arlington, Va., home, and his parents in New Concord, Ohio.

On Jan. 27, Glenn went through final preparations only to be disappointed after the countdown had advanced to within 20 minutes of liftoff. Heavy clouds blanketed the launching area, making vital camera trackage of the rocket impossible.

Glenn climbed out of the capsule after five hours 13 minutes of confinement. Subsequent trouble with the Atlas, caused additional postponements before last week's Atlantic Ocean weather problems. Four earlier dates

(See Glenn, Page 2)

The PUBLIC Interest FIRST

THE STAUNTON LEADER
and
The Staunton News-Leader

Weather
Fair and colder tonight low in the 20s except 15 to 20 mountains. Wednesday fair and a little colder.

VOL. 115, NO. 36 | MEMBER ASSOCIATED PRESS BUREAU OF CIRCULATION | STAUNTON, VIRGINIA, TUESDAY, FEBRUARY 20, 1962 | MEMBER OF THE AUDIT WIRE AND FEATURE SERVICE | PRICE FIVE CENTS

Col. Glenn Kept Personal Date With Destiny Today

CAPE CANAVERAL, Fla. (AP) —John H. Glenn Jr today kept a personal date with destiny, a date he worked unswervingly toward for a long time.

In all ways since his selection as a Mercury astronaut three years ago, Glenn drove himself hard- dedicated and determined to ride into space and contribute to man's knowledge.

So far as anyone could tell, nothing could corrode his iron nerve. All those postponements, including the heartbreaker of Jan. 27, when he spent 5 hours and 13 minutes strapped down in a capsule that wasn't going anywhere, could have unhinged a lesser man. But not Glenn.

Modesty Stood Out

Modesty also stood out all over Glenn's make-up during his long training. In vain, he pleaded with the world to take the spotlight off him and his family and focus it on the worthwhile things to be done, and learned, up there in the skies.

Why was Glenn, a family man with two children, willing to risk his life in a space capsule whirling about the globe at 17,500 miles an hour?

"We've got to do it," he once said. "We're going into an age of exploration that will be bigger than anything the world has ever seen.

"People are afraid of the future, of the unknown. If a man faces up to it and takes the dare of the future, he can have some control over his destiny. That's an exciting idea to me, better than waiting to see what's going to happen."

Glenn, a balding 40-year-old Marine lieutenant colonel, wanted desperately to be the first American space pilot. He lost the call on the first two flights to Alan B. Shepard Jr. and Virgil I. Grissom. For each of these brief suborbital flights, Glenn was the backup astronaut.

He rated his backup experience, in which he worked closely with Shepard and Grissom for weeks before each flight, as invaluable for his round-the-world orbit mission.

Also invaluable was his experience as a combat pilot in World War II and later in Korea. He shot down three Communist MIG fighters in the final days of the Korean War, and after one dogfight returned to base with more than 200 bullet holes in his plane. He won five Distinguished Flying Crosses and an Air Medal with 18 clusters.

After the war he became a top test pilot.

Always very close to his family, Glenn nevertheless decided early that the Mercury program was so important he would live in

(See Destiny, Page 2)

Lt. Col. John H. Glenn Jr.

And Around the Earth He Flew

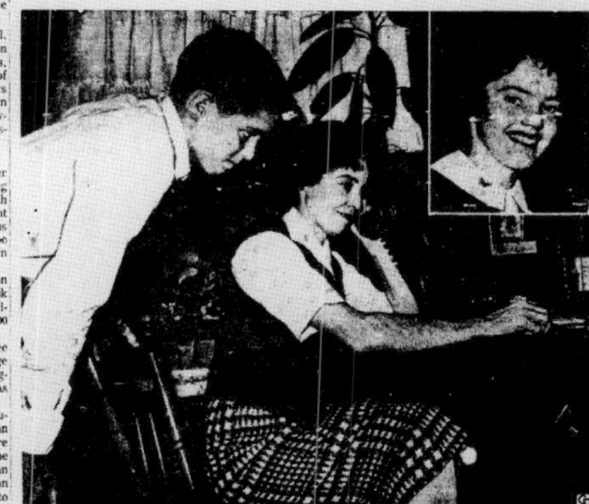

EYES ON SPACE — Here are the wife and children of U. S. Mercury astronaut John H. Glenn Jr., who live in Arlington, Va. The wife and mother is Anna; the son is Dave, 15, and the daughter (inset) is Lynn, 14.

White Collar Pay Hike Urged

WASHINGTON (AP)—President Kennedy urged Congress today to provide a billion dollar pay raise over three years for the government's white collar workers. The aim, he said, is to put federal pay on a par with that outside so that competent people can afford to work for Uncle Sam.

The President said in a special message that he was proposing "federal pay reform, not simply a federal pay raise."

For the whole field of white collar workers, the increase would amount to 10 per cent of the present $10-billion annual payroll. But for individuals, the raises would range from 3.7 per cent to about 33 per cent for the three-year period. The first increase would come Jan. 1.

Kennedy said he is proposing a wholly new, common sense approach to the problem of putting federal salaries on a basis comparable to those in nonfederal service. This would be done for all but the highest-level officials. And for them, Kennedy said, the most vital single element in the proposal is pay adjustments for top executive and professional positions. Many of these top-rank employes, he said, are being drawn away by higher pay outside. Low government wages endanger national security, said Kennedy.

The pay reform would apply to 1,640,000 employes spread throughout the world. It would not affect approximately 660,000 blue collar workers in skilled trades and crafts.

Everybody in the white collar category would get some sort of raise. For the lowest grade, GS-1, the entrance salary of $3,185 would go up to $3,225 next Jan. 1, to $3,265 a year later and to $3,305 in the third step.

The biggest group in any one class is the 166,000 workers in GS-4. Those are mainly clerical workers—file clerks, stenographers or clerk typists. The top salary in this grade would reach $5,475 at the end of the three year salary reform program compared with a present peak of $4,985.

A recent college graduate without experience would start in at Grade 5 at $4,345 under present schedules. Under the new plan he would enter federal service at $4,565 as of next year. The figure would go to $4,690 by Jan. 1, 1965. At this point the top salary for his grade would be $6,130.

In Mental Hospital

Seeks $34,000 For Period 'Lost'

A man who "through error" was detained in a Virginia mental hospital from 1941 until 1958 is asking the state to pay him $34,000.

By request, Delegates George M. Cochran and Felix E. Edmunds have introduced House Bill 538 under which this claim would be paid, if approved by the General Assembly.

Christopher Reid Pforr is the claimant. The history of the case, his detention in a mental hospital, subsequent discharge in court of charges against him, and his claim are set forth in the House bill as follows:

House Bill No. 538, offered Feb. 13, 1962, a bill for the relief of Christopher Reid Pforr; patrons Messrs. Cochran (by request) and Edmunds (by request) — referred to the Committee on Claims:

Whereas, Christopher Reid Pforr was accused of rape on March 19, 1941, in Augusta County, Virginia, the preliminary hearing of which was waived and was held for action by the grand jury, after which he was brought before the Circuit Court of Augusta County; it was then represented to the court by the attorney for the commonwealth that defendant should be confined in a hospital for the insane for proper care and observation; which accusations have at all times been denied by said Christopher Reid Pforr; and

Whereas, on May 20, 1941, he was committed to the criminal insane department of the Southwestern State Hospital, Marion, Virginia, by order of the Circuit Court of Augusta County, for a period of observation and study and determination of his mental condition, which order stated as follows:

". . . there to be confined, observed and examined from time to time by the superintendent in charge and such other officers of the medical staff of said hospital as may be assigned to

(See Seeks, Page 2)

$30,000 Suit Filed In Death of AMA Cadet

The father of an Augusta Military Academy cadet, killed Nov. 9, 1961, when struck by a car while returning from a hayride, has filed a $30,000 damage suit jointly against the school and the driver of the car.

Suit has been brought by George L. Schoechle of Alexandria, father of Peter Warren Schoechle, 14. Named defendants are Robert Fletcher Simmons, Weyers Cave, indentified as the driver of the car which struck the youth and Gen. Charles S. Roller Jr., principal of A.M.A.

The papers were filed in Augusta County Circuit Court by Russell O. Pettibone, an attorney with the Arlington firm of Tolbert, Lewis, and Fitzgerald. Curtis L. Allen, Waynesboro attorney, also has been retained by Mr. Schoechle.

State Police reported at the time of the crash, which occurred on Rt. 11, near its intersection with State Rt. 777, the youth was killed when he either fell or jumped from the wagon on which he was riding. Dr. W. G. Painter, county medical examiner pronounced young Schoechle dead at the scene. He noted death was instantaneous, caused by skull injuries and a broken neck.

Negligence Alleged

In papers filed with the court, Mr. Schoechle alleges the academy "was negligent and careless" in that representatives failed to provide the tractor and wagon with reflectors and warning lights, failed to keep a proper lookout, failed to operate the trac-

(See Suit, Page 2)

News Inside

Glued To Television

ARLINGTON, Va. (AP) — The family of astronaut John H. Glenn Jr. had five television sets ready today to watch his scheduled launching into orbit about the earth.

It meant a day off from school for the children—David, 16, and Lyn, 14.

It meant that Glenn's wife, Annie, 41, was going to stay "glued to the tv," as one friend put it.

It meant excitement, worry and pride, too, but if the repeated postponements of her husband's adventure has brought strain and anxiety to the Glenn family, the astronaut's wife was keeping it to herself.

Mrs. Glenn has said many times that she felt fine during all the waiting for her husband's historic flight and that she had complete confidence in the space project.

Plans at the Glenn's contemporary brick home in Arlington, a suburb of Washington, were for everybody to get up early, everybody to get his own breakfast and everybody to one of the tv sets.

By Public Health Director

Fluoride Hailed at Kiwanis

Members of the Staunton Kiwanis Club were told Monday that "misinformation and fear" keep fluoride out of many public water supplies although fluoridation is "completely safe, effective, economical, and legal".

Speaking to the group was Dr. James B. Kenley, director of the Augusta County, Staunton, and Waynesboro Health Department, who recommended that Staunton City Council add fluoride to its water supply.

In his opinion, judging from figures available in communities comparable to the size of Staunton, it probably would cost about $7,000 for purchase of necessary equipment and some $1,000 each year to add fluoride to the city system. He added the procedure is "very economical", and probably would cost 10 cents per person per year.

PTA Interested

The possibility of adding fluoride to the water supply came up again when the Westside Parent-Teacher Association submitted a resolution to City Council favoring the addition. At that time, Council asked Dr. Kenley to make a study and submit a report. Council has not acted on his recommendation. A similar proposal was turned down some 10 years ago.

Meanwhile neighboring Waynesboro and Harrisonburg have been using fluoride in their water supplies for several years.

Dr. Kenley, introduced by the program chairman, C. M. Moyer Jr., cited the importance of fluoridation in preventing tooth decay. In his opinion, "children drinking fluoridated water from birth have 60 per cent fewer cavities than children drinking fluoride deficient water. Older children benefit also when they begin drinking from a fluoridated water supply".

He observed Staunton's supply contains only about .2 parts fluoride per million parts of water and this "is very little. Anything under .3 is considered insignificant. It is not enough for the body to use effectively".

Dr. Kenley explained "the amount of fluoride needed to prevent tooth decay is one part per million parts of water".

Safety Stressed

Kiwanians also were told fluoridation is safe since "it would take 20 to 80 times the recommended amount daily for between 10 to 20 years to produce crippling fluorosis. It takes eight times the recommended amount daily for 10 years to produce staining of the teeth and a few minor changes in the bones".

There also are a number of safeguards employed to protect the public when fluoride is added. He added: "2,500 to 5,000 times the recommended amount of fluoride would have to be dumped into the water in an in-

(See Fluoride, Page 2)

Grand Jury to Consider Murder Charge

Events Leading Up to Fatal Shooting On Roadside Described at Hearing

A Nelson County man, charged with the murder of a drinking companion entered a plea of not guilty Monday at a preliminary hearing in Augusta County Court. The case was ordered held for grand jury consideration on Feb. 26.

Pettit Carl Miller, 38, of Roseland is charged with killing William Emmett Bayrd, 51, also of Roseland, on Jan. 27 on Rt. 610, between Stuarts Draft and Sherando, following a heated argument.

Three witnesses for the Commonwealth, all of whom were in the party when the shooting occurred, indicated in their testimony that Miller shot Bayrd in self-defense.

Miller did not take the witness stand as no evidence was produced by the defense attorney, Wayt B. Timberlake Jr.

State Trooper E. J. Good, who was called to the scene of the shooting and investigated, said that Miller, Mr. Bayrd, Robert Preston Hite, Richmond; Edgar Bryant, Piney River, and Mrs Anna Bell Armstrong, Deerfield, were together on the night of Jan. 27 when the Nelson County man was slain.

In Gravel Storage Area

Trooper Good said that when he arrived at the scene, he found Mr. Bayrd's body lying in front of Miller's 1953 Ford, which had been parked off the highway in a highway department gravel storage area.

According to the investigating officer, Miller was sitting on the ground, about six feet from the body. The gun used in the shooting, a .25 calibre automatic pistol, was lying between the two men.

The trooper testified that Miller had been drinking and that he admitted having shot Mr. Bayrd with the pistol that was recovered.

Trooper Good said that Miller had been injured. He said his nose was bleeding slightly. He later was taken to the Waynesboro Community Hospital for treatment.

The state policeman said he

(See Murder, Page 2)

February 20, 1962: John Glenn becomes America's first astronaut to orbit Earth. *Microfilm Archives*

View looking north up Central Avenue from Beverley Street, circa the mid to late 1960s. This streetscape would alter dramatically in the early 1980s when Community Federal Savings and Loan (now Community Bank) razed two-thirds of this city block for a parking lot and drive-though. In the process, it displaced a number of profitable businesses and destroyed buildings that housed the first black school in Staunton and the Whitmore Hotel. *Schwartz Collection*

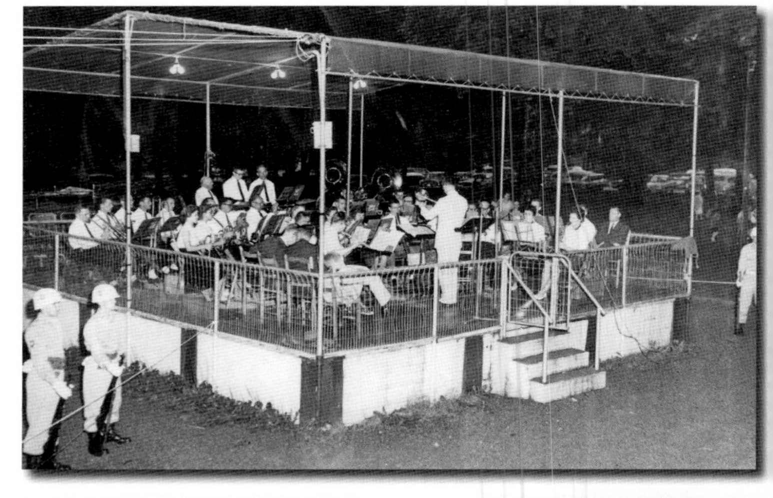

A 1960s photo of members of the Stonewall Brigade Band performing a concert at the old bandstand in Gypsy Hill Park The band still performs on Monday nights throughout the summer, as it has since the 1870s. *Schwartz Collection*

In October of 1960, the city pulled out all the stops to welcome President Dwight D. Eisenhower. Invited to speak by the Woodrow Wilson Birthplace Foundation, Eisenhower agreed because he had long wanted to visit the Mt. Sidney birthplace of his mother, Elizabeth Ida Stover Eisenhower.

The former general who oversaw victory in Europe in World War II visited his mother's birthplace and then swept into Staunton with his entourage on Oct. 27, 1960. Despite rainy skies, thousands of people cheered him as he rode in a car through the streets of Staunton.

Eisenhower toured and spoke at the Wilson birthplace, addressed thousands of admirers from the portico of Mary Baldwin College and, following lunch in MBC's King Auditorium, boarded a helicopter at Northside school for a quick hop back to the Shenandoah Valley Airport in Weyers Cave.
Schwartz Collection

The PUBLIC Interest FIRST

THE STAUNTON LEADER

Weather
Partly cloudy tonight. Saturday, considerable cloudiness. Chance of showers.

VOL. 116, NO. 130 | MEMBER OF THE AUDIT BUREAU OF CIRCULATION | STAUNTON, VIRGINIA, FRIDAY, NOVEMBER 22, 1963 | MEMBER ASSOCIATED PRESS WIRE AND FEATURE SERVICE | PRICE FIVE CENTS

President Kennedy Assassinated

★ ★

Texas Governor Also Shot Down

By Sniper In Dallas, Tex.

DALLAS (AP) — President John F. Kennedy, thirty-sixth president of the United States, was shot to death today by a hidden assassin armed with a high-powered rifle.

Kennedy, 46, lived about an hour after a sniper cut him down as his limousine left downtown Dallas.

Automatically, the mantle of the presidency fell to Vice President Lyndon B. Johnson, a native Texan who had been riding two cars behind the chief executive.

No Immediate Word

There was no immediate word on when Johnson would take the oath of office.

Kennedy died at Parkland Hospital where his bullet-pierced body had been taken in a frantic but futile effort to save his life.

Lying wounded at the same hospital was Gov. John Connally of Texas, who was cut down by the same fusillade that ended the life of the youngest man ever elected to the presidency.

Connally and his wife had been riding with the President and Mrs. Kennedy.

The First Lady cradled her dying husband's bloodsmeared head in her arms as the presidential limousine raced to the hospital.

"Oh, no," she kept crying.

Connally slumped in his seat beside the President.

Dragnet Ordered

Police ordered an unprecedented dragnet of the city, hunting for the assassin.

They believed the fatal shots were fired by a white man, about 30, slender of build, weighing about 165 pounds, and standing 5 feet 10 inches tall.

The murder weapon was reportedly a 30-30 rifle.

Shortly before Kennedy's death became known, he was administered the last rites of the Roman Catholic Church. He had been the first Roman Catholic president in American history.

Even as two clergymen hovered over the fallen President in the hospital emergency room, doctors and nurses administered blood transfusions.

Kennedy died of a gunshot wound in the brain at approximately 1 p.m. (CST) according to an announcement by acting White House press secretary Malcolm Kilduff.

The new President, Lyndon Johnson, and his wife left the hospital a half hour later. Newsmen had no opportunity to question them.

The horror of the assassination was mirrored in an eyewitness account by Sen. Ralph Yarborough, D-Tex., who had been riding three cars behind Kennedy.

"You could tell something awful and tragic had happened," the senator told newsmen before Kennedy's death became known. His voice breaking and his eyes red-rimmed, Yarborough said:

In Anger

"I could see a Secret Service man in the President's car leaning on the car with his hands in anger, anguish and despair. I knew then something tragic had happened."

Yarborough had counted three rifle shots as the presidential limousine left downtown Dallas through a triple underpass. The shots were fired from above—possibly from one of the bridges or from a nearby building.

One witness, television reporter Mal Couch, said he saw a gun emerge from an upper story of a warehouse commanding an unobstructed view of the presidential car.

Kennedy was the first president to be assassinated since William McKinley was shot in 1901.

It was the first death of a president in office since Franklin D. Roosevelt died of a cerebral hemorrhage at Warm Springs, Ga., in April 1945.

30-Year Term For Child Assault

EARL HUNTER HOOVER, who was convicted of attempted rape by a 12-man Circuit Court jury Thursday and given a 30-year term in the state penitentiary, covers his face as he walks from the Augusta County courthouse with Deputy Sheriff James A. Harris. (Staff Photo by Stephenson)

Earl Hunter Hoover of Star Rt. B, Staunton was found guilty of attempted rape of a 12-year-old Negro girl and given a 30-year sentence in the state penitentiary by a 12-man all-white Circuit Court jury Thursday.

Hoover, a white man was charged with raping the Staunton girl on Aug. 30 on a country road leading off the Middlebrook Road, about 2½ miles south of the city limits.

He pleaded not guilty, claiming that he did not remember ever seeing the girl before they met in the police station after the incident.

The jury took the case at 2:53 p. m. and returned with the verdict at 4:42, one hour and forty-nine minutes later. Robert K. Dungan, foreman, handed the decision to Court Clerk Rudolph L. Shaver, who read it.

Hoover turned and watched Mr. Shaver as he read the jury's finding, but showed no emotion. His wife broke into tears. Hoover covered his face as he walked from the courthouse in front of a photographer.

The Negro girl watched from the front steps of the court house lawn as he was taken back to jail by Deputy Sheriff James A. Harris.

Commonwealth's Attorney Philip L. Lotz had asked the jury to find Hoover guilty of rape and sentence him to life in prison.

Hoover's attorney, E. G. Wingfield of Charlottesville, made a motion to have the verdict set aside as being contrary to the law and evidence. Judge William S. Moffett Jr. set Dec. 4 to hear and rule upon the motion.

Approximately 20 persons were in the court room when the jury returned with the verdict, about half were Negroes.

The 28-year-old man was convicted of a forgery count in Staunton Corporation Court on Feb. 5, 1959 and was given two years in the penitentiary, which was suspended, and he was placed on probation for two years.

He was convicted on another forgery count in the same court on March 16, 1961 and given two years to serve. The court also revoked the suspended sentence and ordered him to serve that two years, for a total of four.

Hoover was paroled from the penitentiary on Aug. 28, 1962 and was scheduled to have been released from parole on Feb. 28, 1964.

What Happened To Doctors' Night Calls?

By WILLIAM J. Conway
Associated Press StaffWriter

CHICAGO (AP) — What has happened to doctors' old-fashioned night calls at homes?

This inquiring reporter made a quick sampling at this week's meeting of the Illinois Academy of General Practice.

Talks with seven family doctors from all parts of the state — all of whom make evening visits — left these impressions:

By and large, family doctors still make night calls. But they get fewer calls because of the patient's consideration for the physician's health and his own money. One medical man estimated fees are 30 to 50 per cent higher after dark.

"The truth is we don't get as many night calls as we used to," said Dr. John D. McCarthy of Riverside, "largely because the patients have increased concern for the doctor's welfare and have become accustomed to going directly to the emergency room in a hospital, especially in cases of trauma. It gets the patient under treatment quicker, with better results and less expense to everybody concerned."

Some of the doctors asked anonymity.

"When the price goes up, people don't call you as often," commented a physician from a small town in Northern Illinois. "I'm glad to make them (calls) now at the price I charge for them."

"I wish I had a dime for every time I had to dress and go out on a call," said a medic from a community of 15,000 in Southern Illinois.

A gray-haired physician from a sizable city in the southern half of the state said he makes nocturnal calls.

24-Hr. Flight Around World

SEVEN SHORT YEARS from now, you may be taking a trip around the world aboard a supersonic airliner that is so fast it outraces the sun during its 24-hour journey!

SUCH A UNITED STATES airliner — which would cruise at more than 2,000 miles an hour at 70,000 feet — is not just a science-fiction pipe dream. It is now on the drawing boards and is expected to be flying by 1970.

TO GIVE YOU a preview of your flight of the future, Kevin V. Brown, a veteran aviation writer, has written an absorbing article, "Around the World in 24 Hours", in the Nov. 24 issue of Family Weekly, which appears with your copy of The Staunton News-Leader.

IN THE SAME issue, Mrs. Alan King tells of her hectic—yet heartwarming — years as wife of the popular comedian. In "My Side of the Story", she tells about their growing up in Brooklyn tenements, their marriage when he was 18 and she was 17, their years of struggling to the top, and their happy, often hilarious, life now that Alan has reached the pinnacle of show-business success.

ANOTHER FAMILY WEEKLY article on the lighter side is "Hunters Who Give Me a Pain in My Duck Blind", the lament of a fellow whose choice of hunting companions has often been unfortunate. Among them you will meet George H., the Best-Dressed Gunman on the Housatonic River, and Grant L., who fiddles endlessly with decoys — while the ducks fly away.

ROUNDING OUT the lineup of the Nov. 24 issue features are Melanie De Proft's "Family Weekly Cookbook", Patty Johnson's "I Was Just Thinking", Ann Davidow's "Junior Treasure Chest", and that Family Weekly favorite, "Quips and Quotes".

Area Detention Home Study Group to Meet

An organizational meeting of the juvenile detention home study commission which will have representatives from 10 political subdivisions, is scheduled for Tuesday, Dec. 17.

The session tentatively is scheduled for 2 p.m. in the Staunton City Council chambers in City Hall. A chairman and other officers are to be elected, as well as a course of action chartered.

The group with representatives from Staunton, Waynesboro, Augusta County, Rockingham County, Harrisonburg, Rockbridge County, Buena Vista, Charlottesville, Highland County, and Albemarle County, is expected to make a study concerning the need for a juvenile detention home, size facility needed, probable costs, and other matters pertaining to such a project. Any recommendation made would be taken by commission members back to their respective governing bodies for further consideration.

Those Present

William E. Weddington, chief of the bureau of juvenile probation and detention, is expected to be invited to explain to representatives what help the state would contribute toward construction and maintenance of a home. Several juvenile judges and probation officers are expected to be in attendance.

Location of the proposed home would have to be decided by a committee with representatives from the interested localities.

An interest in construction of a detention home was started last month by juvenile probation officers and the Staunton League of Women voters.

Plans for construction of a home were prepared by a commission in 1958, but the plan died because of lack of support by some of the counties involved.

All the political subdivisions have named their representatives for the commission with the exception of Albemarle County, although supervisors there have approved appointment of two members.

Those Named

Representatives already named are:

Staunton: Police Court Judge J. Forester Taylor; Attorney T. C. Elder, a former Augusta County Court judge; and City Manager C. M. Moyer Jr.

Augusta County: R. E. Huff, supervisor of accounts; Hugh K. Cassell, superintendent of public schools; and R. A. Bowman, executive secretary.

Waynesboro: Andrew Gott, Welfare Department superintendent; and Carter R. Allen, Commonwealth's attorney.

Rockingham County: The Rev. Guy E. Wampler and Don Litten, Harrisonburg attorney.

Harrisonburg: The Rev. Robert Houff and D. Nathan Mims, editor of the Daily News Record.

Rockbridge County: Alex Wilson, member of the board of supervisors, and Mrs. John M. Gunn, member of the League of Women Voters.

Buena Vista: John R. Lynn, member of City Council, and Guy W. Griffin, superintendent of the Welfare Department.

Highland County: R. Turner Jones, Commonwealth's attorney, and Martin Folks, clerk of the Circuit Court.

Charlottesville: James Bowen, city manager, and J. Robert Ponton, member of the welfare advisory committee and City Council.

Tuition Grant Opposition Rises

ROANOKE (AP)—The list of tuition grant opponents lengthens. School principals and supervisors are the latest to speak out. They join their school superintendent, school board members, PTA members, churchmen, taxpayers high and low who lined up against the program soon after its birth four years ago.

Why?

"I'm against public money for private schooling."

"Names of those taking grants read like the social register."

"Only a handful . . . are from desegregated schools, or schools even threatened."

"Pushed to the extreme, this can kill public education as we know it."

No Suprises

These are the reasons; no surprises here. First is the fear the program threatens the public school system. Second, there's class feeling—grant recipients would have mostly gone to private school, anyhow — they're taking advantage of the program to pick up a tax rebate.

The positive regard for the public school is elusive but none the less real—that it is the keystone of life as we know it. Many regard it as almost sacred. They say the public school system must be strengthened, not weakened, and the grant program weakens it.

This is the program put together by a special session of the General Assembly in 1959, extending "scholarships" of up to $275 a year to parents enrolling children in private schools or public schools other than their own.

It was to be a way out for parents who didn't want their sons and daughters in desegregated classrooms.

Backs of the measure defend it as an extension of "freedom of choice." Virginians, they say, always had freedom of choice between public and private schools. Heretofore, the state paid for public schooling. Now, they say, with this legislation, the state also pays for private schooling for those favoring it.

Cost Jumping

So it is against the background that on Nov. 11 Roanoke School Supt. E. W. Rushton tells his board 249 grants are requested this year, that the cost is jumping $20,000 to near $70,000. He calls the jump "alarming," the whole program "questionable." He says money is being spent in ways "never intended by the law." He asks the board to consider dumping the program back into the state's lap, as a gesture, to call attention to the protest.

Board members agreed that tax money pumped into the program in this penny-short city is urgently needed to finance

(See Tuition, Page 2)

Tuition Grants In Area

Augusta County has 36 children attending other schools under the tuition grant program, which will cost $9,450 if all of the students complete the school year, reports Augusta County Superintendent Hugh K. Cassell.

"This is an indication that the program in this county is not growing," added Mr. Cassell. Last year there were 53 students who received tuition grants totaling $12,436.

The largest block of tuition grants paid by the county are for 10 students attending Waynesboro High School. Seven attend Augusta Military Academy. No grants are paid for students at out-of-state schools.

The Staunton Public School System has six students attending other schools under the tuition plan, costing a total of $1,650 if all of the students complete the year. Last year there were four such grants approved.

YULE SEALS AVAILABLE

Christmas Seals are available at The Leader business office for those persons who have not received their seals by mail from the Augusta County Tuberculosis Association.

UF IN NEW OFFICE

The Staunton - Augusta United Fund office is located now on the second floor of the Professional Building in Rooms 204-206. Telephone number remains the same, TU 6-8151.

Diabetes Test Proved Beneficial for Girl, 8

By Leader Staff Writer

Eight-year-old Jacki Lynn Kirby, who has diabetes, is living a normal, active life because the disease was discovered early in life by a simple home test conducted by her mother.

Mrs. Peggy Kirby, 701 D. St., said finding the condition early was an advantage because frequently it is not discovered until a person has gone into a diabetic coma. Noting she found the diabetes when her child was 6½, Mrs. Kirby explained such an early finding has "prevented her from having severe difficulties".

The girl's mother who considers herself "fortunate" in finding the condition used a test quite like the one being advocated for area residents during the Diabetes Week observance sponsored by the Staunton Jaycees.

For Your Check

Tests for all members of this community are available this week at the following places: Hogshead's Drug Store, Peoples Drug Store, Central Drug Store, Terry Court Drugs, Neighborhood Drug Store, and Willson Brothers Drug Store.

Mrs. Kirby offered strong support for tests now available, noting she thought anyone who could get them should. She added: "They don't have an idea what it would mean if they did have diabetes and could find it early enough."

Commenting on her daughter's life, Mrs. Kirby said: "Her life is just as normal as anybody else's as long as she takes care of herself."

She told how she became suspicious of the presence of the disease in her daughter because it runs in her (the mother's) family. When the home test indicated diabetes, she conferred with a doctor who confirmed the presence of it.

Mrs. Kirby said the early finding was important because "the doctor said the condition could have become very serious". Other conditions which can come about if diabetes is not discovered early, said Mrs. Kirby, are such things as heart trouble, blindness, and circulatory ailments.

Watches Diet

Jacki, although she must watch her diet carefully and is required to take insulin daily, attends school regularly at Westside where she is a third grader. In addition, she is active in a majorette group and already is preparing to enter the Staunton, Waynesboro, and Harrisonburg Christmas parades. She also participates in swimming.

Presently Mrs. Kirby gives the insulin injections to her daughter, although the child is being trained to give them to herself.

Despite the condition, Jacki also participated in "trick-or-treat" activities in her community at Halloween. However, the candy received was taken to the nearby Huffer Nursing Home.

The community-wide effort under the direction of the Jaycees, authorized by the Augusta County Medical Society, is being conducted to:

Test every member of the community for diabetes, since over 1,400,000 people in the United States have the condition without knowing it;

Inform everyone about the symptoms of diabetes; and

Persuade those whose tests for diabetes are positive to seek medical care as soon as possible.

Edward L. Irby, chairman of the Jaycee 1963 Diabetes Week campaign noted: "Our diabetes week committee urgently requests everyone in the community to respond to the campaign for diabetes testing during the week. For those among our citizens who have undetected diabetes, early detection and prompt medical care will almost always make it possible for them to continue to lead essentially normal lives."

He said the public has been so receptive to the drive that the Jaycees have ordered 1,500 more detection kits, all that were available from the American Diabetes Association at this time.

Mr. Irby emphasized also that

(See Diabetes, Page 2)

DIABETIC LEADS NORMAL LIFE — Jacki Lynn Kirby, eight, is fortunate in that her diabetic condition was discovered early, and as a result of proper care can lead a normal life, explained her mother, Mrs. Peggy Kirby. Here the girl demonstrates her baton act for her mother. Mrs. Kirby discovered her child's diabetes as a result of a simple home test similar to that recommended by the Staunton Jaycees. (Staff Photo by Reese)

News Inside

Staunton Military Academy cadets compete in a vigorous basketball game. *Sutton Collection*

Night view of a fair in full swing at the old Gypsy Hill Park fairgrounds. View is reflected in the waters of Lake Tams. *Sutton Collection*

The PUBLIC Interest FIRST

THE STAUNTON LEADER

Weather: Considerable cloudiness tonight, with showers. Fair and cooler Friday.

VOL. 117, NO. 214 — MEMBER OF THE AUDIT BUREAU OF CIRCULATION — STAUNTON, VA., 24401, THURSDAY, OCTOBER 29, 1964 — MEMBER ASSOCIATED PRESS WIRE AND FEATURE SERVICE — PRICE SEVEN CEN

FORMER AMBASSADOR to Australia William C. Battle (left) talks politics with the man who introduced him at Wednesday's Young Democratic Club-sponsored charter night and dinner at Ingleside, Del. George M. Cochran (right). At center is John A. Clem III, chairman of the Staunton Democratic Committee. (Staff Photo by Dundore)

Battle Blasts Away At Barry's Position

The former U. S. ambassador to Australia, William C. Battle, Wednesday leveled a salvo of political broadsides at Sen. Barry Goldwater and specifically his vote against the nuclear test ban treaty.

"Just that one vote alone shows and typifies the lengths to which Sen. Goldwater will go to justify his campaign charge that the Democratic administration is soft on communism," Mr. Battle charged.

He said the GOP presidential nominee's "soft on communism" charge has "endangered the health and welfare of the country" and that he has seen "nothing like it since the days of Sen. McCarthy". He also termed the charge "a witch-hunt".

* * *

Mr. Battle's 35-minute attack on Sen. Goldwater came at an Augusta County Young Democratic Club-sponsored charter night dinner and rally at Ingleside's new convention hall before more than 300 persons. The Charlottesville attorney's keynote speech was interrupted by applause a dozen times.

He said he observed "with distress the very, very low level of this whole campaign" and said he was speaking as an American, rather than as a Virginian or Southerner, on behalf of "the man who is most equipped to lead the whole country".

The speaker, son of former Virginia Gov. John S. Battle, said the fact the Virginia delegation to the Democratic National Convention was instructed to "go all the way with LBJ" is an indication that Virginia likes the incumbent President.

Mr. Battle termed the senate record of Sen. Goldwater as "totally negative" and said the Arizona Republican had "failed to sponsor a single piece of major legislation".

He said the nation, under the Democratic administration, has enjoyed "unprecedented prosperity without a recession" and yet has remained "without a doubt the most powerful nation in the world today". Saying that as a former diplomat he was in a position to know, Mr. Battle added, "our military strength is second to none".

Mr. Battle, who was skipper of one of two PT boats which rescued Lt. John F. Kennedy during World War II and who served as Virginia campaign manager for the Democrats in 1960, said there is no comparison between the situations in South Viet Nam and Cuba.

"We are in Viet Nam at the request of the government of South Viet Nam because the country is being actively and aggressively invaded by an outside force," he said. "In Cuba there is no such situation. Just because we don't like a particular government," he said, referring to the Castro regime, "that doesn't mean we can send our army and navy to that country and make it over in our own image."

Mr. Battle declared the problems in both Cuba and Viet Nam were inherited by the Democrats from the previous Republican administration.

"As leaders of the free world, we must be responsible," he stated. "We will remain strong enough to deter aggression and we can compete with commun-

(See Battle, Page 2)

Final Arguments Set Monday in Urban Suit

Final arguments in Staunton's urban renewal case are scheduled to get underway Monday at 10 a.m. in Staunton Circuit Court with Judge Designate Rayner V. Snead presiding. The matter has been pending in the courts since July 19, 1963.

Although it is not known when a decision might be handed down, Judge Snead earlier indicated his ruling might be forthcoming within two days to two weeks after hearing the closing arguments. Indications are the losing side will appeal.

* * *

The controversy reached the court when complainants, nine persons with interests in three parcels, asked the court to decree the project area is "not a slum, blighted, or deteriorated" and that the Redevelopment and Housing Authority may not legally purchase or acquire by condemnation properties there.

R. W. Smith, attorney for the authority, on Oct. 17 filed briefs with the court. Briefs for complainants had been filed earlier by Attorneys J. Sloan Kuykendall and J. Forester Taylor.

Previously some 19 days were spent in receiving testimony from about 76 witnesses and about 240 exhibits were presented to the court for its consideration.

Judge Snead from Washington, Va. was appointed to hear the case after the late Judge J. H. May disqualified himself.

Some of the ultimate legal decisions in the case are expected to have far-reaching effects, particularly since the contention has been made in court that the Virginia redevelopment statutes are not valid.

Gross cost of the pending urban renewal project, Staunton's first, has been estimated at $1.2 million for improving an eight-acre business site.

Motorist Knocked Out For Five Hrs.

A Fort Lee soldier lay unconscious for more than five hours after his car ran off Rt. 11 at Burketown at 11 p.m. Wednesday and plunged into a creekbed, out of sight of passing traffic.

State police said James Harold Tucker, 34, assigned to the military police unit at Fort Lee, regained consciousness about 4:30 a.m. today, climbed to the road and flagged a passing trucker who notified authorities.

The officer said Tucker, who suffered a head laceration and abrasions of the knee, said he would seek medical treatment.

The soldier, who was driving a 1963 model Army auto, was headed north on Rt. 11. For some unknown reason, his vehicle left the road on the right side, went over an embankment, through a fence, and landed in the small creek. The vehicle could not be seen from the road.

Police estimated damage to the car at $700. The investigation of the crash is continuing.

PAUL CARON (left) chairman of the 7th District Young Democratic organization, presents Young Democratic Club charters to (left to right) Leon Klein, Augusta County; Miss Martha Bertrand, Mary Baldwin College, and Dr. James Stayer, Rockingham County. (Staff Photo by Dundore)

Wilson Shrine Named Landmark; Sen. Byrd Honored at Luncheon

Shrine

The Woodrow Wilson Birthplace was designated officially as a registered National Historic Landmark in a special ceremony at noon today at which U. S. Senator Harry Flood Byrd was one of the speakers. Sen. Byrd is vice president of the Birthplace Foundation.

The colorful ceremony was preceded by the inspection of an honor guard by Sen. Byrd and Major Gen. A. A. Sproul, commander of the 29th Division, Virginia-Maryland National Guard.

Cadets of both the Staunton and Augusta Military academies and the Monticello Guards of Charlottesville gave military flourish to the ceremonies.

Sen. Byrd reviewed the color guard and the Roller Rifles of Augusta Military Academy. The national anthem was played by the band of Staunton Military Academy. Also here for the occasion were a unit of the Monticello Guards of Charlottesville in their colorful uniforms of the Revolutionary period.

* * *

At the annual meeting of the trustees of the Woodrow Wilson Birthplace earlier this morning, two Stauntonians, William W. Huffman and Braxton Green, were elected to that board.

Associate members of the Board of Trustees elected this morning included Mrs. James B. Pettis, Mrs. Robert Sterrett and Neal S. Goodloe.

The trustees were told that admission fees at the Birthplace the past year amounted to $14,611. A budget totaling $29,550 was adopted for 1964-65.

Memorial resolutions, honoring former President Herbert Hoover, who died Oct. 20, and Miss Belle Baruch of New York City and Georgetown, S. C., who died recently, were adopted.

President Hoover was an honorary member of the Board of Trustees and Miss Baruch was a very active trustee.

* * *

Following a report by H. W. Tulloch of Waynesboro, chairman of a study for development of the Birthplace, the trustees voted to embark on a long range plan of expansion which eventually will bring the construction of an educational center.

A plan of promotion and financing proposed by Robert L. L. McCormack of Washington was accepted for the next year.

In accepting the plaque designating the Birthplace as a National Historic Landmark, Sen. Byrd said he always had taken great pride in the work of the Woodrow Wilson Foundation.

"And I have always regarded the National Park Service as the finest agency of the federal government," he said.

"The plaque and the certificate are symbols of praiseworthy cooperation between the Foundation and the Park Service in the preservation of this historic edifice and its official exposure to the maximum number of Americans for their inspiration," he added.

* * *

Careful to avoid any comments on his political stand or to "break his golden silence" on the candidate of his choice for the presidency, Sen. Byrd

(See Ceremony, Page 2)

Presentation Highlights Ceremony

Sen. Byrd (l) accepts landmark plaque from Mr. Stratton (Staff Photo by Sutton)

Byrd

Following ceremonies at the Woodrow Wilson Birthplace, where he was the principal speaker incident to presentation of a plaque designating it a national historical landmark under the National Park Service, Senator Harry F. Byrd was honored by a presentation at the luncheon in his honor.

It was a handsome illuminated certificate of citation which read as follows:

"In grateful appreciation of his effective attention to the interests of the Woodrow Wilson Birthplace Foundation, and for continuous service as Charter Trustee and First Vice President, the Foundation makes this presentation to

United States Senator
Harry Flood Byrd

at its annual meeting, Staunton, Virginia, October 29, 1964.. In his consistent devotion to the traditions of the Old Dominion as cradle of the Republic and to representative government, individual liberty and free enterprise; and in his wisdom as State Senator, Governor and United States Senator, he has had few peers. His patriotism, statesmanship and dedication to State and Nation are a lasting inspiration to Americans.

The presentation was made by Maj. Gen. E. Walton Opie, Leader Papers publisher, past president and Charter Trustee of the Birthplace Foundation, on behalf of its members, "and I feel sure", he said, "of the vast majority of Virginians and other citizens of the United States".

The senior Senator from Virginia voiced a hearty "Thanks" for this, the latest of many recognitions accorded him. There were no addresses at the luncheon, which was held at Ingleside. It was attended by

(See Byrd, Page 2)

North Viet Nam Claims U.S. Attack

TOKYO (AP) — North Viet Nam charged Friday "air and naval craft of the U.S. and its agents" again bombed and shelled North Vietnamese territory.

Radio Hanoi, in a broadcast monitored here, said the announcement was made by a spokesman of the North Vietnamese Foreign Ministry in a statement issued Thursday. It said:

"At 1000 hours of Oct. 28, 1964, three jet planes and five T28 aircraft of the United States, coming from the direction of Laos, bombed and rocketed the Cha Lo frontier post, which is situated in the Democratic Republic of Viet Nam territory in Quang Binh Province, at a place two kilometers (1.2 miles) from the Viet Nam-Laos border."

* * *

It added: "At 2300 hours (11 p.m.) of the same day, three naval craft of the United States and its agents, sailing from South Viet Nam, intruded into the territorial waters of the Democratic Republic of Viet Nam, shelled the coastal areas of Quang Binh Province and subsequently fled."

Boy, 17, Goes on Trial For Slaying of Father

The defense attorney for Leonard Herman Pugh this morning said the 17-year-old boy "shot the gun that killed his father in self defense".

Attorney Hampton G. Baylor told an all-male Augusta County Circuit Court jury the boy was in fear of his life when he shot and killed his father on Feb. 24 at the Pugh residence near the Middlebrook Rd. a mile south of Staunton.

The defense also said, in an opening statement, Leonard Trainum Pugh, 44, who was felled with one shot from a .303 British rifle, was a "man of great violence" who "had no respect for others".

* * *

The youth went on trial for murder this morning after entering a plea of not guilty. Judge William S. Moffett Jr. is presiding over the trial. The lanky, youthful appearing boy was sworn with defense witnesses—indicatign he will take the stand in his own defense.

In his opening statement, Commonwealth's Attorney Robert L. Rhea told the jury the state will show the youngster "willfully and deliberately, and with premeditation" killed his father with "no justification and no provocation".

The first witness in the trial was Sheriff John E. Kent who quoted young Pugh as saying, en route to jail following the shooting: "I did not mean to kill him. I meant to shoot him in the leg and stop him. I had run from him for the last time."

Citation for Sen. Byrd

In grateful appreciation of his effective attention to the Woodrow Wilson Birthplace Foundation and for his continuous service as Charter Trustee and First Vice-President this citation is presented to

United States Senator Harry Flood Byrd

Blue Ridge Looms Large as Barrier To Agreement on Joint Juvenile Home Site

The Blue Ridge loomed yesterday as a possible barrier to agreement on a site for an area juvenile detention home.

Charlottesville and Albemarle County, who earlier had withdrawn from the area's Juvenile Detention Home Study Committee, were back yesterday with a proposal for a facility to be constructed on the east side of the Blue Ridge in Albemarle.

James Bowen, Charlottesville city manager, told the committee the two localities are "ready to get started" on building a detention home and had representatives at the meeting to see if "there is any common ground" on which Charlottesville-Albemarle might cooperate with the other areas.

* * *

Because of Charlottesville-Albemarle insistence the home be built on the east side of the Blue Ridge, however, representatives of Rockingham County, an original member of the study committee, said they felt Rockingham would not participate in the project if the home were to be built that far from their area.

The committee, meeting in Staunton yesterday with representatives of Staunton, Waynesboro, Harrisonburg and Rockingham in attendance in addition to the Charlottesville-Albemarle delegation did not rule out an Augusta County site, however.

* * *

At the request of Staunton City Manager C. M. Moyer Jr., chairman, representatives of the four areas agreed to get the governing bodies in their localities to consider resolutions asking the Augusta County Board of Supervisors, which is not participating in the detention home study, to agree to the location of the detention home in the county.

Under present law, a detention home must be located within one of the participating localities. The resolutions would clear the way for the committee to attempt to get the law changed at a December special session of the General Assembly.

* * *

A change in the law might allow the committee to accept the offer of Frank S. Driver of Weyers Cave who has promised to donate a site in that area for a detention home. It would also allow consideration of a site at Waynesboro, proposed at yesterday's meeting.

A. C. Gott of Waynesboro, reporting for the site committee, proposed consideration of a 39.55 acre tract located partly in Waynesboro and partly in Augusta. The site, a former city dump, is located on Rt. 340 at the northern limit of Waynesboro adjacent to the city's Shenandoah Heights School.

Mr. Gott told the committee he feels the tract could be purchased from Waynesbor at "a very reasonable price".

Despite uncertainty created by the Charlottesville - Albemarle proposal, the committee voted to employ Staunton Architect Neal S. Goodloe to update plans on the proposed 20-bed detention home. Mr. Moyer said he had been promised the plans would be ready in about 30 days.

* * *

Mr. Moyer said the plans would allow the committee to come up with two alternates, depending on location, and some figures which could be presented to the governing bodies of the concerned localities. Plans will include a cost estimate on the building.

Earlier, Mr. Moyer had said to the group: "This study has dragged on and on. If we can't do something pretty quick, I'm afraid the whole thing is going to fall apart."

He added: "Whether the home is built east or west of the Blue Ridge, I want Staunton to be a part of it."

Mr. Moyer said he would call another meeting of the study committee when the plans are completed by the architect.

Barry Predicts An Upset

Sees 'Disgruntled Voters Providing Political Reversal

HARRISBURG, Pa. (AP) — Sen. Barry Goldwater kick off a Pennsylvania whistle-s tour today, asserting "millio of unhappy, disgusted Ame cans across this country" w produce the century's bigg political upset next Tuesday.

The Republican president nominee said some people cla he has "just about given up" his battle against Presid Johnson.

But he said there is no tr in that.

* * *

He launched his third r road tour of the campaign af toughening his presidential ch lenge with a charge that Dem crats have Communist back and haven't repudiated it.

The Arizona senator ope his campaign day before a H risburg crowd estimated by lice at more than 8,000.

The Republican nominee the White House took to a ca paign train after a journ through the Midwest and a mand that the Democrats nounce Communists and "th backing." He said Commun publications were "pulling the defeat of Republican can dates."

* * *

Goldwater keynoted a f stop railroad journey to Pi burgh with a complaint t President Johnson had u "false and degrading tric against him.

"He tells the American pub I want to tear up their Soc Security cards," Goldwater s in a speech for Lewistown, Pa "There is not an ounce truth in this smear, and t opponent knows that full we

The whistle-stop tour w Goldwater's third campa foray into Pennsylvania, a st he believes the GOP ticket c carry if the Democrats are h to a 250,000-vote margin in Ph adelphia.

An Oshkosh, Wis., crowd r to cheer him Wednesday wh the Arizona senator brewed i his presidential bid the chal that Democrats have Comm nist backers.

Brandishing a copy of "T Worker," Goldwater told so 1,600 people in a high sch auditorium the Commun newspaper has urged voters "smash Goldwaterism."

New Look Asked At The Vatican

VATICAN CITY (AP) — C dinals and bishops urged Vatican Ecumenical Coun today to undertake a fearl new look at all aspects of tra tional Roman Catholic teach on birth control.

Leo Jozef Cardinal Suenens Brussels, Belgium, put the m ter squarely to the worldw assembly of Roman Catho prelates in St. Peter's, telli them:

"We must not be afraid look at our traditional doctr to see if it represents the fu word. Let us see if there is no new approach that can be ta en."

Other speakers in toda council debate on modern wo problems also urged the asse bly to define more clearly t question of morality and bi control in the council schema the Church in the modern wor All, however, cautioned agai abandoning traditional Chur teaching on this subject.

The speakers, whose remar were reported by a coun press spokesman, dealt with birth control question in gene terms without going into spe ics. This appeared to be in with an admonition by cou presiding officers that "more delicate" points in debate be handled only "n ing."

News Inside

October 29, 1964: The Woodrow Wilson Birthplace is made a National Historic Landmark. *Microfilm Archives*

In the above photo, taken in July 1965, Waynesboro fireman Charles Dooms has collapsed from heat exhaustion while helping fight a blaze at Friendly Tire Co. in Waynesboro. The left photo shows firemen fighting a conflagration at the Big Meal Chinese-American Restaurant in Waynesboro.
Sutton Collection

The PUBLIC Interest FIRST

THE STAUNTON LEADER

Weather Clear and much colder tonight, scattered frost in the interior, low in the 20s. Saturday mostly sunny and cool, high in the 50s.

'OL. 121, NO. 69 — MEMBER OF THE AUDIT BUREAU OF CIRCULATION — STAUNTON, VA., 24401, FRIDAY, APRIL 5, 1968 — MEMBER ASSOCIATED PRESS WIRE AND FEATURE SERVICE — PRICE TEN CENTS

LBJ Postpones Hawaii Trip, Calls for National Restraint

Lone White Man Sought as Slayer

MEMPHIS, Tenn. (AP) — A single white man, following an apparently well planned procedure, was the assassin Thursday of Dr. Martin Luther King Jr., Police Director Frank Holloman said today.

Holloman said the investigation showed the assassin checked into a main street flophouse at midafternoon, shot King from a second floor window of the building three hours later and then disappeared in the resulting confusion.

The murder weapon apparently was a new .30-06 Remington pump rifle with telescopic sights, Holloman said. The assassin also carried a new set of binoculars and a new suitcase.

A .30-06 Remington pump rifle was one of 15 weapons stolen a night earlier from a Memphis sporting goods store, but Holloman refused to say immediately that the stolen gun was the death weapon.

"As far as we know, and from the evidence at this time, there was only one man in the physical area of the slaying," Holloman said.

He said one of the 30 to 40 officers on duty in the vicinity of the motel saw the bullet strike King, and all immediately converged on the scene.

The fatal shot was fired from the window of a common bathroom in the flop-house, Holloman said. King's room was 205 feet away, through trees and across a street but in "clear" view of the window.

Holloman said the assassin was a white male, between 26 and 32 years of age, standing six feet tall and weighing 165-175 pounds. Police radios said he had dark to sandy hair, medium build, a ruddy complexion and was wearing a black suit and white shirt.

Holloman refused to disclose the name the man had signed on the register of the hotel, but said "certain evidence has been found."

The weapon, Holloman said, was sent to the FBI laboratory in Washington for ballistics tests.

Shelby County Sheriff William E. Morris, asked if officers had a palm print from the weapon, replied: "We hope we do."

Memphis Murder Dwarfs HHH Near-Announcement

WASHINGTON (AP) — The violent death of Dr. Martin Luther King Jr. disrupted the 1968 political campaign and some politicians say it could remain a factor through the November elections.

Political leaders, expressing shock and sorrow, also stressed the assassination could spur Congress to pass a pending civil rights bill.

Others viewed the assassination as one more indication of a society too often prone to resort to violence rather than lawful means to settle deep problems.

The immediate plans of the several presidential contenders were not clear but it seemed likely campaigning would be halted for a time.

Sen. Hugh Scott, R-Pa., proposed a week of national mourning.

Vice President Hubert H. Humphrey gave news of the assassination Thursday night to 2,700 people attending the biggest Democratic fund-raising dinner of the year and the affair was abruptly called off.

President Johnson canceled a scheduled appearance at the dinner.

King's assassination dwarfed the biggest political news of the day, which occurred hours before the slaying: Humphrey's near announcement in Pittsburgh that he would seek the Democratic presidential nomination.

The vice president told an audience of labor leaders: "If we stick together a little longer, we will be together a lot longer."

But Humphrey indicated he was withholding his announcement until after Johnson's Vietnam talks in Hawaii.

California Gov. Ronald Reagan, considered a potential contender for the Republican presidential nomination, said King's death was "a shocking act of violence that solves none of the nation's problems."

Reagan added the assassination is more evidence of what he termed a moral sickness affecting the nation.

A Democrat agreed. "We are steeped in violence," said Sen. Frank Church of Idaho. "It is the curse of the land."

Political developments that occurred before King's death included:

—Secretary of Labor W. Willard Wirtz urged Humphrey to run for president. His suggestion was greeted with loud standing applause at a meeting of 1,400 members of the International Union of Operating Engineers in Miami Beach.

Wirtz is the first Cabinet member to endorse a candidate since Johnson withdrew from the race last Sunday.

(See POLITICAL, Page 2)

Coffey Announces For City Council

James W. Coffey Jr. today announced his candidacy for Staunton City Council and thus assured a race in the June 11 city elections.

MR. COFFEY

Mr. Coffey, a 42-year-old Staunton native, has been owner and operator of Staunton Frozen Foods for the past seven years and prior to that was a partner in Staunton Fruit and Produce Co.

In announcing his candidacy, Mr. Coffey pointed out that it was not a "hasty decision", but one which he has been contemplating for some time.

"I have watched the growth of Staunton," said Mr. Coffey, "and foresee its potential growth. I therefore feel it's a moral obligation to take an interest."

A 1943 graduate of North River High School, Mr. Coffey played baseball for Staunton in the old Valley League for 10 years.

He lives with his wife, the former Ivy Claytor of Richmond and three children at 736 Hillcrest Drive.

He is a member of the Beverley Street Methodist Church and

(See COFFEY, Page 2)

Supervisors to Study Use Tax in County

The Augusta County Board of Supervisors is expected to pass a resolution calling for adoption of a local 1 per cent use tax when it meets Wednesday at 10 a.m. in the County Office Building.

Legislation giving local governments the right to impose the tax on materials purchased out of state for use in the county was adopted by the 1968 General Assembly.

The tax would apply primarily to highway and construction materials. It would be imposed on the materials at the point of purchase.

The supervisors have eyed the tax favorably since the legislation was passed, although no great amount of revenue will be realized from it.

* * *

The supervisors are also slated to take action on a Planning Commission recommendation to create a large recreational facility on the county-owned Berry Farm near Quick's Mill.

Plans for the facility, drawn up by a Virginia Tech student, call for a lake, community center, camping areas, nature trail, picnic areas, game areas, amphitheatre, swimming pools, basketball court, and golf and archery ranges.

Set for introduction to the Board Wednesday is the 1968-69 budget. The Supervisors are expected to set a date for a public hearing on the budget.

(See BOARD, Page 2)

News Inside

Rights Leaders, President Confer

WASHINGTON (AP) — President Johnson called on the nation today — all men and all races—to "stand their ground to deny violence its victory" in the wake of the slaying of Dr. Martin Luther King Jr.

The President's statement was issued after a hastily summoned meeting at the White House of civil rights leaders, government officials and members of Congress.

He voiced again his sorrow at the death of the Negro apostle of non-violence, assassinated by a rifleman Thursday night in Memphis, Tenn.

Johnson meanwhile kept in abeyance his plans to fly to Honolulu later in the day for Vietnam policy talks.

The President's statement said:

"The dream of Martin Luther King has not died with him.

"Men who are white—men who are black—must and will join together now as never in the past to let all the forces of division know that America shall not be ruled by the bullet but by the ballot of free and just men."

Johnson said that when he heard Thursday night "the terrible news of Dr. King's death my heart went out to his people—especially to the young Americans who, I know, must wonder if they are to be denied a fullness of life because of the color of their skin."

He said he had called to the White House the leaders of the Negro community for consultation, and went on to say:

"No words of ours—no words of mine—can fill the void of the eloquent voice that has been stilled."

* * *

Those attending the 11 a.m. Cabinet Room meeting, a spokesman said, included:

Bayard Rustin, executive director of the A. Philip Randolph Institute of New York; Whitney Young, director of the Urban League; Mayors Walter E. Washington of Washington and Richard Hatcher of Gary, Ind.; Clarence Mitchell Jr., director of the NAACP's Washington chapter; Mitchell's son, Clarence III, a Maryland state senator of Baltimore; the Rev. Walter E. Fauntroy, vice chairman of the Washington City Council and director of the Washington Chapter of King's Southern Christian Leadership Conference.

Dorothy Height, president of the National Council of Negro Women; Judge Leon Higginbotham of Philadelphia; Bishop George Baber and the Rev. Leon Sullivan, whose Philadelphia job program for the Negro poor has attracted wide attention.

Also participating were Deputy Atty. Gen. Warren Christopher, Supreme Court Justice Thurgood Marshall, Secretary of Housing and Urban Development Robert C. Weaver, Steve Pollak of the Justice Department, Senate Democratic Leader Mike Mansfield, Sen. Thomas H. Kuchel, R-Calif., House

(See JOHNSON, Page 2)

Army Takes 'Precautions'

WASHINGTON (AP) — The Pentagon said today "the Army is taking certain precautionary actions" to be ready for any serious disorders which may develop in the wake of the assassination of Dr. Martin Luther King.

So far, it said, "there have been no requests for any troop assistance from any governor."

The brief statement, given in response to an inquiry, did not go into detail about the precautionary actions being taken by the Army "in accordance with plans developed over the past months among federal, state and local authorities."

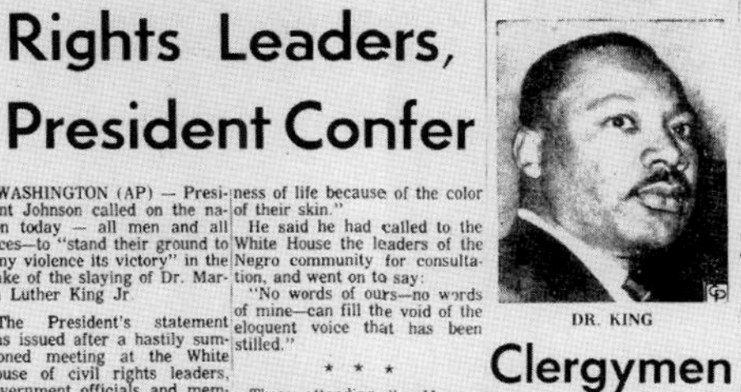

DR. KING

Clergymen Plan Area Memorial

Leaders of the Staunton Area Ministerial Association met this afternoon to plan a memorial service here for Dr. Martin Luther King.

The Rev. William E. Parsons of Churchville, the association leader, said the service will be planned to coincide with Dr. King's funeral.

At the same time, Mr. Parsons, other Staunton area ministers and a spokesman for the NAACP voiced sorrow at the assassination of Dr. King last night in Memphis, Tenn.

"We mourn the loss of a Christian leader, a man who worked for reconciliation, a Negro who sought justice by peaceful means," Mr. Parsons said.

"Dr. King's family lost most by his untimely death. But the nation lost an honored leader, the church lost a pastor and the poor men of whatever race lost a friend," he added. "But soon the nation will turn from sorrow

(See STAUNTON, Page 2)

King Assassination Shocks Entire U.S.

MEMPHIS, Tenn. (AP) — Authorities pressed a manhunt today for the killer of Dr. Martin Luther King Jr. whose assassination Thursday touched off Negro violence in a number of American cities and brought a national outpouring of grief and sorrow.

King, 39, leading advocate of nonviolence and Nobel Prize winner, died in a Memphis hospital Thursday night less than an hour after he was shot in the neck by a white gunman while standing on the balcony of his motel.

President Johnson led the nation in mourning and tribute. In a nationwide television and radio appearance he called upon "every citizen to reject the blind violence that has struck down Dr. Martin Luther King."

But violence flared in Memphis and the convulsive reaction reared also in Nashville, Newark, Washington, Boston, New York's Harlem and Bedford-Stuyvesant and more than a half dozen smaller towns and cities.

Gov. Buford Ellington alerted the Army and Air National Guard of Tennessee and ordered 4,000 troops into Memphis and the same number into Nashville. A curfew, first clamped on Memphis after a King-led march turned into a riot last week, was reimposed.

* * *

King was in the city preparing to lead another march in support of the city's 1,300 striking garbage collectors, most of whom are Negroes. His party was about to go out for dinner when King walked onto the motel balcony.

"And then we heard what sounded like a shot," said the Rev. Andrew Young. "I thought it was a firecracker."

The Rev. Jesse Jackson, who was standing beside King, said the civil right leader's only utterance after the shot was, "Oh!"

"The bullet exploded in his face," said Ben Branch. "It knocked him off his feet."

Solomon Jones, King's chauffeur, said a "man in white clothes" ran from the scene. Police in Tennessee and Arkansas were looking for a young white man, who witnesses said was dressed in white and was driving a late model white car.

Sheriff William Morris said the fatal shot was apparently fired from a "flop-house" facing the front of the motel. Police said a .30-06 Remington rifle and a suitcase were found in the doorway of a building adjacent to the rooming house.

* * *

"The back window of this flop-house faced the front of the motel in which Dr. King was staying," Sheriff Morris said. "We feel the assassin crouched in a second-floor window, sighted through some trees and fired the shot that killed Dr. King."

"He got a straight shot," Morris said. "King was standing on the second floor, leaning over a railing in front of his room. He was talking to two men on the ground. When the shot hit him, it knocked him backward. Officers heard the shot."

Memphis Police Director Frank Holloman said the sus-

(See KING, Page 2)

Violence Erupts In Killing's Wake

By BRIAN SULLIVAN
Associated Press Writer

Violence burst out in cities across the country in the wake of the assassination of Dr. Martin Luther King Jr. as bands of Negroes smashed windows, looted stores, threw firebombs and attacked police with guns, stones and bottles.

A white man was stabbed to death in the midst of violence in Washington, and a Negro died of stab wounds in New York, although it was not known if the latter death was related to the violence.

A white youth died in a fire at Tallahassee, Fla., which police said was started by a firebomb.

Scores were injured, including about 50 in Washington, and several score in New York.

Two Negro students of Mississippi Valley State College at Itta Bena, Miss., were wounded by pellets from shotguns fired by highway patrolmen trying to halt 300 student marchers. Police said shots had been fired from the crowd.

Snipers used guns and bows and arrows against police on the campus of Florida A. & M. University at Tallahassee, but no policemen were hurt.

Tallahassee Mayor Eugene Berkowitz and another city official were treated for minor cuts after rocks shattered the windows of their car.

* * *

In Detroit, two policemen were shot and wounded as they patrolled a Negro section, but that city escaped the street violence that erupted elsewhere.

In Memphis, where King died police shot and critically wounded a man they said had been caught behind a store with a rifle.

More than 90 persons were ar-

(See VIOLENCE, Page 2)

Hookup Said of No Use

Allies Smash Siege at Khe Sanh

SAIGON (AP) — The siege of Khe Sanh has been lifted, a senior U.S. officer said today, although late this afternoon the spearheads of the big relief force was still nearly a mile from the 6,000 Marine defenders of the combat base in the northwest corner of Vietnam.

"We've moved out and taken territory. The basic concept of the enemy besieging Khe Sanh is over," the senior officer said.

"There's no particular value in a hookup. They're within a kilometer and a half of each other. It would be no effort to march together and to shake hands. The important thing now is that we're moving and we have other objectives."

With the 20,000-man relief force of Marines and air cavalrymen bearing down on Khe Sanh from three sides, a 500-man battalion of Marines on Thursday ventured farther outside the two square miles of fortress than any Leathernecks had since it was taken under siege 76 days ago.

The Marine battalion occupied a hill two miles southwest of Khe Sanh for the night and then was attacked before dawn by about 400 North Vietnamese. The Leathernecks drove off the attack, reported the enemy left 93 bodies in the barbed wire around the night camp, and said Marine casualties were extremely light.

It was the heaviest fighting of the five-day-old operation to open Highway 9, the only overland supply route to Khe Sanh, and relieve the base. Most of the enemy dead were killed by dive bombers and artillery.

* * *

U.S. headquarters said no Marines were killed and only two wounded in the two-hour fight.

The hilltop battle pushed the total number of North Vietnamese reported killed in the five-day operation to 180. U.S. losses were put at 24 dead and 211 wounded.

One general in the U.S. command, while not saying specifically what shifts would be made at Khe Sanh, agreed it would be a good assumption that either one of two things could happen in the near future:

—As the enemy reduces his forces around the base, a withdrawal which U.S. officers believe has started, the Marines likely will do the same from the 6,000 men now there, perhaps down to 1,000:

—Or South Vietnamese or U.S. Army troops may replace some of the Marine units. There are now 400 South Vietnamese rangers and another 400 civilian irregulars helping defend the fortress.

The officer said there are still North Vietnamese troops around Khe Sanh but "not in the force they were in a while back."

* * *

"My feeling is that they have a couple of regiments right around there with another regiment close by," he said. "A while back they had two divisions in there."

In round numbers, he said, the North Vietnamese have re-

(See VIETNAM, Page 2)

Full-Scale Campaign Slated in Augusta To Promote Referendum on School Bonds

FISHERSVILLE — A full-scale campaign to promote Augusta County's upcoming $4 million school bond referendum will be launched next week.

The decision to launch the campaign came during a meeting of a school bond referendum committee here last night.

The select group, named by the Augusta County School Board last week, is headed by Dr. Melvin Koogler of Fishersville.

At last night's meeting, the group laid the groundwork for the campaign and discussed plans of how to best inform the voters about the referendum.

More than 15,000 colorful brochures, donated by "citizens interested in better schools", are slated to be distributed in addition to planned talks to various civic organizations in the area.

The brochure contains facts and figures on the overall county school situation and the proposed referendum which would finance a new Wilson Memorial High School, a high school for the Stuarts Draft area, a 24-classroom consolidated elementary school in the southern section of the county to replace Greenville, Spottswood and Middlebrook Elementary Schools, a new gymnasium and renovations at North River Junior High School, and eight-classroom additions to Fort Defiance and Buffalo Gap High Schools.

* * *

The Augusta County Board of Supervisors, which has asked that May 7 be set as the date for the referendum, plans to finance the program with revenue from a utility tax imposed on the first $10 of monthly residential telephone and electric bills and the first $100 of monthly commercial and industrial utility bills, and a business and professional license tax.

Richard A. Bowman, county executive secretary, told the group last night the utility tax would be 15 per cent of the bills. Both he and Supervisor A. R. Hull said that should the bond referendum be defeated, the tax would probably be hiked in order to finance the needed school program.

* * *

District co-chairmen of the committee will be charged with the responsibility of informing the voters of their respective districts on the referendum, it was agreed. Working under them will be precinct captains and their crews.

A number of the brochures are scheduled to be distributed through the schools next week, in hopes the youngsters will take them home to their parents. Principals of the various schools are charged with carrying out this task.

Other members of the special committee are Mrs. Betty Reeves of Mt. Sidney, co-chairman and publicity director.

(See SCHOOLS, Page 2)

Powell Has No Comment

DURHAM, N. C. (AP) — Adam Clayton Powell, who was hospitalized Monday at Duke Hospital left Durham today on a return flight to Bimini in the Bahamas.

Powell had no comment on the assassination of Dr. Martin Luther King Jr., but observers said he appeared "visibly shaken."

The former Democratic representative of New York's Harlem district was hospitalized for what doctors described as symptoms of exhaustion after he failed to appear for a scheduled speech at Duke University.

City Livestock Dealer Has an Unlucky Day

Yesterday was a bad day for Joseph E. Furr, a Staunton livestock dealer.

Two deer, standing in the highway near the village of Ferncliff in Goochland County about 3 a.m. started a series of mishaps that resulted in about $25,000 damage.

Lyle Deaver of Staunton was driving a tractor-trailer, owned by Mr. Furr, loaded with 74 head of grade cattle from Smithfield to Staunton.

Mr. Deaver swerved the truck to miss the deer. When the big rig struck the shoulder, it continued over a 20-foot embankment.

Twenty cattle were killed, mostly from smothering, said Mr. Furr. About 12 others were injured. The remainder scattered about the countryside. All but three were recaptured after hours of work and search.

Mr. Furr was following the tractor-trailer in his new car. Asked by a state trooper to place some flares on down the road, Mr. Furr drove about two miles ahead.

While heading back to the crash scene, two of the frightened cattle ran across the road in front of his car and were struck, causing another $1,000 damage to his vehicle.

Damage to the truck was placed at about $20,000. Value of cattle lost in the wreck amounted to approximately $4,000, according to Mr. Furr. The loss was covered by insurance.

Gov. Godwin Leads State Tributes to King

By THE ASSOCIATED PRESS

Gov. Mills E. Godwin Jr. led Virginians in expressing shock and regret today at the assassination of Dr. Martin Luther King, Jr. and civil rights leaders indicated hope for a conference with state officials to ward off possible racial violence.

Except for a few isolated incidents in Richmond—one case of arson, three false fire alarms and a few window-smashings—the death of King apparently provoked no violence Thursday night.

In Petersburg, the state field director for King's Southern Christian Leadership Conference, Herbert V. Coulton, said he hoped there would be no violence. He said he and SCLC state president Curtis Harris would "be meeting shortly with leaders of Virginia to see if we can curb some of these things before they start."

* * *

By "leaders of Virginia," Coulton said, he meant top state officials and leaders of other civil rights organizations.

Godwin's office in Richmond said the governor had received no request for such a meeting by mid-morning today, but the governor indicated he would agree to the request if made.

Godwin said he has "always been willing to meet with anyone at any time to discuss ways of preventing the outbreak of violence and civil disorder and to maintain law and order in our state."

The governor had commented on the assassination of King only a few hours after King's death in Memphis.

"Like decent people every

(See GODWIN, Page 2)

Carmichael Calls For Retaliation From Negroes

WASHINGTON (AP) — Black power advocate Stokely Carmichael urged Negroes today to arm themselves with guns and take to the streets in retaliation for the assassination of Dr. Martin Luther King Jr.

Carmichael told a news conference he wants black America to "kill" off the real enemy."

"We have to retaliate for the death of our leaders," he said. "The execution of those debts will not be in the courtrooms. They will be in the streets of the United States of America."

"When white America killed Dr. King she opened the eyes of every black man in this country," Carmichael said.

April 5, 1968: Martin Luther King Jr. is murdered. *Microfilm Archives*

Sutton Collection

This series of photographs shows the flood-water damage in Nelson County caused by 1969's Hurricane Camille. More than 27 inches of rain fell in Nelson County, killing an estimated 114 people and causing millions of dollars of damage. *Sutton Collection*

TODAY'S QUOTATION
A crash which cannot be traced to driver-error is almost unheard of.—Wisconsin Highway Safety Com.

THE STAUNTON LEADER

Weather
Partly cloudy with scattered showers and thunderstorms through tomorrow. Low tonight 68 to 73.

OL. 122, NO. 142 — MEMBER ASSOCIATED PRESS WIRE AND FEATURE SERVICE — STAUNTON, VA., 24401, MONDAY, JULY 21, 1969 — MEMBER OF THE AUDIT BUREAU OF CIRCULATION — PRICE TEN CENTS

First Day of New Era Dawns

SPACE CENTER, Houston (AP) — They took their first steps onto the moon cautiously, like prudent boys testing the first ice of winter on a country pond.

When first they walked, they walked carefully and slowly, leaning forward, plodding heavily like tired old cops on a beat in Staten Island.

As they acquired confidence, they walked faster, now with a slow bounce in the one-sixth gravity of the moon. And then they ran and their stride was longer than on earth and their shoes seemed suspended off the strange lunar surface, with something of the floating quality of figures on slow motion film.

When they were still, they seemed very still, as if frozen, and they leaned forward like puppets to be at a lunar form of attention when the president spoke to them from earth.

All the while, the earth was "bright and beautiful" above them. In this first incredible day of an incredible new era one needs to repeat that: the earth was above them.

* * *

In the distance, the lunar surface looked pocked and leathery like the back of a dead alligator. Closer up, it looked like rubble, like earth levelled roughly after a disaster, dead.

* * *

They looked ghostlike on the soundless, airless, mostly colorless moon. Over the curving horizon, only one and a half miles away on a planet smaller than earth, there was the blackness of space and infinity. The foreground was starkly lighted by the sun and the men and their vehicle cast long shadows. It was dawn on the moon and a dawn in the history of man.

Neil Alden Armstrong, formerly of 601 West Benton St., Wapakoneta, a town in Ohio, a state in the United States, a country on the planet earth, extended his left foot onto the moon.

"That's one small step for man, one giant leap for mankind," he said. The first words were fine. History would be content.

Now for the scientists: "The surface is fine and powdery. It adheres like charcoal to the soles of my shoes. You go down only about an inch."

And for the doctors: "There seems to be no difficulty in moving around."

And for the geologists and the

(See STEP, Page 2)

NEIL ARMSTRONG

"That's One Small Step For Man; One Giant Leap for Mankind."

EDWIN ALDRIN

Astronauts Blast Off From Moon Surface

Jubilant Nixon 'Activist in Space'

WASHINGTON (AP) — After a super long distance call to tell America's men on the moon "how proud we all are," President Nixon phoned Mamie Eisenhower and former President Lyndon B. Johnson to share his jubilation with them.

"This certainly has to be the most historic telephone call ever made from the White House," Nixon told astronauts Neil Armstrong and Edwin E. "Buzz" Aldrin Jr.

Millions of television viewers saw Sunday night's telephone conversation through a split picture showing both the President and astronauts.

"For one priceless moment in the whole history of man all of the people on this earth are truly one," Nixon said during his brief message congratulating the astronauts.

* * *

After talking with the astronauts, Nixon called Mrs. Eisenhower at the nearby White House mansion where she is visiting. He disclosed that the widow of the late President Dwight D. Eisenhower had commented earlier that "somebody up there is looking at them too"—referring to the late Gen. Eisenhower.

Nixon telephoned Johnson at his Texas home.

White House Press Secretary Ronald L. Ziegler told reporters the President informed Johnson that "I thought we ought to share this great moment."

Johnson told Nixon, Ziegler said, he had been following the Apollo 11 activities all day and appreciated Nixon's call at the historic moment.

Like people around the world, Nixon watched the television screen intently to see man's first step on the moon.

"It's an unbelievable thing — fantastic," he was quoted as saying at the moment

(See NIXON, Page 2)

ONE OF THE FIRST CHORES performed on the moon by Apollo 11 astronauts was the collecting of lunar surface samples. Edwin E. Aldrin scoops up samples while Neil A. Armstrong takes pictures in this practice session.

Two Americans Open New Frontier of Space

SPACE CENTER, Houston (AP) — Neil A. Armstrong and Edwin E. Aldrin Jr. blasted off safely from the moon and into lunar orbit today, beginning the complex maneuvers to link up with their mother ship. They left behind their footprints in the lunar dust and in the history of man.

Their liftoff began 69 seconds after the command ship, with Michael Collins its lone passenger, passed 69 miles above Tranquillity Base. Seven minutes later, they entered orbit and a 3½ hour chase began.

If all went well, the two ships would link up at 5:32 p.m. EDT, and head for home at 12:57 a.m. Tuesday.

Their thrust lander, which settled them onto the surface Sunday for a 21½ hour stay, served them, too, at liftoff. They left behind the spindly legged lower stage, their launching platform, as a permanent memento of July 20, 1969 — the day man landed on the moon.

It was the first time a rocket had lifted anything from the moon.

* * *

Mission control awakened the moonmen shortly after 11 a.m. following a six-hour rest period. Instruments which monitored Armstrong during the night indicated he slept fitfully. There is only one set of biomedical instruments in the cabin so Aldrin was not monitored.

Sleeping in the cramped quarters of the LM is difficult and Aldrin reported: "Neil has been lying on the engine cover and I curled up on the floor."

Checking of systems and switch settings for the critical liftoff was the No. 1 priority after wakeup.

* * *

A successful liftoff would shoot them into lunar orbit to chase down Michael Collins, orbiting some 65 miles overhead in the Apollo 11 command ship.

Once linked up they plan to fire themselves back toward earth early Tuesday, ending a space odyssey in which they etched their names beside those of history's great explorers, Columbus, Balboa, Magellan, da Gama and Byrd.

Through the magic of television, an estimated 500 million people around the world had a ringside seat to man's greatest adventure.

It was unforgettable.

* * *

Armstrong climbed through the LM hatch and started backing down a nine-rung ladder. On the second rung from the bottom, he opened a compartment, exposing a television camera.

The picture was black and white and somewhat jerky, but it recorded history.

Among scientists, there was elation that the crew had landed in an area with a variety of rocks, a treasure that held at least the hope of a rich payoff in the search to learn more about moon and earth.

As Armstrong planted his size 9½ left boot on the powdery surface at 10:56 p.m. Sunday, he spoke words that will be remembered for all time: "That's one small step for man, a giant leap for mankind."

The camera trained on Aldrin as he stepped on the far shore 20 minutes later and exclaimed: "Beautiful! Beautiful! Magnificent desolation."

* * *

There were other memorable utterances during the day of high adventure.

There were Armstrong's words when Eagle separated from the command ship to start the dangerous descent: "The Eagle is flying."

There were Armstrong's —and man's first words from the moon's surface after touchdown at 4:18 p.m.: "Houston . . . Tranquillity base here. The Eagle has landed."

Or when Aldrin, a deeply religious man, relayed this message to the world shortly after the landing: "This is the LM pilot. I'd like to take this opportunity to ask every person listening, whoever, wherever they may be, to pause for a moment and contemplate the events of the past few hours and to give thanks in his or her own way."

* * *

They planted an American flag and saluted it, but made it plain they came to the moon as ambassadors for all mankind.

They unveiled a stainless steel plaque bearing these words:

"Here men from planet earth first set foot upon the moon, July, 1969, A.D. We came in peace for all mankind."

They left on the moon a disc on which messages from the leaders of 76 nations had been recorded. They will return to earth with them the flags of 136 nations, including Russia. And they left behind mementos for three

(See APOLLO, Page 2)

Piedmont's 370 Pilots Strike

WINSTON-SALEM, N. C. (AP) — Pilots for Piedmont Airlines struck today over the company's plan to reduce from three to two the number of pilots on jet aircraft. The line was knocked out of operation.

All 370 Piedmont pilots, including those who fly propeller-driven craft, walked out as they had threatened to do if Piedmont trimmed the crews on its Boeing 737 jets.

The strike began at 1:30 a.m. in Fayetteville, N.C.

A Piedmont spokesman at Shenandoah Valley Airport told The Staunton Leader shortly before noon today that the strike has not yet affected local service.

According to the spokesman, no schedule flights at the airport have been canceled, although many connecting flights at other locations have.

The pilots, members of the Airlines Pilots Association, refused to fly. About 35 other pilots had driven from Winston-Salem to support them. Winston-Salem is headquarters for Piedmont, which serves mostly southeastern cities.

* * *

Piedmont's president, T. H. Davis, said, "The Boeing 737 was designed and built to be flown by a two-man crew. The 737 and similar jets are now being operated daily by many airlines, both domestic and foreign, with a two-man crew."

* * *

A spokesman for the pilots said no scheduled airlines in the United States use fewer than three men in the 737.

Piedmont had said it didn't intend to discharge the third man, but would reassign the extra crewman to other flights.

At mid-morning, the only Piedmont flights in the air were those en route at the time the strike began, said a Piedmont spokesman, Walter Rollins.

The pilots are "ready at any time to begin meaningful negotiations based on the concept of a three-man crew," a spokesman for the pilots said.

Millions Around World Cheer Moon Walk

LONDON (AP) — Laplanders pasturing their reindeer listened on transistor radios. Japanese stayed up all night to watch on television. Millions around the world hung on every word from the two U.S. astronauts walking on the moon.

In some countries many remained unaware. Communist China, with one quarter of the world's population, did not broadcast news about Apollo 11, nor did North Vietnam or North Korea.

As Neil A. Armstrong's boots scuffed the lunar dust, it was just before sunrise in most of Europe and a crowd of 2,000 still clustered around a giant television screen in London's Trafalgar Square.

At the Jodrell Bank radio observatory, Sir Bernard Lovell, Britain's leading space expert, stopped tracking the progress of the Soviet craft Luna 15 over the moon to watch Armstrong.

"I'm just speechless with amazement," Lovell said. "There is nothing more I can say than that it is absolutely fantastic. One can scarcely believe it is taking place as one sees it."

Crowds in front of tv screens at Paris sidewalk cafes and bars in Rome cheered as Armstrong bounded over the moon's surface and Buzz Aldrin began his descent.

* * *

There was no word from the Vatican on whether Pope Paul VI stayed up to watch the walk, but when the astronauts landed the 71-year-old pontiff hailed them as "conquerors of the moon." He said man faces "the expanse of endless space and a new destiny."

In Venezuela, today is a national holiday, and the bells of hundreds of churches pealed during the walk. A Japanese girl in Tokyo said as she watched a streetside monitor, "It's like a dream, although I know it's not a dream."

Israel Shells Suez

THE ASSOCIATED PRESS

The city of Suez on the southern end of Egypt's Suez Canal came under Israeli artillery fire today, Egyptian officials reported.

The shelling followed air and ground battles along the 103 mile waterway Sunday in the fiercest fighting since the war of June 1967.

"Buildings and streets are being shelled," one official said.

The Egyptians gave no idea when the shelling started or how heavy it was.

* * *

Sunday's action began before dawn with an Israeli commando attack on Green Island, an Egyptian fortress in the Gulf of Suez. Israeli jets followed up 12 hours later, hitting Egyptian positions across the canal for the first time since the 1967 war.

The Egyptians claimed they shot down 19 Israeli jets, one during the Green Island raid and the rest in dogfights along the canal. The Israelis admitted losing two Mirage fighters, but said they shot down five Egyptian planes.

Artillery duels raged for more than six hours up and down the 103-mile waterway. U.N. observers pleaded twice for a ceasefire, but the ground and air fighting continued.

South Vietnam's Battlefields Quiet

SAIGON (AP) — South Vietnam's battlefields were reported quiet today, with only one minor incident reported in the first eight hours after the U. S. moon landing.

The U. S. Command said operations of American troops in the field were proceeding normally. But the only action reported in the first hours after Apollo 11's lunar module touched down was a six-round mortar attack on a South Vietnamese camp a mile south of the demilitarized zone. It caused no casualties or damage.

"There's just not a bloody thing going on," said one officer.

* * *

Little action also was reported Sunday as the lull in the war continued into a fifth week.

The U. S. Command reported 18 enemy shellings from 8 a. m. Sunday to 8 a. m. today, including four attacks on U. S. bases. Five of the attacks caused casualties among the Vietnamese, but there were no American casualties, the command said.

The U. S. Command also announced the closing out of operation Mighty Play, a search-and-clear operation by American and South Korean Marines along the coast seven miles south of Da Nang.

* * *

The operation began July 10 and resulted in 31 enemy killed, the U. S. Command said, with American losses of three killed and 3[illegible] wounded, most of them by booby traps and mines in the coastal dunes. It was the third large Marine operation closed out in the northern provinces in the last week.

A U. S. Marine helicopter hauling South Vietnamese troops was shot down 22 miles southwest of Da Nang, killing nine South Vietnamese, and injuring one American and eight South Vietnamese. It was the 2,862nd helicopter reported lost in the war.

North Vietnamese reported its antiaircraft gunners shot down another pilotless American reconnaissance plane. There was no comment from the U. S. Command in Saigon, which refuses to give any information on operations of such planes over North Vietnam.

South Vietnamese forces reported killing 61 Viet Cong or North Vietnamese in clashes near Dong Ha and Quang Tri, 10 to 12 miles south of the DMZ. The government said four of its troops were killed and six wounded.

Waynesboro Man Dies Of Injuries

A 37-year-old Waynesboro man died early yesterday morning in King's Daughters' Hospital as a result of injuries he received late Saturday night while riding in a car which crashed on I-81, 1.4 miles south of exit 5[illegible] in Rockbridge County.

State Police identified the man as Roy Samuel Mackey of Rt. 2, Waynesboro, a passenger in the car operated by Francis L. Mawyer, also of Rt. 2, Waynesboro.

Police said the car attempted to pass another vehicle when it went out of control, leaving the highway on the left side. The car then struck a guard rail and rolled over on its top, pinning the victim in the car, police reported.

A hospital spokesman said Mr. Mackey died at 3:33 a.m. yesterday from severe chest injuries.

The spokesman said Mr. Mawyer was treated for minor bruises and contusions and released.

The fatality brings Virginia's

(See FATALITY, Page 2)

News Inside

Kennedy Complaint Hearing Set July 28

EDGARTOWN, Mass. (AP) — Police today filed a formal complaint charging Sen. Edward M. Kennedy with leaving the scene of an accident.

The complaint stems from a weekend wreck on Chappaquiddick Island, adjacent to Martha's Vineyard on which this small resort town is located. A young woman was killed and Kennedy injured, though apparently not seriously.

The complaint was filed by Police Chief Domenic J. Arena with the District Court Clerk Thomas A. Teller.

Arena said that an Edgartown lawyer, Richard J. McCarran, had informed the clerk he is representing Kennedy. McCarran asked for a hearing, to which Kennedy is entitled before any summons is issued.

Teller set July 28 for the hearing, which will be held in the Edgartown courthouse.

A crowd of several hundred persons, mostly tourists, filled the street outside the red brick, century-old courthouse as Arena crossed the street from his headquarters in the Town Hall to visit the clerk.

Arena said Sunday he is "firmly convinced there was no negligence involved" in the accident.

"But the matter of the time period after the accident. . .," Arena said. "There is, in my opinion, a violation concerning going from the scene, leaving the scene."

* * *

The mishap occurred between 11 p.m. Friday and 1 a.m. Saturday as Kennedy was driving Mary Jo Kopechne, 28, of Washington, to a landing to catch the ferry back to the Vineyard.

The car skidded off a narrow bridge and landed bottomup in eight feet of water. Kennedy escaped with what a physician said was a mild concussion. Miss Kopechne, former secretary to the late Sen. Robert F. Kennedy, D-N.Y., was trapped in the vehicle and drowned.

Kennedy went to the police 10 hours after the accident. The car had been found by then; two boys going fishing saw its wheels beneath the water.

In a police statement, Kennedy said he was left dazed by the accident. He said he tried repeatedly to rescue Miss Kopechne, but was not able to find her.

* * *

The 37-year-old Massachusetts Democrat and Miss Kopechne had been at a dinner party at a private home on Chappaquiddick attended by several of Kennedy's friends and political associates. Kennedy said he returned to the home after the accident and climbed into the rear seat of a car parked outside.

"I then asked someone to

(See KENNEDY, Page 2)

The 1970s

A Decade of Change

Cleanup operations under way

Area residents were organizing cleanup campaigns today after flooding hit Augusta County following three days of rain. In Waynesboro, residents were being requested to boil water for consumption.

Waynesboro City Manager Charles T. Yancey said the city is busy trying to organize clean up operations. City maintenance employees were only able to get into the city's maintenance shop at 8 o'clock this morning, after Wednesday's flooding left parts of the city under five feet of water.

Authorities Wednesday had evacuated two major sections of the city along South River and the residential Club Court area. The same sections were the hard hit areas of the 1969 floods, which Mr. Yancey described as equal to Wednesday's.

Rumors of imminent breakage of the Coles Run Dam in the Sherando area proved false, but not until after residents, fearful of a repeat of the Nelson County disaster in 1969, had been evacuated after the order went out at 3:15 p.m.

Augusta County Sheriff John E. Kent reported this morning: "Everything is in good shape—there has been no report of loss of life or injury."

Sheriff Kent reported looting in the Coles Run area followed the evacuation and that 12 of his deputies, some working through the night, patrolled the area in attempts to counteract any similar occurences.

The problems in Waynesboro were compounded when one water plant was unable to pump water in the height of the downpour, which had amounted to 6½ inches since Saturday morning. Mr. Yancey noted that one of the top priorities of the clean-up operations will be to open up sewers which were stopped up.

The City Manager also indicated the city's drinking water supply will be chlorinated, as is common in such situations.

The State Highway Department reported that all major roads were expected to be open by noon. Most of the surface water has been receding naturally, and according to the spokesman, no problems are anticipated. U. S. 250 east and I-64 are clear to Charlottesville, he added, discounting reports of continued road closings along that route.

Vepco called the results of the flooding "remarkable", compared with the threat of damage which was feared while rain was still falling. Only minor difficulties were reported to the service department.

Telephone service was interrupted in the area with 51 lines being affected. A spokesman for the C&P Telephone Co. said 101 stations experienced loss of service during the flooding. Kelsie Hughes, C&P Manager, predicted service will be restored by 5 p.m. today.

Leslie E. Ramsey, commercial manager for the Waynesboro-Clifton Forge Telephone Co. in

(See HEAVY, Page 2)

John M. Moore re-appointed to school board

FISHERSVILLE — The Augusta County School Trustee Electoral Board re-appointed John M. Moore to a four-year term during a meeting here Wednesday afternoon, but postponed selecting a successor to Joseph C. Horn until 3 p.m. June 28.

Mr. Horn, senior member and vice chairman of the Augusta County School Board, earlier this month announced that he would not accept reappointment for another term. He has served since July 13, 1943 as North River District's representative.

During the electoral board's meeting, delegations from North River District appeared to endorse Dr. John H. Gum of Churchville and Rollin M. Harshbarger of Mt. Solon for the seat which Mr. Horn will be relinquishing on June 30.

After discussing the appointment for more than an hour, R. Vance McClure, chairman of the board, announced the delay in appointing a successor because the board "doesn't feel it has all the information needed".

Mr. Harshbarger, a native of Weyers Cave, is a general contractor and president of R. M. Harshbarger Inc., a business which he has operated for 28 years. He is a member of the County Industrial Development Authority and the

(See MOORE, Page 2)

Weather outlook

Mostly clear and cooler tonight with lows in the low to middle 50s. Variable cloudiness and cool Friday with a chance of showers. Highs in the low to middle 70s.

News inside today

STAUNTON LEADER

VOL. 124, NO 122 — STAUNTON, VA., 24401, THURSDAY AFTERNOON, JUNE 22, 1972 — PRICE TEN CENTS

Parts of Virginia ravaged by Agnes

By THE ASSOCIATED PRESS

Flood waters ravaged widespread sections of Northern Virginia early today, stranding thousands of motorists and destroying homes as torrential rains up to 12 inches fell in the wake of tropical storm Agnes.

State Civil Defense headquarters in Richmond said it had reports of 11 flood-related deaths, but no figures were available from state police, who keep an official count.

An "emergency situation" existed in parts of Northern Virginia where the National Weather Service reported the "wholesale evacuation of thousands" from their homes. Still more thousands of motorists were stranded, some of them in their automobiles on waterchoked highways.

"This is a terrible situation. I've never seen anything like it," said an officer in hard-hit Prince William County near the Virginia suburbs of Washington, D.C.

"Cars have just been washed off the roads with people in them," he said.

Both Interstate 95 and Interstate 66, which carry heavy traffic into Washington, were blocked in numerous places and hundreds of drivers were stranded on the superhighway with water rising around their vehicles, deputies said.

Officials called early this morning for amphibious military vehicles in an effort to evacuate the stranded motorists after heavy-duty trucks trying to reach them were washed off the roads.

A large barge, hurled along the Occoquan River on roiling flood waters, slammed into the Interstate 95 bridge. The half-mile long bridge was severely damaged, state police said, and was impassable.

One small dam in the county broke Wednesday night and at least one person was reported to have died in the resulting flood. Police said the situation in that area "is so bad we can't even get any units up there."

(See AGNES, Page 2)

Coleman will seek legislative seat

J. Marshall Coleman, a local attorney and life-long resident of Staunton and Waynesboro, announced today that he will seek the Republican nomination for the legislative seat being vacated by O. Beverley Roller of Weyers Cave.

MR. COLEMAN

Mr. Roller, who has represented what is now the 15th Legislative District for seven years, Wednesday announced his resignation in order to serve as northern area supervisor of agriculture education.

Mr. Coleman announced his intention today and said: "The service given to this area by Bev Roller has been really extraordinary. He has distinguished himself as being not only one of the finest legislators from this area, but as one of the best in the Commonwealth. Bev is truly an able and decent person. His presence in Richmond on our behalf will be greatly missed by us all."

Mr. Coleman remarked that "it will be very difficult for anyone to fill Bev's shoes. However, I do feel I can provide hard-working and concerned representation.

"I concluded that I should run for this office," said Mr. Coleman, "after so many friends and acquaintances in this district asked me to make myself available. They nearly all expressed their desire that we continue the kind of representation that State Sen. H. D. Dawbarn, Del. A. R. Giesen and Roller have given us these years. I am humbled by this support. I believe that my association with Sen. Dawbarn and with Dels. Giesen and Roller has given me an understanding of what politics is all about—which is people, and their hopes, desires and problems. Politics is

(See WILL, Page 2)

WATERY RESCUE — Members of the Staunton-Augusta and Lexington rescue squads teamed up to rescue two persons Wednesday when their homes were cut off by the rising waters of St. Mary's River and Spy Run in Southern Augusta County. In top photo, Staunton's Junior squadsman James Carroll inches his way across a downed tree in order to get a rope to the opposite side of the stream. In the center photo, Mrs. A. O. Glander and M. E. Walker stand in the background as the rescue boat gets across the stream. Squadsmen then pulled the boat with the two persons aboard back across and transported the two to safety.

Verona dam need stressed at subcommittee hearing

WASHINGTON (AP)—Two projects in Virginia and Maryland would help meet water needs of towns in the area and the Washington metropolitan region, says Brig. Gen. John W. Morris, Army civil works director.

Morris told a Senate Public Works subcommittee Wednesday the proposed Verona dam in Virginia and the Sixes Bridge project in Maryland have the endorsement of all federal agencies.

He said the two projects, along with an authorized Bloomington project in Maryland, "constitute a system that would meet immediately foreseeable water needs in the metropolitan area."

"In addition, supplemental flows provided by the projects would contribute to maintenance and preservation of the free flowing stream environment in the Potomac River below the metropolitan area's water supplying intakes," Morris said.

He said the Verona dam, estimated to cost $34,350,000, would serve water supply, water quality improvement and recreation needs in Augusta County. He said the Sixes Bridge project, to cost $30,700,000, would serve similar needs in Frederick and Carroll counties.

Concerning water problems in the Potomac River basin, Morris said:

"Flood control problems exist at several localities in the basin, including the Cumberland-Westernport, Maryland, area along the North Branch Potomac River; the Petersburg-Moorefield, West Virginia, area along the upper reaches of the Shenandoah River; the Washington, D. C., area on the Lower Potomac, and several communities including Paw Paw and Harpers Ferry in West Virginia and Hancock, Williamsport and Point of Rocks in Maryland along the Middle Potomac.

"Water supply problems are of increasing concern at a number of communities in the basin, particularly the Washington metropolitan area, where the Corps of Engineers has unique responsibility for water supply."

Of environmental impact of the projects, Morris said "the present ecologic system reflects man's activities in the basin and the original environment no longer exists."

The principal effect of the projects on environmental values, he said, would be inundation and loss of farmland and a small part of the area's natural streams and pastoral scenery.

(See DAM, Page 2)

THESE STUARTS DRAFT YOUNGSTERS enjoy the new swimming hole provided by the rising waters, while parents worried about how high the water would get, endangering their homes.

(Photos by Dennis Sutton)

June 22, 1972: Hurricane Agnes rips through Virginia. *Microfilm Archives*

Waynesboro in the 1950s and 1960s saw unprecedented growth as business and industry poured into the city. While Staunton struggled with a failed "urban renewal" program and seemed bogged down in tiresome arguments over a few old bricks, Waynesboro forged ahead with confidence and vitality.

In 1970, some 30 industries and 22 manufacturing industries helped support Waynesboro's population of 18,500. The city boasted an industrial payroll of $55 million and a buying income of $49 million. With five trucking lines, two railroads, 250 retail stores and retail sales of about $51 million a year, Waynesboro seemed invincible.

But to accommodate this phenomenal growth, Waynesboro had wielded and would continue to wield the wrecking ball without regard to aesthetics, historical or cultural significance, or future economic impact. When the Waynesboro dynamo began to slow in the 1970s as foreign competition contributed to an overall industrial decline in the United States, some – but not many – began to see the detrimental effects of having equated progress with the wrecking ball for so many years.

Even with a national industrial slow-down, Waynesboro was still regarded as a business model for cities throughout the commonwealth. Augusta County, which philosophically allied itself more with Waynesboro than Staunton, also grew during the 1970s and, on Jan. 27, 1970, rezoned a 225-acre tract of land at Interstate 64 and Va. 608 near Fishersville for what would become Augusta Expo.

In 1972, Blue Ridge Community College received approval from the Virginia General Assembly for a $2 million expansion program that would include the construction of a modern library, student activities area and much-needed expansion of classroom space. Also that year, the entirety of Interstate 64 was completed in Augusta County with the finish of the Afton portion of the highway.

Stuarts Draft would be identified as one of the county's areas for high-level growth, and began to fulfill that expectation in the 1970s with road improvements, school construction, the establishment of a rescue squad, and retail development such as the 1975 construction of Broadmoor Plaza shopping complex. Three industrial plants – Nibco of Virginia, Skyline Plastics Corp. and Hollister Inc. – were all opened in Stuarts Draft, which would see even greater growth in the coming years.

Although Staunton's "urban renewal" project had been an abysmal failure that initially contributed more to the city's decline than its development, the overall economic picture was not bleak. By the mid 1970s, Staunton recorded $20 million in new construction within the city – most notably a series of modern, low-slung buildings in the demolished Central Avenue area – and saw its taxable property increase by more than 40 percent.

A city prospectus published mid-decade noted that Staunton's economy also benefited from a number of new industries including textile and apparel plants, electronic parts, bakery and dairy products, beverages, printing, concrete blocks, metal castings and framework and farm and industrial machinery.

On July 4, 1970, Staunton's most famous sons – The Statler Brothers – held the first of what would become an internationally popular event in Gypsy Hill Park. The free "Happy Birthday, U.S.A." concert featuring Harold and Don Reid, Phil Balsley and Lew DeWitt would draw 3,000 people that first year. By the time it ended with the July 4, 1994 concert, some 100,000 people from around the world descended upon Staunton for the event.

Other stories that occupied area residents in the 1970s included the June 1972 flooding by Tropical Storm Agnes; 1973's rumblings from Augusta County that it wanted to move its offices out of Staunton; the 1974 moving of all blind students from the Virginia School for the Deaf and the Blind to the Virginia School at Hampton; the abandonment in 1975 of the old Western State Hospital site for a newer one just east of the Staunton city limits; the 1977 going-under of Staunton Military Academy and the demolition of Staunton's old Capuchin Monastery; and, in 1979, the sale of the Staunton Leader to Multimedia Inc. of Greenville, S.C., a move that ended private ownership of newspapers in the city.

Above, the Goodyear blimp lands in Augusta County as part of a commemoration of the 50th anniversary of Smith's Transfer in Verona. Below, Thornrose Cemetery in Staunton from the observation cab of the blimp. Notice the blimp's shadow on the ground. *Sutton Collection*

U.S. evacuating Americans from Saigon

SAIGON (AP) — U.S. helicopters swooped down on Saigon rooftops and the Tan Son Nhut airport today and began evacuating most of the remaining 800 to 900 Americans. Some of the Americans fought off South Vietnamese desperately trying to flee before Communist-led forces take over.

America's 30-year involvement in the Indochina war was ending in wild and tragic scenes, with U.S. Marines and civilians using pistol and rifle butts to smash the fingers of Vietnamese trying to claw their way over the 10-foot wall of the U.S. Embassy.

Some tried to jump the wall and landed on the barbed wire. A man and a woman lay on the wire, bleeding as helicopters lifted off the embassy roof. People held up their children, asking Americans to take them over the fence.

At the airport, angry Vietnamese guards fired at busloads of evacuees and shouted, "We want to go, too." U.S. fighter-bombers flew air cover high over the city for the evacuation.

The Pentagon said 81 helicopters and more than 800 Marines were used to ferry evacuees to aircraft carriers in the South China Sea. Defense Secretary James R. Schlesinger said more than 4,500 Americans and Vietnamese had been evacuated six hours after the operation began.

Vice President Nguyen Van Huyen renewed calls for a cease-fire but denied Tuesday night that the government had reached any agreement with the Viet Cong. He said a government delegation met twice during the day with a Viet Cong delegation at Tan Son Nhut but the Viet Cong group said it was not qualified to make political decisions.

Huyen said one of the demands of the Viet Cong — the removal of all Americans — was already being met and that the demands for abolishment of the Saigon government and the army were being considered.

President Ford ordered the airlift after President Duong Van Minh made a radio speech ordering all Americans assigned to the U.S. defense attache's office out of the country within 24 hours.

At the same time, South Vietnamese air force men began a mass flight from their homeland. The Thai Foreign Ministry said 74 planes carried about 2,000 Vietnamese to Utapao Air Base in southern Thailand.

Civilian officials of the South Vietnamese government were also reported fleeing as rumors spread that the Viet Cong and North Vietnamese would soon march into the city.

In Washington, some congressional Democrats criticized the U.S. evacuation as coming too late and unnecessarily risking American lives.

"If there is a number of Americans at the very end that get trapped or killed, I think there will be an investigation," said Sen. Frank Church, D-Idaho.

"I think it's been too slow," said Sen. Hubert H. Humphrey, D-Minn. and vice president during the big Vietnam buildup of the Johnson administration. "We lost two Marines last night. I really think it's inexcusable, this delay."

The two Marines were killed in shelling at Tan Son Nhut that preceded the evacuation.

As the Americans pulled out, South Vietnamese police and soldiers looted buildings they had occupied. They carried out refrigerators, furniture, air-conditioners and other household goods.

STREET SCENE IN BELEAGURED CAPITAL — Neighbors inspect homes damaged in overnight shelling Tuesday as they gather in a Saigon street to discuss the war. Shelled buildings and the rubble left by rocket fire is now a common sight in the besieged capital. (AP Wirephoto)

THE STAUNTON LEADER

VOL. 128 NO. 84 STAUNTON, VA., 24401, TUESDAY AFTERNOON, APRIL 29, 1975 PRICE TEN CENTS

Refugees face cool reception

By THE ASSOCIATED PRESS

The welcome awaiting thousands of Vietnamese refugees being brought to the United States apparently will be a generally chilly one.

Three military bases will temporarily house the refugees during a period of 90 days or more, a Pentagon spokesman announced Monday. The bases are Camp Pendleton, Calif., Ft. Chaffee, Ark., and Elgin Air Force Base in Florida.

The announcement drew cool reactions in the three states.

"I have serious questions about the policy we're pursuing in the evacuation program," said Sen. John L. McClellan D-Ark., chairman of the Senate Appropriations Committee. "The Congress should have been consulted more fully before such a massive refugee program of Vietnamese people was launched.

In Niceville, Fla., where the refugees are expected to arrive at Eglin on Wednesday, the local reaction was dismal.

"We have one of the highest unemployment rates ever, and a recession that's going into a depression," said one local resident who called a radio station talk show. "Now, I'm going to have to pay for them, too.

"They can't speak English and they have no trade," the male caller said. "I would like to round them up and send them back."

"We should be at the airport and not let those refugees off the plane," said one female called "because we're going to have to feed them."

The federal government said that about 38,000 refugees had been evacuated from Indochina as of Monday — 12,800 were evacuated to the Philippines, 1,700 to Wake Island and 23,400 to Guam.

Deputy assistant secretary of state for congressional relations, Samuel Goldberg, said that the refugees would later be settled in all parts of the country.

He said the State Department is encouraged by the response of volunteer organizations that want to find homes for the refugees.

In California, where almost 1,000 refugees have arrived at Camp Pendleton, Gov. Edmund Brown Jr. sharply criticized "haphazard" federal plans to relocate, even temporarily, the thousands of homeless war victims in the state.

He said California cannot afford more unemployment which the refugee influx would spur.

Perhaps the harshest criticism came from Rep. Burt L. Talcott, R-Calif., whose district includes Camp Roberts near San Luis Obispo. He said in Washington that he was "pleased to announced" that neither Roberts nor Camp San Luis Obispo will be used to shelter the refugees.

"Generally my district was more positive, understanding and compassionate than some other areas," he said.

DEMOLITION CHARGES SET — South Vietnamese troops ready demolition charges on a bridge on the highway connecting Bien Hoa and Saigon Monday. Government forces hoped to slow the advance of enemy armor by blowing up the span. (AP Wirephoto)

Guard surrenders after slaying two

JOHANNESBURG, South Africa (AP) — A South African security guard took 21 persons hostage in the Israeli consulate, killed two persons and wounded at least 33, then surrendered early today after 21 hours.

David Protter, a 26-year-old Jew who fought for Israel in the 1973 Arab-Israeli war, said he had a grievance against the Israeli government. He said he wanted to be flown to Israel to talk to Premier Yitzhak Rabin.

First police reports said six terrorists had taken over the fifth-floor consulate Monday. Officials said they did not correct the report until after Protter surrendered because he threatened to kill all the hostages if it became known he was acting alone.

Armed with three revolvers, two submachine guns and some hand grenades, Protter hid inside the consulate before dawn Monday. He launched his takeover by telling each staff member arriving for work that he was conducting a security exercise and locking him up.

When his Israeli superior, security officer Giora Raviv, objected, Protter shot and killed him.

The other man killed was a South African employe, Edwin Malpo.

Consul-General Arieh Bustan said that when he arrived at 9:50 a.m., Protter asked him to accompany him to the vault for the security exercise. There he saw a guard lying on the floor, and Protter trained a revolver and light machine gun on the consul, telling him he was a hostage.

Commercial Attache Michael Ram said Protter wired the building with 165 pounds of explosives tied to an electronic detonator. He added to his hostages by capturing children of consulate staff who arrived after attending morning movie shows.

Bids will be sought on post office

STUARTS DRAFT — Bowing to the wishes of the community, the U.S. Postal Service is having second thoughts about moving the Stuarts Draft Post Office to Broadmoor Plaza Shopping Center.

As a result of a two-hour meeting last Friday, postal officials announced today that the planned immediate move has been postponed and bids will be sought for a facility to house the postal service here.

Al Sarno of Roanoke, district manager for the U. S. Postal Service, said that facility specifications will be posted

(See POST OFFICE, Page 2)

New water, sewer rates for county approved

Most Augusta County Service Authority water and sewer customers will find an increase in their bills after July 1.

During a joint meeting Monday night, both the Board of Supervisors and the authority adopted new water and sewer rates for all areas of the county with the exception of the Weyers Cave Sanitary District.

During the hearing it was explained that the increase — the first in the minimum service since 1957 — was necessary to meet rising costs.

"Our costs have been going up every day," said ACSA Chairman Robert Warner, who indicated that the new rates should cover projected needs for the next five years. He hinted, however, that at the end of this period, the authority might find it necessary to hike rates again if the present inflationary trend continues.

The minimum bi-monthly water rate (for those using 7,000 gallons or less) will jump from $7 to $7.50 for the single-family residential user. After 7,000 gallons, the fee will be 80 cents per 1,000 gallons or the next 23,000 gallons. The cost for the next 20,000 gallons will drop to 75 cents per 1,000 gallons; 65 cents per 1,000 gallons for the next 150,000 gallons; and 40 cents per 1,000 over 200,000 gallons.

The minimum per unit for multi-family units will be $5.

Sewer rates took a somewhat higher jump for residential customers. The bi-monthly minimum jumped from $5.25 to $7.50 for 8,000 gallons. The next 42,000 gallons will cost the customer 80 cents per 1,000 gallons; the next 150,000 will cost 65 cents per 1,000; and over 200,000 will cost 50 cents per 1,000.

Single-family water connections will jump to $350 and those for a small business will go to $500. Water connection fees for apartments, trailers and-or multi-family dwellings will be: $350 for the first unit; $250 each for the next 24 units; and $200 each for over 25 units.

Motels will be charged $125 per unit and restaurant connection fees will be based on the seating capacity, with the minimum fee being $700.

Single-family sewer connections will cost $500 and those for small businesses will be $700. Sewer connection fees for apartments, trailers and-or multi-family dwellings will be: $500 for the first unit; $300 each for the next 24 units; and $200 each for over 25 units.

Sewer connection fees for motels will be $175 per unit and the fee for restaurants will be based on seating capacity, with a minimum $1,000 fee.

During the hearing only one person, Tom Reese of Wayne District, appeared to ask questions about the rate changes.

William L. Hart, authority engineer-director, noted that the increased costs are needed to keep the system self-supporting.

"The service authority is not supported by taxes," Mr. Warner stated. "All operating funds have to come from sewer and water service."

(See RATES, Page 2)

Waynesboro to buy high-rise site

WAYNESBORO — Waynesboro City Council, following an executive session Monday night, authorized the city manager to obtain options on three lots as a site for a proposed high-rise building for elderly residents.

The three parcels of land would comprise a site 150 feet wide at one end and one block long. It is situated on the south side of 11th Street, across from the City Building, between Wayne and Market avenues.

The land is occupied by the old Lutheran church on the corner of 11th Street and Wayne Avenue, a house next door fronting on Wayne, and the Scout hut at the corner of 11th Street and Market Avenue.

Funds for the options will come from the city's reserve for contingencies fund. Money for site acquisition will be federal funds under the Housing and Community Development Act of 1974. The city has been assured of a $150,000 grant for this purpose from the U.S. Department of Housing and Urban Development.

Henry E. Thurston, executive director of the Waynesboro Redevelopment and Housing Authority, attended the executive session and conveyed to council the RHA's approval of the proposed site.

The RHA would be the managing agency for the home. Its operational costs would be subsidized by state and federal monies. Funds to build the home would come through the Virginia Housing Development Authority, provided the VHDA approves the project as developed by the city and the Eco Corp., a Reston consulting firm under contract to the city.

Preliminary discussion about the proposed home indicates it may be eight or nine stories high and contain 100-150 units, a city official said.

During its regular session, council adopted a tax rate ordinance for the calendar year 1975. Tax rates remain unchanged.

An ordinance was introduced to make an additional $15,200 available for general relief for the fiscal year ending June 30, as requested by G.O. Pendergraft Jr., superintendent of the Department of Social Services. He said the city will be reimbursed 62.5 per cent of the appropriation by the state, and that the amount "will get us through June 30 if we restrict it to the District Home".

The councilmen received copies of a proposed ordinance to control erosion and sedimentation where the contour of land is changed. The ordinance has been recommended for adoption by the City Planning Commission.

By state law, the ordinance must be adopted prior to July 1. As drafted, the city's erosion and sediment control ordinance is virtually identical to those of Staunton and Augusta County. Representatives of the three jurisdictions worked together to achieve uniformity in the three ordinances, and the result has been approved at the state level.

Councilmen were informed of planned expenditures of federal revenue sharing

(See WAYNESBORO, Page 2)

REFUGEES FLEE BIEN HOA — Thousands of refugees walk toward Saigon along the road from Bien Hoa Monday. They fled the town to escape a devastating North Vietnamese shelling which left the town in flames. (AP Wirephoto)

Weather

Cloudy tonight, with a chance of showers; lows in the upper 40s to low 50s. Cloudy Wednesday; highs in the mid-60s to low 70s.

News inside

April 29, 1975: The U.S. evacuates Saigon, ending American presence in Vietnam. *Microfilm Archives*

These two photographs show an honor guard and a formation at Augusta Military Academy in Ft. Defiance. The academy closed its doors in 1984 as a result of hard economic times. *Sutton Collection*

THE STAUNTON LEADER

VOL. 129 NO. 132 STAUNTON, VA., 24401, TUESDAY AFTERNOON, JULY 6, 1976 PRICE TEN CENTS

Statlers, Tammy Wynette draw thousands to city

THE STATLER BROTHERS entertained a large enthusiastic crowd at Happy Birthday U.S.A. festivities at Gypsy Hill Park Monday. Hanging behind the stage is a large American flag hemmed by students in the sewing department at Woodrow Wilson Rehabilitation Center. (Photo by Dennis Sutton)

Statlers big hit with the hometown folk

By CHESTER B. GOOLRICK III
Leader Staff Writer

Climaxing a day which resembled nothing less than a festival, the Statler Brothers and Tammy Wynette celebrated the nation's bicentennial with a concert before an enormous crowd at the old Staunton fairgrounds Monday night.

The crowd, estimated to be the largest in the seven-year history of Happy Birthday U.S.A. (as high as 40,000, according to some members of the committee), had been gathering for two days for the festivities sponsored each year by the Statler Brothers, the Staunton group which has risen to the pinnacle of success in the country and western music world.

So it was fitting that when the Statlers finally appeared on stage around 8:30 p.m., decked out in red, white and blue suits, the crowd, which filled the fairgrounds and overflowed onto nearby streets and into front yards above the field, was estatic.

Performing their most familiar tunes, including "Flowers on the Wall", the song that made them famous more than a decade ago, '"Susan When She Tried", "Class of '57", "Whatever Happened to Randolph Scott", "Thank You World" and others, the Statlers drew long applause and whistles and cries of appreciation after each of their numbers.

The songs, so familiar to many in the crowd that they could be seen singing along with the group, draw heavily from nostalgia over the era of the middle and late 1950s, years of cowboy movies, high school pranks and first dates. It is a world of idealized youth and innocence which has not yet been marred by the hard lessons of adulthood and disillusionment. A line from "Class of '57", a song about the troubles that overtake most members of a high school class explains: "Things get complicated when you get past 18".

The Statlers, winners of many major country music awards since their discovery by Johnny Cash, pleased the crowd with their music and comic antics which found lead singer Don Reid playing straight man to brother Harold's buffoonish antics.

But it was the two religious numbers the group sang, including the old hymn '"How Great Thou Art" and their a capella version of "America the Beautiful" that brought the most response, sending waves of applause and cheers through the crowd.

Miss Wynette, one of a triumvirate of female country music singers (the other two are Loretta Lynn and Dolly Parton), sang many of her most famous songs about broken romances and hard times.

(See STATLERS, Page 2)

TAMMY WYNETTE wooed the thousands at the Happy Birthday U.S.A. celebration Monday night with a number of her hit songs. (Photo by Dennis Sutton)

Pennsylvania woman first for celebration

Mrs. Mary Parks of Pleasant Gap, Pa., celebrated her own July 4 birthday by arriving at the fairgrounds five days early for Happy Birthday U.S.A.

As loyal a fan of the Statler Brothers as you could find, Mrs. Parks camped in her car with her three small children, from Wednesday until the show Monday night "to get a front row seat".

She declined an offer from the Statlers to put her family into a local motel. "We like camping in the open and fixing our own food" she said, and the youngsters nodded in approval.

It was the second year Mrs. Parks occupied the No. 1 parking space on the football stadium lot near the barn. Sunday was Mrs. Park's 39th birthday, she said, "and I couldn't think of a better way to spend it".

Thousands brave rain to attend services

By BILL BROWN
Leader Staff Writer

He "flew halfway across the United States to talk 15 minutes" to a Happy Birthday U.S.A. vesper audience that braved rain and cold weather to hear him. But, judging by his warm reception, both sides felt the effort was worthwhile.

Dr. Leslie Parrott, president of Olivet Nazarene College in Kankakee, Ill., was the featured speaker Sunday night at vesper services which had been delayed 45 minutes by rain.

A sudden downpour that started at 6 p.m. canceled a concert from 7-8 p.m. by the Wilson Memorial High School band, and almost dispersed an earlier crowd of 3,000 which filled the fairgrounds baseball outfield for gospel concerts throughout Sunday afternoon.

The crowd had begun to build again by 8:45 p.m. when the Rev. Freeman Hamrick asked the audience to stand for the "Star-Spangled Banner" and the invocation by the Rev. John W. Cowan of First Presbyterian Church.

A 100-voice community chorus representing 35 community churches, presented "My Country 'Tis of Thee" and "Battle Hymn of the Republic" before Staunton Mayor Frank R. Pancake extended a welcome and greetings from the city.

"Traditionally, Staunton's favorite sons have, on the day before their annual July 4 program, turned first to Almighty God and asked his blessings on this celebration," the Mayor said.

Happy Birthday U.S.A. President Charles P. Blackley seconded the Mayor's welcome and acknowledged the help given this year by the Staunton Bicentennial Commission, "including the giant Garrison flag suspended between light poles over the main stage, a large shelter tent and fireworks."

Commission Chairman Paul O. Hirschbiel and Executive Director Kenneth T. Linkous were recognized, together with James E. Crosby who emceed Monday's program.

Following several more selections by the community chorus, Kenneth B. Frank, principal of John Lewis Junior High School, read the scriptures and evening prayer was conducted by the Rev. John Sawyer of St. Paul's United Methodist Church.

Dr. Parrott was then introduced by the Rev. Gene Fuller, Virginia district superintendent of the Church of the Nazarene.

Using "The New Spirit of '76" as his subject, Dr. Parrott emphasized that "this civilization cannot continue to survive materially unless it survives spiritually".

He differentiated between "man's biological nature and man's spiritual nature," saying that anyone could understand the former "by reading a driver's license". The spiritual side is more difficult to understand, he said, but there have been leaders in every generation who understood the spirit of their era and could interpret it for others.

As examples, he cited the musician, Handel, and Thomas Jefferson "who caught the true spirit of democracy and, with 56 others, pledged their lives, fortunes and sacred honor to pursue it in the Declaration of Independence".

"Americans — even the early Puritans — have not all been pious and reverent", he continued, "but spiritual ideals have run like a thread through American history." He called Presidents Coolidge and Wilson more recent examples of true spiritual leaders.

"What this country needs today is a revitalization of spiritual ideals, of old-fashioned integrity based on responsibility", he continued. "You don't have to memorize the Bible to know what's right

(See VESPERS, Page 2)

GUEST SPEAKER at the Happy Birthday U.S.A. vesper services Sunday night was Dr. Leslie Parrott, president of Olivet Nazarene College in Kankakee, Ill.

Weather

Fair tonight; partly cloudy and pleasant Wednesday in the north. Lows tonight in the 60s; highs Wednesday in the mid-80s. Considerable cloudiness tonight and Wednesday in the west and south, with a chance of afternoon thundershowers. Lows tonight in the 60s; highs Wednesday in the

Local persons among those naturalized

Area residents were among the 105 immigrants naturalized Monday during Charlottesville's traditional July 4 ceremony at Monticello where President Gerald Ford gave the welcoming address.

Local persons naturalized included John Dickie of Augusta County, his wife Jean, their two sons Robert and John, their daughter, Mrs. Ruby Sherer, and Linette Santos of 1908 Baylor St.

The 105 immigrants from 22 countries were sworn in by Supreme Court Justice Lewis F. Powell before a crowd of about 8,000 on the back lawn of Monticello.

Following the oaths, President Ford was introduced by Gov. Mills Godwin as the "spokesman for all Americans". President Ford told the new citizens that they had given Americia a diverse "birthday present beyond price — yourselves, your faith, your loyalty and your love".

"There is still something wonderful about being an American," President Ford said. "If we cannot quite express it, we know what it is... Why not call it patriotism?"

President Ford is the first President since Truman to visit Monticello where he was flown by Marine helicopter. The President received a warm welcome to which he responded by grinning and waving to the crowd which had gathered to greet him.

Mr. Dickie, director of management at Amercian Safety Razor, said the President's appearance "put a cap" on a weekend of celebrations and the naturalization ceremony that made him an American. He added that he and his family have had a sense of belonging to the community, however, since the day they arrived from Scotland in 1968.

Miss Wynette released from local hospital

Country music singer Tammy Wynette was hospitalized after a performance here Monday night at the Happy Birthday U.S.A. celebration.

A King's Daughters' Hospital spokesman said Miss Wynette complained of abdominal pains and was admitted for observation.

The popular singer was released from the hospital early this morning and was expected to continue on to Wilmington, Del., where she is scheduled to give her next performance.

Also treated at the hospital last night was Claude E. Dull, a 523 Grubert Ave. man whose hand was badly injured when fireworks went off prematurely as he was assisting with the fireworks display following the performances at Gypsy Hill Park.

Mr. Dull, 68, was taken to the hospital where he was treated for a broken left hand and lacerations.

Verona man becomes fatality

CHARLOTTESVILLE — A 25-year-old Verona man died here Monday afternoon from head injuries he sustained June 24 in a late-night car crash on Va. 798 east of Verona.

The man, James C. Turner Jr., died at 5 p.m., according to a spokesman for the University of Virginia Hospital. He never regained consciousness after the crash which occurred when his car went out of control and struck an embankment.

Mr. Turner was first taken to King's Daughters' Hospital and then transported here.

Mr. Turner's death is the eighth on Augusta County highways to date this year.

The body is at Jones Funeral Home; arrangements will be announced. Friends are being received at the home of his parents, Mr. and Mrs. James C. Turner at 103 Anthony St.

News inside

(Two sections today)

FLAG PLAZA DEDICATION — Participating in Sunday's dedication of the bicentennial flag plaza near the Thomas D. Howie Memorial Armory were members of the 116th Military Police Detachment. (Photo by Dennis Sutton)

Flag plaza dedicated in Gypsy Hill Park

Multi-colored flags of the 13 original colonies were fluttering in the wind by the time Sunday's Happy Birthday U.S.A. dedication ceremonies ended at Staunton's attractive new bicentennial flag plaza, located near the armory in Gypsy Hill Park.

Presented to the city by the Staunton Bicentennial Commission, the simple flag memorial is the only one of its type in the United States, according to bicentennial officials who developed the concept and supervised its design and construction.

Flags of the first 13 colonies, each on its own pole, flank the American flag, with the official bicentennial and city of Staunton flags subordinated to Old Glory and Virginia. A landscaped concrete foundation and plaza extend from the base of the flag poles, and are decorated only with wooden benches and two commemorative plaques.

Music by the Stonewall Brigade Band preceded the dedication which opened at 3:30 p.m. with the national anthem, raising of the colors and pledge of allegiance, led by Brig. Gen. Kenneth T. Linkous, executive director of the Staunton Bicentennial Commission and master of ceremonies Sunday.

The American flag, raised first, was a gift of Staunton VFW Post 2216, in memory of World War II casualty, Sgt. Earl P. Talley, Co. L, 116th Infantry, Virginia Army National Guard. It was presented by VFW Post Commander George Wimer. Mr. Wimer also presented the official flag of the American Revolution Bicentennial Authority which was hoisted under the American flag.

With appropriate background music by the band, the flags of the 13 colonies were raised in the order of their first permanent settlement, starting with Virginia which was founded at Jamestown in 1607. Staunton's flag flew under it.

Sgt. Maj. Woodrow W. Ashby and members of the 116th Military Police then hoisted the flags of Massachusetts (1620), New Hampshire (1623), New York (1624), Connecticut (1633), Maryland (1634), Rhode Island (1636), Delaware (1638),

(See PLAZA, Page 2)

July 6, 1976: The Statler Brothers bring Tammy Wynette to Staunton for the annual "Happy Birthday, U.S.A." celebration. *Microfilm Archives*

Students at Thomas Jefferson Grammar School are treated to cake and ice cream in June 1979 to commemorate the last day of school – and the last day of the old school as a working facility. The building would sit empty for years until it was renovated for use as the Staunton City Library. *Waynesboro Collection*

Carter declared victor over Ford

WASHINGTON (AP) — President-elect Jimmy Carter's long, once-solitary journey from Plains, Ga., will carry him to the White House in January with a victory forged from the traditional Democratic party coalition of the Old South and industrial North.

Carter was declared the victor over President Gerald Ford early today when his electoral vote total reached 272, two more than the 270 needed for election.

Wisconsin and Mississippi were the states that established the Democratic candidate's majority in The Associated Press tabulation.

Three states — Oregon and Maine, where Ford held a slim lead, and Ohio, where Carter was ahead — remained too close to call. If Ford were to carry all three, Carter's victory margin would remain just two electoral votes.

The lead in California passed back and forth through the night with Ford finally declared the winner near daybreak.

Returning to Plains from his election headquarters in Atlanta, Carter received a tumultuous, emotional welcome from a crowd that included most of the town's 683 residents.

See complete election charts and results on Page 6.

Beaming his now-famous smile, Carter told the crowd, "I told you I didn't intend to lose."

But when he tried to continue speaking, his voice choked, he turned his head and then embraced his wife, Rosalynn, who was sobbing.

"It was a long night," he said when he regained his composure. "But I guarantee you, it's going to be worth it to all of us."

The latest returns showed Carter carrying 22 states and the District of Columbia with 272 electoral votes. Ford had 25 states with 231 electoral votes.

The popular vote totals from 96 per cent of the nation's precincts gave Carter 38,848,599 and Ford 36,980,456.

(See CARTER, Page 2)

Election news inside...

THE SENATE: The Democrats again clinch solid control. See story on Page 7.

THE HOUSE: Republicans gain some seats. See story on Page 7.

THE GOVERNORS: New faces include a Rockefeller, a woman scientist and a prosecutor of the Daley political organization. See story on Page 6.

THE STAUNTON LEADER

VOL. 129 NO. 217 | STAUNTON, VA., 24401, WEDNESDAY AFTERNOON, NOVEMBER 3, 1976 | PRICE TEN CENTS

Byrd victorious in re-election race

By GEORGE M. MAYS
Leader Staff Writer

U.S. Sen. Harry F. Byrd Jr., favored by both political observers and oddsmakers, was given a decisive mandate by Virginia voters Tuesday to serve another six-year term.

SEN. BYRD

Facing perhaps his strongest opposition since he was first appointed in 1964 to fill the unexpired term of his father, Sen. Byrd captured an overwhelming 57 per cent of the vote statewide.

With 1,837 of the state's 1,854 precincts reported, Sen. Byrd had 871,674 votes; Democrat Elmo R. Zumwalt 586,703, and Independent Republican Martin H. Perper 68,990.

Retired Adm. Zumwalt, who shattered many crusty naval traditions, received 38.5 per cent of the vote, and Mr. Perper, a Falls Church Republican, received 4.5 per cent.

While it wasn't the biggest victory in Sen. Byrd's long political career, it was more than enough to continue unbroken the state's 44-year tradition of having a Byrd in the Senate.

Sen. Byrd, an apple-grower, newspaper publisher and former state legislator, retained the family seat as a Democrat in 1966, but rebelled against a party loyalty oath in 1970 and won a full six-year term as an independent.

In the 1970 Senate election, Sen. Byrd won over Democrat George C. Rawlings and Republican Ray Garland of Roanoke. In that election, Sen. Byrd received 54 per cent of the vote; Rawlings got 31 per cent, and Garland received 15 per cent.

As election returns started rolling in for the 6th District, there never appeared to be any question about voters favoring the

(See BYRD, Page 2)

HAIL TO THE CHIEF — President-elect Jimmy Carter is applauded as he waves to the celebrating crowd at Atlanta, Ga., early today.
(AP wirephoto)

Liquor by drink voted in Staunton

Sunday closing law to remain

By JOHN A. MILLER
Leader Staff Writer

"Yes" for liquor by the drink in certain Staunton restaurants. "No" to abolishing the city's Sunday closing law.

That was the verdict of Staunton voters on the two referendum questions placed before them Tuesday.

It was an overwhelming vote in the case of liquor by the drink, with 4,349 or 63.8 per cent for and 2,468 or 36.2 per cent against the measure. Voters in all five wards voted decisively in favor of it.

The final tabulation showed that 3,716 Staunton voters asked that the Sunday Closing Law remain on the books, while 3,269 voters opted for repeal. All five wards voted for retention.

The margin for the law that forbids the sale of certain items on Sunday was trimmed from the 58.6 per cent voting for its retention in 1974 to 53.2 per cent Tuesday.

An intensive last-minute advertising campaign was mounted on both sides of the controversial closing law. Those supporting abolition of it argued that a person should have the freedom to choose whether or not to shop on Sundays. Persons favoring retention of the law argued that Sunday should be kept a family day relatively free of commercial trade.

The statute authorizing the serving of liquor by the drink will become effective 30 days after Circuit Judge William S. Moffett Jr. enters an order proclaiming the results of the election. Eligible establishments will have to show at least 50 per cent of their gross receipts as food sales and that they can seat 50 or more persons.

Those opposed to liquor by the drink contended that it would encourage alcoholic consumption and consequent law enforcement problems. Supporters of the measure argued that it would revitalize the restaurant business in the city and add to tax revenues.

Area supports Ford, record number votes

By ROY T. STEPHENSON
Leader Staff Writer

Area voters turned out in record numbers Tuesday and supported President Ford in his unsuccessful election bid with 56.9 per cent of the unofficial vote count.

In Staunton nearly 83 per cent of the registered voters went to the polls. Augusta's turnout was 86.5 per cent.

Staunton, Waynesboro, Lexington and Augusta and Highland counties gave the edge to President Ford, while Rockbridge, and Bath counties and the city of Buena Vista went with the winner, Gov. Jimmy Carter.

Staunton election officials, who had a difficult time processing the returns, reported today that 7,936 of the 9,564 registered voters went to the city's five precincts. Long lines of voters were still waiting to get to the machines at the 7 o'clock closing hour.

Of the 17,114 registered voters in Augusta's seven magisterial districts, 14,809 cast ballots. Middle River had the highest voting percentage with 88.4. The district has 15.1 per cent of the county's registered voters.

Wilson precinct was first to report to the central reporting station in the county registrar's office. The call came at 7:35 p.m. Stuarts Draft was the last to report at 9:38. Staunton's Ward II (Shelburne) reported its returns at about 11:40 p.m. The city's Ward III returns were reported first at 9:30.

Eighty-five per cent of Rockbridge County's 5,833 registered voters turned out on a day that was definitely favored by the weather, one fact that may have contributed to Gov. Carter's victory. About 89 per cent of Lexington's 2,327 qualified voters went to the polls. In Buena Vista, 84 per cent or 1,868 of the 2,233 registered voters cast ballots.

About 80.7 per cent of Waynesboro's 7,363 registered voters went to the voting places. Five thousand, nine hundred and forty three ballots were cast.

(See LOCAL, Page 2)

Butler retains 6th District seat

By GEORGE M. MAYS
Leader Staff Writer

For the second time in two years, incumbent U.S. Rep. M. Caldwell Butler Tuesday edged out Warren Saunders of Bedford to retain the 6th District House of Representatives seat.

Rep. Butler, a 51-year-old Republican and former member of the Virginia House of Delegates, had been favored to win the race and did so by capturing 62 per cent of the vote in the district.

Mr. Saunders, a Bedford businessman and investor who was making his second run for the seat as an American Party candidate, garnered 38 per cent of the vote.

With 214 of 217 precincts counted, Rep. Butler had 89,889 votes to 54,676 for Mr. Saunders.

First elected to the House of Representatives in 1972 to fill the unexpired term of former Rep. Richard H. Poff, Rep. Butler, a Roanoke attorney, edged out Democrat Willis M. Anderson and Independent Roy R. White in that race.

Two years later, Rep. Butler faced opposition from three opponents — Roanoke Democrat Paul Puckett, Independent Tim McGay of Goshen and Mr. Saunders. In that race, Rep. Butler garnered 54.2 per cent of the vote, while Mr. Saunders received only 19.8 per cent.

In the just-ended campaign, Mr. Saunders had sought to link Rep. Butler with the Washington establishment, but the Republican largerly ignored his opponent during a campaign that was characterized by little head-to-head confrontation.

In what may have been a first, both the winner and loser spoke from the same platform — their victory and concession statements dovetailing each other.

Calling it a "fun campaign", Rep. Butler said following his victory that he hopes "to be a better congressman as a result of it".

Rep. Butler carried most of the voting wards in Staunton, Waynesboro and Augusta County, but apparently because of his opponent's opposition to the proposed Verona dam, he failed to carry New Hope and Crimora. In addition, Mr. Saunders was the favorite of the voters in Spottswood and Craigsville.

A breakdown of the voting in political subdivisions follows:

(See BUTLER, Page 2)

LOCAL ELECTIONS AT A GLANCE

Areas	Ford	Carter	Byrd	Perper	Zumwalt	Butler	Saunders
Staunton	4,681	2,951	4,504	523	2,263	4,491	2,235
Augusta County	8,452	5,626	8,945	980	3880	7,351	5,574
Waynesboro	3,528	2,209	3,609	173	1,790	3,550	1,595
Highland County	629	493	921	43	160	724	303
Rockbridge County	2,157	2,525	3,024	151	1,396	2,762	1,722
Buena Vista	771	993	1,058	48	533	1,069	511
Lexington	1,026	945	1,203	30	671	1,343	458
Bath County	888	1,029	1,418	82	415	1,198	601
Totals	22,132	16,771	24,682	2,030	11,108	22,488	12,999

STAUNTON REFERENDA

Sunday Opening Yes	Sunday Opening No	Liquor by Drink Yes	Liquor by Drink No
3269	3716	4349	2468

Woodrum Station roof falls, 2 injured

By Mark S. Miller
Leader Staff Writer

Two women were injured when a large portion of the ceiling at Woodrum Station of the Staunton Post Office on W. Frederick Street caved in Tuesday at 2:40 p.m.

Miss Barabara K. Kuykendall, 18, of Rt. 1, Verona, and Mrs. Alice Taylor, 76, of 817 N. Augusta St., both patrons of the post office, were transported by the Staunton-Augusta Rescue Squad to King's Daughter's Hospital where they were treated for minor injuries and released.

Interviewed at the hospital, Miss Kuykendall said there was plaster all over the floor of the post office when she walked in. "I asked if they were working on the ceiling," she related, and C.W. Ergenbright, a postal worker, reportedly told her they weren't. "I said I thought the ceiling was going to fall in and then it did," she recalled.

When the ceiling collapsed, the young woman was trapped along the wall until the plaster settled. "It was dark, it was dusty and then I ran. When I got to the door I fell and this woman tried to help me up," Miss Kuykendall related. Pausing for a moment, she added: "There was plaster all over the floor when I walked in and I can't understand why they didn't see it."

Mrs. Taylor was near a postal window when the ceiling dropped. "I had just left the window after getting my money order when it knocked me down," she said when

(See CAVE-IN, Page 2)

STAUNTON POSTMASTER W.G. Elkins Jr. surveys the damage following the cave-in of a large portion of Woodrum Station's ceiling Tuesday afternoon. Two women were slightly injured, and the building has been closed pending an investigation and repair.
(Photo by E. Topping)

Weather

Considerable cloudiness tonight; lows between 30 and 40. Partly cloudy and a little cooler Thursday; highs in the 40s and 50s.

News inside

(Three sections today)

Five of six amendments approved

By MARK S. MILLER
Leader Staff Writer

Five of the six proposed amendments to the Virginia Constitution were approved by voters in Tuesday's election, with the amendment to strike the restriction against certain public officials and employees from serving as election officers and assistant or substitute registrars voted down.

Of the six amendments, five concerned election laws and one dealt with property tax exemptions. With 1,397 of the state's 1,854 precincts counted and completed, results are:

Amendment 1 (approved): "Shall Sections 1 and 2 of Article II of the Constitution of Virginia be amended to eliminate length of residence as a qualification to vote and to extend the time a voter may vote in his precinct after

(See AMENDMENTS, Page 2)

November 3, 1976: Election Day. Jimmy Carter becomes President and Stauntonians go for liquor-by-the-drink. *Microfilm Archives*

In the predawn of December 3rd, 1978 the Southern Crescent passenger train, making its run from Atlanta to Washington, D.C., was progressing a few miles south of Charlottesville. At 5:40 AM the train derailed for then undetermined reasons about 2 1/2 miles north of Shipman in Nelson County. Of the 81 persons on board six passengers and crew were killed and 60 were injured in the crash. Over 100 rescue personnel from 20 different squads responded to the scene. It took crews 11 hours to free a cook trapped under a stove in the dining car. As a final resort a bulldozer was used to rip the car apart to free the man after two previous attempts to free him had failed. Oddly, Southern had petitioned the FTC to discontinue passenger service prior to the accident but the petition had been denied. *Sutton Collection*

Sutton Collection

The 1980s

Era of Growth

"Urban renewal" – the official catchphrase of the 1960s – was replaced in the 1980s with the term "economic development." Business and industrial growth, annexation, consolidation and the expansion of the tax base obsessed area officials to the point that hardly a day passed when local newspapers in Staunton and Waynesboro didn't carry at least one story devoted to "economic development" in some form or another.

In the 1980s, Staunton city officials began laying the groundwork for a future annexation of Augusta County land by decrying the lack of acreage available for industrial development. Even though a developer from Delaware bought up the land at the eastern base of Betsy Bell and Mary Gray mountains – and was urged by the city to pave it over – many felt it wasn't enough.

But something had to be done. The early 1980s saw a regular decline in area construction; retail sales lagged; and as many as 3,000 people moved out of Staunton in 1980 alone, headed for areas with a more promising job market.

Increasingly, annexation seemed to be the answer, although a consolidation of county and city services was forwarded as a solution. After a typically long and involved process, Staunton eventually won the right to buy 11.1 square miles of county land in an annexation agreement that would take effect on Jan. 1, 1987.

Other developments in the decade include:

- In January 1980, the U.S. Postal Service announced its plans for transferring Staunton mail processing operations to Charlottesville.
- Augusta County voters in 1980 narrowly approved Sunday beer sales, with 8,049 voting for and 7,402 against.

Inside today

(Two sections)
Abby .... Page 14
Classifieds .... Pages 29-31
Comics .... Page 28
Entertainment .... Page 28
Farm .... Page 27
Lifestyle .... Pages 13-15
Obituaries .... Page 2
Opinions .... Page 4
Sports .... Pages 17-23

Weather

Mostly cloudy today with showers and thunderstorms. Highs in the low- to mid-80s. Mostly cloudy tonight with thundershowers likely. Lows in the low- to mid-60s. Seventy percent chance of rain. Complete weather on page 2.

Richard Petty wins 200th race

Page 17

McEnroe plays flawlessly

Page 17

THE DAILY NEWS LEADER

VOL. 137, NO. 132 — STAUNTON, VA., 24401, THURSDAY, JULY 5, 1984 — 20 CENTS

daybreak

Use permit nixed

The Augusta County Board of Zoning Appeals Tuesday nixed a special use permit sought by Meridian Care Centers Inc. for a residential care facility at Weyers Cave for brain-injured people.

During a public hearing in June on the permit, five Weyers Cave residents expressed opposition to the facility. Page 25.

General promoted

The Soviet general who reportedly gave the order last year for fighters to shoot down a South Korean airliner with heat-seeking missiles has received a promotion.

Army Gen. Vladimir L. Govorov, head of the "Far Eastern Troops" division, has been named a deputy defense minister. Page 6.

Fire claims 14

Fourteen people were killed and seven injured when an old, three-story rooming house in Beverley, Mass., erupted in flames before dawn Wednesday.

Several people reportedly jumped from windows or were rescued over ladders. One man was dead on arrival at Beverly Hospital from injuries he sustained in a fall from a top-floor window. Page 6.

Cancer discovery

The discovery that cancer apparently can grow from two single cells that go awry, not just one, could complicate the search for new ways to treat the disease, scientists say.

Scientists had previously assumed that all tumors grew from a single cell that, because of a genetic foul-up, grew out of control and spread. Page 6.

Bumpers considered

Walter F. Mondale is considering Arkansas Sen. Dale Bumpers as vice presidential running mate, but Bumpers is apparently trying to decide whether he would want the position before submitting to a public interview, Democratic sources say. Page 2.

Ron Witherow and Trish Cason were the top winners in Wednesday's Happy Birthday U.S.A. race around Gypsy Hill Park.

The race attracted 142 participants, which was a record number of entries. Page 17.

Stauntonian to compete

Staunton's Tim Randolph will be entering the national Long Driving Contest in Birmingham, Ala., in August.

Randolph won the Regional Long Driving Contest at Baltimore's Hillandale Country Club last weekend. Page 17.

Red Sox take win

It took a tremendous grand-slam homer from Jim Rice to give the Boston Red Sox a 13-0 victory over the Oakland A's Wednesday. Page 21.

74,000 on hand for celebration

Most states represented at celebration

By BILLIE BARLOW
Staff Writer

People from 48 states and 14 foreign countries converged on Gypsy Hill Park July 4 at the 15th annual Happy Birthday U.S.A. celebration hosted by the Statler Brothers with their guest Mel Tillis.

With good spirits abounding in the audience and on stage, the estimated 74,000 people were once again entertained by the Statlers' latest and greatest: "Bed of Roses," "Flowers on the Wall" and "Atlanta Blue," with "Elizabeth" bringing the fans to their feet.

Tillis and his band followed the Statlers on stage with favorites such as "Ruby Don't Take Your Love to Town," "Detroit City," "Burning Memories" and "Send Me Down to Tucson."

The "Happy Birthday" crowd made nearly a million people Tillis had entertained on the Wednesday. He arrived from a performance at the Washington Monument with a few minutes to spare before making his appearance in Staunton.

For much of the crowd Happy Birthday U.S.A. was a day-long affair. There was the parade, horse shoe competition, softball, and carnival games. But the evening performance was what many were waiting for. The ball park grounds were covered with lawn chairs early, and some of the most loyal fans, in order to get a front row seat, had camped near their chairs for 24 hours.

Judy Malinowski of Shenandoah, Pa., and Sharon Butler of Pasadena Md., have camped on the front row for seven years, and Donna Cox, of Staunton has been there every July 4 since she was two years old.

Ms. Malinowski likes the "down to earth, clean" music of the Statlers. She and Ms. Malinowski have been to 63 Statler shows in New York, Maryland, Virginia, Pennsylvania, and West Virginia.

For Frank and Erma Rowe of Craigsville, July 4 in Staunton is a 40-year tradition. They have attended every celebration, and came to the fairgrounds to celebrate before the Statlers started hosting the event in their hometown in 1970.

Donald W. Duncan, originally of Craigsville and now of Chester, has followed the Statlers' progress since the 1960s.

"I'd come if they charged," he said. "I saw those guys when they were nothing. I don't see how anyone couldn't like them."

Fans came from Alaska, California, Maine, and Florida. The 14 foreign countries represented included England, Venezuela, Japan, and Portugal.

The fans waiting in the ball park for the evening performance were entertained by Kim and Karmen

(See CELEBRATION, page 5)

HOMETOWN PERFORMANCE — Staunton's Statler Brothers perform for the hometown crowd Wednesday evening during the annual Happy Birthday U.S.A. celebration. This year's crowd was estimated at 74,000 plus. (Photos by Dennis Sutton)

Long wait pays off for some fans

By PATRICK KELLY
Staff Writer

It's a game of strategy and patience that demands a quick burst of speed and assertiveness at the end. It's call "The Line."

And each year the line is played by thousands of people who wait as many as 18 hours to make sure they put their lawn chairs as close as possible to the Happy Birthday U.S.A. stage in Moxie Memorial Baseball Stadium.

There is no question about it. The ultimate prize is a front row seat where the Statler Brothers, Mel Tillis and other performers can be seen up close.

If they don't get the front row, the fans in the line know they did not settle for a seat on Thornrose Avenue where the performers appear to be mere specks, not giants of county music.

The four lines in the stadium started to form as early as noon Tuesday. These people were a hardy lot. They were willing to wait for hours so they could be in position when a whistle blew at 6 a.m. Wednesday to signal the opening of the gates.

"When the whistle blows, I just run. I don't think about what's behind me," said Karen Collins 28, of Raleigh, N.C.

Ms. Collins said she was disappointed when she was in the eighth row last year, her first time at the celebration. "This year I'm going to get the front row," she said.

She got in position with her lawn chairs about noon on Tuesday. During the vesper service Tuesday night she kept her position. After the crowds had left, she was at the front of one of the lines.

At 5:30 a.m. Tuesday, as she continuously snapped the buttons on her Statler Brothers jacket, she said she was very nervous about getting a good seat and had thought of little else for three weeks. A "fanatic" Statler fan, she said letters spelling "Statler" are on her car's North Carolina license plates.

Robert Divis of Chicago was also at the front of his line. He got in position at 12:30 p.m. Tuesday. Last year he was several hundred people back.

"I'm doing this because my family members are big Statler fans," Divis said. Although his dedication meant he had only a few hours sleep since Sunday, he claimed "you don't feel it."

"I think he forgets why he's here after awhile," his wife, Alice, said. She said their goal was the front row.

Walstein Dofflemyer of Baltimore, Md., and his friends arrived at 11 p.m. Tuesday and he expected they would still be back at least 20 rows. "If it weren't for the

(See FANS, page 5)

SPECIAL GUEST of the Statler Brothers at the Happy Birthday U.S.A. celebration was Mel Tillis.

Former Staunton pastor speaks at vesper service

By JOHN WELLS
Staff Writer

God and country were the theme used by a former Staunton minister at this year's Happy Birthday U.S.A. vesper service Tuesday night in John Moxie Memorial Stadium.

The Rev. Carl H. Douglas Jr., pastor of Blacksburg United Methodist Church and former pastor of Christ United Methodist Church in Staunton, used the opportunity to offer a lesson in history.

"I am attempting to talk about God and country both although they are not the same by any means," he began. "I hope that the roots of this country are based on an idea — and the idea is God."

The greatest ideas, said Douglas, are always the simplest, and he quoted the prophet Micah as saying that God requires three things: to do justice, to love kindness and to walk humbly with God.

"Thomas Jefferson and the men who framed the idea that already existed concerning this country did it with great simplicity," he said.

"They touched on that which was basic — an idea inherent in the grain of God's creation."

That idea, as phrased by Jefferson, is that all men are endowed by their creator with certain unalienable rights.

"That means that you have something given to you that is not alien to you, that is inherent in your creator," the pastor said.

He praised Jefferson for his support of religious liberties, and remarked that of all his accomplishments, this was one of only three the former president chose to have inscribed on his tombstone.

"You and I have a heritage we

(See SPEAKER, page 5)

Parade considered to be best ever in Gypsy Hill Park

By JOHN WELLS
Staff Writer

Staunton's 15th annual Happy Birthday U.S.A. was an old-fashioned Fourth of July celebration, and was considered by many to be the best parade Gypsy Hill Park has ever seen.

The weather was cool for the morning event, especially in the generous shade supplied by trees that lined the parade route. Featured in the hour-long event were antique cars, floats, fire units, high school bands and majorettes.

The parade wound through the park, as politicians, clowns, beauty contest winners and Shriners, resplendent in their fezzes, waved to the crowds that lined the road in large numbers.

Some of the Shriners whizzed by in noisy groups of mini-cars, making figure eights and circles as they passed.

One agitated bystander, clutching a barking dog, appeared to be distressed by this display, and repeatedly shouted, "Y'all slow down and be careful! Don't hurt anybody!"

Numerous representative animals walked or rode past, including Woodsy the Owl, Smokey the Bear, McGruff the Anti-Crime Dog, the WHSV Bee and the G-83 Gorilla.

Even Abner, the Staunton United Revitalization Effort mouse, had his head removed temporarily from the SURE office window to ride by, swathed in red, white and blue.

Parade awards were announced by Kenneth T. Linkous, chairman of the event.

Winners included the Buffalo Gap Ruritan Club "Little Miss Baby Doll Summer" float, best of parade; Miss Augusta County Pre-Teen log house float, first place, Virginia Gun Owners & Sportsmen Alliance, second place, floats; Chesapeake & Potomac Telephone Co., first place, Shoney's-Captain D's Restaurants, second place, commercial floats; the WTON "U.S.A. Calendar Girl" float, first place, Staunton Coca-Cola "Street Shiek Break Dance" float, second place, theme floats.

Other awards went to the Staunton-Augusta County Chamber of Commerce covered wagon, Judge's Award; the Marine Corps League float, Independence Day Award; the Acca Temple Shrine mini-cars, Chairman's Award; Augusta County Fire Department, Best Appearing Emergency Award; Buffalo Gap Sportsmen Club, Best Booth Award, and "The Florettes" majorette corps and color guard, Special Marching Award.

July 5, 1984: "Happy Birthday, U.S.A." hits record attendance – 74,000 from around the world. *Microfilm Archives*

- In 1982, Community Federal Savings and Loan (now Community Bank) demolished two-thirds of a city block in the heart of the historic district for a drive-thru and parking lot.
- Waynesboro attorney Henry Tiffany and six passengers in the private airplane he piloted died in January 1983 when he collided over the Atlantic Ocean with an Air Force F-4 jet fighter.
- In 1984 the Daily News Leader ended a tradition of afternoon editions by becoming a morning newspaper.
- Augusta Military Academy closed its doors in 1984 as the result of hard economic times.
- On December 31, 1985, Waynesboro added 6.5 square miles to its city borders in an annexation of land from Augusta County.
- Area officials rated the year 1985 as "average to above average" and predicted that economic development would continue as the area's major issue. One Staunton City Council member, however, noted that Leggett's decision to close its West Beverley St. store was "another nail in the coffin of the downtown area."
- The Museum of American Frontier Culture was created in 1985.
- Georgia businessman Vic Meinert would arrive in Staunton in 1986 and would, eventually, single-handedly save the C&O train station and turn it into a spectacular, economically vibrant enterprise.
- An agreement was reached in 1986 by the Augusta County Board of Supervisors to study moving its offices to the old Smith's Transfer site in Verona.
- Much attention in 1987 was given to a proposal by Augusta Hospital Corporation– which owned both King's Daughters' Hospital in Staunton and Waynesboro Community Hospital – to close the facilities and build a new regional hospital in Augusta County.
- In 1989, the P. Buckley Moss Museum opened in Waynesboro.

Perhaps the biggest story of the 1980s – one that would affect all residents in Staunton, Waynesboro and Augusta County – was that of plans to close community hospitals in Staunton and Waynesboro and build a new regional facility in Fishersville. Despite a Daily News Leader poll that showed 528 of 615 respondents wanted King's Daughters' Hospital and Waynesboro Community Hospital to remain as they were, Augusta Hospital Corp. – which owned the unprofitable hospitals – voted unanimously for the new facility in 1989.

The vote didn't happen without a fight. While Waynesboro quietly went along with the idea of a regional hospital, forces in Staunton fought it tooth and nail. Petitions, letter-writing campaigns, recriminations, calls for resignations, charges of conflict of interest, heated public hearings, press conferences and huge headlines marked every step of the way toward the abandonment of KDH.

A citizens' group, the Committee for Health Care Awareness, was established to fight the closure, and the issue literally split legislators, citizens, physicians and other health-care providers into two frequently hostile, always very vocal camps. Yet, despite efforts to save KDH, they were essentially wasted in the face of the hospital's continued poor financial performance and AHC's zoning successes with the Augusta County Board of Supervisors and Certificate of Need successes with the state health commissioner.

The Staunton Fire Department tests a pumper engine in Gypsy Hill Park in this July 1983 photo. *Sutton Collection*

Aerial view of the crowd at the "Happy Birthday, U.S.A." celebration, circa the 1980s. *Sutton Collection*

The Statler Brothers in a circa 1980 photograph. From left are Harold Reid, Lew DeWitt, Phil Balsley and Don Reid. *Sutton Collection*

The First Presbyterian Church in Waynesboro is gutted by fire in this May 4, 1983, photo. The sanctuary, which was built in 1911, was destroyed. *Sutton Collection*

October 1983 photo of the Augusta County Fire Department battling a blaze at the 23,000-square foot Powell & Company Inc./Southern Stainless Equipment Co. plant in Fishersville. The fire leveled the building, causing more than $1 million in damage. *Sutton Collection*

Weather

Mostly sunny and cool today. Highs near 50. Clear and continued cold tonight. Lows near 30. Mostly sunny and warmer Thursday. Highs 55 to 60. Complete weather on page 2.

Highland couple's home used for voting
Page 3

Notre Dame football fans restless with Faust
Page 17

THE DAILY NEWS LEADER

VOL. 137, NO. 220 — STAUNTON, VA., 24401, WEDNESDAY, NOVEMBER 7, 1984 — PHONES: Staunton 885-7281, Waynesboro 949-7113 — 20 CENTS

India unrest

Opposition political and religious leaders warn that the Indian capital of New Delhi remains a tinderbox and call on the government of Prime Minister Rajiv Gandhi to take firm measures to protect Sikhs from marauding Hindus. Page 5

Polish priest

Polish officials on Tuesday said three officers of the secret police had been charged with killing a pro-Solidarity priest. The government said the priest probably died of strangulation and that the accused men said he showed no sign of life when he was thrown into a reservoir. Page 10

Space shuttle

Space shuttle Discovery is readied for a Wednesday morning launch and an eight-day flight in which its astronauts will chase and capture two satellites that are whirling around Earth in useless orbits. Page 10

World's Fair

The world's fair in New Orleans, plagued by debts and low attendance since it opened in May, filed for protection from creditors under Chapter 11 of the federal bankruptcy laws. The fair's marketing director estimated the exposition will be at least $100 million in the red by the time it closes Sunday. Page 7

Endangered flock

A mysterious ailment that has killed seven of the world population of 170 whooping cranes since September, including two deaths last weekend, has been traced to a virus transmitted by insects. Page 11

Wall Street

Stocks surged ahead Tuesday in surprisingly active trading, and the Dow Jones industrial average climbed to its highest level since January as the nation elected its next president. The market wrote history of its own by being open on the day of a presidential election for the first time since organized securities trading began in the United States nearly 200 years ago. The Dow Jones average of 30 industrials spurted 14.93 to 1,244.15, its highest point since Jan. 23, when it closed at 1,244.45. The measure is up 36.77 over the past four sessions. Page 27

Faces murder charge

A Waynesboro man is being held in Augusta County jail today after he allegedly shot and killed his wife Monday night.

Jimmy G. Fisher, 40, of 1812 Shenandoah Ave. is charged with murder and the use of a firearm in the commission of a felony and is being held in lieu of $100,000 bond for the first charge and $10,000 for the second. Page 3

Reagan wins by landslide

WASHINGTON (AP) — President Reagan swept to runaway re-election over Walter F. Mondale Tuesday night, but Republicans struggled to translate his landslide into significant gains in Congress.

Mondale conceded defeat, telephoned his congratulations to Reagan and told cheering supporters in St. Paul, Minn., "He has won. We are all Americans; he is our president and we honor him tonight."

The GOP renewed its control of the Senate, even if by a reduced margin, and were gaining in the House. But Democrats successfully battled against the Reagan tide in district after district to protect their large majority.

The president's victory was convincing; he and Vice President George Bush came close to the 50-state sweep they sought. Mondale won the District of Columbia and claimed victory in his home state of Minnesota.

Reagan won 37 states with 381 electoral votes, led in 7 more with 89. In The Associated Press count, the electoral votes of South Dakota pushed his total past the 270 majority mark.

Mondale's running mate, Geraldine Ferraro, hailed Mondale in a concession from New York City, saying he won another battle — "That battle for equal opportunity ... he opened a door that will never be closed again" by naming her first woman on a national ticket.

Sen. Paul Laxalt, Reagan's campaign chairman, said, "We've got at least a reasonable chance to have the most historic landslide in all American history."

No matter what the margin, Mondale told his supporters, "I'm at peace with the knowledge that I gave it everything I've got."

"This fight didn't end tonight. It begins tonight," he said.

Mondale praised Ms. Ferraro and said, "We didn't win, but we made history and that fight has just begun."

The president got news of his victory in Los Angeles, where he and his wife watched the returns in a Century Plaza Hotel suite equipped with four television sets.

He told reporters he hoped to participate in a summit with the Soviet Union during a second term in office.

The president insisted all day he was superstitiously avoiding predictions, but felt confident enough to outline his goals for a second term in an interview with the Washington Post. He said he would push again for congressional approval of a balanced budget amendment to the Constitution and the right to veto individual sections of spending bills, two measures he wants to help reduce federal spending.

He also renewed his call for a defense system in space designed to shoot down missiles.

With votes counted in 48 percent of the precincts, Reagan was polling 58 percent to 41 for Mondale.

The largest popular vote in history belonged to Lyndon Johnson, elected with 61.05 percent of the vote in 1964. Ironically, Reagan emerged as a conservative spokesman for Republican Barry Goldwater during that campaign.

Reagan's strength was signalled in advance in the public opinion polls, and the returns validated those forecasts from the time the first ballots were tallied in the east.

The story was somewhat different in Congress.

Democrats counted one Senate gain, in Tennessee, where Rep. Albert Gore captured the seat vacated by retiring Republican leader Howard Baker.

(See REAGAN, page 5)

Consolidation defeated

By PATRICK KELLY
Staff Writer

Augusta County voters approved the consolidation referendum, but Staunton voters dealt the death blow to the plan by rejecting it Tuesday.

Staunton is expected to move quickly to annexation proceedings under a backup plan.

Seventy percent of county voters approved the referendum, but it was rejected by 65 percent of city voters. The referendum, which asked voters to simply vote "for" or "against" consolidation, lost in each of the city's wards and won in all of the county's precincts.

Of the county's 22,883 registered voters, 19,652, or 86 percent, voted. Of those, 12,692, or 70 percent, voted for consolidation and 5,456 voted against it.

In Beverley Manor District, the vote was 1,425 for and 449 against; Middle River, 1,979 for and 818 against; North River, 2,150 for and 786 against; Pastures, 1,616 for and 689 against; Riverheads, 1,884 for and 892 against; South River, 1,583 for and 751 against, and Wayne, 2,055 for and 1,071 against.

Of the city's 9,897 registered voters, 8,309 voters, or 84 percent, voted in the election. There were 5,057 city votes against consolidation and 2,72 for it.

In Ward I, Bessie Weller Elementary, the vote was 611 for the plan and 1,62 against; Ward II, Shelburne Junior High, 717 for and 1,146 against; Ward III, Thomas D. Howie Memorial Armory, 500 for and 911 against; Ward IV, Robert E. Lee High, 392 for and 887 against Ward V, 345 for and 724 against, and Ward VI, absentee ballots, 15 for and 327 against.

City and county voters had to approve the plan to create a tier city of Staunton in a consolidated Augusta County. Rejection by either side was enough to defeat it.

City Council will meet at 8 this morning to discuss what action the city will take as a result of the referendum's outcome.

According to the consolidation backup plan, Staunton may annex 12.25 square miles of land without contest by the county. The land contains 2,952 people, including 320 students.

The financial settlement will have to be worked out, and most observers agree it probably will be one to two years before annexation can take place.

The land Staunton may annex is the smallest of the three sites the city and county agreed could be annexed. The amount depended on which side, or both rejected the plan. The backup annexation plan was not in the consolidation plan, but was agreed upon when Staunton and Augusta County agreed to seek to study consolidation on March 21, 1983.

If Staunton decides to proceed with annexation, its first step would be to instruct its lawyers to have a three-judge panel validate the March study agreement.

If Staunton annexes the 12.25 square miles of county land, the county has predicted its real estate tax rate will go up 6 cents per

(See CONSOLIDATION, page 5)

WATCHING THE RETURNS — President and Mrs. Reagan are glued to the television as they watch the returns giving him a landslide re-election victory Tuesday night, from their suite at the Century Plaza Hotel in Los Angeles. (AP Laserphoto)

Staunton likely to annex

With the defeat of the consolidation plan, Staunton City Council appears headed for annexation.

Tuesday's consolidation referendum won in the county but was defeated in Staunton. Since both sides had to approve the consolidation plan, the referendum was defeated.

Regret and pleasure at the defeat were voiced by both sides, but it was clear that council will pursue the annexation of 12.25 square miles of the county. The city and county had agreed that the city could annex, without contest by the county, one of three sites if consolidation was rejected. Under the plan, the city will get the smallest of the three amounts.

"I am disappointed in the outcome of the referendum. I think we have lost an opportunity to provide a better form of government for Staunton and Augusta County," said Staunton Mayor Hugh B. Sproul III. "However, I accept the mandate of the people and I will work as diligently as I can to pursue annexation of the agreed-upon area. Council will meet at 8 Wednesday morning to implement the next step in the process."

Usually voters make the right choice, Sproul said. "I hope they're right this time. Certainly I'm going to forget about consolidation and jump on the annexation bandwagon."

Sproul said council's first step will be to ask a three-judge study panel to validate the March 21, 1983 agreement between the city and county to study annexation. The agreement contained the annexation backup agreement.

"I've waited two years for this night," Councilman Dolores Lescure said.

"With the support that we have received tonight, city council has a green light to proceed on the annexation course we began in 1982," she said. She said the city's effort to expand its borders could have turned out better, but the area will more than double the size of the 9-square-mile city, which is "certainly a step forward for Staunton's growth."

"I believe we can go forward now with talks on annexation and seriously consider combining some services. Both the city and county have much to gain by sharing and working together. I am ready to start tomorrow," Mrs. Lescure said.

"At the first opportunity I'm prepared to vote to move on to annexation," Councilman James H.

(See REACTION, page 5)

Warner is easy winner for Senate

By THE ASSOCIATED PRESS

Area votes mirrored the sentiments of the rest of the state Tuesday by overwhelmingly re-electing Virginia Sen. John W. Warner.

WARNER

Approximately 36,140 area voters cast their ballots for the incumbent Republican, while only 8,683 voted for Democrat Edythe C. Harrison. Warner garnered 81 percent of the area vote, while 19 percent went for Ms. Harrison.

Warner won Staunton with 82 percent of the vote against Ms. Harrison's 18 percent. Total votes were 6,306 for Warner and 1,372 for Ms. Harrison. In Augusta County, Warner took 85 percent of the vote with Ms. Harrison garnering 15 percent. Vote totals were 15,563 for Warner and 2,698 for Ms. Harrison.

Waynesboro voters approved Warner with 81 percent of the vote. Ms. Harrison received 19 percent. Vote totals were 4,681 for Warner and 1,077 for Ms. Harrison. In Buena Vista, 72 percent of the voters cast their ballots for Warner with the remaining 28 going for Ms. Harrison. Vote totals were 1,363 for Warner and 521 for Ms. Harrison.

In Lexington, 66 percent cast their ballots for Warner, while 34 percent voted for Ms. Harrison. Vote totals were 1,341 for Warner and 691 for Ms. Harrison. Rockbridge County voters also went for Warner with 76 percent siding with the Republican and the remaining 24 percent for Ms. Harrison. Vote totals were 4,300 for Warner and 1,466 for Ms. Harrison.

In Highland County, 73 percent of the voters went with Warner while 27 percent voted for Ms. Harrison. Vote totals were 991 for Warner, and 368 for Ms. Harrison. Bath County voters also went for Warner with 77 percent on the Republican side and 23 percent for Ms. Harrison. Vote totals were 1,595 for Warner and 490 for Ms. Harrison.

Warner, celebrating his victory in Richmond Tuesday night, urged

(See SENATE, page 5)

Olin defeats Garand

Incumbent U.S. Rep. James R. Olin, D-6th, won re-election Tuesday night in a close race against former state Sen. Ray L. Garland of Roanoke.

OLIN

Olin, 64, won re-election to his second two-year term in the U.S. House of Representatives with apparently no ill effect from President Ronald Reagan's coattails.

Locally with 39,412 people voting in the congressional race Garland, 54, carried the area with 55 percent or 25,209 votes compared with Olin's 45 percent or 20,640 votes.

Garland won Augusta County with 62 percent, or 11,479, compared with Olin's 38 percent, or 7,152 votes.

Garland won Staunton with 56 percent, or [illegible] votes, compared

(See HOUSE, page 5)

STAUNTON

ANNEXATION AREA
IMMUNITY AREAS

WITH THE DEFEAT OF the consolidation referendum, Staunton may now pursue annexation, without opposition by Augusta County, of 12.25 square miles of land. If Staunton does annex the land, Verona and Fishersville would get permanent immunity from annexation. The dark area shows the land Staunton may annex while the lined areas show the Verona and Fishersville immunity areas.

Area voters join tide for Reagan

Staunton, Waynesboro, Augusta County and other area voters kept up with the state and national flow Tuesday as they cast an overwhelming number of votes to re-elect President Ronald Reagan.

Reagan won an significant mandate from Virginia voters for another four years in the White House. With 1,811 of 1,958 precincts reporting, Reagan had 1,207,359 votes, or 63 percent, and Democrat Walter Mondale 722,296, or 37 percent.

As substantial majorities of voters from the other states cast their ballots for the incumbent, voters from six local cities and counties cast 34,906 or 73 percent of their votes for Reagan, 12,379 for Mondale, and 286 for Independent Lyndon L. La Rouche.

Staunton voters cast 6,137 or 75 percent for Reagan, 2,012 for Walter and 47 for LaRouche; Augusta County voters cast 15,274 or 79 percent for Reagan, 3,895 for Mondale and 116 for LaRouche; and Waynesboro voters cast 4,465 or 73 percent for Reagan, 1,579 for Mondale and 35 for LaRouche.

The climate was similar in surrounding areas. In Highland County the support of 997 voters or

(See AREA, page 5)

November 7, 1984: Ronald W. Reagan defeats former Vice President Walter Mondale by a landslide. *Microfilm Archives*

A February 1983 blizzard rages through Staunton, creating near white-out conditions. This view looks south on Augusta Street. *Sutton Collection*

May 5, 1983 photo of a bi-plane spreading pesticides in the Mint Spring area.

Two-horse team of Howard & Speck of Ebensburg compete at Augusta Expo in this July 27, 1983 photo. The team won first place.

THE DAILY NEWS LEADER

VOL. 142, NO. 266 STAUNTON, VA. 24401, THURSDAY, NOVEMBER 9, 1989 Staunton 885-7281 Waynesboro 949-7113 25 CENTS

BRCC lists priorities

By TED CAGE
Staff Writer

WEYERS CAVE — Physical plant maintenance and renovations will be priorities for Blue Ridge Community College on the 1990-1992 Virginia Community College system-wide legislative initiative, reported BRCC president Dr. James Perkins at a regular board meeting Wednesday night.

"The renovation of existing buildings is our highest priority, because they are 22 years old (and in need of service)," said Perkins.

BRCC will place the allocation of $650,000 for the replacement of mechanical heat and cooling pumps in the highest legislative priority group, based on recommendations by the State Council for Higher Education.

The system-wide initiative will ultimately become part of the governor's budget after it passes through the state legislature.

BRCC's maintenance funds will come from the VCCS's maintenance reserve fund.

Other BRCC legislative priorities include construction funding for a new $1.4 million science and technology center, which is ranked in BRCC's fourth priority group but is not likely to make it through the legislative process this year, said Perkins.

"We could try to amend the legislative package to include the science and technology center through a sponsor, but the odds are slim," he said. But "we are optimistic about getting the center funded in the next legislative initiative as it moves up our list of priorities — the state has given us pre-planning money (for the project)," he added.

System-wide, increased funding to support enrollment growth will be the highest legislative initiative priority, said Perkins.

"The highest priority of the sys-

(See BRCC, page A2)

VICTORY CLAIMANT — Virginia Democratic gubernatorial candidate, L. Douglas Wilder, gestures in front of a Virginia flag during a press conference in Richmond Wednesday. Wilder claimed victory after votes showed him leading by 7,000 votes. (AP Laserphoto)

Wilder savors win; Coleman demands recount

RICHMOND (AP) — Republican J. Marshall Coleman said Wednesday he would demand a recount of the closest governor's race in Virginia history, but Democrat L. Douglas Wilder was already relishing the historical dimensions of his apparent victory.

"It starts coming home to you, something happened last night," Wilder said at a news conference the morning after he claimed victory as the nation's first black elected governor.

Just what happened was not absolutely certain, although Wilder still clung to a lead of 5,500 votes out of more than 1.7 million cast. With all 1,967 precincts reporting, unofficial results showed Wilder with 896,283 votes to Coleman's 890,750 votes.

Because the margin was within one-half of 1 percent, Coleman had the right under state law to demand a recount. At a news conference in McLean, he said he would do so.

"The outcome, although still in doubt, has given me a responsibility, for plainly I am the trustee of the votes of more than 880,000 Virginians who supported me in this contest. I have a responsibility to them and to all Virginians to ensure the person with the most votes is declared the winner," Coleman said.

"I congratulate Doug Wilder on a hard-fought campaign and if he is certified the winner, he will have my full support," he added.

But, he continued, "For the good of the next governor, whoever he may be, and for the good of the commonwealth, it is essential that there be complete confidence in the integrity and accuracy of the results."

The State Board of Elections will meet Nov. 27 to certify the results of Tuesday's vote, which board Secretary Susan Fitz-Hugh said was the closest contest for governor ever in Virginia.

Coleman will have until Dec. 7 to request a recount. Mrs. Fitz-Hugh said as far as she knew, no such recount had ever been conducted in a statewide election. She had no estimate of how long it would take to tally the votes a second time.

Wilder's running mates for lieutenant governor and attorney general, Donald S. Beyer Jr. and Mary Sue Terry, both won by substantial margins, prompting questions about the role that race played in the campaign.

But Wilder dismissed such speculation, saying the election answered "the subliminal question" about the importance of race.

"I'm saying it is not and was not a factor in the results because I was elected," he said. "I said if I won by 50.1 percent of the vote, I'd be happy. That's why you see me happy."

Wilder also dismissed questions about whether people were saying one thing in pre-election polls and exit polls, all of which showed him leading by a comfortable margin, and then voting a different way.

The same polls showed Beyer well behind his Republican opponent, Edwina P. "Eddy" Dalton. Wilder said. Beyer won 54 percent to 46 percent.

Wilder also said he intended to serve as a full-time governor rather than get involved in national Democratic politics as a potential black rival to Jesse Jackson.

"I don't think you're going to see me being in confrontation with anybody," he said. However, he added that if he were asked and had the time, he would campaign for Democrats in other states. He also would not rule out a bid for federal office in the future.

He said his victory showed national party leaders that "Democrats don't need to make special appeals to special groups" because mainstream candidates can win.

"The mandate is that in Virginia, we are prepared to move and we don't care what that person looks like," he said.

Wilder, who used Coleman's opposition to abortion in television advertising, said it would be wrong to say that his candidacy was based on that single issue.

Phone book cover is hot item

By SAM CARTER
Staff Writer

WAYNESBORO — Though usually not an item prized by art collectors, phone books are being framed in Waynesboro.

Richard Curry, who owns a craft center here, says he has been deluged with customers who want to frame the cover of the June 1989 Waynesboro phone book. The cover bears a painting by a favorite local artist, P. Buckley Moss.

"I've framed over 250 so far; 60 in the last week and a half . . . Some people are getting stocked up for Christmas," said Curry.

The painting, entitled "Shenandoah Heritage," depicts an Amish man and woman standing in front of snow-covered scenery with a powder blue sky above.

A representative of the P. Buckley Moss Museum here said the depiction is a particularly positive one, with the eggs the woman holds in her basket representing hope for the future.

Mrs. Moss allowed the painting to be reproduced on the phone book cover free of charge. The original, which is valued between $10,000 and $20,000, stands in the atrium of the museum.

"A lot of people who normally could not afford the art are proud to own this one," said Curry.

Margie Campbell, a resident of the city, had two made for herself and several others for acquaintances.

"We know Pat Moss. My children played with her children, and I like her work a lot," she said.

About 35,000 copies of the 1989 phone books were printed, but supplies have been rapidly dwindling, said Carl Rosberb, an official with Clifton Forge-Waynesboro Telephone Company.

"We are monitoring the supply. We may need to reorder before the 1990 directory, which we've never had to do before," said Rosberb. CFW allows about two directories for each customer and a directory per phone for each business.

"People are requesting more telephone books than normal. Local hotels are requesting more because people coming through the area are taking more than they usually do," said Rosberb.

Because Yellow Page advertisements cover the costs of printing, an additional printing wouldn't require increases on customer phone bills, Rosberb said. But the CFW official encouraged people not to take the covers.

The directory cover was a way to highlight Moss' work in conjunction with the P. Buckley Moss Museum, which opened this year, said Rosberb.

Mrs. Moss' husband, Malcolm Henderson, who spoke on her be-

(See COVER, page A2)

KAY ROBERTSON, an employee at Curry's Craft Shop in Waynesboro fits a mat on a telephone book cover. The P. Buckley Moss print on the cover has become a hot item for framing. (Photo by Vincent Lerz)

Waynesboro woman killed

Members of the Dooms Volunteer Fire Company check through the wreckage of a car which struck a tree near Crimora about 8:20 p.m. Wednesday, killing the driver of the car, Michelle Renee Rexrode, 21, of 1034 N. Delphine Ave., Waynesboro. Ms. Rexrode reportedly was pronounced dead on the scene. She was reportedly traveling south on U.S. 340 when she lost control of the car which ran off the right side of the road and struck the tree. The crash is under investigation, said Virginia State Police Trooper R.L. Edwards. (Photo by Danielle McMillion)

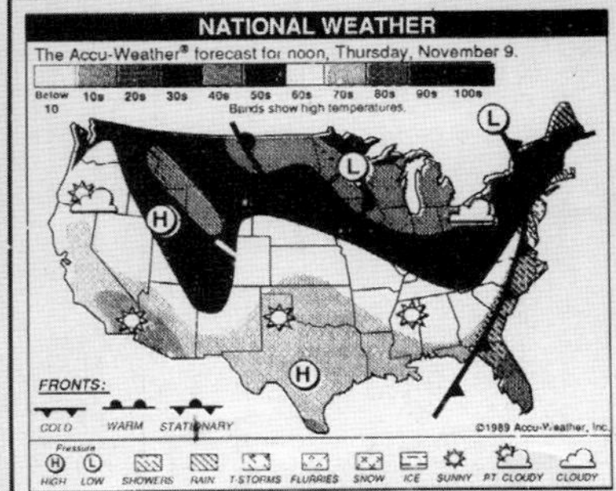

INSIDE

(Four sections)

WEATHER

Showers likely this morning with partial clearing in the afternoon. Highs near 60 but falling in the afternoon. Chance of rain. Mostly cloudy, breezy and turning colder tonight. Complete weather on page A2.

November 9, 1989: Douglas Wilder wins the Virginia gubernatorial race by fewer than 7,000 votes. *Microfilm Archives*

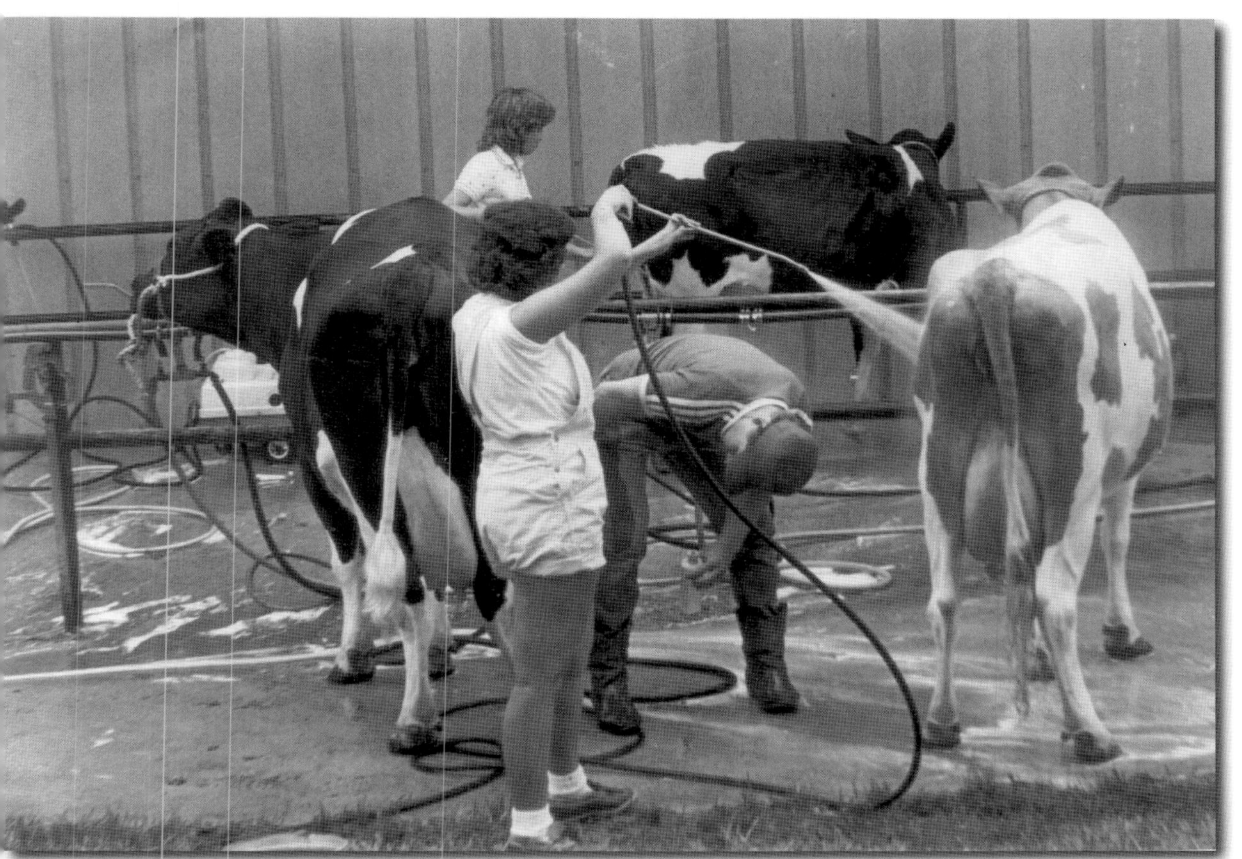

Grooming of dairy cattle at Augusta Expo in July 1983. *Sutton Collection*

A wax figure of President Woodrow Wilson is carried into the Birthplace in Staunton by John McFerren of the Natural Bridge Wax Museum. The wax figure was on loan to the Birthplace. *Sutton Collection*

On Aug. 29, 1983, Jimmy James – ringmaster of Clyde Beatty-Cole Brothers Circus – placed a wreath at the Thornrose Cemetery grave of Eva Clarke, a performer who was killed in 1906 while a circus was in Staunton. The ceremony pictured here, under the auspices of the Circus Fans of America, also featured Cherie Cunningham, Tom Weasel Weiss, Chris Baltzley and Chris Peters of the circus, and J.C. Coffman of the CFA. *Sutton Collection*

Workers replace Chesapeake & Ohio railroad tracks between Staunton and North Mountain, in this September 1983 photo. *Sutton Collection*

At 7-ft. 1-in., Ralph Sampson of the University of Virginia nearly always had the height advantage in early 1980s college basketball contests. Here he snatches the ball from Duke University player Jay Bilas.
Sutton Collection

1989 photo of Nancy Sorrells feeding poultry at the Museum of American Frontier Culture's American farm. *Sutton Collection*

June 16, 1983 photo of Virginia Sen. Chuck Robb signing a poster for 11-year-old Curtis Johnson of Goshen, at the site of the future Augusta Correctional Center. Looking on is William Choquette of Gilbane Building Company. *Sutton Collection*

Mrs. Joseph M. Greene of Harrisonburg – a.k.a. the Tooth Fairy – makes an appearance for Dental Health Month (February) 1981 at Mary Baldwin College Laboratory. *Sutton Collection*

The 1990s

Rebirth and Balance

While Staunton was rapidly becoming a national example of how historic preservation could serve as a vital component of "economic development," the city – which had doubled its size in 1987 with the annexation of 11 square miles – looked to a number of avenues for continued growth and prosperity. These included new development both on the city's periphery and within its historic core.

Some of the most visible growth took place in Staunton's northern quadrant with the establishment of the Green Hills Industry and Technology Center, an industrial park situated on land owned until 1987 by Augusta County. In 1993 Virginia Power became the first business concern to break ground in the park, and the following year Gov. George Allen helped break ground for a $15 million Best Buy distribution center.

Other development that drew attention – not all of it favorable – included the almost demonic strip-development of Richmond Road. Bulldozers roared constantly as huge tracts of land were sheared off at the eastern base of Betsy Bell Mountain for a Wal-Mart "supercenter" and a new Lowe's. Banks, restaurants and a host of other businesses followed their lead.

Downtown, the focus was on attracting new business and filling as many as 70 vacant buildings. Meanwhile, Georgia businessman Vic Meinert had transformed the C&O train station in Staunton from a vandalized, burned-out derelict slated for demolition into one of the city's most vibrant and important attractions.

AUGUSTA COUNTY'S NEWSPAPER

THE DAILY NEWS LEADER

VOL. 144, NO. 14 — STAUNTON, VA., 24401, THURSDAY, JANUARY 17, 1991 — 25 CENTS

WAR U.S. bombers hit Baghdad

At a glance

Here are Wednesday's developments in the Persian Gulf war:

— The United States launched air attacks against Iraq and Kuwait from Saudi Arabia.

— "Operation Desert Shield" was renamed "Operation Desert Storm," which U.S. officials said included U.S.-allied forces and began 7 p.m. EST.

— Marlin Fitzwater, quoting a statement from President Bush, said: "The liberation of Kuwait has begun."

— Oil prices shot up $3 per barrel in cash trading behind closed doors as war with Iraq began.

'Liberation of Kuwait has begun,' Bush says

CENTRAL SAUDI ARABIA (AP) — The United States launched air attacks early Thursday against Iraq, hurling its mighty Air Force against an Arab power that for five months has held Kuwait in defiance of the rest of the world.

"The liberation of Kuwait has begun," President Bush declared in Washington.

In Baghdad, television reporters said bombs were falling on the center of the Iraqi capital. They said explosions shook the ground, an oil refinery 10 miles away was in flames, and flashes of light brightened the night sky — apparent anti-aircraft fire.

"Operation Desert Shield" became "Operation Desert Storm" around 12:50 a.m. (4:50 p.m. EST) as F-15E fighter-bombers took off from the largest U.S air base in central Saudi Arabia and streaked north. "This is history in the making," said Col. Ray Davies, the base's chief maintenance officer.

The offensive included U.S.-allied forces and was aimed at Iraqi troops in both Iraq and Kuwait, U.S. officials said. British news reports said Royal Air Force Tornado GR1 fighter-bombers had joined the air assault.

There was no immediate word on whether ground attacks had been mounted against the dug-in Iraqi army in Kuwait. Nor was there any immediate sign of an Iraqi attack on Israel, as Iraq had threatened.

The early-morning assault was the climax to a crisis that built over more than five months, as Iraq's President Saddam Hussein, whose forces stormed Kuwait in a lightning invasion Aug. 2, rejected world condemnation and dismissed international economic sanctions designed to force him out of the occupied emirate.

Less than three hours after the U.S. jets were launched, reporters in Dhahran, Saudi Arabia, a staging base for the U.S. force, said air raid sirens sounded an alert of a possible Iraqi missile attack. The "all-clear" later sounded with no word of an attack.

The American warplanes took off in pairs, disappearing in red dots that winked out as they gained altitude. The aircraft were heavily loaded with bombs and underwing fuel tanks for the long trip north. They also were armed with cannon and air-to-air missiles for self-defense.

"We've been waiting here for five months now. Now we finally got to do what we were sent here to do," Col. Davies said.

Later, in Baghdad, ABC and CNN reporters said there were "flashes in the sky." Explosions and machine-gun fire could be heard in the background of their reports. "The night sky filled with a hail of bullets from anti-aircraft guns," CNN's John Holliman said.

The U.S.-led attack came one day after the Tuesday midnight deadline set by the U.N. Security Council for an Iraqi withdrawal from Kuwait. After that, the council declared, the assembled international military force would be free to drive the Iraqis from the conquered oil-rich enclave.

"The liberation of Kuwait has begun," White House spokesman Marlin Fitzwater said in Washington, quoting Bush. "In conjunction with the forces of our coalition partners the United States has moved under the code name Operation Desert Storm to enforce the mandates of the United Nations Security Council.

"As of 7 o'clock p.m. Operation Desert Storm forces were engaging targets in Iraq and Kuwait."

Right to the end, Iraq had remained defiant. Saadi Mehdi Saleh, speaker of Iraq's legislature, said on Wednesday that Saddam — already de-facto military commander — would "from now on direct the battle." Saddam later met with his ruling Revolutionary Command Council.

Saleh said in an interview Wednesday that Iraq was ready for talks with the United States if U.S. forces were withdrawn from the Persian Gulf. But he reiterated Iraq's threat to use chemical weapons if attacked.

On Wednesday, many of Baghdad's 3.8 million residents, fearful that war was about to befall their ancient city, continued their flight into the countryside.

In Saudi Arabia on Wednesday, as skies cleared after 36 hours of rain in the desert, mile-long convoys rumbled north past abandoned private cars in 60-degree temperatures, and twin-rotor Chinook helicopters swooped low. More than 1 million soldiers were ready for battle — almost [illegible] in the U.S.-led coalition, and more than a half-million Iraqi troops in southern Iraq and Kuwait.

Anti-war protests continued around the world Wednesday. In Germany, hundreds of thousands of students marched in Berlin, Munich and other cities for a fifth straight day carrying banners saying "No blood for oil!" Hundreds of protesters blocked traffic in Boston.

One of the first condemnations of the U.S.-led attack came from Cuba's U.N. ambassador, Ricardo Alarcon, who said in New York the offensive "deals a death blow to the new international order."

The oil market, as expected, reacted sharply to the word of war. In New York, oil prices soared some $8, to more than $40 a barrel, in cash trading behind closed doors as hostilities exploded in the world's greatest oil-producing region.

MESSAGE TO SADDAM — An F16 fighter assigned to the 138th Tactical Fighter Squadron at a base in Central Saudi Arabia Wednesday carries a 6,000-pound bomb with a message to Iraqi President Saddam Hussein. Planes from the base were reportedly involved in the bombing of Iraq. (AP Laserphoto)

'We will not fail,' President vows

WASHINGTON (AP) — President Bush summoned American and allied forces into war with Iraq on Wednesday night, declaring that with Operation Desert Storm. "The battle has been joined" to free Kuwait. Military officials said the initial attack was an aerial assault that met little resistence.

Related stories on page A6

Hostilities were well under way when Bush spoke to the nation at 9 p.m. EST. "We will not fail," he vowed as F-15E fighter bombers were marking strategic military targets across Iraq and Kuwait.

The president expressed hope "this fighting will not go on for long, and that casualties will be held to an absolute minimum." About 100 anti-war protesters maintained a vigil outside the White House.

Bush marshalled a potent international alliance to challenge Iraq's occupation of the oil-rich kingdom of Kuwait and issued his war order less than 24 hours after the expiration of a United Nations deadline.

Within moments of Bush's comments, Defense Secretary Richard Cheney told reporters that the first foray was conducted by hundreds of American, British, Saudi Arabia and Kuwaiti aircraft. "So far there has been no air resistance" from the Iraqis, Cheney said.

He provided no details on casualties, but said reporters were "very encouraging," and said the battle plan was designed to "focus on military targets, to minimize U.S. casualties, and to do everything possible to avoid injury to civilians in Iraq and Kuwait."

Bush spoke slowly, somberly, unsmilingly, and stumbled over several words. He said "all reasonable efforts" to resolve the Persian Gulf by diplomacy had failed, that Iraqi President Saddam Hussein "met every overture of peace with contempt."

One hundred and fifty Saudi aircraft were in the first wave, according to embassy spokesman Fred Dutton, who called the attack "saturation bombings" of Iraq. A Pentagon official said "a wave of Cruise missiles" were fired from U.S. Navy ships at preprogrammed targets in Iraq.

Bush said he had been assured by Army Gen. H. Norman Schwarzkopf, the American military commander in Saudi Arabia, that the air operations were succeeding. Bush said no ground forces were involved in the assault against Iraqi positions in Kuwait and Iraq.

BUSH

War brings tight security at airport

By DAVID BOTKINS
Staff Writer

WEYERS CAVE — The Shenandoah Valley Regional Airport will increase security here as a direct result of the war with Iraq.

Virgie Duff, airport manager, said Wednesday the Federal Aviation Administration has issued a mandate that all airports tighten security across the country in case of terrorist attacks.

Mrs. Duff said the Rockingham and Augusta County Sheriff's departments will share the duty of providing an armed officer for the airport prior to each takeoff.

Details remain to be worked out about scheduling of the officers but their primary purpose will be to screen passengers prior to boarding flights, Mrs. Duff said.

During the airport commission meeting Wednesday night, Roger Roberts of Shenandoah Flight Service and Greg Grow of Tri-Star Aviation, private charter services based at the airport, asked the commission to consider giving them discounts on fuel purchases.

Commission Chairman A. Erskine Sproul said the budget wouldn't allow giving fuel discounts and costs were already lower than other nearby airports.

"We are all business people here," said Roberts. "You have to do what you have to do and we as operators may have to relocate.

"It seems like sometimes there is a monologue going on here and not a dialogue; we would like you to look at things and not just give us a blanket rejection," he said.

Local reaction mixed

By CINDY CORELL
Staff Writer

Hours after U.S. forces led an attack on Iraq, area residents expressed mixed emotions about the starting war — Operation Desert Storm.

When television reports on the attack began shortly before 7 p.m., shoppers quickly gathered around the large selection of TV sets at Montgomery Ward. Salesperson Dottie Wilkerson said the people in the crowd were at first stunned, then emotional.

"A couple people were just standing there crying," Ms. Wilkerson said. "Then a lot of people out in the mall heard about it and they crowded in here too."

Within an hour of the mall's 9 p.m. closing a few shoppers still milled through and any conversations were of one subject, war.

In the food service court of the mall, a few people sat at tables finishing up coffee and soft drinks. As they waited for the mall to close, they visited with one another and the mood was at once somber and anxious.

Some were glad for the attack, they felt Saddam Hussein deserved the attack in payment for his aggression against the smaller neighboring country of Kuwait Aug. 2.

"Let's fight," said Edgar P. Smith of Staunton. "I'm not surprised about it; that's what we're over there for."

Don Marton of Staunton agreed. "I think they ought to do and get it over with," he said. "Shoot them and get it over with."

David Snyder and Thomas F. Clemmer, both of Staunton, were

(See REACTION, page A2)

NATIONAL WEATHER

The Accu-Weather® forecast for noon, Thursday, Jan. 17.

FRONTS: COLD, WARM, STATIONARY

INSIDE

(Two sections)

WEATHER

Mostly sunny and breezy today; highs 45 to 50. Fair skies, brisk winds and colder tonight; lows around 30. Mostly sunny Friday; highs 45 to 50. See complete weather on Page A2.

January 17, 1991: The Gulf War, launched against Iraq for its invasion of Kuwait, begins with air attacks. *Microfilm Archives*

In the spring of 1997, Staunton City Council began toying with the idea of reverting from a city to a town and uniting with Augusta County. The idea was abandoned in the face of stiff public opposition.

In 1998 – one year after it celebrated its 250th anniversary – Staunton embarked on a project it called "Our Big Dig – A New Foundation for An Old Community." This massive street improvement process included burying utility lines, installing brick sidewalks and replacing unsightly, concrete light- and traffic poles with fixtures based on antique designs. At this time the city also replaced water and sewer lines in the downtown.

One year later, the touring performance group Shenandoah Shakespeare moved its corporate headquarters from Harrisonburg to Staunton, and announced plans to build a replica of Shakespeare's Blackfriars Theater on South Market Street.

Waynesboro, ever the industrial and business leader, courted and won a new development that would be known as Eagles Nest – a residential area featuring homes with taxi-ways leading directly to an airplane runway. The 1992 development of this aviation village, which was part of a $5 million project, was the largest in the state.

In April 1992, a massive two-lane pile-up on Afton Mountain near Waynesboro killed two people and injured 44. The fog shrouded mountain became what one eye-witness called "a scene from hell" when nearly simultaneous accidents in both the eastbound and westbound lanes of I-64 resulted in rapid, devastating pile-ups. As many as 100 cars were involved in the accident.

The year 1992 was also important for Waynesboro in that it lost the Correctional Training Academy and Genicom's corporate headquarters. But better times were ahead for Waynesboro. In 1994 it began to look for ways to tap into the historic preservation wellspring, and that year city agreed to purchase the Plumb House on Main Street and renovate it. The 1806 Plumb House would become a museum.

As the decade drew to a close, Waynesboro also began to fill up the great gash it had created in one of its eastern slopes, and to seek historic district designation from the commonwealth.

And, as a sort of exclamation point to the statement Waynesboro was making about itself, Fairfax Hall – the once-elegant finishing school for young women that had begun life in 1890 as the Brandon Hotel – underwent extensive renovations to convert it to a retirement facility.

1992 photo of Genicom Corp. in Waynesboro. This was the original site of the Valley Airport established by Col. C.C. Loth.
Waynewsboro Collection

Gulf war used in area high school courses • Page B1

AUGUSTA COUNTY'S NEWSPAPER

The Sunday News Leader

101ST YEAR, NO. 8 STAUNTON, VA., 24401, SUNDAY, FEBRUARY 24, 1991 Staunton 885-7281 Waynesboro 949-7113 75 CENTS

Ground war begins

Bush calls it 'final phase' of Kuwait liberation

DHAHRAN, Saudi Arabia (AP) — Allied forces struck Iraqi troops in a long-awaited land offensive early Sunday after Saddam Hussein ignored a White House ultimatum to pull his army out of occupied Kuwait.

The attack, following weeks of practice by allied armored, air and amphibious forces, marked the start of the biggest U.S. ground engagement since Vietnam and America's first desert land war since World War II.

President Bush briefly addressed the nation Saturday night to announce that he had ordered the military to use "all forces available, including ground forces, to eject the Iraqi army from Kuwait."

The Pentagon canceled its briefings, a staple of news on the war. It said any details it released on the offensive would aid the enemy.

But the Kuwait News Agency quoted an Arab military source as saying allied forces retook the Failaka island, which dominates the entrance to Kuwait harbor. The agency, run by the exiled Kuwaiti government, said allied forces destroyed Iraqi tanks and took prisoner from 500 to 1,000 Iraqi troops.

Arab military sources in Riyadh said some 250 Iraqis had surrendered in the first hour of the attack, which began at 4 a.m. local time. They gave no details.

Capt. Ahman Al-Sabah, a pilot and member of the Kuwaiti royal family, said in a television interview he thought it would take ground troops three to four days to enter Kuwait City, 50 miles north of the Saudi border. He said he expected "thousands and thousands" of Iraqi troops to surrender.

In London, Prime Minister John Major said British forces would join the land drive and President Francois Mitterrand ordered French ground troops to engage "in the liberation of Kuwait."

There was no immediate reaction from Baghdad, where state radio was playing popular music and chants from the Koran when the invasion started.

Iraq's deputy ambassador to the United Nations predicted a long war.

"Iraq will not surrender," said the official, Sabah Talat Kadrat.

The U.N. Security Council convened Saturday night for consultations but diplomats said there was little the council could accomplish.

The assault came [illegible] days after the United States and coalition nations began a relentless air campaign against Iraqi forces. More than 100,000 missions have been flown against Iraqi troops and military and economic targets in Iraq.

The coalition's attacks began after an international trade embargo and diplomatic initiatives from a host of nations failed to convince Saddam Hussein to pull Iraq's troops from Kuwait.

U.S. military officials in Saudi Arabia late Saturday night spoke of increasingly fierce clashes with Iraqi forces just inside Kuwait, including a two-day battle in which 33 Iraqi armored vehicles were destroyed and 200 prisoners taken.

The battle, which had been the longest engagement of the war, began Thursday when about 500 Marines on a reconnaissance patrol were attacked just inside Kuwait. Lt. Gen. Walter E. Boomer, commander of the 80,000-plus Marine ground troops in Saudi Arabia, described it as "progessing obviously toward an offensive."

See related Persian Gulf war stories and photos on page A3.

Balance of Power in the Gulf

	IRAQ	U.S.	ALLIES
Troops	555,000 regular army 480,000 reserves (As of Jan. 15, Iraq had 545,000 troops deployed in Kuwait and southern Iraq)	More than 532,000 (At the peak of the Vietnam War in 1968, 545,000 Americans were involved)	271,030 (approx.)
Tanks	5,500 (By Feb. 18, the allies said they had destroyed at least 1,400 tanks)	More than 2,000	1,710 (approx.)
Combat Aircraft	700 (As of Feb. 22, 91 aircraft have been destroyed, 137 have flown to Iran)	1,300	500 (approx.)
Warships	No significant navy	More than 100	110 (approx.)

EYES TO THE FRONT — Saudi troops on an armored personnel carrier near the Kuwait border look toward suspected Iraqi positions Saturday as the waiting continued at the border. Smoke from burning oil wells in Kuwait darkens the midday sky. (AP Laserphoto)

Pastor, professor, consultant vie for Council seat

By NATALIE AUSTIN
Staff Writer

A pastor, college professor and former journalist have their names in the hat for a seat on Staunton City Council.

Resumes were distributed to council members Saturday to begin the process of selecting a successor for the seat of R. Eric Staley, who resigned effective Feb. 28.

Applicant Dr. C. Phillip Johnson has the support of the Staunton branch of the National Association for the Advancement of Colored People and at least two members of council.

The NAACP has criticized council for accepting applications for the seat rather than selecting Johnson, who trailed Staley in the May 1990 election by only 64 votes. NAACP representatives also criticized the lack of minority input in local government and said council is opening itself up to charges of racism.

Councilmen G. John Avoli and Douglas C. Wine have indicated their support for Johnson due to

(See COUNCIL, page A2)

Panel to study election system in Staunton

By NATALIE AUSTIN
Staff Writer

A committee of Staunton residents will be appointed to study the city's election system, including whether minorities have fair access to the political process and if voting wards should be implemented.

The action came after City Council heard a report on redistricting Saturday during a special workshop meeting.

Results of the 1990 census showed two of the city's voting precincts are potentially above limits allowed in the Code of Virginia, explained City Attorney Desmond C. Wray Jr.

The state requires at least 500 and no more than 5,000 qualified voters within a precinct area and that the areas be divided as equally as possible with regard to population.

Staunton elects council members at-large so the purposes of the city's election wards are merely to provide polling places.

"The at-large system is suspect if complaints are made that it doesn't accord minorities access to the political process," said Wray.

Wray said a committee should be appointed, including minority representation, to look at how the census has affected the districts. Council is slated to formally authorize the redistricting committee at its meeting Thursday followed by appointment of committee members March 14.

The committee will be charged with making recommendations concerning any changes in the city's present districts or if the city should instead go to election by wards, rather than at-large, Wray said.

Public hearings on any changes would follow and the plan submitted to the state Board of Elections and the U.S. Justice Department for clearance.

"The mere fact we've received clearance doesn't preclude citizens from bringing action if they feel the plan is unfair. Sufficient input from minorities in the city will be looked at," Wray said.

According to Staunton Assistant City Manager Richard A. Anzolut Jr., the population of those 18 and

(See SESSION, page A2)

Susie Audibert of Dogs East Search and Rescue shows police a rock found during a search around two houses on Fayette Street Saturday, apparently for the remains of Rebecca Ann Crist, who disappeared May 3, 1988. The remains of Raymond O. Fauber, 63, who lived at 309 S. Fayette St. were found in the basement of the house Feb. 8. Two members of his family were charged in connection with his murder. He had been missing since Sept. 18, 1988. (Photo by Vincent Lerz)

NATIONAL WEATHER

The Accu-Weather® forecast for noon, Sunday, Feb. 24.

Bands show high temperatures.

FRONTS: COLD WARM STATIONARY

©1991 Accu-Weather, Inc.

INSIDE

(Four sections)

WEATHER

Partly sunny today; highs in the mid-40s. Fair tonight; lows in the upper 20s. Increasingly cloudy Monday with a chance of rain; highs mid- to upper 40s. See complete weather on Page A2.

Police's search for second body on Fayette St. unsuccessful

By CINDY CORELL
Staff Writer

Staunton police brought search dogs, a backhoe and the local medical examiner to 309 S. Fayette St. Saturday morning, apparently searching for another body.

The search was unsuccessful.

The remains of Raymond O. Fauber, 63, who had lived in the house, were found in the basement Feb. 8. He had been missing since September 1988. His son-in-law, Robert C. Asbury, 31, has been charged with first-degree murder in connection with Fauber's slaying and remained in Augusta County jail Saturday.

Raymond Fauber's wife, Margaret R. Fauber, 55, was charged with a misdemeanor in the slaying, being an accessory after the fact. Mrs. Fauber and her daughter, Michelle Asbury, were also charged in connection with forged checks owned by Fauber. Mrs. Fauber remained in the county jail Saturday, and the charges against Mrs. Asbury were dropped in exchange for her husband's statement about Fauber's death and what happened to his remains, according to Staunton Commonwealth's attorney Raymond C. Robertson.

Also missing since 1988 is Rebecca Ann Crist of West Beverley Street.

Neighbors and her family said they believe police were searching for her remains Saturday morning.

Alice Cale of Churchville, Ms. Crist's sister, and her husband, Jeff Cale, were at the scene Saturday morning.

"It's her sister they're looking for," Cale said, pointing at his wife.

Madelaine Crist, the missing woman's mother, was driven by the scene by friends as police were packing up to leave. A distraught Mrs. Crist didn't get out of the car.

Police wouldn't confirm that the search was related to the Crist case.

"We just executed a search warrant," Police Chief G.L. Wells said. "If we had found something,

(See SEARCH, page A2)

October 24, 1991: American ground troops move against Saddam Hussein's Iraqi army in Kuwait. *Microfilm Archives*

Rescue workers help a firefighter at a May 9, 1990 blaze at the Vesuvius Baptist Church. Six fire companies turned out to fight the fire. Shortly after they got the blaze under control, another fire erupted at the Mt. Carmel Presbyterian Church in Steeles Tavern. Both fires were the work of an arsonist, who later was apprehended. *Sutton Collection*

Virginia Fall Foliage Festival among top 100 • Page 3

AUGUSTA COUNTY'S NEWSPAPER

THE DAILY NEWS LEADER

VOL. 144, NO. 53 STAUNTON, VA., 24401, MONDAY, MARCH 4, 1991 Staunton 885-7281 Waynesboro 949-7113 25 CENTS

Iraqis agree to Allies' conditions

MILITARY LEADERS MEET — U.S. Gen. H. Norman Schwarzkopf, the top allied commander, walks with Iraq's Lt. Gen. Sultan Hasheem Ahmed toward a tent Sunday in Safwan for the start of a meeting to set the terms of a permanent cease-fire. Surrounding the military leaders are armed soldiers providing security for the meeting. (AP Laserphoto)

Safwan Air Base

Iraqi military commanders accepted [illegible] permanently ending the Gulf War.

IRAQ IRAN Basra Persian Gulf Bubiyan I. Kuwait SAUDI ARABIA Khafji 25 miles 25 km

Faylakah Island

U.S. troops capture 1,405 Iraqi soldiers, including a brigadier general and 49 other officers on the Kuwait island.

AP

SAFWAN, Iraq (AP) — Allied and Iraqi military leaders agreed Sunday to a tentative cease-fire and a quick release of war prisoners in a dramatic meeting of commanders at a captured desert airstrip in southern Iraq.

"I am very happy to tell you we agreed on all matters," U.S. Army Gen. H. Norman Schwarzkopf told a crowd of soldiers and journalists after the two-hour meeting in a tent beside the crushed-stone runway.

He announced that a "symbolic release" of POWs would be made immediately to show good faith, and that "all detainees," including several thousand Kuwaiti civilian hostages held by Iraq, would be treated as war prisoners.

Iraq's U.N. ambassador, Abdul Amir al-Anbari, said in New York that Iraq had released 10 POWs already, among them six Americans, "including one of them the young lady that was captured." Pentagon officials said they had received no confirmation of any releases from the Red Cross in Geneva.

Schwarzkopf, the U.S. commander in the Persian Gulf, and other allied chiefs refused to say whether they had learned how many POWs are held by Iraq. The U.S. command knows of at least nine Americans. The only woman U.S. soldier listed as missing in the war is Army Spc. Melissa Rathbun-Nealy, 20, of Grand Rapids, Mich.

Schwarzkopf said U.S. troops would withdraw from occupied southern Iraq as soon as a permanent cease-fire was signed and Iraq has complied with U.N. resolutions. Those resolutions say Iraq must, among other things, rescind its annexation of Kuwait and accept liability for war damages in the emirate.

About 12 hours after the meeting in Safwan, Baghdad Radio announced that Iraq accepted the tougher U.N. conditions. That acceptance could clear the way for a permanent cease-fire in the Persian Gulf War.

In return, the U.N. Security Council on Sunday authorized mercy flights into Baghdad of food, medicine and water purification equipment.

In other developments:

—Iran's official radio reported violence between Iraqis and government forces during demonstrations against Saddam Hussein in at least four cities. Tehran radio said refugees fleeing Iraq for Iran reported "severe clashes" in the cities of Basra, Al-Amarah, Nassiriya and Kut. Washington repeatedly has urged Iraqis to overthrow Saddam, but U.S. officers say they don't know whether civil unrest in Iraq has become widespread.

—Saddam began the long process of rebuilding his war-torn nation and refurbishing his image as a regional leader to be reckoned with. Baghdad Radio reported Sunday that he led two meetings dealing with the restoration of Iraqi communications, the first report of his activities since Tuesday.

—A woman pilot and three other U.S. soldiers were killed in a helicopter crash in northern Saudi Arabia, U.S. military officials said Monday. Army Maj. Marie T. Rossi, 32, of Oradell, N.J., was the first woman pilot reported to be killed in the Gulf War. Officials in Saudi Arabia did not provide details of the Saturday crash, two days after the allies declared a cease-fire.

—French President Francois Mitterrand on Sunday proposed an unprecedented meeting of the leaders of the U.N. Security Council member nations to discuss Middle East issues such as the Palestinian-Israeli conflict.

In Safwan, two Iraqi army lieutenant generals, Sultan Hasheem Ahmad and Salah Abbud Mahmud, led the eight-member Iraqi delegation to the tent rendezvous. U.S. sources identified Ahmad as Saddam's deputy chief of staff, or third-ranking man in the defense establishment. Mahmud was the Iraqi 3rd Corps commander, the sources said.

A third man at the table, Brig. Taha Muhammad Ahmad, served as interpreter, and the rest of the Iraqi delegation sat in chairs behind their spokesmen.

Schwarzkopf and the allied Arab commander, Saudi Lt. Gen. Khalid bin Sultan, faced the Iraqis across the small wooden table that had notepads, teacups, two tape recorders and a bottle of water for each participant. A can of diet cola also was placed at Schwarzkopf's seat.

Other allied commanders — including British Forces chief, Lt. Gen. Sir Peter de la Billiere, French Lt. Gen. Michel Henri Roquejeoffre, and Arab officers — sat on metal folding chairs behind the two top allied leaders.

Witnesses described the mood of the meeting as businesslike, with a stern Schwarzkopf mincing no words in outlining the allied demands.

One source said the Iraqis were "slightly arrogant, but obviously wanting to get it over with."

Schwarzkopf, standing with Khalid at an outdoor podium afterward, told the crowd that the Iraqis had come "to discuss and cooperate with a positive attitude." If the atmosphere is maintained, the American general said: "We are well on our way to a lasting peace."

He said the Iraqis agreed to other key allied demands, including help in locating land mines in Kuwait and sea mines in the Persian Gulf. Operations to remove the mines will begin immediately, Schwarzkopf said.

Military prepares to receive POWs

WASHINGTON (AP) — American POWs returning from Iraq will receive thorough medical tests and debriefings on their treatment, including possible torture, at the hands of their Iraqi captors, Pentagon officials said Sunday.

Americans who have spent up to six weeks in captivity may already be on the first leg home. Iraqi Ambassador to the United Nations Abdul Amir al-Anbari said 10 foreign POWs, including six Americans, had been released.

Pentagon officials said the State Department had learned that Iraqi Foreign Minister Tariq Aziz had informed al-Anbari of the releases and the ambassador in turn had conveyed the message to Thomas Pickering, U.S. ambassador to the U.N.

However, neither the U.S. Central Command in Riyadh nor the International Committee of the Red Cross in Geneva could confirm that the POWs, said to include one American woman, had been released.

Nine Americans are among the 13 known POWs. The 66 listed as missing in action include 45 Americans, among them Army Spec. Melissa Rathbun-Nealy, 20, of Grand Rapids, Mich., the woman the Iraqis may have released.

Those freed will first go to a still-classified medical facility for what could be several weeks of intensive medical observation and treatment.

Jet crashes in Colorado Springs

COLORADO SPRINGS, Colo. (AP) — A United jetliner with 25 people on board crashed in flames as it approached the Colorado Springs airport early Sunday. There were apparently no survivors, authorities said.

"We can't even find a chair," said El Paso County Sheriff Bernie Berry. "There's not a great deal of that airplane left."

United Flight 585 en route from Denver crashed at 9:55 a.m. four to five miles south of the airport, the Federal Aviation Administration in Washington said. There were 20 passengers on board and a crew of five.

The FAA and the airline said all aboard apparently were killed. The plane narrowly missed houses and apartment buildings; at least one person on the ground was injured.

The United States Olympic Committee said two committee employees and a coach with the U.S. Cycling Federation were aboard the plane. United officials said a list of victims probably will be released Monday.

"There does not appear to be" any survivors, said Dick Meyer of the FAA's public information office in Seattle. Chicago-based United said in a statement that "at this time there are no reports of survivors" aboard the twin-engine Boeing 737-200.

Raphine woman dies in I-81 crash

RAPHINE — A Raphine woman was killed in a two-vehicle crash Sunday on I-81 near exit 54 between Raphine and Fairfield.

Sarah Harris Doyle, 69, of Rt. 1, Raphine, was killed at 1:50 p.m. when the vehicle in which she was a passenger was struck while the driver attempted to pull back into interstate traffic. The car had stopped in the emergency lane during a rain storm, according to Virginia State Police.

Mary Henderson, of Rt. 1, Lyndhurst, the driver of the car, was also injured in the crash and was transferred to the University of Virginia Medical Center where she was listed in critical condition Sunday night.

Another passenger in Ms. Henderson's car, Murlin B. Monger, was admitted to Stonewall Jackson Hospital and is in stable condition, according to a hospital spokesman.

The crash occurred when the vehicle driven by Ms. Henderson had pulled off to the side of the interstate during a rain storm.

While trying to get back into the flow of traffic, Ms. Henderson's vehicle was struck by a southbound vehicle driven by Joseph Marks, 29, of Clementon, N.J. He was transferred to U.Va. and is listed in guarded condition.

The crash remains under investigation, according to Virginia State Police.

CRASH SCENE — Four Waynesboro men were killed in this two vehicle collision on Va. 20 south of Scottsville Saturday night. The crash occurred when the northbound pickup skidded sideways into the southbound lane and was struck broadside by a Chevrolet Blazer. (AP Laserphoto)

Crash claims lives of four Waynesboro men

SCOTTSVILLE — Four Waynesboro men died Saturday night as the result of a two-car crash on Va. 20 south of here in Buckingham County. Four others, all Buckingham and Cumberland county residents, were seriously injured in the crash.

Mickey Harmon Brown, 32, his brother, Carl Allen Brown, 21, and Mitchell Blaine Male, 26, all of Waynesboro, were killed at 6:15 p.m. The crash occurred when the pickup being driven by Mickey Brown and heading north in a curve on Va. 20, skidded sideways into the southbound lane and was struck broadside by a Chevrolet Blazer.

A fourth man, Kevin Ashby Hubbard, 21, of Waynesboro, was pronounced dead on arrival at the University of Virginia Medical Center.

According to Trooper R.A. Cox the vehicles came to rest with the nose of the Blazer imbedded several feet into the passenger side of the pickup's cab.

The driver of the Blazer was Robert Paul Ingle, 30, of Cumberland. He was treated at the University of Virginia Medical Center and released, according to a hospital spokesman.

Other passengers in the Blazer were Robert's brother Mark Ingle, 18 and Charles Banton, 19, both of Cumberland. Banton was transported to U.Va. Medical Center and is listed in critical condition, according to a hospital spokesman.

Another passenger, Ernest Steve Palmore, age unavailable, of Buckingham, and Mark Ingle were also transported to U.Va. and are listed in satisfactory condition.

The crash remains under investigation according to Cox. He said the curve where the pickup and Blazer collided has been the scene of numerous crashes.

Bumgardner to hear Henderson trial

By SCOTT M. LANGSTON
Staff Writer

WINCHESTER — Circuit Court Judge Rudolph Bumgardner III of Staunton was appointed by the state Supreme Court to preside over the capital murder trial of Ronald Lee Henderson.

Henderson, 25, of Marlinton, W.Va., is being tried here March 25-29 for the Jan. 5, 1990 murder, abduction and robbery of 19-year-old James Madison University student Leanne Whitlock of Roanoke.

Bumgardner will replace Augusta Circuit Court Judge Thomas H. Wood who withdrew at the request of Henderson's attorneys.

In their motion for Wood to remove himself from the trial, defense attorneys said Wood gave his opinion of how the murder occurred which indicated a belief that two people were involved.

Wood withdrew Feb. 25 to avoid any problems later if Henderson is convicted, he said.

"I think it's good news," said Waynesboro attorney Jeffrey A. Ward, who is one of Henderson's attorneys. "It will help to have someone new look at the case. Bumgardner is an excellent judge and he should keep things moving along."

Bumgardner presides over Staunton and Waynesboro circuit courts so Ward said things will be "convenient."

"All the attorneys and the judge will be together," he said. "It will help with procedure and pre-trial motions."

Some of those pre-trial motions are tentatively scheduled to be heard March 13, said Ward.

The defense will ask Bumgardner to find the death penalty unconstitutional because it is "cruel and unusual punishment."

They also will ask it not be considered because inadequate instruction can be given to the jury on how to consider the penalty and Henderson's prior record can be introduced during the sentencing phase.

The defense also asks for extra juror strikes, money to help transport witnesses and money to hire a special investigator.

NATIONAL WEATHER

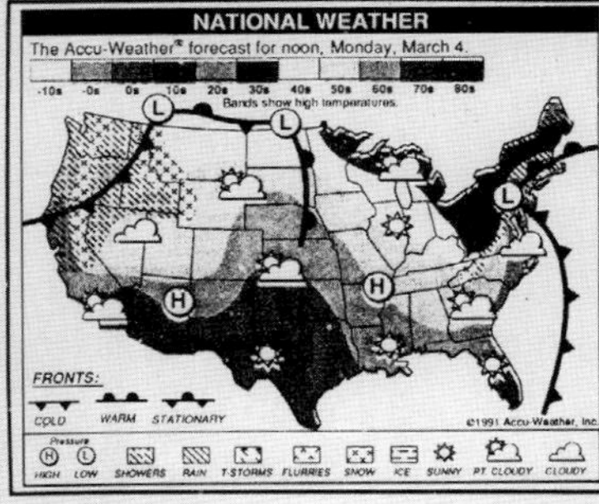

INSIDE

(One section)

WEATHER

Today windy with rain ending early morning but remaining mostly cloudy. Highs around 50. Chance of rain early 70 percent. Tonight, clearing breezy and colder. Lows in the low to mid-30s. Tuesday, partly cloudy. Highs in the upper 50s. See complete weather on Page 2.

March 4, 1991: Iraq admits defeat. *Microfilm Archives*

April 4, 1990 photograph of John Lane, rector of Trinity Episcopal Church, handing Staunton police officer Wayne Hamilton a palm leaf as the officer assists with traffic control for a Palm Sunday procession through downtown Staunton. *Sutton Collection*

Spotlight on the election • Pages C1-3

SERVING STAUNTON, WAYNESBORO AND AUGUSTA COUNTY

THE DAILY NEWS LEADER

VOL. 145, NO. 262 STAUNTON, VA., 24401, WEDNESDAY, NOVEMBER 4, 1992 Staunton 885-7281 Toll Free 1-800-79DAILY 25 CENTS

THUMBS UP — Democratic presidential candidate Gov. Bill Clinton of Arkansas gives final thumbs up as he leaves Dunbar Community Center after voting in Little Rock on Tuesday. (AP Photo)

Clinton wins!

12-year GOP reign ends

By DAN BALZ and ANN DEVROY
The Washington Post

Arkansas Gov. Bill Clinton, riding a wave of voter sentiment to revitalize the economy and change the country, was elected the 42nd president of the United States Tuesday in a broad electoral victory that ended 12 years of Republican rule in the White House and restored one-party government in Washington.

Clinton, 46, captured states from coast to coast as the voters turned President Bush out of office after one term. Texas independent Ross Perot, whose campaign shook the political rafters this year, was running third in what appeared to be the best performance by a third-party candidate since 1924.

Driven by their anxiety over the economy, voters abandoned a president whose leadership in the Persian Gulf War had briefly raised his popularity to record levels. He was winning barely 40 percent of the vote.

Clinton won pluralities of voters in every age group and every level of education and won among all but the wealthiest voters, breaking the presumed Republican "lock" on the electoral college map and winning back many of the voters who abandoned the Democratic Party beginning with Ronald Reagan's election in 1980.

But with Perot at about 17 percent and dividing the anti-Bush vote, Clinton was winning only about 45 percent, making him the first minority president since Richard M. Nixon in 1968.

In a gracious concession speech to his supporters in Houston around 11:15, Bush said, "Here is the way I see it. The people have spoken. We respect the majesty of the democratic system."

Bush said he had telephoned Clinton to congratulate him. "Our entire administration will work closely with his team to assure the smooth transition," Bush said, adding, "... America will always come first. We will get behind this new president and wish him well. ... Stand behind our new president."

He made no mention of Perot.

Clinton's supporters in Little Rock, Ark., massed outside the historic Old Statehouse where he announced his candidacy in October 1991, broke into cheers when the networks projected Clinton as the winner. Thousands of Clinton friends, allies and party faithful gathered in the Arkansas capital Tuesday to celebrate the biggest night the Democrats have had since Jimmy Carter won the presidency 16 years ago.

Perot was the first of the three candidates to appear before his supporters Tuesday night, conceding to Clinton at 10:30, even before the networks projected the Democrat as the winner. "The best is in front of us," Perot told his cheering audience in Dallas, calling on them to work with the new administration, for the time being.

With his supporters chanting "'96, '96," Perot told his allies to "team up and try to make it work now." He called on his supporters to "give it a world-class best effort" to work with the new Democratic administration to address the nation's problems.

In Tuesday's returns, Clinton swept economically hard-hit New England, according to network projections, only the second Democrat in this century to do so. He won New Hampshire and Vermont, which had not voted Democratic since 1964, along with two states Bush has called home and once counted as his: Connecticut, where he grew up, and Maine, where he has a vacation home.

The Democratic ticket rolled through the big states of the East and Midwest, capturing New York, New Jersey, Pennsylvania, Michigan, Illinois and Missouri, according to projections.

See *CLINTON*, page A2

Area backs Bush

By CINDY CORELL, SCOTT HELM, and SAM CARTER
Staff Writers

The Old Dominion was a patch of solid ground in the landslide that elected Bill Clinton president on Tuesday.

Following a historically Republican bent, the state and three area localities supported President George Bush.

But many voters dissatisfied with conventional politics cast their ballots for Independent H. Ross Perot.

With 98 percent of the precincts reporting across the state, Bush won 45 percent of the popular vote, Clinton 41 percent and Perot 14 percent.

Augusta County reported 60 percent for Bush, Clinton 24 percent and Perot 16 percent.

In Staunton, Bush won 56 percent, Clinton 31 percent, and Perot 13 percent.

Waynesboro reported 56 percent for Bush, 30 percent for Clinton and 14 percent for Perot.

Local Democratic and Republican leaders differed on the impact a Democratic president will have, but many agreed voters were seeking a change.

Ray Ergenbright, chairman of the Staunton Republican Committee, said he was pleased with Virginia's support of Bush.

About 10:30 p.m., he was hoping for a Republican majority in Congress where he says the work really counts on a domestic agenda.

See *AREA*, page A2

Goodlatte buries Musselwhite in 6th

By DAVID BOTKINS
Staff Writer

The 6th District U.S. House of Representatives seat will be filled by a Republican for the next two years.

Robert Goodlatte, a Roanoke attorney and GOP political operative for several years under the tutelage of former U.S. Rep. M. Caldwell Butler, R-6th, buried his Democratic opponent Steve Musselwhite with more than 60 percent of the vote district wide.

"It feels great to win," said Goodlatte from a Roanoke Days Inn lobby pay phone. "I'm overwhelmed by the margin of victory. The voters elected me because I stand for real change in the Congress."

Goodlatte said a Bill Clinton presidency will not deter him from working toward his articulated conservative agenda.

Goodlatte plans to consult retiring U.S. Rep. James Olin, D-6th, and Butler during his transition prior to being sworn in in January in Washington, D.C.

Goodlatte swept the Staunton, Augusta County and Waynesboro vote. In Augusta County with 24 of 26 precincts reporting by press time, Goodlatte had 13,863 votes to Musselwhite's 4,722. Unofficial totals in Staunton's five wards had Goodlatte with 5,484 votes to 2,372 for Musselwhite.

The unofficial vote totals in Harrisonburg and Rockingham County mirrored the margins in Staunton and Augusta. 12,800 for Goodlatte in Rockingham compared with 4,164 for Musselwhite; in Harrisonburg Goodlatte had 5,464 to 2,791 for Musselwhite.

In Waynesboro and Highland County, Goodlatte won by almost 2-1 margins.

Musselwhite won very few localities across the district. Those he did carry were close and traditionally Democratic. Musselwhite carried the heavy labor areas of Clifton Forge, Covington and Buena Vista.

He also carried Lexington and vote-rich Roanoke City, but only by 1,000 votes. Goodlatte carried Roanoke County 19,221 to 12,880 with 99 percent of precincts reporting.

Reached at a Holiday Inn in Roanoke, Musselwhite said he was surprised at the margin of his loss.

"We are looking to see what happened; I am surprised," he said.

See *6TH*, page A2

GOODLATTE

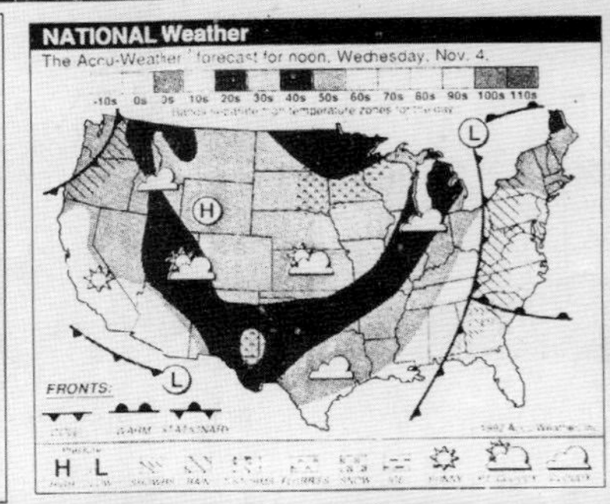

VOTERS SPENT 13 hours going to the polls on Tuesday in record numbers. Here at T.C. McSwain Elementary School candidates worked the crowds by erecting signs and passing out more campaign literature. (Photo by Dennis Sutton)

Meals tax on menu

By CHRISTINA NUCKOLS
Staff Writer

Proponents of a county meals tax toasted their success Tuesday night, as Augusta became the 53rd locality in the state to institute the measure.

The vote passed with 58 percent or 11,215 voters in favor. Forty-two percent or 8,019 county voters were opposed to the tax.

Supervisor Chairman Charles W. Curry of North River said the tax's passage is a double mandate for county officials.

"The voters have spoken very clearly that they want their real estate rate protected and that they support education," he said.

In 1989, a similar referendum failed by a margin of 77 percent to 22 percent. Curry said this year's referendum avoided the same fate because supervisors stipulated that 90 percent of the revenues from a meals tax will go toward school capital improvements, with the remainder to be funneled into regional tourism.

Of a total school capital improvement package of $28 million, supervisors have authorized the sale of $2.33 million in bonds for five small projects. Curry said the passage of the meals tax will be one factor in preparing the way for moving forward with the remainder of the projects, which includes construction of two new elementary schools and major renovations to Fort Defiance High School.

See *MEALS*, page A2

News capsules

Gag rule rejected

WASHINGTON (AP) — The Bush administration may not enforce a rule restricting federally funded family planning clinics from counseling patients about abortion, a federal appeals court ruled Tuesday.

A three-judge panel of the U.S. Circuit Court of Appeals here said the revised gag rule, permitting only doctors at the clinics to discuss abortion with patients, was adopted illegally.

The Department of Health and Human Services adopted the modified rule without giving the public adequate opportunity to challenge it, the appeals court said.

Women in combat

WASHINGTON (AP) — A presidential commission recommended Tuesday that military women not be allowed to participate in ground combat.

However, it said the armed services should have greater leeway in defining what comprises modern-day fighting.

The 15-member Commission on the Assignment of Women in the Armed Forces concluded three days of hearings in sharp dispute over the future of the 200,000 American women in uniform.

A complete summary of election returns, along with stories on the school board election referendum, Staunton city sheriff race, Staunton Circuit Court clerk race, state bond referenda and Waynesboro commissioner of revenue race are featured on pages C1-3.

NATIONAL Weather

The Accu-Weather forecast for noon, Wednesday, Nov. 4.

-10s 0s 0s 10s 20s 30s 40s 50s 60s 70s 80s 90s 100s 110s

FRONTS:

H L

INSIDE

(Four Sections)

WEATHER

Cloudy through Thursday with a chance of rain. Highs today in the mid- to upper 60s. Lows tonight in the upper 40s. Highs Thursday in the mid- to upper 50s. See complete weather on page A2.

Craigsville council takes steps to improve creek • Page A3

SERVING STAUNTON, WAYNESBORO AND AUGUSTA COUNTY

THE DAILY NEWS LEADER

VOL. 149, NO. 216 | Classified 885-7387 Circulation 885-7348 | STAUNTON, VA., 24401, SATURDAY, SEPTEMBER 7, 1996 | Main Office 885-7281 Toll Free 1-800-79DAILY | 50¢ Newsstand 20¢ Home Delivery

Fran deluges area with rain

By PAUL BERGEN, RONDA COX, MICHAEL HEWLETT and DAVID NIVENS
Staff Writers

Tropical Storm Fran's leaden clouds cracked open to reveal silvery-blue sky Friday evening as Gov. George Allen toured flooded Waynesboro, and Augusta County-area residents began cleaning up.

Throughout the area, more than 200 displaced residents spent the day in shelters, with many likely to stay the night. In Augusta County and Staunton, road crews were clearing away fallen trees and preparing to assess damage in expectation of federal emergency aid.

About 10,000 people lost power in Virginia Power's Blue Ridge District, which includes Staunton, Augusta County and Waynesboro, said Phil Sparks, the director of community relations at Virginia Power in the western part of the state. About 9,800 Shenandoah Valley Electric Cooperative customers also lost power.

"It's going to be a long day and a long night and another long day and long night," said Sparks, estimating how long it would take to get everyone's power back on.

Allen visited downtown and Club Road areas where the swollen South River filled basements with mud-brown water and debris. "Unofficially," the river reached an level of 13.5 feet, said City Manager Schuyler Giles, four feet above flood stage, and it appeared to have begun receding Friday night.

"These hundred-year floods that come every six months, that's got to change," said Waynesboro resident John Durgin.

"It's clear this is a disaster area," said Allen, who was joined by fellow Republicans Sen. John Warner and Rep. Bob Goodlatte, as well as Waynesboro and Augusta County officials. Earlier in the day, he had declared the state a disaster area, making it eligible for federal aid.

Seeing sand-bagged storefronts downtown, he said, "Obviously these people are resourceful. They haven't just sat around and complained about the weather."

He also said he would look into why the city has experienced delays in trying to get a permit to dredge the river.

Talking to Club Road resident Mike Sobczak, whose basement was filled with water to the top of the stairs, Warner noted that the house lay in a flood plain.

"When you build a house in a flood plain, you're running a risk like when you build a house on the San Andreas Fault," Sobczak agreed. But he said his homeowners insurance company was being uncooperative, with Sobczak's claim from the January flood still not settled.

"The governor and I will look into that," Warner promised.

Allen, visiting flooded areas throughout the state, had intended to fly into Eagle's Nest Airport near Waynesboro, but cloud cover over Afton Mountain forced him to take a State Police cruiser from Albemarle County.

Before leaving, he visited the Red Cross shelter at Kate Collins Middle School, where manager Walter Lonas said he expected 15 people to stay the night, although almost 40 spent the day there.

Among those were five students and two instructors who were on the last seven-mile leg of a six-week hike on the Appalachian Trail when they had to be rescued by State Police.

"We made it to Wintergreen. We got a ride to here," said 13-year-old Kareem Shelton, sitting in the Kate Collis cafeteria. "I was laying down, and I heard something — pow! — and a lot of tree limbs were breaking and stuff. ... I thought it was a gunshot at first."

Staunton declared a state of emergency at 7:20 a.m. Friday. Assistant City Manager Richard A. Anzolut Jr. said many areas of the city experienced high winds and power outages at a number of major intersections.

"There's been a lot of street flooding," Anzolut said. "We're encouraging people to stay home if at all possible."

Anzolut said that all non-life threatening calls were being handled through the Emergency Operations Center set up at the city fire department. No city emergency shelters have been set up, Anzolut said.

The Salvation Army was housing 40 people in its gymnasium, including displaced residents of the Beverley Hotel, which experienced flooding Friday.

Street Supt. Don Kirby said that clearing the trees from the city streets was his department's main priority.

Beginning at 6 a.m. Friday, the crews cleared the trees, and cleaned up mud slides on Richmond Road and Old Greenville Road.

WELCOME TO STAUNTON, if you can get into the city. Friday was not a good day to enter the city under the railroad bridge at Greenville Avenue and Richmond Road. More than 7 inches fell on the city during the morning hours, flooding several low lying areas and cutting off traffic on several major arteries.

(Photo by Mark Miller)

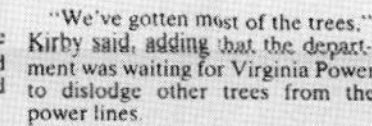

"We've gotten most of the trees," Kirby said, adding that the department was waiting for Virginia Power to dislodge other trees from the power lines.

Kirby said flooding was the city's biggest priority, with many of the city's main thoroughfare's shut down because of excessive water.

"We've got half of the town blocked," he said, adding that many motorists are running barricades.

Kirby said the public works crews are prepared for more bad weather.

"We're planning on working all weekend," he said, adding that Friday's trash routes should be taken care of by this morning. "We're going to get the right-of-ways cleaned out and the streets cleared."

Although the average rainfall in Augusta County was between 6 and 9 inches, the rain gauge at Upper Sherando Lake topped out at 14-1/2 inches, according to John McGehee, the county's assistant director of emergency services.

He said the worst hit areas of the county were those lying at the foot of the mountains. The county declared a state of emergency at 7:30 a.m.

"The worst problems are in the western part of the county and in Sherando," McGehee said.

Four National Guard members helped evacuate people in Augusta County.

Pete Combee, commander for the western sub-area for the National Guard, said the Guard took most of the people to North River Elementary School.

"We aren't looking at this as a real heavy requirement," he said. "The community still has to assess the damage and what they need."

The Virginia State police had 10 men out helping people with various problems.

Sgt. Joe Rayder said their lines were overwhelmed with calls about roads being flooded. "We've been pretty busy helping with evacuations and roads."

Most of the manpower were concentrated at Va. 252, Va. 42 and U.S. 250.

About 170 people were staying at eight shelters set up in Augusta County schools, including 68 at Churchville Elementary, 50 at North River Elementary and 41 at Buffalo Gap High School.

"That's a considerable amount of people at shelters for us," McGehee said.

Telephone service was cut off to Craigsville, where 25 people moved to the elementary school for the day.

The Department of Social Services was assisting with shelters at North River and Churchville, said Red Cross' Lynn Murphey. In Rockbridge County, Red Cross opened eight shelters.

"We want people to have a dry place if they need it," Murphey said.

Red Cross workers were asking people to bring pillows and blankets with them and any medications. Food was provided.

See **FLOOD**, *page A2*

More photos on page A3

A TRUCK plows through water in Brands Flat Friday after rains from Tropical Storm Fran caused streams, creeks and rivers in Augusta County to overflow their banks. At one point Friday, among the roads that were closed to traffic by high waters or fallen trees included U.S. 11, U.S. 250 and Va. 254, according to county officials.

(Photo by Mark Miller)

Flash flooding claims Highland resident

By SANDY HEVENER
Special Writer

McDOWELL — Flash flooding in the McDowel/Doe Hill area Friday claimed the life of Thelma Botkin, 53, according to the Highland County Sheriff's Office and Emergency Services.

Sheriff Herbert Lightner said when Ms. Botkins's husband, Glen Botkin Jr., returned home and discovered she was missing he called for help. Members of the Highland County Rescue Squad and Fire Department found her about 1 p.m.

"She apparently was moving a four-wheeler to higher ground and did get washed away," said Lightner.

Lightner said the road, Va. 619 in Botkin Hollow, had been closed by flooding and workers engaged heavy equipment to complete rescue efforts.

Attending physician, Dr. Carolyn Ferrari, was unable to release the cause of death by press time, but a source close to the victim gave the apparent primary cause of death as severe head injuries and drowning a secondary cause. The victim apparently received the head injuries when washed downstream. The four-wheeler was about 30 yards away.

The Sheriff's office and Emergency Services reported no other injuries caused by anything related to the severe weather.

As of 5:45 p.m. Friday, U.S. 220 north to West Virginia and U.S. 250 east to Augusta County remained closed. About 25 percent of Highland's secondary roads were also closed at that time.

Harley Gardner, Highland's emergency services coordinator, reported no major damage to any dwellings but minor damage to some homes with all affected dwellings inhabitable. About 20 families were evacuated and several families placed in shelters through Red Cross services.

Areas evacuated included New Hampden, Mustoe, Bolar, the Williamsville gorge area and parts of the McDowell area.

Britain bows to Russian opposition on Iraq resolution

By JOHN M. GOSHKO
The Washington Post

UNITED NATIONS — Britain bowed to unyielding Russian opposition Friday and gave up its drive for a Security Council resolution criticizing Iraq for its military offensive against Kurdish rebels.

It was the first major setback here for U.S. policy toward Iraq since the 1991 Persian Gulf War, and reflected the unraveling of the international coalition that supported Washington in that conflict.

Had the resolution passed, it would have rebuked President Saddam Hussein's government for renewed mistreatment of Kurds in northern Iraq. It also would have been a tacit endorsement of President Clinton's attempt to punish Saddam by launching U.S. cruise missile attacks against Iraqi air defense installations earlier this week.

But efforts to get majority support in the 15-nation council foundered in the face of Russian threats to veto the resolution on grounds that it failed to mention the U.S. involvement in the latest fighting.

During four days of backroom negotiation, the proposed criticism of Iraq was watered down substantially. That was not enough to sway Moscow, however, which was a dependable U.S. ally during the Gulf War but now has become more an advocate of flexibility in dealing with Saddam's regime.

The United States did not co-sponsor the resolution. Nevertheless, the proposed draft was squarely in line with the U.S. argument that Saddam's government is a rogue regime that must be held to a tough standard and if necessary punished to make it behave.

The Security Council's failure to act in the current situation marked the first time that it has not gone along with the U.S. position on a significant issue involving Iraq since the latter's August 1990 invasion of neighboring Kuwait. At that time, in response to Washington's urging, the council created the framework for the U.S.-led military coalition that forcibly expelled Iraq from Kuwait. Since then, the council has kept Iraq under crippling economic sanctions to pressure it to surrender its weapons of mass destruction and yield on other issues.

The United States had sought to keep a certain distance from the failed resolution by emphasizing that it was a British initiative. Still, U.S. Ambassador Madeleine K. Albright left no doubt that Washington was not pleased by the council's failure to give its blessing to Clinton's action.

"We consider that an unfortunate result because there clearly was broad support for a resolution that criticized the Iraqis," she said. "It shows that sometimes the council is not the most effective way to deal with this. . . . We stand by what the United States did to deal with the problem in the northern (areas) . . . . and it's just unfortunate that at this stage the council was not able to speak on the subject."

In the course of the negotiations, it became clear that the United States no longer can expect its hard-line attitude toward Iraq to be backed by many of the other countries that lined up behind it in 1990 and 1991. While Britain has remained a staunch supporter, France made clear it had serious reservations about U.S. moves in recent days, and many Arab countries that aided the 1991 campaign to free Kuwait either remained silent or were openly critical of the U.S. missile attacks.

There were a variety of reasons for these changes. France and Russia both have potential financial and commercial interests in Iraq worth billions of dollars. Arab governments fear that attacking Saddam might create sympathy for him among populaces swayed by Arab nationalism. And many governments feel that the United States was on shaky legal grounds when it argued that existing U.N. resolutions gave it the green light to fire missiles against Iraq.

In this week's negotiations, all of these factors came together to make clear that the U.N. membership now is too divided about the proper approach to Iraq to simply fall in line behind the United States. Stephen Gommersall, the acting British ambassador, said his government was leaving its proposed resolution on the table, but he acknowledged that "the council is not ready to take a decision on Iraqi oppression of its people."

Russian Ambassador Sergei Lavrov argued that any resolution should have called for a halt to all military action, including the American, rather than attempt to give the U.S. moves a legal underpinning by criticizing only Baghdad.

He noted that the Iraqis have withdrawn most of their forces from the north and added: "The situation has evolved in northern Iraq so it is not necessary to call on anyone to withdraw. Also it is too early to start assessing from the perspective of history the right or wrong of what happened there."

INSIDE

(Two Sections)

WEATHER

Today, variable cloudiness with a 40 percent chance of showers and thunderstorms. Highs 80 to 85. Southwest winds 10 to 15 mph. Tonight, variable cloudiness. Lows in the mid to upper 60s. Chance of rain 30 percent. See complete weather, page A8.

September 7, 1996: Hurricane Fran batters Virginia with flood waters. *Microfilm Archives*

Sludge battle has 10-year history • Page C1

SERVING STAUNTON, WAYNESBORO AND AUGUSTA COUNTY

The Sunday News Leader

107TH YEAR, NO. 35 | Main Office 885-7281 Toll Free 1-800-79DAILY | STAUNTON, VA., 24401, SUNDAY, AUGUST 31, 1997 | Classified 885-7387 Circulation 885-7348 | $1.25 Newsstand

VMI board gets good report on female rats

LEXINGTON (AP) — Virginia Military Institute's transition to a coeducational school has been smooth so far, Superintendent Josiah Bunting III told VMI's governing board Saturday.

VMI welcomed a freshman class of 30 women and 430 men on Aug. 18. Two females and 27 males have dropped out.

Bunting told the Board of Visitors that the integration of women, ending a 158-year all-male tradition, has been a team effort.

"I have the sense ... of being assigned here as the coach of a great football team with virtually every position being very deep and very skilled," he said.

He said the mission has been to assimilate women into the cadet corps "in a way that preserves the raw essentials of a VMI education and keeps intact our reputation for principled excellence and denies neither gender the reasons for which they enrolled."

Board members said they were pleased with the smooth transition, but they realized the academic year is young.

"I don't think it's over 'til it's over," said board member Rhett Clarkson of Richmond. "I'm still looking over my shoulder."

Said board member Anita Blair of Arlington: "It all seems very positive so far. ... But everybody understands it's a long process."

The board's cadet corps committee was told Friday that the female "rats," as VMI freshmen are called, are handling the harsh physical and mental discipline as well as the males.

"VMI has not changed," said Commandant of Cadets James N. Joyner Jr., a 1967 graduate. "The policies that we have in place are good and workable, and I feel very strongly that the corps understands what we're about ... and understands the seriousness of what we're doing."

Regimental Commander Timothy O. Trant III, a senior from Disputana and the highest-ranking cadet, told the committee that "the cadre appears to be completely gender-blind." The cadre is the group of upperclassmen assigned to train the rats.

Clarkson asked if women were really being treated as harshly as men.

"Yes, sir," Trant said.

The U.S. Supreme Court ruled in June 1996 that VMI would have to admit women if it continued as a state-supported school.

INDEX

Four sections

WEATHER

Today, partly sunny. Highs in the mid 80s. Light winds. Tonight, variable cloudiness. Lows in the low to mid 60s. Light winds. Labor Day, partly cloudy with a 30 percent chance of late day showers. Highs in the mid 80s. See complete weather, page A2.

Music, history celebrated on Staunton's 250th birthday

By HEATHER BURKEY
Staff Writer

STAUNTON — Some residents and visitors celebrated the city's 250th birthday Saturday inside city hall by learning about the city's history and listening to the relaxing melodies a musician created on a hammered dulcimer and a flute.

Others sat just outside city hall listening to loud music coming from the bandstand and bought acrylic paintings, glass vases, wooden bird houses and animal woodcarvings from booths set up along Beverley Street.

Staunton resident Glynda Barker said history is what the 250th anniversary means to her.

"There's so much history in this area," she said. "I feel like the baby boomers are going to bring it back by participating in renovations of the older houses and by going to auctions."

Mrs. Barker is restoring a house at 303 Berkeley.

"I never cease to be amazed at just how interesting the history of this city is," said Sergei Troubetzkoy, a historian who displayed tidbits about Staunton inside city hall.

"I think people who grow up in a community tend to overlook the significant events that took place in their own community. They forgot about, for example, William Haines."

Haines, who appeared in 50 films and has a star on Hollywood's Walk of Fame, was born in 1900 at what is now 419 N. New St.

"He's just one of many people from this community who really made an impact out of the city."

Troubetzkoy said Haines, who left Staunton when he was 17, became an interior designer after he stopped making films.

"It shows that anyone can make it big. He's someone who became a household name and had no entrees into Hollywood or into the interior design business."

Someone living in Staunton right now could become the next movie

star or president of the United States, he said, referring to Woodrow Wilson.

Troubetzkoy said some Staunton residents may not know the local Stonewall Brigade Band is the nation's oldest continuous band supported by a municipality. The band serenaded Ulysses S. Grant and performed for Wilson numerous times. The Stonewall Brigade Band, which began in 1855, is still performing today.

"That's something to be proud of," Troubetzkoy said.

Alexander H. Stuart, who lived on Church Street, was the first secretary of the interior of the United States under Millard Fillmore.

Staunton has looked at its own past to maintain its heritage, Troubetzkoy said. Staunton held a Beverley Street carnival on Labor Day in honor if its 150th birthday, he said.

"Here we are Labor Day weekend 100 years later having a birthday."

The Rev. A.D. Mason traveled with his wife about 125 miles from Harpers Ferry for the city's anniversary celebration.

Mason said he wanted to participate in the city's birthday to honor the community that raised more than $3,000 and gave his family furniture after the Church of the Nazarene and his family's basement apartment burnt down in 1950.

"The community was great to me when we had the tragedy," he said. "We just wanted to come down and see what they're doing for the celebration."

Later in the afternoon, a crowd ate birthday cake at the Johnson Street parking lot and listened to more music.

BRUCE HAMMER, of Staunton, takes a bite of some fried chicken off of his picnic lunch Saturday on Beverley Street. The street and Wharf area in downtown Staunton were shut off to traffic so that Staunton could host its 250th Birthday Celebration with food, crafts, music and games that will continue through today.

(Photo by Sherri Sturgis)

Ex-ASR president, John Baker, dead at 77

By HEATHER BURKEY
Staff Writer

DURHAM, N.C. — A co-worker remembers former American Safety Razor officer John Raymond Baker Jr. as an excellent manager with exceptionally high standards.

Baker, who died Thursday at the age of 77, joined the Philip Morris Co. in the 1960s and eventually became the president and CEO of American Safety Razor in Verona. When Philip Morris sold the American Safety Razor division in 1977, Baker led ASR employees in buying the company from Philip Morris. Baker sold his interest in ASR in 1984 and retired to Saddleback Farm in Afton.

Baker's leadership extended beyond ASR. He served as president of the Country Club of Staunton.

Earl Howell, who worked under Baker for about eight years serving as corporate development manager and division manager for industrial blades, called Baker "an extraordinarily bright and capable manager."

Howell said Baker made a good manager because he had a "tremendous attention to detail, a genuine feel for business, an ability to prioritize and just a keen analytical mind."

He said Baker was an important mentor to him.

Baker was an active reader, Howell said.

"He always stayed current with the latest business developments."

Howell said Baker's passion was sailing. He sailed in a number of competitions and was interested in the design, construction and racing strategies of his boats.

"He was a very high energy kind of person who placed value on doing things well whether at work or sailing," Howell said.

Baker is survived by his widow, Brenda Vaughn Baker of Durham, and a sister, Janet Baker Gage of South Chatham, Mass. A service will be conducted at 2 p.m. Wednesday at the family's residence, 4 Stoneglen Court in Durham with a private burial.

Booker T. Washington alumni honor scholars

By DAVID NIVENS
Staff Writer

STAUNTON — Alumni of the former Booker T. Washington High School recalled their alma mater with love Saturday as they gathered to honor local scholars and to celebrate the alumni association's 25th anniversary.

Young alumni heard stories of the old days during a banquet at Ingleside Hotel Resort.

Kenneth L. Jones, Class of 1923, marveled at the accomplishments of the graduates. The class of 1923 was the school's first.

"It is the reputation of these people that matter," said Jones, who was one of only two young men to graduate in 1923's class of seven.

Jones took classes in three rooms. That's all the school had for the seven students and for teachers and offices, Jones said.

For many years, the school was so small, graduation ceremonies were held in local churches. In 1923, students finished school after 11th grade.

"If we wanted to go on to college, we had to go to another high school," Jones recalled.

Jones then split his time between work and school until he went on to West Virginia State College where he graduated in 1934. Jones returned to Staunton to teach before going to Langston University in Oklahoma where he was executive secretary to the president for four years.

"I don't know what I would have done without the school," said Arthur R. Ware Jr., who was Title I administrator for Staunton City Schools from 1966-78. "It is important for us to remember what it was all about."

Ware was a member of the Class of 1928.

"We are proud to carry on," said the former school principal.

The school closed in 1966 as Staunton and the rest of the country grappled with the reverberations of the Brown vs. Board of Education decision that declared segregation morally wrong.

ROSALIE C. VICKERS of the Booker T. Washington Alumni Association talks Saturday with alumni scholarship winner Natasha Jones at Ingleside Resort where the association celebrated its 25th anniversary.

(Photo by Sherri Sturgis)

But alumni have not forgotten the building that is being used as a community center. The Class of 1947 gave the city of Staunton two benches to place at the building for the city's 250th anniversary.

The Booker T. Washington Scholarship Fund awarded these scholarships Saturday:

- Natasha Jones, daughter of Mr. and Mrs. Herbert Jones, thanked the association for her $2,000 alumni scholarship to attend Shenandoah University in Winchester. She will take studies for a major in business.

"I want to thank my family who made me hit the books," she said. "I thank God for my parents and family for this."

Miss Jones also received a certificate of recognition from the Community Involvement Awareness group for her work at the Booker T. Washington Community Center.

- Jacquline Wormsley, daughter of Wanda and D.C. Wormsley, was the winner of a $1,000 scholarship to attend Virginia Tech from the Washington, D.C. chapter. She will study environmental science.
- Caleris Lang, the daughter of Iris and Winfred Lang, got a $800 scholarship from the Class of 1947 scholarship fund to attend Old Dominion University. Miss Lang's mother was the association's first scholarship winner in 1974.

Diana seriously injured in car crash

By JOCELYN NOVECK
Associated Press Writer

PARIS — Diana, Princess of Wales, was seriously injured in a car crash early Sunday that killed her boyfriend, Dodi Fayed, and the chauffeur, police said.

The crash happened shortly after midnight in a tunnel along the Seine River at the Pont de l'Alma bridge, while paparazzi followed her car, a police spokesman said on condition of anonymity. The high-speed pursuit ended in a crash in the tunnel that trapped several people in a pileup, France Info radio reported.

Fayed, son of the billionaire Egyptian owner of London's prestigious Harrod's department store, was killed in the accident along with the chauffeur, the spokesman said.

•BULLETIN: At presstime, the Associated Press reported that Princess Diana had died.

The fourth person in the car, a bodyguard, was also seriously injured in the crash, the spokesman said. He would not say where Diana or the bodyguard were hospitalized.

Dodi and Princess Diana's close friendship became clear to the outside world over the past five weeks, as the couple took a series of holidays together in the Mediterranean.

Newspapers reported Diana first

See **DIANA,** *page A2*

August 31, 1997: Staunton celebrates its 250th anniversary. *Microfilm Archives*

Medical waste discovered in second Va. landfill, A3

THE DAILY NEWS LEADER

Serving Staunton, Waynesboro and Augusta County

50 cents

Saturday
February 13, 1999
109th Year, No. 38

Special Report:
IMPEACHING A PRESIDENT

Perjury
55 - 45
Not Guilty - Guilty

Obstruction
50 - 50
Not Guilty - Guilty

NOT GUILTY

Senate votes end historic impeachment saga; censure unlikely; Clinton 'profoundly sorry'

Gannett News Service

WASHINGTON — The Senate acquitted Bill Clinton of perjury and obstruction of justice charges Friday, but somber and even angry senators from both parties warned the president not to regard their refusal to remove him from office as vindication of his conduct.

Inside
■ See how senators voted, A6 ➥
■ Check listings for Sunday news shows, A6 ➥
■ Acquittal in the long shadows of Mr. Lincoln, A4 ➥

Within two hours of the vote, Clinton appeared in the Rose Garden to note gravely that the Senate had "fulfilled its constitutional responsibility" and to apologize once more for his conduct.

"I want to say again to the American people how profoundly sorry I am for what I said and did to trigger these events and the great burden they have imposed on the Congress and on the American people," Clinton said.

For only the second time in the 210-year history of the presidency, the Senate found itself in the uncomfortable position of having to decide a president's fate. In 1868, Andrew Johnson escaped conviction by a single vote.

"Senators, how say you?" Chief Justice William Rehnquist, presiding over the trial as required by the Constitution, solemnly asked after each of the articles was read.

Instead of the usual yay or nay, the senators stood when their names were called to respond "guilty," or "not guilty." Some pronounced their verdicts loudly and vigorously, some could not be heard despite how still and attentive the senators and standing-room only crowds were.

Article I, which charged Clinton with lying to a grand jury about his affair with former White House intern Monica Lewinsky, was defeated 55 to 45. Article II, alleging Clinton obstructed justice by trying to conceal the affair, failed 50 to 50.

Ten Republicans joined all 45 Democrats in voting down Article I and five Republicans helped the unified Democrats defeat Article II.

Rehnquist solemnly announced the verdict:

"The Senate having tried William Jefferson Clinton, president of the United States, upon two articles of impeachment exhibited against him by the House of Representatives. And two-thirds of the senators present not having found him guilty of the charges contained therein, it is

Please see NOT GUILTY, back page this section ➥

The Associated Press

President Clinton heads back to the Oval Office after making a statement to the press following his acquittal on all charges in the Senate impeachment trial Friday.

America needs healing not a censure fight

Pastors call for reconciliation

By David Nivens
Staff Writer

STAUNTON — With President Clinton's impeachment trial over, the call has come for a healing — a reconciliation.

The Senate set aside any ideas of censuring Clinton, in hopes of reconciliation. President Clinton also asked again Friday for forgiveness.

In his remarks, U.S. Sen. John Warner, R-Virginia, put it eloquently, drawing from the words of World War II President Franklin D. Roosevelt:

"Today at another grave point in history, our rendezvous with destiny is to join together not unlike 60 years ago. The nation needs our support; the president needs our support ... A censure process by the Senate only delays

Please see CENSURE, back page this section ➥

Clinton to commit U.S. troops to Kosovo

Decision depends on Serbs and ethnic Albanians reaching an agreement

The Associated Press

WASHINGTON — President Clinton will announce today the United States is prepared to contribute ground troops to a NATO peacekeeping force in Kosovo if Serbs and ethnic Albanians agree to a political settlement, a senior administration official said Friday night.

Clinton will discuss his plans in his radio address, the official said.

Sen. John Warner, R-Va., chairman of the Senate Armed Services Committee, hinted at Clinton's decision. "There's going to be a serious announcement by the president on Kosovo ... what we're going to do," Warner said on CNN's "Larry King Live."

Warner said he had talked with Pentagon officials and Senate colleagues, and that the Senate would be supportive.

Asked about Warner's comment, National Security Council spokesman David Leavy said Clinton, in his radio address, would "continue his conversation with the American people about the U.S. national interests and the stakes in Kosovo."

Any decision to send U.S. troops would depend upon Serbs and ethnic Albanians reaching an agreement to end their fighting, U.S. officials said.

The parties have an informal deadline of Feb. 20 for reaching an accord and Secretary of State Madeleine Albright is flying to Paris today to assess peace talks between the two sides. Officials said it was not a foregone conclusion that there would be a settlement despite the threat of NATO military intervention if one isn't reached.

"Depending on the character and composition of a political settlement, the president is prepared to contribute U.S. ground forces to a potential implementation force," the senior administration official said. Some reports have suggested as many as 4,000 U.S. troops.

Pentagon officials said earlier Friday that the United States would send 2,200 Marines to Kosovo in the first stage of any peacekeeping mission if there's a need to move quickly and U.S. troops are involved.

More than 2,000 people have been killed and hundreds of thousands have been driven from their homes in clashes in Kosovo between ethnic Albanian separatists and Serbian security forces.

"There has been no decision made to send troops and there won't be until there's a peace agreement," Col. Richard Bridges, a Pentagon spokesman, said Friday.

Britain and France are serving as co-hosts for the talks at Rambouillet.

Seller of domain name 'eflowers.com' gets flowers for life

The Associated Press

HOUSTON — Marc Ostrofsky is off the hook for life when it comes to Valentine's Day gifts for his wife.

The Houston entrepreneur agreed to sell the Internet domain name "eflowers.com" to Flowers Direct of Tampa, Fla., with one special condition: a bouquet of flowers to be delivered to his wife, every month, for life.

Ostrofsky bought the "eflowers.com" name for $70 two years ago. Ever since, he has been hounded by florists wanting to buy it.

On Thursday Ostrofsky finally agreed to sell the name for $25,000, a 50-cent commission from each order placed through eflowers.com and the flowers for his wife.

Sara Ostrofsky received her first delivery Thursday. But she may not be the only lucky lady for long.

On Friday, Flowers Direct began offering to deliver flowers to anyone's loved one, once a month, for life, for $2,500.

Inside Today

Mark Miller/The Daily News Leader

Matt Fitzgerald, Wilson

Hornets clinch Skyline District Title

➥ Details on page B1

Arafat revives statehood idea

➥ Details on page A8

Happening Today

Folktales and stories

STAUNTON — Olive Sheffey will present "African-American" Folktales and Stories for Children" at 2 p.m. at Frontier Culture Museum. The snow date is Feb. 27. For information, call 332-7850.

Benefit dance

STAUNTON — The Staunton Junior Woman's Club will sponsor a Valentine's dance from 8 p.m.-midnight at the Thomas D. Howie Memorial Armory. Trademark will perform. Tickets are $35 a couple and are available at the Bookstack.

History program

STAUNTON — A black history program will be held at 6 p.m. at the Booker T. Washington Center. Participants will provide information concerning local businesses and individuals who made contributions in the past.

Valentine's dance

VERONA — Verona Volunteer Fire Department will hold a Valentine's Dance from 9 p.m.-1 a.m. For information, call 248-3877 or 248-7573. The cost is $25 per couple and I.D. is required.

Weather

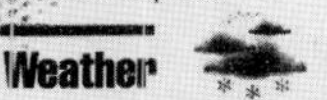

Windy and cold with limited sunshine and a few flurries today. Highs 27-33. Turning out partly cloudy and cold tonight. Lows 17-22. Sunshine mixing with a few clouds Sunday.

➥ Details, page A12

Index

TODAY

Confident March into a New Millennium

Staunton, Waynesboro and Augusta County marched into a new century and a new millennium with renewed confidence in the future.

Staunton forged ahead as a center for historic preservation and cultural awarenss with the 2001 opening of the Blackfriars Playhouse and continued work on the R.R. Smith Center for History and Art. Additionally, new life was breathed into the rapidly declining Stonewall Jackson Hotel, life that saw it reborn as a first-class hotel and conference center.

In April 2002, the National Trust for Historic Preservation announced that Staunton had earned a Great American Main Street Award for its successful efforts in revitalizing its downtown – reflecting a rebirth that heralds a bright and promising future for the Queen City of the Shenandoah.

Waynesboro, too, despite its reputation as a manufacturing town, hopped on the historic bandwagon when a five-block quadrant of the city was approved as a historic district by the Virginia Department of Historic Resources. The city also saw an increase in new business activity and a major turn of events at a Waynesboro landmark – the $4.4 billion sale of DuPont's Invista division to Koch Industries.

The construction of a Wal-Mart Superstore and accompanying retail outlets seemed to cap Waynesboro's statement that, as an economic force to be reckoned with, it was here to stay.

Augusta County continued in the 2000s a trend begun a decade earlier – improving the physical condition of its schools and roads while, at the same time, planning and building a new jail at its government complex in Verona. This move marked another step in the gradual shift away from Staunton and in reducing the county's functioning offices there to only those affiliated with the courts.

While Staunton, Waynesboro and Augusta County frequently – and naturally –seem driven by different visions, priorities and political viewpoints, few who live here can doubt the overall quality of life provided by a unique historical, commerical and agricultural symbiosis.

ELECTION 2000

Wednesday
November 8, 2000
110th year, No. 268

The Daily News Leader

Serving Staunton, Waynesboro and Augusta County

50¢

TOO CLOSE TO CALL

Presidency hinges on Florida absentee votes, irregularities

The Associated Press

Democratic presidential candidate Al Gore steps out of the voting booth near his home in Elmwood, Tenn., Tuesday.

By Jon Frandsen and John Yaukey
Gannett News Service

WASHINGTON — In a wildly unpredictable and close election that reflected a sharply divided nation, Texas Gov. George Bush rolled up impressive victories in the heartland, the South and a handful of Democratic states and Vice President Al Gore won California, the Northeast and key industrial states.

As of 1:30 a.m. EST, Bush was holding a narrow lead over Gore nationwide — with 78 percent of the vote counted. Bush had 49 percent, or 40,031,480 votes, to Gore's 48 percent, or 39,448,402.

After polls closed all across the nation, the outcome appeared to hinge on a handful of states that were too close to call: Florida, Wisconsin, Oregon and Iowa. However, it was clear Gore could not win without capturing Florida.

It was unclear whether Green Party candidate Ralph Nader might throw some key states to Bush, but he was expected to do better in the Pacific Northwest states that had not been decided. But nationwide he was pulling only 2 percent.

"It's going to be a long night," Bush said, watching returns from the private living quarters of the governor's mansion. "But this is exciting. Evidently, the turnouts are big, and that's good for America. A lot of people spoke."

"Florida is the key. ... It is white-knuckle time here," said Mark Fabiani, deputy campaign manager of the Gore campaign.

Some history was made early in the evening: Hillary Clinton became the first first lady to go to the Senate from the White House — winning in New York even though she and President Clinton bought a house there just last year so she could make the race.

The tight race was a dramatic and fitting end to a crucial election that has been contested all year

Please see RACE, back page, this section

The Associated Press

Republican presidential candidate Texas Gov. George W. Bush talks to reporters while watching election returns on television in the Governor's Mansion Tuesday evening.

Stay Tuned

If the presidential race is decided before late afternoon, The News Leader will publish an Extra edition, available at news racks and newspaper dealers throughout our area.

The News Leader went to press at 2 a.m. today with the latest possible election results in order to serve customers who want early-morning delivery.

Late night tests patience

Area voters watch presidential race, cheer Allen

By Kristie DiSalvo
Staff Writer

STAUNTON — "Say goodnight, Al," Cliff Fretwell yelled at the TV around 10 p.m. in the Elks Lodge. A member of the city Republican Committee, Fretwell watched as a TV anchor told viewers that Florida had swung back to Bush.

Emotions jumped from disappointed to elated Tuesday night as Republicans awaited the fate of George W. Bush. It was a roller coaster for both parties as Electoral College votes trickled in and most states were still "too close to call" by 10 p.m.

By 11:30 p.m., most of the Republicans that had crammed in front of the two blaring TVs in the lodge had gone home — a clear winner had not been named and the fate of several states still hung in the balance.

They returned home confident with at least one race — Chuck Robb's U.S. Senate seat had fallen to former Gov. George Allen.

But the Democrats, on the other hand, were harder to find. They spent election night alone, some at home, others at bars. They did not expect Gore to win, according to Tracy Pyles, a Democrat and member of the Augusta County Board of Supervisors.

At the Baja Bean Co. in downtown Staunton, Democrats and Republi-

Please see EMOTIONS, back page, this section

Electoral College Breakdown

Current status		
Candidates need 270 electoral votes to win the election. Here is how votes stand:	Al Gore	226
	George W. Bush	242
	Not decided	70

Note: As of 12:26 a.m. EST.

ALLEN

Va. Senate race follows U.S. trend

By Dawn Linsner
Staff Writer

Former Gov. George Allen edged incumbent Charles S. Robb out of his Senate career and a 23-year undefeated run in politics Tuesday by a 4 percentage point margin. But for local voters, even Democrats, the win did not come as a big surprise.

"Robb just wasn't aggressive enough," said Tracy Pyles, a Democrat and member of the Augusta County Board of Supervisors.

According to complete, but unofficial totals at midnight, Allen had 52 percent of the vote to 48 percent for Robb.

The win gave the Republicans a victory they considered crucial to retaining control of Congress. The race has been tight from the outset, one that both parties felt could go either way, but the seat's return to Republicans increased the GOP's majority in the Senate.

Allen

"When I look at Robb, I see a good background in politics... when I look at Allen, I see a good background in reality," said Rhonda Eustler, 32.

Detailed Story, Page A2

GOP CONGRESS

Hastert confident of control

Dems make gains; Republicans ahead

The Associated Press

WASHINGTON — Republicans battled Democrats for continued control of the House Tuesday, winning five seats in the East but giving two back in New York and Oklahoma. Democrats looked to California for offsetting gains.

"We're looking pretty good," said Speaker Dennis Hastert, hoping for two more years of GOP control.

On a night extremely kind to incumbents, three Republican lawmakers easily turned aside well-financed Democratic challengers in Kentucky.

Clinton

Two House Democrats were turned out of office. Rep. Sam Gejdenson lost a bid for an 11th term in Connecticut, and first-term Democrat Rush Holt lost in New Jersey by fewer than 1,000 votes out of 280,000 cast.

Republicans also won Democratic open seats in Pennsylvania, New York and Virginia.

Voter News Service projected Republicans would retain control, based on interviews with voters as they left the polls.

Well after 1 a.m. in the East, the national trend showed Republicans had won 202 seats and were leading for 21 more, with 218 required to seal control. Democrats had won 180 seats and were leading for 30 more.

Hillary Clinton won her race for the Senate from New York.

Detailed Story, Page A4

Inside Today

Surfin' with Sam
Our uncle is on the Web
Details in E section

Vincent Lara/The Daily News Leader

Robert E. Lee's Fairland Ferguson (32) guards Harrisonburg's Alex Johnson during Lee's 63-30 win.

Details on B1

Weather

Plenty of clouds today with a shower or two in spots. Highs 66-70. Mostly cloudy tonight with rain late. Lows 52-56.

Details, Page A12

Index

Our commitment: We correct all errors of fact as soon as we learn of them. Corrections and our policy run daily on Page A2.

We print using at least 25% recycled paper fiber and earth-friendly soy color inks.

7 91564 54321 7

November 8, 2000: The Presidential election hangs in the balance with no clear winner. *Microfilm Archives*

Built in 1925 at a cost of more than $3 million, the Stonewall Jackson Hotel was once the luxury destination for travelers coming to Staunton. In 1929 a proposed expansion of the hotel led to the demolition of the historic Virginia Hotel adjacent to the Stonewall Jackson, but the Depression killed the plan. In 2004, after many years of decline, the Stonewall Jackson Hotel became the target of an ambitious renovation and revitalization project. *News Leader Photo*

"The Wayne Theater on Main Street in Waynesboro. No longer in use as a theater, the building is being reclaimed as a performing arts center. *News Leader Photo*

Photo of a reception to raise funds for the renovation of Waynesboro's Wayne Theater. *News Leader Photo*

Daily News Leader photo of the city's new parking garage and, behind it, the Stonewall Jackson Hotel. The garage was built on the site of the historic Virginia Hotel, which was demolished in 1929 for an expansion of the Stonewall Jackson. The expansion never happened due to the Great Depression. *News Leader Photo*

Staunton's parking garage at the intersection of South New and Johnson Streets. Locally designed, the structure won national recognition for architectural concept. *News Leader Photo*

The Stonewall Jackson Hotel, Market Street entrance, before renovations in 2004 that saw demolition of the adjacent townhouses. *News Leader Photo*

Wednesday
September 12, 2001
The Daily News Leader
111th year, No. 219

The News Leader

Serving Staunton, Waynesboro and Augusta County • www.newsleader.com

AMERICA UNDER SIEGE

50¢

'Unyielding anger'

America reacts: As shock subsides, rage begins to burn

The Associated Press

Far from the smoke and rubble, Americans everywhere reeled from the blow of Tuesday's terrorism. Then, as the shock subsided, anger flooded in.

"We will respond," vowed Sen. Richard Durbin, D-Ill. "America's been attacked. Those who attacked us will pay a price."

"I feel like going to war again. No mercy," said Felix Novelli of New York, a World War II veteran who served aboard the USS Intrepid aircraft carrier. "We have to come together like '41, go after them."

For many citizens, from homemakers to lawmakers, the terrorist attacks in New York and Washington were a devastating bolt from the blue. People gathered around big-screen TVs in public places, transfixed by the unbelievable horrors they were watching. Some sobbed. Some shook their fists in anger. Others just stood there, paralyzed.

"I'm numb," said Corinne Zuege, 49, of West Lafayette, Ind. "This is such a tragedy. They always said there would never be another Pearl Harbor, and here it's happened on our shores."

Delaware Gov. Ruth Ann Minner ordered schools and state agencies to close early, as the state's National Guard units moved to high alert.

"I'm still in shock over today's events," she said. "I have hung my head in sorrow and I have prayed in earnest over what will

Please see ANGER, back page this section ➡

Bakersfield Californian, Casey Christie

Steve Swarts in downtown Bakersfield, Calif., reacts to the attacks in New York and at the Pentagon.

Inside

- More national stories and photos, **A2-3, A6** ➡
- Area residents want justice for victims, **A4** ➡
- Former Verona man sees tower crash, **A5** ➡

Vincent Lerz/The News Leader

Robert Ingram, assistant Commonwealth's attorney of Waynesboro, bows his head during a prayer vigil at the St. John's Episcopal Church on Tuesday night.

Churches offer refuge

By Dawn Linsner and Kristie DiSalvo
Staff Writers

WAYNESBORO — Throughout the day, community churches became a place of refuge. Many in the area turned to their houses of worship to express concern, questions and disbelief about the morning's reports.

It was impossible to enumerate the range of emotions present in the sanctuary at St. John's Episcopal Church Tuesday night, eight hours and hundreds of miles away from the morning's terrorist attacks.

One woman lifted a tissue to her eyes as the congregation sang, "O God, our help in ages past." Another clasped her young daughter's waist, bringing her near. A man in another pew held

Please see CHURCH, back page this section ➡

Index

We print using at least 25% recycled paper fiber and earth-friendly soy color inks.

7 91564 54321 7

ATTACK ON THE TWIN TOWERS

In a horrific sequence of crashes and collapses, the 110-story towers of the World Trade Center were obliterated early Tuesday, the epicenter of a coordinated terrorist attack that included another direct hit on the Pentagon and a crashed jet in Pennsylvania.

'It was like a war zone'

A low-tech plan

Two flights leaving Boston for Los Angeles 15 minutes apart – American Airlines Flight 11 and United Airlines Flight 175, carrying a total of 157 people – were hijacked.

(1) At 8:45 a.m., American Airlines Flight 11 crashed into the face of the north tower of the World Trade Center, about 20 stories below the top of the building.

(2) At 9:03 a.m., the second hijacked jet – United Airlines Flight 175 – streaked into the south tower, sending a fireball out the other side.

Sealing off the scene

As emergency crews rushed to lower Manhattan, authorities sealed off the island, stranding a population in disbelief.

Damaged, then destroyed

As people evacuated the area, emergency crews mobilized and authorities pushed pedestrians out of the surrounding blocks. But the casualties and damage of the initial crashes multiplied horribly when the crippled towers toppled.

Severely weakened by the impacts, the towers probably fell, say experts in skyscraper construction, when intense heat from the ensuing fires melted crucial steel supports.

At 9:50 a.m., the south tower – the second tower hit – collapsed as floors caved onto one another. The fire spread to adjacent buildings, including the 47-story 7 World Trade Center.

Then, at 10:29 a.m., the north tower collapsed. Just before nightfall, the evacuated 7 World Trade Center collapsed.

A day of terror

7:59 a.m. American Airlines Flight 11, a Boeing 767, departs Boston for Los Angeles with 92 people on board.

8:01 a.m. United Flight 93 departs Newark International Airport for San Francisco with 45 people on board.

8:14 a.m. United Airlines Flight 175, a Boeing 767, departs Boston from Logan International Airport for Los Angeles with 65 people on board.

8:45 a.m. American Airlines Flight 11 crashes into the north tower of the World Trade Center in New York City.

9:03 a.m. United Airlines Flight 175 crashes into the south tower of the World Trade Center.

9:31 a.m. President Bush calls the crashes an "apparent terrorist attack."

9:40 a.m. American Airlines Flight 77, a Boeing 757, crashes into the west side of the Pentagon in Washington, D.C., collapsing a side of the building. It was en route from Dulles Airport to Los Angeles with 64 people.

9:49 a.m. The Federal Aviation Administration shuts down airports nationwide.

9:50 a.m. Two World Trade Center — the second tower hit — collapses.

10:29 a.m. One World Trade Center collapses.

10:37 a.m. United Airlines Flight 93 from Newark, N.J., to San Francisco crashes 80 miles southeast of Pittsburgh, in Shanksville, Pa.

10-11:30 a.m. Government buildings around the country are evacuated, including the Capitol and the White House. The United Nations closes down. The Securities and Exchange Commission closes all U.S. financial markets for the day.

2:51 p.m. The U.S. Navy sends missile destroyers and other equipment to New York and Washington, D.C.

5:25 p.m. A third building collapses, 7 World Trade Center.

AP Graphic

September 12, 2001: America reacts to the destruction of the World Trade Center towers by terrorists. *Microfilm Archives*

The principal stars of the Fortune-Williams Festival in Staunton: Linda Williams, Jimmy Fortune (formerly of The Statler Brothers) and Robin Williams. *News Leader Photo*

The Cabell House on East Beverly Street is the oldest existing exposed log structure in Staunton. Pictured at the home are Alysia Tate and Pamela Brown.

Sunday
October 27, 2002
The Sunday News Leader
112th year, No. 44

The News Leader

Serving Staunton, Waynesboro and Augusta County • www.newsleader.com

$1.25

Inside Today

The Associated Press
Virginia Tech quarterback Bryan Randall (3) launches a pass during first-half action with Temple.

Virginia Tech Hokies scatter Temple Owls to win 20-10

➥ Details on Page B1

Fall back

Daylight-saving time ended today at 2 a.m., so don't forget to set your clocks back one hour.

AP

Angels' strong rally brings on Game 7 of the World Series

➥ Details on Page B1

Staunton's favorite sons, the Statler Brothers, end their touring career among their die-hard fans at home in Virginia.
Literally and figuratively, they decide to go out on their own terms ...

SPECIAL REPORT INSIDE Pages A2-3

With Amazing Grace

Mark Miller/The News Leader
Don Reid, right, reaches out to fans with Phil Balsley and Harold Reid in the background during the Statler Brothers' final concert in Salem. The evening was bittersweet for the singers and the fans as the quartet closed the book on 38 years of touring. Jimmy Fortune also greeted fans off camera to the right. Thousands attended the group's farewell performance.

Weather

High pressure will promote mostly sunny skies today. Tonight will be mainly clear and cool. Sunshine will mix with clouds Monday and Tuesday.

➥ Details, Page A12

Index

➤ **Our commitment:** We correct all errors of fact as soon as we learn of them. Corrections and our policy run daily on **Page A2.** ➥

We print using at least 25% recycled paper fiber and earth-friendly soy color inks.

Witness nabbed in sniper case

Virginia to charge two suspects

The Associated Press

Inside
■ Alleged sniper's life filled with flux, frustration.
Page A6 ➥

RICHMOND — A man sought as a material witness in the Washington-area sniper shootings was arrested Saturday, and prosecutors announced plans to charge the two suspects in Virginia, the second state where 17-year-old John Lee Malvo could face the death penalty.

Virginia prosecutors will charge the men Monday to cover one killing and one wounding there, said William Neely, Spotsylvania County, Va., Commonwealth's Attorney.

Neely said he will seek the death penalty for John Allen Muhammad, 41. Malvo could face death, but Neely said his sentence would depend on his role in the shootings.

Virginia and Alabama — where the pair are charged with killing a woman outside a liquor store in September — allow the death penalty for crimes committed at age 17.

Earlier Saturday, a third man, believed to be the co-owner of a blue Chevrolet Caprice the suspects were found in a day earlier, was arrested and held as a material witness.

Nathaniel O. Osbourne, a man of Jamaican descent who has lived in Camden, N.J., was arrested at a home in Flint, Mich. He was to appear in court Sunday but was not considered a suspect in the shootings, FBI Agent Barry Maddox said. According to the New Jersey Department of Transportation, Muhammad and Osbourne bought the blue Caprice from Sure Shot Auto Sales Inc. in Trenton on Sept. 10.

The Associated Press
Nathanel O. Osbourne, of New Jersey, is shown in this undated handout photo released by the FBI.

Valium likely used in raid

The Associated Press

Inside
■ Moscow counts dead, braces for more violence.
Page A8 ➥

Military experts and toxicologists say Russian commandos probably pumped a gas containing Valium into a Moscow theater to subtly disable and disorient heavily armed Chechen rebels prior to Saturday's dramatic assault.

Russian authorities didn't identify the gas used in the operation, which freed hundreds of hostages but also resulted in the deaths of more than 100 captives and rebels. Officials claimed none of the hostages were killed by the gas.

Several nations, including the United States, have developed a variety of non-lethal incapacitating agents, which can also induce choking, nausea or blurry vision, depending on their recipes.

According to some hostages inside the theater, they realized they were becoming sleepy and confused; but no one reported seeing a vapor cloud, smelling a chemical or experiencing the sort of irritating symptoms associated with tear gas and pepper spray.

Experts said the Russians may have released a gas concentration of a powerful sedative like Valium or may have used a form of BZ gas, a hallucinogenic drug widely researched in the 1960s that works more slowly.

"The thing that pops into my mind is aerosolized Valium," said Dr. Christopher Holstege, medical toxicology director at the University of Virginia. "But there isn't much literature out there on it. There is talk of using it as a riot control agent."

Others said the agent used by the Russians didn't seem to be like anything that has been part of the U.S. arsenal.

"It's no surprise that the Russians have that kind of stuff," said Ron Madrid, a former Marine and an expert on non-lethal weaponry at Pennsylvania State University. "They spent 30 years putting it together. We're prevented from doing that by treaty and executive order."

Russian television reported the gas was dispersed through the theater's ventilation system. Workers were seen digging around sewers and steam pipes near the theater in the first day of the crisis.

One Interfax News Agency employee among the captives in the theater said the rebels appeared ready to kill all the hostages, "then something happened."

Fighter plane rescued from clutch of ice flies for first time

The Associated Press

MIDDLESBORO, Ky. — Hibernation is officially over for Glacier Girl.

After spending a half-century in the heart of a Greenland glacier, the World War II fighter plane flew Saturday for the first time since it was pulled piece by piece from beneath 268 feet of ice and snow.

With propellers whirling and 1,275-horsepower twin engines humming, test pilot Steve Hinton raced the P-38 Lightning down the runway and lifted it into a gray sky for a 30-minute flight before an estimated 20,000 spectators in this small eastern Kentucky town.

"Seeing that plane lift off was just thrilling," said Brad McManus, who had piloted one of the P-38s that crash-landed with the recovered plane on July 15, 1942. "It's a moment in time, a very special moment."

The plane, one of the war's fastest, was among six fighters and two bombers forced by foul weather and low fuel to crash-land on the frigid glacier. It took rescuers on dog sleds 10 days to reach the 25 crew members but all of them got out safely.

The warplanes were left behind to be slowly buried in snow and ice They might have been forgotten except for people including Middlesboro businessman Roy Shoffner, who had become enamored with the piston-engined, propeller-driven P-38s as a youngster. Shoffner, too young for the war, imagined flying one of the planes, which could reach 405 mph at altitudes of up to 35,000 feet. The United States built 10,113 P-38s, but just 24 survive and only a few are still flying. The restaurateur, former banker and 1950s Air Force fighter pilot recovered one of the P-38s in the summer of 1992.

The Associated Press
Steve Hinton, a pilot from Ontario, Calif., waves to the crowd as he climbs aboard Glacier Girl at the Middlesboro Airport in Middlesboro, Ky.

October 27, 2002: Front page coverage of The Statler Brothers and their final concert in Salem. *Microfilm Archives*

News Leader Photo

This series of photographs shows activities at Riverfest – an annual, spring festival in Waynesboro sponsored by the Waynesboro Department of Parks and Recreation. The event was begun as a way to highlight the city's natural and recreational assets and to encourage repeat visitors. *News Leader Photo*

Sunday
February 2, 2003
The Sunday News Leader
113th year, No. 5

The News Leader

Serving Staunton, Waynesboro and Augusta County • www.newsleader.com

$1.25

Ilan Ramon

William McCool

Michael Anderson

Kalpana Chawla

Laurel Clark

Rick Husband

David Brown

Columbia disintegrates in meteoric flash; Crew dies; Tile damage under scrutiny

Dr. Scott Lieberman/Tyler Morning Telegraph via AP

Debris from the space shuttle Columbia streaks across the sky over Tyler, Texas, Saturday. Columbia broke apart in flames at 200,000 feet.

The Associated Press

High over Texas and just short of home, space shuttle Columbia fell to pieces Saturday, raining debris over hundreds of miles of countryside. Seven astronauts perished — a gutwrenching loss for a country and world already staggered by tragedy.

The catastrophe occurred 39 miles above the Earth, in the last 16 minutes of the 16-day mission as the spaceship re-entered the atmosphere and glided in for a phere and glided in for a landing in Florida. In its horror and in its backdrop of a crystal blue sky, the day echoed one almost exactly 17 years before, when the Challenger exploded.

"The Columbia is lost," said President Bush, after he telephoned the families of the astronauts to console them.

"The same creator who names the stars also knows the names of the seven souls we mourn today," Bush said, his eyes glistening. "The crew of the shuttle Columbia did not return safely to Earth but we can pray they are safely home."

The search for the cause began immediately. One focus: possible damage to Columbia's protective thermal tiles on the left wing from a flying piece of debris during liftoff on Jan. 16.

The loss of seven explorers of space's dark reaches — shuttle commander Rick Husband, Michael Anderson, David Brown, Kalpana Chawla, Laurel Clark, William McCool and Ilan Ramon — brought a new round of grief to a nation still in mourning after the terrorist attacks of Sept. 11, 2001.

And again, Americans were forced to confront the risks of space, along with the glories.

"The reality of what these people do has often escaped me," said Charlie Dillon, 52, of Denver. "But they are frontiersman, they're out there making my life better and creating endless possibilities for my children."

NASA appointed an independent commission to investigate. The agency said the first indication of trouble Saturday was the loss of temperature sensors in the left wing's hydraulic system.

The spacecraft had just re-entered the atmosphere and had reached the point at which it was subjected to the highest temperatures.

NASA officials said they suspected the wing was damaged on liftoff, but felt there was no reason for concern. They cautioned that it may have had nothing to do with the accident.

Authorities said there was no indication of terrorism; at 207,135 feet, the shuttle was out of range of any surface-to-air missile, one senior government official said. Security was extraordinarily tight on this mission because Ramon, Israel's first astronaut, was among the crew members.

Television footage showed a bright light followed by white smoke plumes streaking diagonally across the brilliant sky. Debris appeared to

Please see COLUMBIA, back page, this section ➡

SPECIAL REPORT

- Witnesses report exp osions, find debris. ➡ **Page A2**
- Problems began on wing during liftoff. ➡ **Page A3**
- Worried nation faces more bad news. ➡ **Page A4**
- Challenger memories flood back. ➡ **Page A5**
- **OPINIONS:** The future doesn't belong to the faint-hearted. Editorial & Cartoon ➡ **Page B10**

Stay Current

- Continuing coverage can be found at www.floridatoday.com and linked from www.newsleader.com .
- If you know of a local angle on the story or are planning a memorial, call Cindy Corell at 213-9123.

Index

SPORTS: Some wrestling programs on the mat.

➡ **Page B1**

Weather

A mix of clouds and sunshine today with an increasing south wind in the afternoon.

➡ **Details, Page A12**

➤ **Our commitment:** We correct all errors of fact as soon as we learn of them. Corrections and our policy runs today on **Page A6.** ➡

We print using at least 25% recycled paper fiber and earth-friendly soy color inks.

Disaster teaches another generation risks of space

By Brad Zinn/staff
bzinn@newsleader.com

STAUNTON — Twelve-year-old Kelley Harris learned about the 1986 Challenger space shuttle disaster just last year when a teacher at Beverley Manor Middle School taught it as a history lesson.

"I remember thinking, 'I can't imagine what it would have been like,' " Harris said. "Now I can."

After Harris woke up Saturday morning, her mother directed her to the television set, where the Columbia tragedy played out before her.

"I was shocked," Harris said. "I didn't think anything like that could happen again. I was really sad for the families."

Harris said she was "amazed" at the thought of space exploration last school year as a sixth-grader. Saturday's events haven't altered that view. "I think I could do something like that," she said.

It's that amazement that Shelburne Middle School science teacher Mary Ann Plogger taps when she teaches a unit on space and our solar system about this time each school year.

Plogger said she has rethought how the lessons will continue next week.

She spent Saturday videotaping President George W. Bush's remarks to the American public, and said she'll piece together news reports of the Columbia tragedy for her students.

"A good way to talk about it will be in the classroom," she said.

Plogger, like just about everyone else who was around in 1986 when the Challenger spacecraft exploded, remembers where she was the exact moment she learned about that disaster: Checking her mail in the student lounge of Mars Hill College in Asheville, N.C.

"It's going to be like that for them," she said of her students. "They've never experienced some-

Please see DISASTER, back page, this section ➡

Radar snaps path of shuttle debris

Weather radar stations emit energy toward the sky. When this energy strikes an object, a portion of the energy is reflected back toward the station. Stronger reflected signals indicate denser objects encountered by the radar. This radar image shows the shuttle Columbia plume strewn over Texas and Louisiana.

SOURCE: National Weather Service AP

February 2, 2003: Columbia becomes America's second space shuttle to disintegrate in flight. *Microfilm Archives*

Thursday
March 20, 2003
The Daily News Leader
113th year, No. 68

The News Leader

SPECIAL EDITION

Serving Staunton, Waynesboro and Augusta County • www.newsleader.com

50¢

FIRST STRIKE

U.S. unleashes bombs on key Iraqi targets

Three U.S.S. Donald Cook-based Tomahawk Land Attack Missiles are fired Thursday morning from the Red Sea. The Associated Press

Reuters

President George W. Bush announces war.

Bush: 'No outcome but victory'

USA TODAY

President Bush's speech announcing that a U.S.-led attack on Iraq had begun.

My fellow citizens, at this hour American and coalition forces are in the early stages of military operations to disarm Iraq, to free its people and to defend the world from grave danger.

On my orders, coalition forces have begun striking selected targets of military importance to undermine Saddam Hussein's ability to wage war. These are opening stages of what will be a broad and concerted campaign.

More than 35 countries are giving crucial support, from the use of naval and air bases, to help with intelligence and logistics, to the deployment of combat units. Every nation in this coalition has chosen to bear the duty and share the honor of serving in our common defense.

To all of the men and women of the United States armed forces now in the Middle East, the peace of a troubled world and the hopes of an oppressed people now depend on you.

That trust is well placed.

Please see BUSH, back page, this section ➡

Full brunt of attack still ahead

The Associated Press

The United States launched the opening salvo Wednesday night of a war to topple Saddam Hussein, firing cruise missiles and precision-guided bombs against selected targets in Baghdad.

"This will not be a campaign of half-measures and we will accept no outcome but victory," President Bush said in an Oval Office address shortly after explosions ricocheted through the pre-dawn light of the Iraqi capital.

Anti-aircraft tracer fire arced across the Baghdad sky as the American munitions bore in on their targets. A ball of fire shot skyward after one explosion.

Saddam's state-run television broadcast a message of defiance to Americans in return: "It's an inferno that awaits them. Let them try their faltering luck and they shall meet what awaits them."

The missiles struck less than two hours after the expiration of Bush's deadline for Saddam to surrender power or face war.

Bush described the targets as being of "military importance," and one White House official said the attack was the result of fresh intelligence that prompted an earlier-than-planned opening strike.

One military official, speaking on condition of anonymity, identified them as "leadership targets," members of the regime's ruling group. Saddam later defiantly addressed his country on television.

Even so, it was clear from Bush's words — he called it the opening stages of a "broad and concerted campaign" — that the war to topple the Iraqi dictator and eliminate his weapons of mass destruction.

BEVERLEY

Going to War
The Homefront

Early reports prove confusing

By Dawn Medley and Maria Longley/staff
dmedley@newsleader.com
mlongley@newsleader.com

STAUNTON — The only sound coming from the student center at Mary Baldwin College was of young women bubbling with chatter Wednesday night, until President George Bush started to speak at 10:15. Then the quiet hum of a soda machine was the only background noise.

"I have to trust that it has been well-thought out and we know what we're doing," said Jenna Wood after the four-minute address.

At the Staunton Fire Department, it was much the same story.

With most of the shift out on a call, the Staunton Fire Department on Augusta Street was quiet except for the drone of a television correspondent's voice.

TV news had been on all day. Seated in the shift commander's office, firefighter Gary Mullis followed the latest developments of the U.S.'s first

Please see REPORTS, back page, this section ➡

Special Report Inside

Get updates every 15 minutes around the clock at www.newsleader.com

7 91564 54321 7

Tech alumni speak out.

■ Furor grows over Tech ending affirmative action
➡ Details on Page A6

Nick Vander Lann is fouled.

■ Watson, U.Va. top Brown in NIT tip-off
➡ Details on Page B1

➤ Our commitment: We correct all errors of fact as soon as we learn of them. Corrections and our policy run today on Page A6. ➡

March 20, 2003: The U.S. launches air attacks on Iraq in the start of the second Gulf War. *Microfilm Archives*

Friday
September 19, 2003
The Daily News Leader
113th year, No. 223

The News Leader

Serving Staunton, Waynesboro and Augusta County • www.newsleader.com

50¢

Inside Today

The Associated Press
Virginia Tech's Michael Crawford tackles Texas A&M quarterback Reggie McNeal on Thursday during the first half.

Hokies hit Texas A&M like hurricane in 35-19 win

➥ Details on Page B1

Note To Readers

Today you will be reading much about the people and places affected by Hurricane Isabel. Production of The News Leader, unfortunately, was one of the businesses affected.

An electrical transformer in Staunton was damaged Thursday evening, killing power for much of the downtown, including The News Leader building. Staffers quickly implemented Plan B, taking necessary equipment to the Daily News-Record in Harrisonburg to finish assembling the paper and print it. All departments of the paper worked hard to bring you this edition, but we were unable to include several regular features, including our opinion page, and were forced to relocate others.

Throughout the day today, you can check www.newsleader.com for calendar listings and the latest updates.

Please bear with us as we make the best of this weather emergency.

Weather

Windy at times today with rain tapering to showers. Highs 74-79. Any showers ending this evening with clearing skies overnight. Lows 52-56. Sunny and nice Saturday.

➥ Details, Page A12

Index

➤ **Our commitment:** We correct all errors of fact as soon as we learn of them. Corrections and our policy run daily on **Page A2.** ➥

7 91564 54321 7

Isabel lashes Valley

Storm dumps 19½ inches of rain on Sherando; Staunton hunkers down overnight; Waynesboro expects downtown flooding today

By Mike Emery, Chris Lassiter, Maria Longley and Rob Longley
Staff Writers

The power of Tropical Storm Isabel left many local residents powerless, but the worst could come today, especially in Waynesboro.

The state's power outage hotline listed 19,680 local residents without power at 11:40 p.m. in Staunton, Waynesboro and Augusta County, plus part of Rockingham County.

The storm contained a solid area of rain extending a couple of hundred miles over western Virginia, according to Michael McAuliff, an Accuweather meteorologist.

"Tropical air funneled into the center of the storm, rising up the mountains," McAuliff said. "You guys are just in the wrong place at the wrong time."

Local experts are expecting the worst is yet to come.

The tropical storm dumped more than 12 inches of rain in the Sherando Lake area upstream from Waynesboro and city officials late Thursday were expecting the South River to flood sometime early this morning.

"We are monitoring the river very closely, and at this point we are anticipating it will flood," City Manager Doug Walker said shortly before 11 p.m.

Isabel was expected to lash the areas with as much as 6 additional inches overnight.

The city was advising residents in low-lying areas to evacuate, and public safety crews spent much of the night informing homeowners in Waynesboro's flood zone of the impending flood.

"Things are really starting to happen in Augusta County," Barbara Watson, a meteorologist with the National Weather Service, said at 8 p.m. "We've already had 15 inches in some places and it's going to continue for the next six hours. So we're very concerned about the South River and flooding."

Mark Miller/The News Leader
Strong winds forced a tree on Walnut Street to fall on Staunton resident Mike Crawford's Pontiac minivan Thursday evening.

Mark Miller/The News Leader
When the power failed in Staunton, in some downtown spots about 6:30 p.m. Thursday, city workers resorted to low-tech methods of controlling traffic at Beverley and Augusta streets.

At 8 p.m., the eye of the storm was over Emporia and was on a track that would take it over Charlottesville late Thursday or early Friday. Winds at Shenandoah Valley Regional Airport were gusting at more than 40 miles per hour, with sustained winds of 25 miles per hour.

"You could see sustained winds of around 40 miles per hour later in the evening," said Watson.

Power outages were sporadic around Waynesboro, Walker said, and damage from winds was "minimal."

The city closed several streets due to localized flooding in low-lying areas, he added, and street lights in some parts of the city were out.

The advance warning gave local businesses plenty of time to prepare.

In Staunton's Historic Wharf, where businesses saw extensive damage during last month's floods, sandbags were piled several feet high along storefronts.

However, Cool Spot coffee shop on New Street appeared to be the only business with plywood boarding up its storefront. Spray painted on the wood was "Hurricane Isabel Central." Owner Lester Bowers wasn't taking any chances.

"I lived in Key West before I came here. I've been around the high winds and I know what they can do," he said.

Bowers worried about debris damaging his front windows. "It's not so much the wind but the people who don't take it seriously and leave their trash cans and other things outside," he said. "People can laugh but I wouldn't be laughing if a trash can lid came crashing through my window."

At 11 p.m., Dominion Virginia spokesman Phil Sparks said about 1.4 million customers of the company's total 2.2 million had no power, he said. Many of those customers are located along the coast in cities like Virginia Beach, where 99 percent of customers lost power.

"We've never seen this much devastation in our service area," Sparks said.

Additional outages were expected throughout the night and the company planned to send out workers to restore power this morning.

"We're asking customers not to go near any downed lines and to be patient," he said. "We will restore power to all of those people within the next few days."

By late last night, about two dozen power lines and more than 20 trees were down throughout the city, said Doug Cochran, Staunton customer relations coordinator.

City workers have been clearing roads of debris throughout the night and would continue today, he said. City creek levels had reached the banks and no flooding had been reported yet, but the worst of the storm was still to come.

Continuing

■ Check our Web site, www.newsleader.com, throughout the day for any updates.

Inside

■ More storm coverage, A3 ➥

1 million without power as storm churns through Va.

The Associated Press

RICHMOND — More than 1.6 million electric customers were without power Thursday as Hurricane Isabel churned through Virginia with winds gusting to more than 60 mph, and officials feared it could bring the coast's worst flooding in 70 years.

The Category 2 storm was responsible for at least seven deaths in Virginia. The hurricane moved onto North Carolina's Outer Banks early Thursday and passed through Virginia later in the day, weakening to tropical storm strength by Thursday night. The National Weather Service reported gusting winds nearing 70 mph in Virginia Beach, with sustained winds in the range of 40 mph elsewhere in the state.

President Bush and the Federal Emergency Management Agency committed federal disaster aid to localities affected by Isabel. Dominion Virginia Power reported 1.6 million customers without power in Virginia, and another 100,000 customers in North Carolina.

East coast battles Hurricane Isabel

Position: **37.7° N, 78.0° W**
Movement: **NNW at 23 mph**
Sustained winds: **65 mph**

As of 11 p.m. EDT Thursday

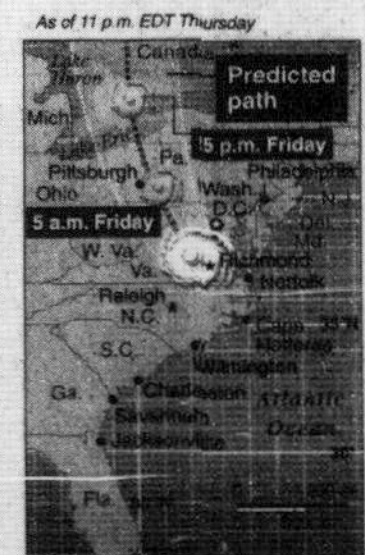

SOURCE: AccuWeather AP

Eastern Augusta County battered by rain, floods

No injuries logged

By Tim Harrington/staff
tharrington@newsleader.com

The Blue Ridge Mountains caught Isabel like wind in a sail and, by 1 a.m., the storm had dumped almost 20 inches of rain in some parts of eastern Augusta County.

Dozens of families fled to shelters at Stuarts Draft Elementary and Kate Collins Middle schools, and several other were at Clymore Elementary and Beverley Manor Middle schools.

About 7 p.m., Anita Harris, assistant director of Staunton-Augusta-Waynesboro Social Services, and her volunteer staff had attended to three people who left their low-lying home in Stuarts Draft and then went to stay with family in Crimora.

"It's kind of good not to see people here," she said.

Mark Miller/The News Leader
Jeff Messer of Wilson Volunteer Fire Department closes off a road after evacuating people from Creekside Mobile Home Park in Sherando.

Please see SHERANDO back page this section ➥

Construction of the Blackfriars Playhouse on South Market Street. This facility now houses off-the-road productions of Shenandoah Shakespeare, a world-class performing company with headquarters in Staunton. *News Leader Photo*

A performance at the Blackfriars Playhouse in Staunton. *News Leader Photo*

VHSL STATE BASKETBALL CHAMPIONSHIPS

LEE HIGH 96
GREENSVILLE 57
AA BOYS

The News Leader
SPORTS
SUNDAY, MARCH 14, 2004 — SECTION B

ALTAVISTA 54
RIVERHEADS 37

LEEMEN TAKE THE FIFTH

1931 1967 1984 1990 2004

Lee High pummels Greensville County for Group AA title

By Hubert F. Grim III/staff
bgrimiii@newsleader.com

RICHMOND — Tyler Crawford, you and the rest of the Leemen can shed those tears of joy.

You are the state Group AA champions.

Crawford had said last week he wanted the tears in his last game in a Robert E. Lee uniform to be joyous and not sorrow.

And, boy, were the tear ducts flowing, not only for Crawford, but the rest of the Leemen..

The Leemen saved one last woodshed performance for the for most important game of the season, crushing the previously unbeaten Greensville County Eagles 96-57 in the championship game Saturday night at the Siegel Center.

Lee's one-and-only goal coming into the 2003-04 campaign was to bring the state title back to Staunton for the fifth time.

Mission accomplished in grand fashion.

Except for a slipup against Group AAA Culpeper in the semifinals of the Daily Progress Christmas tournament, the Leemen were unbeaten, ending the season on a 23-game winning streak. The 30-1 record set a school mark for most wins in a single season.

The Leemen made Greensville look like anything but a team that entered the game with a 29-0 record, and a No. 2 ranking all year behind Lee.

After a 10-all tie following a dunk by the Eagles' Jamar Walton, the reigning Group AA player of the year, it was all Lee, all the time.

Daryl Taylor, the hero of Friday night's dramatic win over Salem with his last-second shot, buried his second 3-pointer of the first quarter to ignite an 11-0 run. The Eagles never got the deficit under double figures the rest of the game.

As Lee slowly put distance on the scoreboard, one could easily tell the Eagles were ready to go home.

"I had no doubt the team would be focused," Lee coach Paul Hatcher said when asked about a possible letdown after Friday's emotional win. "These guys have played every game expecting to win, and tonight was no different."

Taylor made sure of that point, popping a 3-pointer less than 10 seconds in to the game.

Eli Crawford and Taylor had monster games in driving Lee to its third title in the Hatcher era. Crawford matched his career high, set in the Region II championship, with 25 points, while pulling down 13 rebounds among the physical Eagles. Taylor added 22 points.

Tyler Crawford was hampered for the second straight

Please see LEEMEN, Page B3 ➡

AA BOYS

■ More Lee High photos, B2 ➡
■ Lee celebrates its win, B3 ➡

Mark Miller/The News Leader
Robert E. Lee's Eli Crawford scored 25 points Saturday.

Mark Miller/The News Leader
Robert E. Lee's Travis Stuart celebrates with Lee fans after the Leemen beat Greensville County, 96-57, Saturday night to win the Group AA state championship. The win is Lee's fifth state championship and completes a 30-1 season.

Riverheads falls prey to Hunt

Altavista star helps deny Gladiators state championship

By Steve Cox
Sports Writer

RICHMOND — The third time proved to be the charm for Altavista and star point guard Kenny Hunt.

After being denied a state title the past two years by Nandua, the Colonels were determined not to leave the Siegel Center without the big trophy. Surprisingly, it was Altavista's smothering defense, not its high-powered offense, that made the difference Saturday against the Riverheads Gladiators.

The Colonels (26-3) held the Gladiators to just 22 points in the first three quarters en route to a 54-37 victory and the elusive Group A state title. The win also capped a sweep for the high school as the girls' team won its state title game, defeating Radford 50-39, just before the boys took the floor.

"I guess today A-town is Titletown," head coach Mike Cartolaro said after his team defeated the Gladiators. "It's great for our school and community to leave here with both trophies."

The Gladiators (24-5) went toe-to-toe with the Colonels in the Region B title game won 65-56 by Altavista, and another close game was anticipated in Saturday's rematch.

However, a 21-9 second-quarter advantage for the Colonels put Riverheads in a 31-17 halftime hole, and the Gladiators were unable to mount a serious charge in the second half.

The Gladiators were determined to keep Hunt under wraps and did so with a variation of a box-and-one that basically had one player guarding Hunt man-to-man and a second waiting to help if Hunt tried to penetrate. The tactic worked for most of the

Please see RIVERHEADS, Page B5 ➡

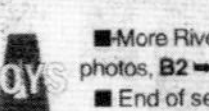

■ More Riverheads photos, B2 ➡
■ End of season hurts players, B5 ➡

Vincent Lerz/The News Leader
Riverheads' Josh LaPorte fights for possession against Altavista's Alan Grzenda on Saturday during the Group A state championship game.

Mark Miller/The News Leader
Riverheads' Jonathan Cash watches his team's hopes for a state title evaporate Saturday in Richmond.

March 14, 2004: Robert E. Lee High School's basketball team wins its fifth state championship since 1931. *Microfilm Archives*